THE MOTORING CENTURY

The Story of the Royal Automobile Club

Front endpaper: The Great Gallery of the RAC
clubhouse in Pall Mall.

Back endpaper: The Members' Lounge at the RAC
clubhouse in Pall Mall.

Original pen and ink drawings by Hanslip Fletcher, RA,
1946.

THE
MOTORING
CENTURY

The Story of the
Royal
Automobile
Club

PIERS BRENDON

BLOOMSBURY

First published in Great Britain 1997
Bloomsbury Publishing Plc, 38 Soho Square, London W1V 5DF

Copyright ©1997 The Royal Automobile Club Ltd
Text copyright ©1997 by Piers Brendon

The moral right of the author has been asserted

A CIP catalogue record for this book is available from the British Library

ISBN 0 7475 3034 3

10 9 8 7 6 5 4 3 2 1

Produced by NB Design

Designers: Nick Buzzard, Louise Dick
Editor: Richard Dawes
Picture research: Anne-Marie Ehrlich, Tamara Griffiths
Motoring consultants: Malcolm Jeal, Nigel Fryatt
Literary consultant: Andrew Best

Printed in Great Britain by Butler & Tanner Ltd, Frome

CONTENTS

ACKNOWLEDGEMENTS

When the Chairman of the Royal Automobile Club, Jeffrey Rose, invited me to write its history he said that he wanted a '"warts-and-all" account'. I replied that I would not accept the commission on any other terms. This book, based on full access to the RAC's archives, is the result of that agreement. It is a wholly independent work. Only in the last three chapters have I tempered freedom of expression with the need to respect commercial confidentiality and the feelings of the living, to say nothing of the laws of libel. My first thanks must therefore go to Jeffrey Rose. He has not only given me cordial assistance and unfailing support, he has always encouraged me to make up my own mind.

The same applies to Neil Johnson, who has been involved with this project from the start. Since becoming Chief Executive of the RAC towards the end of 1995, he has made time in the midst of a hectic schedule to talk to me about the whole organisation, past, present and future. I am heavily in his debt.

Like the foregoing, the following senior members of the RAC have not only talked to me at length but have been kind enough to read some or all of my typescript and to make valuable comments on it: Richard Bensted-Smith, Neil Eason Gibson, Tim Keown, Alan Levinson, Michael Limb, Brian McGivern, Ian Mavor, Sir John Rogers and David Worskett. Together their knowledge of the organisation is encyclopaedic and I have generally accepted their corrections on matters of fact and frequently (though not always) in cases of interpretation. I am deeply grateful to them.

I owe further gratitude to many of the Senior Hundred and to other members of the RAC who were free with their reminiscences. They are too numerous to mention individually but some I cannot omit. Harry Stanley gave me splendid hospitality and shared family memories that went back to the very origins of the Club. The same is true of John Crampton, whose father was a founder member. Robin Montgomerie-Charrington and John Hogg offered me a fund of anecdotes over memorable meals. Lord Iliffe made his father's memoir available and allowed me to quote from it. John Fingleton sent me some useful information about Sir Charles Rose, the Club's Edwardian Chairman.

I must also express my appreciation to those who discussed the important roles they had played, or were playing, in the RAC. Sir Clive Bossom was exceedingly frank and friendly. Arthur Large was open and generous with his time, as was David Livermore. I learnt an enormous amount from Norman Austin, Eric Charles, Nick Cranfield, Frank Richardson and Jack Williams. Dean Delamont's memories were enthralling. So were those of Tony Lee and Phil Drackett. Andrew Knight was a liberal host and a fascinating raconteur. I also benefited from the vivid recollections of Mrs Rosie Ramsay, daughter of the Club's founder, Frederick Simms.

Everyone I met on the staff of the RAC treated me with unstinting courtesy and candour. In particular, I must thank those 165 employees, past and present, who completed (and sometimes more than completed) the questionnaire I sent out through the good offices of Andrew Reeve and the Motoring Services organisation. They provided me with an incomparable body of material, on which I have drawn heavily. Once again, I cannot mention them individually. But I must include the names of those currently working for the RAC, in various capacities, who went out of their way to help me in person: Simon Allen, Graham Barker, Emma Beaufrere, John Bidgood, Paul Burgess, Martin Connor, Philip Corrick, Paula Crewe, Julie Gaukroger, Paul Gowen, Rob Hadgraft, Gerrie Johnson, Marcia Langdon, Terry Lankshear, Alec Leggett, Paul Simmons, Hayley Watson and John Wright. Last but not least, I must express my appreciation to Joan Williamson, the Club Librarian. Together with her assistant, Moira O'Farrell, she provided aid and support well above the call of duty.

Thanks are also due to others who have contributed to the book in different ways: Johnny Bell, P. N. Furbank, Gerald Lovell, Lord Montagu of Beaulieu, Brian Palmer, Alistair Ross and Trisha Stewart. Nigel Fryatt cheerfully allowed me to dip into the deep well of his professional knowledge, to the book's consistent advantage. Malcolm Jeal not only provided accurate information about many of the photographs, but also read the text, commented on it with formidable erudition and corrected a humbling number of mistakes. I am grateful to my colleagues at Churchill College for their forbearance during the protracted period of the book's gestation. The staff of the many libraries and archives where the research was carried out were uniformly obliging. But I must single out, as usual, those at the Cambridge University Library, itself the finest resource a writer could have.

Three people allowed themselves to be dragooned into doing extra research on my behalf: Paul Lavelle, who was simultaneously working for a First, which he duly got, in the Cambridge History Tripos; my son George, who also undertook the arduous task of compiling the index to my notes; and my wife Vyvyen, who endured the long hours I devoted to the RAC with her customary benevolence and stoicism. The book is richer for their sterling efforts. It has also been shaped by the deft hand of Nick Buzzard, who not only designed it in its present form but was an immense source of strength during the writing. He was expertly assisted by Louise Dick and by Anne-Marie Ehrlich, who did much of the picture research.

Finally, I must pay warm tribute to Andrew Best, without whose dedicated labour this book might not have seen the light of day – it certainly would not have done so as it stands. He has nursed and nurtured it with inestimable patience and skill, reading every chapter as it emerged from the word-processor, decorating the text with elegant and incisive comments, and saving me from countless *faux pas*. I could not be more grateful to him.

PIERS BRENDON
Cambridge, 1997

INTRODUCTION

THE ROYAL AUTOMOBILE CLUB is Britain's oldest and most influential motoring organisation. From the advent of the horseless carriage to the age of the stretch limousine, it has been the 'Parliament of Motoring'. This book, which combines text based on a wealth of new material and illustrations drawn from many original sources, is the Club's centenary history. But the book gives both more and less than a full account of the RAC: less in the sense that it is not a total record of the work of the institution; more in that it makes the Club the focus of a larger story, one which traces the controversial journey of the car through 100 years of Britain's national life. It is a story that has never before been told.

Of course, there have been countless books and journals about the machines themselves: celebrations of distinctive models, motor reminiscences, biographies of manufacturers, surveys of the industry. Whole libraries have been devoted to motor sport and its champions. Transport studies abound. But there is only a single scholarly account of *The Motor Car and Politics* (written by William Plowden) and one popular, pictorial volume, commissioned by the RAC itself in 1981, on the social history of the automobile. There is also a good, though somewhat parochial and deferential, seventy-fifth-birthday tribute to the Automobile Association (AA). Compared with the prolific literature on the role of the car in America over the past century, Britain has a virtual blank.

Yet from the moment pioneer motorists set off from London to Brighton in 1896, each contraption shaking (as one observer noted) 'like a blancmange at a dance-supper', the automobile began to invade the imagination and metamorphose the life of its time. It has been an engine of change more potent than the locomotive and, with half a billion now on the planet, more ubiquitous than the aeroplane. It has revolutionised the static, isolated society of the past and brought mobility to the masses – in 1890 the average distance a Briton travelled was 13 miles a year, whereas in 1990 it was 13 miles a day, nearly all that distance by courtesy of the car. The automobile has spawned new industries and transformed old patterns of behaviour. It has improved access to culture, leisure and health. It has encouraged the emancipation of women and augmented the freedom of men. It has altered the very topography of the kingdom, reshaping cities, extending suburbs and opening up the countryside. Whether as consumer durable, phallic symbol, producer of wealth, instrument of pleasure, marque of status, motor of progress or emblem of liberation, the automobile is the true icon of the twentieth century.

On the other hand, this prized possession is, in Colin Buchanan's famous phrase, a mixed blessing. The automobile has had a shattering social impact, causing accidents, pollution and congestion. It has weakened the bonds of family, locality, even morality – one puritan described cars as 'mobile houses of prostitution'. The car has not just eroded but degraded public transport, making trains, for example, seem fit only for those who come from the wrong side of the tracks. It has posed new problems of urban blight. It has criss-crossed the countryside with concrete and, as a recent RAC report observes, it threatens rural peace by making it accessible to millions. By a notable irony, the apotheosis of individual freedom has also enhanced the power of the state, producing additional taxes, a welter of restrictions, tighter planning controls, wider police surveillance.

Here, then, is a fascinating, important and paradoxical phenomenon. It is made up of many separate strands and forms a rich historical tapestry that has touched almost every aspect of life. Woven into its fabric from the start was the Automobile Club, on which King Edward VII bestowed the royal title in 1907. Most early motorists joined the Club, which at once became the arbiter of automobilism in all its aspects.

It promoted the new movement by arranging trials, fostering touring, teaching driving, issuing road maps, dispensing propaganda, approving garages and hotels, organising insurance and legal assistance, and eventually establishing Road Patrols to help its Associate (as well as its full) members. It became the governing body of motor sport, initiating the Tourist Trophy, the oldest regularly run race in the world. It set standards, devising, for example, the formula by which horsepower was measured. It advised governments, directing (and often resisting) the incursions of the state. It also faced an awkward new situation with the minions of the law, formerly respectful of the rich but now pursuing affluent automobilists with every means at their command – Scotland Yard's first Flying Squad carried egg-bombs filled with green and white paint to hurl at fugitive vehicles.

Actively resisting speed-traps and other forms of 'police harassment', the AA (which was formed in 1905) soon gained more members than the RAC, which condemned 'scorchers' and 'motorcads'. Yet, partly because it was no mere lobby but an élite which espoused responsible automobilism (thus helping to preserve its privileged position), the RAC enjoyed by far the greater prestige. Its palatial Edwardian clubhouse in Pall Mall was the Vatican of motordom. Its word was law on everything from automobile etiquette to engineering refinement. It was the Jockey Club of motor racing. Everyone who was anyone in the world on wheels belonged to the Royal Automobile Club. For at least the first twenty-five years of its existence, the history of the RAC was virtually synonymous with the history of motoring in Great Britain.

But as the car boomed and the nation was gripped by what *The Times* called a 'fever of mobility', the Club gradually sank into magisterial lethargy. During the 'golden age of motoring' between the two world wars, when the automobile was changing the face and character of Britain, the RAC dwelt chiefly on its own Edwardian glories. Anyway the aristocracy of automobilism felt ambivalent about middle-class motoring. It was proud that its pioneering labours had borne such copious fruit. But it was concerned that what had been an exclusive pleasure should now be pursued by the bourgeois multitude, who adopted the 'week-end' habit, preferred golf to church and aped the fashions of their betters. Despite the RAC's decadence, though, it grew in dignity and respectability, counselling the Ministry of Transport on everything from the Highway Code to the Belisha beacon, from driving in the blackout to defeating petrol black marketeers.

Part of the Club's problem during its middle age was lack of vigorous leadership. In the six decades between 1912 and 1972 it had only three chairmen, each of whom grew very old in office. The last of these, it is true, did achieve a certain revival in the RAC's fortunes during the postwar years, a period which saw the end of austerity motoring and the beginnings of mass motoring. He campaigned successfully for motorways and recommenced motor sport in Britain, which grew hugely in popularity thanks to television. The RAC's motoring services also made progress, largely as a result of the better equipping of its tough, omnicompetent Road Patrols, whose adventures were legion. But during the 1960s and 70s the Club was caught in a seemingly inexorable spiral of decline. Like the domestic motor industry, the RAC seemed to be terminally afflicted by the 'British disease'. The malady culminated in a dramatic crisis, here fully documented for the first time, which almost extinguished the Club.

Its renaissance during the 1980s and 90s, during the chairmanship of Jeffrey Rose, is one of the most extraordinary sagas in modern corporate life. The RAC's motoring services were revolutionised, becoming the most technologically advanced in the world, setting new standards of service which the AA struggled to match and attracting an enormous increase in membership. Its clubhouses – the one at Pall Mall acquired a country cousin at Woodcote Park, near Epsom, in 1913 – were renovated to become more luxurious and profitable than ever before. The motor sport division is now so successful that the RAC plans to market its expertise abroad. And, at a time when the automobile is under sustained attack from environmentalists, the RAC has pioneered 'green' motoring policies.

The current onslaught is by no means unprecedented. In the glow of centennial nostalgia it might seem that the automobile speedily became accepted as a vehicle of progress and that its recent critics have become so vociferous only because it has multiplied so unconscionably. This is a myth. As the following pages reveal, the motor car has always been a cause of contention. From Edwardian 'motorphobia' via interwar strictures on 'carbarians' and postwar denunciations of this 'bad machine', to the 'automotive nightmare' of the 1990s, the car has been fiercely condemned as well as ardently championed. Despite the appearance of smooth, effortless acceleration in public esteem, its ride has always been bumpy.

For 100 years, from early hopes of 'Autopia' to contemporary fears of 'Autogeddon', the Club has been in the eye of the storm surrounding the automobile. Often it has been wrong: the RAC's stubborn opposition to car seat belts, for example, was one of the most inglorious episodes in its history. Often it has been right: the continuing campaign against 'bull bars' and for side-impact bars shows a proper concern for road safety despite the impulses of fashion and the incentives of economy. But whatever its day-to-day policies, the Club has almost always upheld the principle of responsible motoring. Furthermore, where equivalent organisations overseas have withered or died, it has triumphantly survived.

This book is a portrait of the RAC set against the background of the 'Motoring Century'. It is not the chronicle of a business, let alone a bureaucracy. It is not a catalogue of rallies run and races won. A book could be written about the RAC's Byzantine relations with motoring organisations overseas and the international bodies in charge of motor sport; but that book is not this book. This is a composite biography of a living institution. It aspires to evoke the character of the Club, itself a microcosm of a significant section of British society over the past hundred years. Clubs are assemblages of people and the following pages contain cameos of many of the RAC's most important and interesting personalities, especially when they were involved with the career of the motor car. Therefore this is essentially a human story, in which men loom larger than machines.

It is written in the same spirit as the *History of the Travellers' Club* (1927) by Sir Almeric Fitzroy, who aimed to 'give space and form to the ideas these dumb stones insensibly embalm'. The history of a club is difficult to pin down for it is 'associated with an indestructible aura, distinct and yet intangible, the force of which is felt from generation to generation, but in no sense susceptible of definition'. Aura of club is even more elusive than attar of club, which is said to consist of the smell of bowler hats, studded leather chairs and ashtrays full of cigar butts. But the RAC presents a peculiarly challenging problem because it is not just a club and it has no single ethos. Like Gaul, it is divided into three parts: clubhouses, motoring organisation and motor sport. Moreover, the development of automobilism and the automobile, with which the Club has been so intimately associated, must be included in what aspires to be a coherent chronological record.

Words alone, within the confines of a single volume, could hardly do justice to this multi-faceted story. Moreover, to produce a purely verbal account would be to ignore the striking pictorial history of the automobile and its Club, preserved in the archives at Pall Mall and elsewhere. So this book has been designed to integrate – yet to separate – words and illustrations in a way that is original, attractive and compelling. Its left-hand pages are devoted to unbroken text, with nothing to distract the reader or interrupt the flow. The pictures appear on right-hand pages, where they often supplement the prose account, giving form to those who people the narrative and illustrating it by means of graphic images. But they also complement it with visual essays, adding a spectacular dimension to the volume. Thus sometimes where the writing concentrates narrowly on the Club, the illustrations continue to present the wider motoring picture. Similarly, where Club matters (such as the evolving style of RAC badges and trophies) lend themselves to pictorial treatment, photographs tell the tale.

Together text and illustrations cast twin beams on the automobile age, as though catching it in the headlights of its distinctive creation. But they shine most brightly on the RAC itself. In sum, therefore, this book attempts to capture the substance and the spirit of the Club, giving a faithful (though by no means exhaustive) account of its history in the context of the motoring century.

CHAPTER ONE

HORSELESS CARRIAGES

*Motoring in Britain got off to a dramatic start. But behind the
scenes the new movement was shaken by personal rivalries and
retarded by commercial machinations. Champions of horseless
carriages decided that only an independent organisation could
give automobilism stability and a sense of direction.*

RED LETTER DAY

*Founded in 1895, a year
before motorists were free
to drive on British roads,*
The Autocar *celebrated
'liberty day' with a
crimson edition.*

THE MORNING OF SATURDAY 14 NOVEMBER 1896 was cold and wet;
but nothing could dampen the spirits of spectators or drivers as motor cars
mustered for their first legal journey along English roads. It was a momentous occasion, the stuff of dreams and the seed of myths. The Tory
government had just repealed the 'Red Flag Act', so called because it
required a man to walk in front of road locomotives warning of their
approach with a red flag. The Motor Car Club determined to celebrate the
new freedom. It had recently been founded by a daring automobile entrepreneur called Harry J. Lawson and his colleague, Frederick R. Simms, a
talented engineer who was later to create what became the Royal
Automobile Club. They organised and advertised an 'Emancipation Run'
for self-propelled carriages from London to Brighton. So, on that dank
morning, an immense crowd gathered around the starting-point, the Hotel
Métropole, a flat-iron building (now offices) which overlooks the Thames
at the corner of Whitehall Place and Northumberland Avenue. The police,
who had not anticipated such a multitude, hastily summoned reinforcements. They struggled
to make way for the snorting iron monsters, to clear a path for progress.

Some thirty-two motor vehicles assembled, perhaps as many as half of all those in
the country at that time. They presented a weird and novel spectacle. There were bizarre
contraptions like the 'Britannia' bath chair, the red parcels van which looked as though it
would collapse if loaded with anything heavier than a hatbox, and the Pennington four-seater
tricycle which eventually reached Brighton by train. There were Bollée tandems resembling
'land torpedoes', whose exhausts sounded like naval guns. There were machines whose hot-tube
ignition burners caught fire when lit by flares, giving a lurid aspect to the scene. There were

dogcarts, phaetons, victorias and landaus, which bucked and shied without benefit of horses. Such 'oil cans', 'steam kettles' and 'skeletons on wheels' provoked good-natured chaff from the onlookers. But fears lay behind the jeers. The rumour spread that 'an organised massacre of cab-horses was contemplated'. 'Bill,' shouted one cabby to another, 'my old gee's off to the knacker's yard afore the year's out, blest if she won't.' Other spectators, though, admired the modern mode of travel. 'No fellow would ride behind a 'bus horse while he could glide along like that,' exclaimed a City gentleman. Many who stood in the rain that day felt that they were witnessing the dawn of an era, the beginning of a 'great and beneficial … revolution in the life, habits and methods of locomotion of the people'.

Motorists in the Hotel Métropole would have agreed, though most of their energies were devoted to sustaining themselves for the rigours of the road with a breakfast consisting of half a dozen courses, including fish and pheasant, served with wine. None expected their initial journey to run smoothly. As one of the speakers told his 150-strong audience, cars were in their infancy and drivers were inexperienced because they had been victims of the restrictive code. However, its repeal was a triumph which indicated the shape of things to come. It was a triumph, moreover, famously marked during the course of the meal. With a flourish Lord Winchilsea, chairman of Harry Lawson's Great Horseless Carriage Company, tore the red flag to shreds and trampled on the pieces. His gesture was loudly cheered though its symbolic force was somewhat impaired by the fact that he had to cut through the hem with a penknife. Afterwards, at about half past ten, drivers forged their way through the throng and mounted their vehicles. Passengers took their seats, which were said to have sold for as much as £50 apiece. Some faced forwards and some back; but all, as one journalist noted, faced the future.

In the foremost car, a hooded Panhard-Levassor dogcart which had won the 1895 Paris–Bordeaux–Paris Race and now sported the purple and gold banner of the Motor Car Club, sat Harry Lawson. Short and stout, pop-eyed and wax-moustached, he was a flamboyant figure, especially when dressed in the Motor Car Club uniform. This consisted of a double-breasted blue serge coat with brass buttons and gold and silver braid, set off by a navy-blue cap with a white top, glossy peak and badge. The ensemble, embellished by a blue and crimson armlet, was deemed vulgar. It also caused confusion: one distinguished member of the Club, perhaps Simms, was hailed in the street as 'Inspector'. It also attracted ridicule. The French engineer Léon Bollée likened it to the uniform of a Swiss admiral. Others described it as a cross between the garb of a Hungarian band leader and the dress of a steward on an excursion steamer. A journal founded by Lawson's chief rival as a motoring pioneer, Sir David Salomons, noted that this 'fantastic costume [was] more usually associated with the Whitechapel holiday element at Margate during the summer season'. Lawson wore it with supreme self-confidence. He drove off first when, two minutes after the order 'Start your motors' had provoked a salvo of explosions, the signal was given to go. Riding in the vanguard, Lawson looked every inch the pilot of progress.

The concourse moved forward at a snail's pace. The roads were thick with mud and yellow fog still lingered over the Thames. The environs of Whitehall Place were congested with equine traffic – carts, hansom cabs, private carriages and omnibuses. There were also several coaches whose red-faced, brown-coated Jehus seemed determined to 'demonstrate that the

MOTORING GETS STARTED

The Emancipation Run begins in Whitehall Place on 14 November 1896. On the right is the Panhard-Levassor (bearing the banner of the Motor Car Club) which won the 1895 Paris–Bordeaux–Paris Race. The Panhard had tube ignition and three speeds, the top one giving nearly 20mph. It pioneered the layout – front engine, middle passenger compartment, rear-wheel drive – which became standard. Harry Lawson, in the MCC uniform, is at the tiller and beside him sits his driver, Otto Mayer. Next is the Cannstatt-Daimler called 'Present Times', containing Frederick Simms and (inside) Gottlieb Daimler himself. Following this is the historic Panhard-Levassor which won the Paris–Marseilles–Paris Race.

journey to Brighton was still the affair of the horse'. The bicycling boom being at its height (so much so that in 1896 seventy members of White's formed a club to pursue the fashionable hobby), cyclists had rallied in their thousands to act as flying escorts to the motorists. The cars also had to pick their way through a dense mass of humanity such as only the vast metropolis of London could furnish. The Embankment was a sea of people. Many were respectable men in top hats and frock coats. There were also quite a few ladies: one or two sported 'rational dress'; others fainted in the crush. Westminster Bridge was so packed that mounted police had to clear a passage. The streets of Lambeth, Vauxhall and Kennington were equally crammed, though the faces were paler and surmounted with flat caps. Wan women and girls in threadbare dresses waved from windows and doorways. Gaunt youths in broken boots climbed lampposts, sat on roof-tops, clung to chimney-pots. Old men who had seen the advent of trains held aloft children who would witness the coming of spaceships. Chugging through the slums in his enclosed phaeton, the writer Jerome K. Jerome speculated about the thoughts of their inhabitants:

> 'We have seen many changes come,' the faces seem to say, 'and each change we have seen preceded with the same banner, "The Benefit of Humanity and the Happiness of the Masses." Yet here, in our dark hovels, we eat the husks that you leave us, and sometimes we starve because we are too weak to struggle for the husks. What will this new thing bring to *us*?'

To judge from the raucous applause which greeted the cavalcade as it spread out and speeded up along the wider thoroughfares of Brixton, most people thought that the new means of locomotion would be a universal blessing. Every twenty yards or so amateur photographers with box cameras leapt out to snap the convoy. At the top of Brixton Hill, where Lawson's vehicle suffered a temporary breakdown after shedding a cylinder bolt, a party of undertaker's men *en route* to a suburban funeral cheered the cars – though theirs, reporters thought, might have been a professional enthusiasm. Through Streatham and Norbury excitement and delight were writ large on the countenances of those who lined the streets. In Croydon the crowd, less thick by now, pelted the cars with flowers and rice. It also roared with laughter when two policemen on horseback galloped in vain pursuit of a Daimler which was exceeding the new speed limit of 12mph – by now indeed the procession had become a race, as Lawson, intent on drumming up the kind of prestige generated by French races, had secretly planned. Reigate, where the Prince Regent had been wont to break his four-and-a-half-hour coach journey to Brighton and the motorists in their turn stopped for luncheon at the White Hart, was *en fête* with flags and bunting. A sign proclaimed, 'Reigate welcomes Progress'. Gaitered farmers and smocked labourers, after expressing their amazement and satisfying their curiosity about these horseless vehicles, seemed to endorse the message. It was echoed in later stages of the odyssey. At Crawley a huge blue and white banner proclaimed 'Success to the Motor Car'. Finally, Brighton hailed those who completed the course with the portentous inscription: 'Centuries look down upon this, your immortal ride.'

Only about twenty horseless carriages finished the ride and there was confusion about who arrived first. Some gave the palm to the Bollée brothers, while others declared that the American

REIGATE WELCOMES PROGRESS

The small town was in an 'uproar', according to The Autocar, *as 'every shade and degree of the great British public were out awheel and afoot to see the autocars on their initial legal journey in this country'.*

LAWSON'S FELLOW TRAVELLERS

Among the associates of Harry Lawson (seated centre), here pictured on the Monday after Emancipation Day, are Otto Mayer (back row, far left), J. S. Critchley (next to him), Charles McRobie Turrell (back row, sixth from left), H. O. Duncan (back row, second from right) and Charles Harrington Moore (front row, far right). All had vested interests in horseless carriages.

Frank Duryea had won. He and his passenger certainly looked like pace-setters: they reached Brighton 'carrying enough mud on their hats, faces and clothes to start a small estate'. After he returned to the United States Duryea exhibited his successful car at Barnum & Bailey's circus, between an Indian elephant and the ape-man from Borneo. But then motor cars were generally regarded as freaks. So it came as little surprise that many had fallen by the wayside. It was also understandable that certain drivers, as dusk approached and a gale began to blow, decided to complete their journey by train, and that some secretly took their cars with them – endeavouring to disguise his own misdemeanour, Colonel Bersey made 'frantic efforts to discover mud with which to clothe' his battery-driven brougham. Vehicles with pneumatic tyres had suffered frequent punctures, while solid wheels got stuck in tramlines. Electric cars had been unable to recharge their cells. Other machines had run out of water or fuel. Still others had met with mechanical breakdown. Often they underwent the indignity of being rescued by horses, parked in stables and attended by blacksmiths.

FRAUD ON WHEELS
The American inventor Edward Pennington made extravagant claims for spurious products like this three-wheeled four-seater. Lacking a carburettor and supposedly fired by a 'long-mingling spark', it was billed as 'the only machine that will not blow up'. Even more fantastic was 'Pennington's Flying Cycle'. Yet he deceived many, including the wily Lawson himself, before going bankrupt in 1900.

Harry Lawson's ebullient self-esteem armoured him against criticism. In any case he had issued a press release proclaiming the event a brilliant success two days before it took place. As the stragglers, including the Cannstatt-Daimler known as 'Present Times' containing Frederick Simms, puffed and shuddered to the finish, he repeated this verdict, which was at first widely endorsed. During a dinner held at Brighton's Hotel Métropole and presided over by the Mayor, Lawson saluted the new Locomotives on Highways Act, which had banished the red flag, as 'the Magna Charta [*sic*] of Motor-Cars'. And he portrayed the occasion as a victory for applied science over the brute forces of obscurantism. 'Thank goodness this day has come at last,' he declared, 'a day of the great deliverance of our roads and highways from the reign of quadrupeds and the rule of – well, other animals.' It was a victory, moreover, which promised employment to millions as well as an undreamed-of improvement in the quality of life for all.

Lawson's oratory seemed to ring true at the time and it even strikes a chord today. Drivers and passengers who had just completed the 'Emancipation Run' were buoyed up by the dizzy afflatus of the motoring experience. Having ridden comets which outstripped their tail of bicyclists, they exulted in raw power. Having dodged pedestrians like quicksilver, they rejoiced in magical manoeuvrability. Having whirled through the countryside on limbs of steel, they succumbed to the delirium of speed. As Jerome K. Jerome wrote, 'the lust of motor-careering was in our blood'. For different reasons later generations, who measure velocity in terms of fuel-injected overdrive, are almost equally thrilled by the Brighton Run. Re-enacted each year by the Royal Automobile Club, it is 'the world's biggest motoring spectacle'. It attracts two million onlookers, four times the number who watched the event in 1896. For a modern audience, especially for those who don period costume and toast the 'old crocks' (a term their owners much resent) with champagne as they set off from London, the Brighton Run has become a gigantic exercise in automotive nostalgia. It stirs folk memories of a simpler, purer age. It harks back to a time when motoring was a perpetual adventure. It conjures up the romance of the

THE NEW PENNINGTON AUTOCAR.

The above is an illustration of the New Pennington Autocar, constructed to carry four persons only but which has actually run with nine people on, the same being fitted with Pennington Non-puncturable Pneumatic Tyres.   The vehicle complete weighs less than 2½ cwts.

WHAT THE PRESS SAYS:

The *Paris Herald*, dated 10th May, 1896, in describing the **Exhibition** at the Imperial Institute, of the **largest display** of **Auto-motor Cars** ever held in the **World,** says that the **PENNINGTON MOTOR** is "**immensely lighter and speedier than any other pattern yet made,**" and that "**its qualities of lightness of weight, facility of direction, and freedom from smell and oscillation are beyond question.**"

THESE ARE FACTS!

NO VIBRATION, FIRE, SMOKE, OR ODOUR.

HEATED AND LIGHTED BY ELECTRICITY.

These Autocars are on exhibition at the National Show, Crystal Palace, London, S.E.

For Prices, Address:

E. J. PENNINGTON, Motor Mills, COVENTRY.

Regarding Foreign Countries, Address:

Wm. BAINES, 5 & 6, Gt. Winchester Street, LONDON.

open road. It resounds with echoes of 'Genevieve' and 'Chitty-Chitty Bang-Bang'. Legend, however, has obscured truth. These rose-tinted views of the past are about as misleading now as Harry Lawson's inflated rhetoric was a century ago.

TO SEE WHY, it is necessary go back a few years and look at what led up to the Brighton Run. Harry Lawson, born the son of a nonconformist minister in 1852, had cashed in on the bicycle boom. He professed to have invented the safety cycle and did indeed patent a modern-style machine; but more authentic products of his quack ingenuity were the patent lever-driven low-seater, said to be less like a penny-farthing than a penny-ha'penny, and the disastrously elongated 'Crocodile'. By the early 1890s, though, Lawson aimed at nothing less than cornering the market in automobiles. He regarded the new vehicle as an 'El Dorado in embryo', irresistible to one for whom money-making was 'the breath of life'. Lawson's method was not so much to manufacture cars as to acquire and exploit their 'master patents'. The scheme was spurious, nefarious and vaultingly ambitious. Frederick Simms, who became consulting engineer to Lawson's companies, must have recognised the truth of *The Autocar's* statement that 'there can be no such thing as a master patent upon a self-propelling carriage' because it would be swiftly overtaken by new inventions. Nevertheless, Simms participated in his schemes. According to his admirers he became in the process 'the Adam' of the motoring movement, the supreme progenitor who 'threw his whole life into the cause of automobilism'.

Born in 1863, the same year as Henry Ford, Simms was brought up in Hamburg. His grandfather had moved there from Birmingham to set up a business, so young Simms served an engineering apprenticeship in Germany, birthplace of the motor car. Afterwards he met Gottlieb Daimler and at once grasped the glittering possibilities of the petrol engine. Ingenious, industrious and full of what his daughter called 'heavy-weather seriousness', Simms acquired some of the foreign patent rights and tried to exploit them in England. But he encountered one obstruction after another. For fear of an explosion he was apparently refused permission to use his engine to power a cocoa-making machine at an Earls Court exhibition. He was even forbidden to take a petrol-driven boat on the Serpentine, though he became the first man to do so on the Thames. By 1893 Simms was having a hard time, not least because of the defalcations of a business associate. Several dunning letters to him survive, one threatening a writ unless he at once paid the sum of £20 7s 3d to a cabinet manufacturer. Simms was at the time renting a workshop, for twenty-five shillings a week, under a railway arch close to Putney Bridge station. Yet it has some claim to the blue commemorative plaque, unveiled by RAC chairman Wilfrid Andrews in 1964 , to mark the 'birthplace of the motor industry in Britain'.

That Simms could be hailed as its founding father was the result of a visit from Harry Lawson's solicitor in 1895. To the astonishment of the ambitious engineer, the lawyer offered him £25,000 (later increased to £35,000) for the British patent rights to Daimler engines. The deal with Lawson and their subsequent collaboration made Simms's fortune. Thereafter this imposing figure, with his domed brow and prominent nose, could adorn himself in elegant suits. He could purchase fine wines, of which he became a connoisseur. He could indulge his taste for zither-playing, tea-drinking and chamois-hunting on the two estates he acquired in the

1929

1896

1996

1950

1981

RUNNING FOR A CENTURY

The Brighton Run, revived as a newspaper stunt in 1927, has been organised by the RAC since 1930 with the help of various sponsors. The commemorative event has grown in popularity and in dignity – witness the disappearance of the vulgar man with the red flag. Distance lends enchantment to the dawn of motoring and these programme covers show a sport turning into a ritual. At the 1996 Centenary Run, which attracted a record number of contestants, Lord Winchilsea re-enacted his great-grandfather's tearing-up of the red flag.

1954

1974

1955

1957

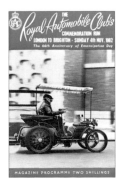

1962

1967

Austrian Tyrol, which he would motor round like a 'regal personage'. (Hermann Goering later occupied a neighbouring estate but even he was not treated with the 'almost feudal respect' which local people accorded to Simms.) Between 1895 and 1897 Simms gravitated round Lawson at the centre of motordom. According to one authority, it would require 'the analytical mind of a trained accountant and the pen of a Gibbon to do justice to the atmosphere of chicanery and hornswoggling' which enveloped Lawson and his satellites. Like many others in the fledgeling motor business, Simms later distanced himself from Lawson; but at the time he advanced the cause of his aspirant monopoly with much flair and little scruple.

He advised Lawson on the purchase of other 'master patents'. Simms assisted when Lawson, trumpeting their worth, floated a series of companies to profit by them. He himself acquired a considerable stake in these ventures (becoming a major shareholder in the Great Horseless Carriage Company, for example) and declared that they were in good and reliable hands. Simms was a huckster after Lawson's own heart. In July 1895 he had presented as an objective account (for the *Saturday Review*) what was really 'the first commercial promotion of a motor car in Britain'. He described how 'whole villages turned out to behold, open-mouthed, the new marvel of locomotion' driven by the Hon. Evelyn Ellis. Later hailed as one of the 'automobile Hampdens' bent on defying a bad law, Ellis, a breezy, bearded ex-sailor, had a major holding in Daimler. The car, actually a primitive vehicle 'not unlike a four-wheeled dogcart', was puffed by Simms as one which emitted 'neither heat, smoke, soot, nor smell'. Later, in the same vein, Simms exaggerated Daimler sales. He announced, for instance, that several had been bought to carry the mails in Ceylon, which was not the case.

In addition, Simms campaigned for the repeal of the 'Red Flag Act'. But in truth the red flag was virtually a dead letter. It had been introduced in 1865 to secure the future of, and to make the roads safe for, lumbering traction engines. However, although it was still demanded by some local authorities, it had ceased to be a statutory requirement as early as 1878. Nor was it much to blame for the backwardness of the British motor car, which, as Herbert Austin once said, suffered at this time from so many involuntary halts that speed hardly mattered. The red flag was nevertheless a potent emblem of repression, which Lawson's acolytes brandished energetically. Lord Winchilsea disclosed their true motives when he remarked, after tearing it up at the Hotel Métropole, that trade would now follow the destruction of the flag.

With the skill of a born showman Lawson fostered this trade for several months before the 'Emancipation Run'. Assisted by Simms and others, he organised competitions and exhibitions, which mainly featured foreign cars, because the British motor industry was at that time little more than a gleam in his eye. Lawson imported 'anything that would astonish the crowd'. 'What I want,' he informed his French agent, H. O. Duncan, 'is some motor-cycles or motor-cars that will run for half an hour or so, and they must not break down in the middle of the exhibition!' Lawson painted glowing pictures of the happy horseless age that was to come, once penning what seemed a fanciful 'sketch of Piccadilly Circus of the future with motor cars, cabs and buses crossing and re-crossing in every direction'. He suborned the press, inveigling journalists like Henry Sturmey into his enterprises and exacting editorial support in return for advertisements. He helped to initiate the practice of appointing titled

LOOK, NO REINS

*The tiller, as featured in the
1891 Serpollet steam carriage
(right), gave male drivers an
arm-wrenching experience and
virtually prevented women from
driving at all. Even the upright
steering-wheel, visible in the
1895 petrol-driven Jeantaud
(below), was a notable advance.
Significantly most automotive
progress came from abroad,
though these vehicles seem
incomplete without shafts
and horses.*

folk to the boards of his companies – apparently the going rate was £10,000 for a duke, £5,000 for an earl. Lawson plastered London with 'posters showing horseless vehicles doing everything except flying'. And he got Simms to write catalogues forecasting the imminent fulfilment of the dream of countless generations, the 'invasion of the air around us' and the transfer of traffic 'to the skies'.

Such Utopian (yet uncannily accurate) claims brought Lawson and Simms into conflict with that other great champion of the motoring movement, Sir David Salomons (1851–1925). A wealthy, liberal Jew, prominent in City life, Salomons was also a keen amateur electrical engineer. He had fitted up his beautiful house, Broomhill, near Tunbridge Wells, with an elaborate workshop and he also constructed the first properly equipped 'motor house' (i.e. garage) in England. Here Salomons, an inveterate smoker who kept racks of ready-filled pipes to hand and whose grey, Mephistophelean whiskers were stained yellow by nicotine, loved to tinker with machinery. He was eager to spread technical knowledge, having met a woman at Peugeot's works in Paris who expressed surprise that engines were not wound up before starting. Salomons' advice to fellow motorists reveals as much about him as about early cars: 'The first thing to be done by the purchaser of a mechanical carriage is to have it completely dismantled under his eyes, and to thoroughly comprehend the whole mechanism.'

The fact that British cars, insofar as they existed, were even more primitive than French and German ones, Salomons considered a national disgrace. Typical of the nation's backwardness, he reckoned, was one press suggestion that, since cars' tiller steering was so cumbersome, engines should provide their power while mules should be attached in front to give direction. Unless Britain kept abreast of other countries in what would prove to be 'the bloodless revolution of the end of the 19th century', he warned, 'we shall find ourselves a third rate power'. Accordingly Salomons became the most influential and energetic campaigner for the 'Emancipation Act'. In October 1895 he held the first British motor show at Tunbridge Wells, for which, as Mayor, he was able to secure the co-operation of the police. The Chief Commissioner promised that 'any policeman you happen to pass will have his back turned to you', and obliging constables even evicted a couple of velocipede bath chairs which gatecrashed the proceedings. Simms helped to make the exhibition a success: 5,000 spectators admired the antics of Count de Dion's steam tractor and barouche, Evelyn Ellis's Daimler-engined Panhard-Levassor and George Bouton's 'one "mouse-power" tricycle'. But when Salomons announced that he was setting up a club to propagate the gospel of motordom, Simms offended him by claiming that he had suggested the idea. In an early expression of epistolary disgust from Tunbridge Wells, Salomons informed *The Autocar* that 'the starting of an association was "cut and dry" before I had the pleasure of meeting Mr Simms'.

Salomons was altruistic and philanthropic. Simms had an eye for the main chance and could not be 'regarded as reliable'. So it has been easy to assume that the magnanimous amateur was more credible than the calculating professional. However, an unpublished letter from Sir David Salomons survives among Simms's papers arranging for Simms to help at Tunbridge Wells and saying, 'In France, the Comte de Dion has started a Club somewhat similar to the one you suggest. We might talk it over when you come down here and discover the best way of carrying out the movement.' Evidently, therefore, Simms did deserve at least some of the

SALOMONS' SHOW

*Sir David Salomons at the tiller of his Peugeot (a worthy rival
to the pre-eminent Panhard) during the first British Motor
Show, held at Tunbridge Wells in October 1895. It attracted
enormous interest. Afterwards the* Daily Chronicle *damned
restrictions on cars as 'absurd' and forecast a time when 'Hyde
Park in the season will simmer with benzine'.*

credit for the first British motoring organisation, the Self-Propelled Traffic Association (SPTA), which Salomons inaugurated in December 1895. The fact is that Salomons never wished to share the limelight. High-minded and warm-hearted, he was also mean-spirited. Unlike Lawson, Simms did not even become a member of the SPTA council. This was the only time Salomons became associated with Lawson and he swiftly regretted it. Within a month he was accusing the entrepreneur of trying to make the SPTA 'a company promoting concern'.

Salomons blocked that attempt and Simms accordingly announced the formation of a rival body, the Autocar Training Club. For some reason this was still-born and instead, in January 1896, Simms sired the Motor Car Club. He solemnly stated that this Club, of which Lawson became Chairman, had not been 'formed for any trade purposes whatever'. Salomons was sceptical and accused Simms of playing a 'double game, of promoting his business interests through the front of a disinterested motor users' organisation'. The Club Secretary, Charles Harrington Moore, replied on Simms's behalf, saying that the Motor Car Club could do without Salomons' support and casting doubt on his 'patriotism' – which was probably a coded anti-Semitic slur.

In view of Simms's later club-creating activities, the dispute is an important one. But its rights and wrongs are not difficult to discern, even though St John Nixon, Simms's biographer and friend, did his best to substantiate Simms's account. In his aptly entitled book *Romance Amongst Cars* (1938) Nixon declared that Lawson managed for a long time to 'deceive those behind the scenes' at the Club – notably Simms and Harrington Moore – about its true nature. Yet Nixon also said that Lawson could 'hardly hope to deceive a child into believing that the [Motor Car] Club was run merely as a club and not as a very useful adjunct to his own business'. Nixon's argument therefore falls to the ground. He himself, in any case, is an untrustworthy advocate – one early motorist described him as 'a liar' and an 'impudent, insolent fake'. In truth Lawson hardly bothered to hide the fact that the Motor Car Club was a means of advancing what he called at its inaugural dinner 'the most wonderful industries that God has ever blessed mankind with since the world began'.

Lawson subsidised the Club to the tune of £6,000 a year. He ran it from his office at 40 Holborn Viaduct, whose 'glorious … shop window' he once urged Simms to placard 'from top to bottom with Daimler Motor Co Ltd'. Although 'ostensibly social in its aims', said motoring enthusiast John Scott Montagu (later second Baron Montagu of Beaulieu), the Club was dedicated to commercial ends. The racing driver S. F. Edge agreed: the Club was a 'one-man show' in which 'Lawson's word was law'. Everyone in the business recognised that the Motor Car Club was a 'private propaganda organisation'. Plainly Simms was claiming independence for the Club in order to invest it with an authority that it did not deserve.

As the motoring movement gathered pace during 1896 relations between Salomons and Lawson, and their rival clubs, grew even worse. Salomons was enraged when Lawson mailed him a company prospectus which seemed to imply Salomons' endorsement – it was, as Nixon said, like 'sending the Koran to Friedrich Nietzsche'. Lawson's exhibitions outshone those of Salomons. At the Imperial Institute Evelyn Ellis took Edward Prince of Wales for a ride on a Panhard-Levassor – Simms was much concerned when Ellis backed His Royal Highness up a steep wooden ramp as 'the combined weight of the two occupants was no small matter'.

ON THE EDGE

S. F. Edge was an outstanding British racing driver and one of the most formidable personalities of early motordom. But even he (accompanied here, in 1896, by his first wife and a friend) was shaken by the turbulence of the bounding Bollée.

KING OF THE ROAD

Even as Prince of Wales, Edward VII gave important encouragement to the motoring movement. But he never learnt much about cars and did not even know that internal combustion engines were fuelled by petrol – his nephew the Kaiser thought they ran on potato spirit. When things went wrong Edward would growl at his chauffeur: 'This should not be!'

By contrast, at the Crystal Palace Salomons could not persuade Lord Salisbury to take a spin on his Peugeot – the Prime Minister thought that 'it might make him seasick'. Salomons declared that Lawson's 'master patents' were not worth the paper they were written on and he had no illusions about the purpose of the Emancipation Run. Its commercial aim was indeed obvious to those who looked below the surface. In the words of Lawson's sharp and natty adjutant Charles McRobie Turrell, who probably suggested this automobile extravaganza, 'no finer or cheaper advertisement could be imagined for ensuring the success of his company flotations'.

Salomons was not alone in trying to expose these enterprises and, despite Lawson's flim-flam artistry, the Emancipation Run actually signalled the imminent collapse of his grand design. So many cars broke down and the performance of the others was so erratic that, after the initial excitement had died down, they were much discredited. The *Daily Mail,* noting that there had been one accident in which a child was injured, described the event as a 'comparative fiasco'. Its proprietor Alfred Harmsworth (later Lord Northcliffe), who was already an enthusiastic motorist, considered its results so poor that 'the less said the better'. The most influential motoring journalist of his day, H. Massac Buist (nicknamed 'the massive beast'), also concluded that the first Brighton Run had been a pitiable 'fiasco'. Worse still, from Lawson's point of view, 'ridicule' was compounded by anxiety about 'company promoting sharks'. The chaotic arrangements, and the plausible suspicion that he had tried to fix the result for his own commercial purposes, prompted press warnings against 'the unscrupulous company promoter'.

Far from taking the hint, Lawson used the Emancipation Run to promote his most outrageous flotation. In his speech at Brighton he descanted on the vast fortunes made during the 'railway mania' and the 'millions and millions of pounds' scooped up by those who had bought bicycle shares. Yet trains were inflexible compared to motor cars and the bicycle was 'a comparative toy'. Investors in the horseless carriage would therefore reap riches beyond the dreams of avarice. A week later Lawson floated his reorganised British Motor Syndicate. He published a dazzling prospectus, decorating it with artists' impressions, extolling the triumph of the Brighton Run, promising almost unlimited profits and soliciting another £1 million. Lawson's prospectus was subjected to damning criticism. Salomons denounced it and found its author 'guilty of discreditable conduct'. Its drafting, said the fashionable *Pall Mall Gazette*, 'would be a disgrace to a playbill'. That journal, like others, exposed Lawson's ineffable compound of audacity and mendacity. It also condemned the 'clever mixing up of a social club with a money-making syndicate … which is not so clever but that it is transparent'.

Later Simms claimed that he himself 'practically' decided to quit the Motor Car Club and to found what became the Royal Automobile Club during the Emancipation Run. It was only at this time, he said, that the Motor Car Club 'began to be exploited for business'. This assertion is specious. And St John Nixon's further assertion – that Simms had almost single-handedly 'saved the British motor industry from ruin while it lay there in its cradle' by keeping it out of the 'clutches of Lawson' – is sheer fantasy. The fact is that Simms was consulting engineer to the British Motor Syndicate and remained closely involved with Lawson at least until the following July. However, he grew increasingly uneasy as the price of shares in Lawson's companies collapsed. Furthermore, the failure of promotional gimmicks like the

PUFFING AND GLOWING

In the 1890s many experts thought petrol dangerous. Steam had an excellent record and the 1891 Serpollet steam carriage (above) was a serviceable vehicle. Electricity, silent and clean, powered the 1897 Jeantaud dogcart (right) and promised to be the energy of the future. But both these 'mechanical travellers' had disadvantages and they were rapidly overhauled by the internal combustion engine.

'Motor Derby' indicated that the Motor Car Club was on its last legs. In the spring of 1897 aristocratic directors like Lord Winchilsea resigned from the boards of Lawson's companies and these were reconstructed. A few months later, after Lawson had ceased to be chairman, Simms left the board of the Daimler Motor Company. Lawson himself struggled to sustain his tottering empire. For a time he even had some success, especially with electric cabs known as 'humming birds'. But electric tramways finally proved his downfall: in 1904 he was found guilty of what the judge called 'an ingenious system of fraud carried out over a long period'. Lawson was sent to prison for a year, with hard labour.

Sir David Salomons, who reiterated that he had 'no pecuniary interest whatever' in the manufacture of motor cars, might have expected his star to wax as Lawson's waned. But, curiously enough, he too was eclipsed in 1897. It was partly that he harped so much on his own righteousness. Insisting that officers of the SPTA such as E. Shrapnell-Smith, Secretary of the Liverpool branch, should not hold shares in motor companies, Salomons boasted, 'The place I have occupied in regard to self-propelled traffic is so exceptional that it is difficult to believe that I have not some ultimate interest in the movement.' More important, Salomons made the mistake of publicly favouring steam cars over petrol-driven machines. Having staked his reputation, he backed the wrong horseless carriage.

SO, BY MID-1897, with its leaders bickering and discredited, British motordom seemed to have lost both its will and its way. The public, which had once been prepared to speculate on vehicles allegedly propelled by 'pendulums', 'gravity' and 'a system of levers', was now reluctant to invest in cars. Automobile exhibitions flopped. The very word was a matter of dispute: some pronounced it 'automobuyle' and others 'automobilly', while scholars objected to it as an improper fusion of Greek and Latin. Contemporaries heeded the warning of Lord Kelvin, one of the most distinguished scientists of his day: 'it was not in reason that … vehicles, propelled by a series of explosions, and using an engine not on a solid base, could reach a practical and permanently useful stage'. In its edition marking Queen Victoria's Diamond Jubilee the *Illustrated London News* celebrated the technical progress of the age with articles on steam and electricity, whereas the car rated only a single mention. The old Queen herself never entered a motor car (though she possessed an electric vehicle – a victoria) and expressed the conventional wisdom about them. She told her Master of Horse, after seeing a picture of her eldest son in a motor car: 'I hope you will never allow any of those horrible machines to be used in my stables. I am told that they smell exceedingly nasty and are very shaky and disagreeable conveyances altogether.' What was needed to restore confidence and a sense of direction, maintained the press, was a 'really independent' body like the Automobile Club de France. It alone could champion the cause of all motorists. Frederick Simms took the cue.

At the end of July 1897 he announced the formation of the 'Automobile Club of Great Britain' ('and Ireland' was added later). With considerable effrontery he equated the SPTA and the Motor Car Club, saying that each had done good work but had 'turned out more or less a single man's institution'. Consequently there now prevailed 'a kind of stagnation' and 'almost

THE PASSING OF THE HORSE

F. R. Simms and Charles Harrington Moore take part in a symbolic drive at Eastbourne's Battle of Flowers, a fête held in May 1896. The girls with the ribbons indicate that this is a horseless carriage, while behind the Cannstatt-Daimler walks a horse with a cloth on its back bearing the letters R.I.P. Reports of its death were exaggerated.

MOTOR PIONEER

The Hon. Evelyn Ellis, in his Daimler-engined Panhard-Levassor at the Tunbridge Wells Show, 1895. Ellis was among the first to drive a car (illegally) in England, but he backed the Automobile Club reluctantly. One of Ellis's passengers wrote that the car was sure to be popular because it 'never requires to be fed … [is] unsusceptible to fatigue … [and] climbs at a faster pace than a pedestrian'. The RAC purchased this vehicle in 1910 and presented it to the Science Museum in London.

an unkindly feeling towards motor carriages'. Here he was on safer ground. After the high hopes that 'a motor millennium' was at hand, the outlook for 'automobilism in this country was dark as dark could be'. But finally, slipping back into the brazen manner of Harry Lawson, Simms asserted that the Automobile Club of Great Britain was an 'accomplished fact'.

It is true that Simms had canvassed the tiny band of late-Victorian 'autocarists', as they were sometimes called, and had gained some influential support. For example, Fred Horner, owner of the *Whitehall Review*, wrote to him: 'there is decided room for such a *cercle*, especially as it will undoubtedly tend to the improvement and ultimate perfection of the motor as a means of independent locomotion; with this idea I am in entire sympathy'. Another enthusiast added: 'I think it is a capital idea to form a club identified with the new industry but quite independent of any of the companies.' Simms had also obtained the adherence of Harrington Moore, who that summer passed with the delicacy of a cat from the Secretaryship of the moribund Motor Car Club to the Secretaryship of the nascent Automobile Club. Moore, who was paid an honorarium of twenty guineas a month, had even translated the rules of the Automobile Club de France. These were to be adapted and adopted by its British counterpart. It was, stressed Simms, to be 'essentially a members' club'. It was to be 'conducted independently of any personal interest' for the purpose of 'social intercourse' and the promotion of automobilism. The latter would be accomplished through tours, exhibitions, competitions, races, the dissemination of information and the establishment of an associated body, known as the Motor Union, open to all. The Club's headquarters would be at 4 Whitehall Place, which Simms announced that he had rented for £400 a year. For all his swagger, though, the British Automobile Club was anything but an accomplished fact. As a correspondent of *The Autocar* complained, Simms had no 'magician's wand' to create it out of nothing. The journal itself deplored the 'apparently hole-and-corner manner' of the Club's inception.

The truth is that probably no club in history has been formed in such comically inauspicious circumstances. Simms's patrician friend Evelyn Ellis had always been against the idea. He belonged to half a dozen clubs, he said, and could drive his car quite well without another one. Even so, Ellis reluctantly agreed to act as chairman at an initial meeting on 10 August 1897. He then said:

> Gentlemen, I have been asked to take the Chair at this meeting to form a Club to further the interests of motoring. My own opinion is that it's not wanted, but as I'm here I propose the first resolution: that we form ourselves into … into … an Automo-bi-le Club, [adding *sotto voce*] what a silly name.

The proposal was unanimously adopted. Ellis therefore continued: 'Well, gentlemen, you all know this kind of thing can't be done without money, so my next duty is to invite you to subscribe to a guarantee fund. If any of you are willing to subscribe, will you please hold up your hands?' There was an ominous silence and no hands appeared. Then Simms softly intimated that he would be responsible for £1,000. In a stage whisper, Ellis replied: 'Well, I think you're very silly, Simms.'

Sir David Salomons thought Simms a knave rather than a fool. At best he might simply be intending to create a smart club for motoring swells. But Salomons feared the worst – that

FREDERICK RICHARD SIMMS

*The founder of the Automobile Club, as portrayed by Mark Milbanke in
1923. He never received the knighthood to which many felt he was
entitled, perhaps because of his questionable commercial activities, perhaps
because people were not certain whether he was a crank or a genius.*

Simms aimed to start another disguised promotional organisation. Salomons' journal expressed his suspicions in polite language: 'Without impugning in the slightest degree the *bonâ fides* of Mr. Simms, we think that his connection with the commercial side of automobilism would operate as a deterrent to many who would otherwise gladly associate themselves with such a movement.' Then, desperate to avoid more contamination by commerce, Salomons acted with an odd mixture of rashness and circumspection. In mid-August, when Simms had gone to hunt 'the wily chamois' in the Tyrol and his solicitor was shooting grouse in Scotland, the press reported that *another* Automobile Club was being started. Suspecting 'mischief', Harrington Moore investigated. He reported to Simms: 'the Pirate Automobile Club was registered on August 17 by Messrs Lumley & Lumley, the solicitors of the Self-Propelled Traffic Association. This looks like the cloven hoof of Sir David Salomons again.' Furious that his old enemy had stolen a march on him, Simms sought counsel's opinion. In September Percy F. Wheeler QC advised that Simms, having invested financially in the new club, could apply for an injunction to restrain Salomons from commencing or carrying out business under the name Automobile Club of Great Britain. Wheeler added presciently that Salomons would be unwilling to have the transaction discussed before the bench as he 'would not come into court with clean hands'.

The legal mills began to grind. Harrington Moore swore an affidavit that Salomons had been notified of Simms's proposal and, being 'greatly annoyed at the said Club having been formed without his cooperation', was trying to 'render it a failure'. In his turn Salomons avowed that he had no memory of receiving the circular announcing Simms's plan and that Lumley & Lumley had acted on the instructions of the Automobile Club de France, which had long pressed him to create an English equivalent. He concluded with his familiar refrain: his interest was 'entirely in the public interest and in no way to benefit myself financially'. But this was a feeble defence. On 29 October a jubilant Moore informed Simms (now in Stuttgart) that Salomons had 'caved in', his counsel admitting privately that 'they had no case'. So Salomons relinquished his putative rights to the club title. And Moore, who in the heat of the battle had accused him of 'unworthy tactics' and 'obvious malice', now suggested that Simms should extend an olive branch. He would thus 'remove a source of ill-feeling which can have no other than an injurious effect on the progress of mechanical traction in this country, which all parties have at heart'. Simms, having twice been wronged by Salomons over the formation of a club, proved implacable. In particular, he refused to accept Moore's emollient formula whereby Salomons was to dissolve all 'unfriendly sentiments' by acknowledging that the whole affair had been a misunderstanding.

Perhaps Simms's bitterness stemmed in part from a guilty consciousness that Salomons understood him all too well. It would have been surprising if he had not had pecuniary motives for founding the new Club. Certainly its amateur status and its relations with the motor trade were always problematic. There was a nice ambiguity about being 'interested' in motor cars; and the issue of whether that interest could be commercial as well as intellectual would become a well-gnawed bone of contention in the Club. Yet Simms may also have refused a reconciliation because he felt that Salomons had misjudged him. For it is clear that Simms was not just out to make money. He had other creative interests, to which financial considerations were often subordinated. Simms, as his daughter says, was 'above all an inventor'. Some of his notions were

No. 169, March 27, 1914.]   The Royal Automobile Club Journal.   257

AN ELECTRICAL TRAFFIC-WARNER.

UNDOUBTEDLY one of the most urgent needs of the present time is some means whereby the driver of a car can warn followers in traffic that he is about to stop or change his course, and so prevent accidents. There have been numerous attempts to produce such an apparatus, but almost all have failed because of their complicated nature and the impossibility of keeping the many rods and levers in adjustment. In order to overcome mechanical difficulties, an electrical signalling apparatus has been placed on the market by Simms Motor Units. The means adopted to warn a following driver that the vehicle preceding him is about to turn is that of causing an

THE COMPLETE TRAFFIC WARNER WITH REAR LIGHT AND NUMBER PLATE ILLUMINATOR

arrow to appear pointing to the left or to the right. The construction of the warner is such that the arrow is practically invisible, in the daytime as well as at night-time, until the lamp behind it is illuminated. An ordinary four-volt battery will supply sufficient current for lighting the lamps, which may be separate and placed one on either side of the car or combined in a single casing. To enable the arrows to be illuminated, the steering wheel is provided with two switches, one on the left and one on the right, the driver pressing the switch corresponding to the direction in which he is turning. When necessary it can be arranged so that the mere fact of moving the steering wheel a certain number of times to the left or to the right causes the arrows to be illuminated.

A more elaborate system, emanating from the

same source, provides for additional signals that indicate the intention of a preceding driver to slow up or to stop. In this instance, combined in one casing are left-hand and right-hand arrows, the signals "Slow" and "Stop," a red rear light, and a side light for illuminating the number plate. The system of control for direction is the same as in the smaller system, while to give warning of an intended stoppage there is a switch

THE SIMMS TRAFFIC WARNER, SHOWING LEFT-TURN AND RIGHT-TURN SWITCHES, WITH LAMPS AS SEPARATE UNITS AND COMBINED.

interconnected with the clutch pedal which causes the warning sign "Slow" to appear when that pedal is depressed. The "Stop" signal comes into action whenever the rear-brake lever is applied.

LIGHT CAR RELIABILITY TRIAL, 1914.

THE interest shown in the forthcoming Light Car Reliability Trial has given rise to a number of inquiries as to the centre from which the trial will be run. This was not published in the Regulations, the only information given being that the 1,000 miles would be covered by six daily runs from a centre. Harrogate has now been selected. This town provides excellent hotel accommodation, and the country around is suitable for a trial of this kind.

Speed Records at Brooklands. — Successful attempts were made on March 18th on the 60 h.p. class records at Brooklands, when J. Chassagne, driving a 177 h.p. twelve-cylinder Sunbeam car, covered the half-mile in 15·03 sec. (119·6 m.p.h.) and the mile in 29·82 sec. (120·73 m.p.h.), both being considerable improvements on existing records.

Found. — On the road between Festiniog and Portmadoc, Rudge-Whitworth wire wheel with tire and case. Loser should communicate with the Secretary of the R.A.C., 89, Pall Mall, London, S.W.

INVENTOR EXTRAORDINARY

Simms was often so far-sighted that he was way ahead of his time, as his early car indicators and tank prototype suggest. The 'war car', fitted with a four-cylinder engine, 6 mm armoured-steel plate, a Maxim gun and two pom-poms, attracted no interest from the War Office when he demonstrated it at the Crystal Palace in 1902. However, his work on magnetos, largely a German preserve before 1914, helped to provide Britain with an independent supply of these vital components during the First World War.

unsound and he lacked the mental stamina and business skill properly to realise the rest. But this otherwise orthodox Victorian, full of prejudices against the Church of Rome, discourse on the benefits of empire and maxims about the dignity of labour for men and the need for women to guard their tongues, was an individual of rare vision and originality.

Simms created many 'original designs' which car makers have 'universally adopted', notably magneto ignition. On this he worked for years with Robert Bosch, showing 'a great deal of courage, lots of enthusiasm, and an eye for the possibilities of the automobile', if not 'a rigorous conception of … clean business dealings'. He made Simms-Welbeck cars, lorries and marine engines. He invented the first rubber bumper. Simms produced a prototype indicator which he called a 'traffic warner'. He patented a motor plough and a caterpillar tractor. He devised motorised Maxim guns and armoured ancestors of the tank described as 'locomotive forts'. He provided technical equipment for Captain Scott's Antarctic expedition. He patented various aeronautical devices including the joystick, gyroscope and airbrake. Simms was responsible for innovations in insulators, pneumatic tyres, taximeters, telephones, cable-cars, railway ticket machines, even cocktails – he once came up with a 'jelly cocktail' which his family pronounced 'disgusting'. He claimed to have coined new terms, like 'petrol' and 'motor car' (as opposed to 'motorfly', 'electrobat', 'autokinetic', 'non-equine'). Such claims were fanciful but he certainly minted the expression 'motour' (i.e. tour by motor car) which, like other hybrids, did not survive. Most of all, though, Simms had a passion for founding clubs.

He pursued this passion throughout the autumn of 1897, undertaking 'mountains of delicate work' to bring the Automobile Club of Great Britain into full existence. Simms arranged for the decoration and furnishing of the commodious (some said 'cavernous') ground-floor rooms at 4 Whitehall Court. He organised the provision of service and supplies, including 'liquors, cigars and refreshments, and other articles of consumption'. He called preliminary meetings to discuss matters like storing members' cars – they agreed that the 'expenses of stables' should be shared. He decided that the entry fee should be four guineas and the annual subscription two. He set up the Club's holding company, Automobile Proprietary Ltd. He held 'daily conclaves' with Moore, who later claimed to have played a far from auxiliary part in the preparations. Certainly the cheeky, cheerful Moore – he was known as 'Moore the Merrier' – did more than merely sustain Simms. He also tried to ensure that the new Club was not regarded as another one-man band. In a letter to the press Moore declared that Simms had long disassociated himself from Lawson and had

> resolved to attempt the organisation of a Club which should be entirely free from
> personal interest or self-aggrandisement and, being governed by themselves and not
> by or in the interests of any one man, should, like the Automobile Clubs of France and
> Belgium, be a truly national institution, devoted only to the best interests of what
> must surely become one of the greatest industries of this great country.

But if, as the years went by, Moore increasingly emphasised his own role, he did acknowledge Simms's 'initiative, pluck and foresight' in founding the Club. Its great merit, he added, was to have been 'absolutely free of the taint of Financialism' at a time when 'faith in the future of motor-cars was practically non-existent'.

ROGER WALLACE QC

The first chairman of the Automobile Club. He urged its members to take the advice of Shakespeare's Hotspur: 'Let good manners be your speed.' Simms paid tribute to the 'immensity' of Wallace's achievement in guiding the Club through its difficult formative years.

ACGBI HQ

The cover of the menu for the 'light luncheon' before the inaugural meeting of the Automobile Club of Great Britain and Ireland features the proud building in part of which it was first housed.

THE INAUGURAL RUN

Charles Rolls drives the leading car in the first parade of the Club's vehicles, immediately after its formation in 1897. In the next sits (as passenger) Henry Mulliner, who lived until 1967, the longest-surviving founder member of the Club. He is followed by F. R. Simms driving a Cannstatt-Daimler.

Anything but the remorseless Juggernaut of legend, the British car had made little progress since its maiden run to Brighton. It needed a powerful push. So in November Simms announced the inaugural meeting of the Club, urging that in order to match Continental success 'it is of the utmost importance that those who are prominently interested in the movement should rally round one institution, which, in a national sense, should represent the true interests of automobilism in Great Britain'. His exhortation was timely, for Harry Lawson, though already sinking himself, was trying to take the wind out of Simms's sails. Early in December he and the new Secretary of the Motor Car Club, Charles Jarrott, staged another run from Whitehall Place, this time to Richmond. About forty horseless carriages took part, drawing large crowds. Afterwards Lawson made a witty, impudent speech, saying that he liked the horse except when it pretended to be a motor. 'When you nail iron to his feet; when you put iron in his mouth; when you strap him in iron in the shafts … the poor thing has positively become an infringement of the British Motor Syndicate's patents.'

By contrast the inaugural meeting of the Automobile Club of Great Britain and Ireland was an understated affair. It was preceded by a light luncheon at the Hotel Métropole which consisted of consommé, lobster, *foie gras*, *contrefilet*, chicken, pheasant, partridge and Charlotte Russe. Then, in the early afternoon of Wednesday 8 December 1897, the 120-odd automobile enthusiasts adjourned to 4 Whitehall Court. The pioneering motorist Roger Wallace QC took the chair; indeed, he became first Chairman of the Club, from 1897 to 1904. The rules were adopted. The future programme was agreed. Thanks were expressed to Simms for the 'spirited manner' in which he had guaranteed the first year's expenses. In reply he modestly paid tribute to Moore. Finally some members who possessed motor vehicles (most did not) rode along the Embankment as far as Battersea to demonstrate them. They included two gleaming Arnold carriages powered by Benz motors, two smart electric omnibuses which bystanders dubbed 'the elephants', several handsome Daimlers and the famous Panhard No. 6, fitted with a Daimler-Phoenix four-cylinder engine, and driven by its new owner, the Hon. C. S. Rolls. The display, like the début, was not especially impressive. Yet, supported by over 160 eminent members (a figure that rose to 380 within a year), the Automobile Club was destined to last. It was scarcely an exaggeration to say, as *The Autocar* did a quarter of a century later, that its history 'is the history of the automobile movement in this country'.

SPEED MERCHANT

*Charles Rolls in Panhard No. 6, the car that
had won the 1896 Paris–Marseilles–Paris
Race. He bought the car from Lawson after the
Emancipation Run for £1,200.*

MOTORING ON THE MAP

*Early members of the Automobile Club were often sportsmen,
adventurers, daredevils. But they were also practical pioneers
of a revolutionary mode of transport. And, as the horseless
carriage began to turn into the motor car, they were eager to
prove its worth.*

**BADGE OF
DISTINCTION**

*The talisman of
motordom, which
members could wear in
their lapels.*

BEFORE THE FIRST WORLD WAR motor cars were luxuries that only the
prosperous could afford, so the Automobile Club attracted affluent
members – an open secret of its success. 'I doubt,' wrote an Edwardian
journalist, 'if there be collectively a wealthier club in the world.' But even
in an age that was given to the 'worship of wealth', cash was supposed to
be matched by cachet. The Automobile Club was a gentleman's club. As
its first full-time Secretary, Claude Johnson, said, 'Anyone interested in
automobilism is eligible for membership, though, naturally enough, we
observe some social restrictions.' This meant that candidates were
blackballed if they came from the wrong side of the class divide – lacked
the correct 'background', were too obviously 'in trade', had a 'common'
appearance, 'ran out of aitches' and so on. Thus the Club decided that 'a
working manager was not eligible for election'. It also refused to admit 'professional cycle
riders', one of whom was proposed by founder member S. F. Edge. Yet, as if to prove that the
restrictions were elastic, Edge himself had been a professional bicycle rider (and a pugilist)
before going into the car business and becoming a victorious motor-racing driver.

The career of Charles Jarrott, another founder member, followed a similar pattern.
According to a well-informed, if malicious, early motorist:

> It pleased Charles to wear a high collar and ape the manners of more fortunate people,
> and talk nonsense about Oxford, Cambridge or any other university whose name he
> heard mentioned; but Charles was educated, *if* he was, at what was called a 'church'
> school [in] Pimlico …. [Charles mimicked] what he regarded as a gentlemanlike
> accent … while he remained moderately sober.

In general, though, founder members of the Club – and thus the leading dramatis personae of early motordom – were outwardly respectable. But they were not entirely conventional.

At their head were the aristocrats, noble by birth and often adventurous by inclination. Lord Carnarvon, for instance, was a horse-racing old Etonian who, like many of his peers, regarded driving primarily as an exciting new sport. Carnarvon soon developed a reputation as 'a motor scorcher' and special traps were set to catch him. 'Clouds of dust as high as the neighbouring trees,' said a policeman who had calculated his speed as 24mph, 'rose up as his car whizzed along the road.' In 1901 Carnarvon had a serious accident which so affected his health that he was obliged to spend much time in the warm climate of Egypt. He thus became the patron of Howard Carter, who in 1922 discovered the tomb of Tutankhamun. Another patrician founder member was Charles Rolls, son of Lord Llangattock. Tall, thin, with bright, bird-like eyes and a ragged, drooping moustache, he was another motoring 'dare devil'. He was also notoriously mean, preferring to sleep under his car than to pay hotel bills and taking his own sandwiches into the Club dining room – it retaliated by imposing a sixpenny table charge. Not content with terrestrial thrills or with the immaculate products of his partnership with Henry Royce, Rolls eventually took to aviation and became the first Briton to be killed in an aeroplane crash.

Rolls was not alone, incidentally, in exploiting his social position to sell cars. Other early Club members, such as Montague Grahame-White and Major Sherwin Holt, did the same. Before the First World War, as the writer Ian Hay said, it was an inexplicable but indisputable fact that 'You may sell motor cars for a living and remain a gentleman.' Acquiring mechanical knowledge, though, was a more ticklish business. When George Cornwallis-West, one of the Club's brightest social ornaments, wanted to find out what made his single cylinder de Dion go – on one occasion when it refused to do so he had felt it necessary to hire a special train – he took a job in a Paris garage under the name of Smith.

Still more prominent among the blue-blooded early members of the Club was Frank, Earl Russell. He was the elder brother of Bertrand Russell, who wrote that their parents had regarded Frank as 'a limb of Satan' and that he 'set out to live up to this reputation'. Frank was duly sent down from Oxford for 'malpractices' and later imprisoned for bigamy. But though raffish, choleric and litigious, his eyes glittering behind gold-rimmed spectacles, his paunch thrust forward like a challenge, Earl Russell claimed to be 'by profession an electrician'. Certainly he loved engines, bought cars to which he gave exotic names like 'Pegasus' and soon learnt the joys of speed. When number-plates were introduced he stayed up all night in order to obtain the first registration – A1. As a result the police were readily enabled to identify Russell, much to his indignation, as a 'hooligan driver'.

The Hon. Rupert Guinness was altogether more staid, though he was less a member of the peerage than the 'beerage'. He also became a member of parliament and a pioneer exploiter of the car for political purposes. During elections he transformed his bottle-green, yellow-wheeled de Dietrich into a striking advertisement for the Conservative party. It had 'blue across its roof, blue wheels, and blue mudguards, with blue rosettes and portraits of the candidate making a frieze around the car'. Guinness shocked his parents by refusing to keep a carriage when he got married in 1904: he relied on stately motor cars with enough roof space

RIVALS ON THE ROAD

Whether racing or selling cars, Charles Jarrott (here at the wheel of an eight-horsepower Panhard) was often in contention with his passenger, S. F. Edge. Jarrott, who liked to shoot rabbits from his speeding vehicle, thought Edge 'rather too inclined to consider his neck'.

ROLLS BEFORE ROYCE

Charles Rolls was a skilled engineer and a dealer in Panhards like this one, as well as a daredevil driver. Here he looks surprisingly smart. Usually he wore rough clothes for motoring and was mostly visible, said Lord Montagu, as a pair of boots under a car.

to allow him to wear a top hat. Later he inspected his estates in a *deux-chevaux* Citroën, replacing the horn and calling his prize cattle home with 'a device that gave out a lowing sound'.

Among the less socially elevated early members of the Club were a number of journalists. They played an important role, none more so than Alfred Harmsworth. Having begun his career as the editor of *Bicycling News* in Coventry, where (his employer found) 'self-reliance, ambition and abounding energy were his chief characteristics', Harmsworth had gone on to become a powerful press magnate. Motor cars were good for the circulation, in more senses than one – the new sensation of driving at speed, he found, was like 'being massaged in a high wind'. Harmsworth championed these 'vehicles of the future' at a time when many journals were ignoring or attacking them. Thus he helped to root out 'the astounding prejudice displayed at that time in England', though, in search of sensation, his *Daily Mail* often pandered to the very same prejudice that he condemned. Harmsworth sustained, perhaps even saved, the Club with generous donations. He also threw his weight behind Claude Johnson, declaring that the Club's first Secretary, 'as much as any man, developed motoring in Great Britain'.

Other journalist members assisted in that development. In the *Automotor Journal* Stanley Spooner fearlessly exposed 'unscrupulous commercial exploiters' of the horseless carriage. During the first ordinary meeting at Whitehall Court, on 9 February 1898, Arthur Walter, chief proprietor of *The Times*, said that the Club should display motoring pictures and photographs, put maps at the disposal of members and compile a register of professional drivers. Henry Sturmey, editor of *The Autocar*, became the first man to drive a car from John O'Groats to Land's End, in 1897. Charles Cordingley founded the *Motor Car Journal* to boost his automobile exhibitions, in which the Club for a time had a stake. Henry Norman MP, an enthusiastic amateur mechanic, was owner of *The World's Work*, which was soon 'singing the swan song of the horse' – one rendition went, 'It's all U.P. with the old G.G.'

Many other early members of the Club had some kind of commercial interest in mechanical traction. Harvey du Cros had set up, with John Boyd Dunlop, the world's first pneumatic tyre factory. The consulting engineer Edward Manville was a director of Daimler and built tramways all over the world. Paris Singer, a generous benefactor of the Club, founded the City & Suburban Electric Carriage Company. E. S. Shrapnell-Smith, who resigned from the Self-Propelled Traffic Association and became a stalwart of the Club, was manager of the Road Carriage Company. Frank Lanchester, an edgy, fidgety man, worked with his brother Fred, an engineering genius who would produce cars which gave an experience like 'riding on velvet'. Two famous coach-builders who soon saw that their future lay in making motor bodies were 'Georgie' Thrupp, an admirer of 'graceful lines' in chorus girls as well as cars, and Henry 'Mingy' Mulliner, who was the last founder member to die – in 1967, aged ninety-seven. Less reputable was the director of the so-called Motor Car Emporium, Dr E. C. Lehwess, who in 1902 attempted to drive his huge yellow Panhard 'Passe Partout' round the world, getting stuck in a snowdrift at Nizhny-Novgorod. Eventually he had to resign from the Club for various misdemeanours including the attempted bribery of a policeman. But perhaps the most blatant scoundrel to become an early member was Charles Yerkes, the American 'Rapid Transit King' who masterminded the financing of London's electric underground railway. He made Lawson look like a philanthropist. Yerkes was pilloried in two novels by Theodore Dreiser as

MOTORING MOGULS

Leading figures in the automobile world, brought together in this montage during the early 1920s, were proud to be members of the Parliament of Motoring.

From left to right, standing:
D'Arcy Baker (Fiat), W. R. Morris (Morris), Hamilton Hobson, Sir W. M. Letts (Crossley), S. F. Edge, F. Shorlands (Straker-Squire), H. J. Vane (Napier), James Sealy-Clarke, Sir A. S. Mays-Smith, F. S. Bennett (Cadillac), Charles Jarrott, F. W. Hatter (Holweiss), J. Starley (Rover), A. Brown, Malcolm Campbell (Itala), F. Pullinger (Arrol-Johnston), L. Walton (Vauxhall).
Seated:
F. Lanchester (Lanchester), Sir Herbert Austin (Austin), Claude Johnston (Rolls-Royce), Col. A. Cole (Humber), A. McCormack (Wolseley), E. Maverick (Daimler), E. M. C. Instone.

a rapacious social-Darwinist tycoon, a lobster in a world of squids. After the death of this 'distinguished member' in 1905, the Club *Journal* paid tribute to his 'brilliant and romantic, if chequered, career'.

By contrast, many more or less disinterested scientists and engineers were quick to join the Club. Best known among them was Hiram Maxim, the American designer of the machine-gun, which helped to preserve British dominion over palm and pine. During the early 1890s Maxim had tried to perfect a steam-driven flying machine, though it proved too heavy to get off the ground. He turned to experiments with motor-car engines, being a 'chronic inventor' to match Frederick Simms himself. At Whitehall Court he often 'electrified the assemblage with entirely irrelevant, but particularly interesting historiettes'. A number of technically inclined military officers also became founder members. Colonel R. E. B. Crompton, for example, had the distinction of straddling the Crimean War – he was in the trenches as a cadet aged only ten, before going on to Harrow – and the Great War, during which he constructed tanks for Winston Churchill. In India he had driven the first steamer, a ferrous leviathan called the 'Blue Belle', along the Grand Trunk Road. An expert on highways of all sorts, Crompton did as much as any Club member to prepare British roads for the motor age. The Club's most eminent soldier, though, and its second Chairman, was Brigadier-General Sir Henry Holden (as he became). He was head of the Royal Gun Factory at Woolwich, 'the man upon whom the empire depends for its straight-shooting guns'. In 1895 Holden had built a four-cylinder, air-cooled motor-cycle with electric spark ignition, which bore his name. Later he drew up the plans for Brooklands racetrack and helped to create the 'Magician' car self-starter.

Hoping that it would always remain 'a Club of good fellows who met together for fighting the Battle of Automobilism', Crompton would later recall the 'scrappings' and 'larks' they had got up to in the early days. Yet the breadth of technical expertise encompassed by the founder members of the Club (to say nothing of the depth of the scientific papers read there) was remarkable. W. J. Crampton, who christened one of his early cars 'Fireworks', installed electricity in Sandringham. Mervyn O'Gorman, who described motor-cycling as the 'nearest approach to the thrill of hunting I know', later became superintendent of the Royal Aircraft Factory. W. Worby Beaumont had experience of railway, dock and foundry work. He was also editor of *The Engineer* and became adviser to the Metropolitan Police on the subject of horse-less carriages, about which he wrote with formidable erudition.

Most founder members, though, were simply users of cars. They were gentlemen, professional people, company directors, lawyers, accountants, stockbrokers, plus one or two doctors and clergymen. Some were captains of industry. The dapper merchant miller Mark Mayhew was a Vice-President of the Club and organised the Motor Volunteer Corps in 1903. The exquisitely *soigné* Alfred Bird, 'father of the Custard Powder', had been an amateur bicycle champion and served on endless Club committees to promote what a hostile witness called 'the aggrandised proliferation of road-pests'. The wine merchant Frank Hedges Butler, the Club's first treasurer, sustained his portly person during the vicissitudes of infant motoring with 'Bath Oliver biscuits and one or two bottles of dry sherry'.

Such members, though they would probably have had a smattering of mechanical knowledge, were unable 'to execute their own repairs'. A few were invincibly ignorant. On a ride

CHARLES HARRINGTON MOORE

*Formerly Secretary to Lawson's Motor
Car Club, Harrington Moore helped
Simms to found the Automobile Club –
mostly, it was said, by dint of 'cheek
and smiles'. Moore developed
considerable commercial interests in
motoring and criticised grandee
amateurs on the RAC's Committee.*

CLAUDE JOHNSON

*The first Secretary of the Automobile Club
(until 1903) who later became the business
brains of Rolls-Royce, Johnson was a model of
ability, industry and integrity. No one was
more responsible for the early progress of the
British motoring movement.*

MERVYN O'GORMAN

*A pillar of the Club and an authority on
motoring until the 1950s, O'Gorman was a
man of wit, culture and originality. He warned
Edwardian motorists that those who looked like
scorchers, with heads down and hats jammed
over their eyes, would certainly be arrested and,
if caught near Andover, would 'probably be
hung'. But he also inspired the Highway Code.*

with Frank Butler, Worby Beaumont found that the car kept stopping and starting because a wire was only making intermittent contact with the terminal, its screw having gone. 'Does that matter?' asked Butler. 'That screw was always getting loose, so I threw it away.' Yet technical ineptitude did not disqualify figures like Butler from making a sterling contribution to the Club. Sir David Salomons, himself a founder member despite his antipathy to Simms, went so far as to say that the Club owed its success not to 'handle-named gentlemen' but to 'forty hard-working men with a certain amount of business instinct and tenacity'.

In fact, as Harmsworth said, much of the credit was due to one man, Claude Johnson. Simms, Moore and others described Johnson as an 'organising genius' and he certainly 'coupled with a keen and creative imagination the ability to do and to get things done'. Johnson's father worked most of his life for a pittance in the Science and Arts Department at Kensington Museum. Claude, born in 1864, was thus brought up in humiliating shabby-genteel circumstances. The family was a loving one: there were plenty of 'rags', sing-songs, picnics, walking tours and trips to see the Christie Minstrels. But his parents were also intensely pious and the youthful Claude suffered agonies of terror about the Day of Judgement, especially during black London fogs. Later he was hostile to 'semi-pagan fanatics, religious maniacs and German bigots'. He had a wry sense of humour and waxed irreverent about 'Onward Christian Soldiers' which, he said, seemed to have strayed into *Hymns Ancient and Modern* from *The Yeomen of the Guard*. Claude developed pronounced tastes in art as well as music. But he had little chance to indulge them at St Paul's School, where he was sent thanks to heroic sacrifices by his parents, or at the Imperial Institute, where he became a clerk at the age of nineteen. Shortly afterwards an elopement, productive of many children but little happiness, further cramped Johnson's style. But his industry and efficiency were soon noticed, not least during the Motor Exhibition at the Imperial Institute in May 1896. Johnson became convinced of 'the undreamed of potentialities of automobilism' and he accompanied the Emancipation Run on a bicycle. The following year Harrington Moore secured his services as Club Secretary.

Well over six feet tall, with a cliff-like forehead, a luxuriant moustache, large capable hands and an intimidatingly taciturn air, Johnson was an impressive figure. Although never a dandy, he was very clothes-conscious and, earning ten shillings per new member on top of an annual salary that rose to £1,000, he dressed impeccably. His eldest daughter remembered 'ginger Harris or off-white hairy tweed, white socks, silkiest of shirts, flowing yellow-and-white silk ties and, more often than not, red morocco slippers when not walking or golfing'. Johnson's wavy brown hair was perfectly groomed and he always smelled of bay rum or eau-de-Cologne. He wore his bowler hat at a slightly rakish angle.

Like his equally handsome friend Alfred Harmsworth, Johnson had an eye for the ladies. For a time the two men employed attractive sisters, Rose and Nelly Thornton, as their secretaries. Both were 'new', emancipated women and Nelly went on from her post in the Automobile Club to become Lord Montagu's mistress. She also posed in the nude for sculptor Charles Sykes, whose Flying Lady statuette was to adorn the bonnet of Rolls-Royce cars. Johnson, who himself later became the managing partner – 'the hyphen' – in Rolls-Royce, said that the mascot was intended to convey the spirit of the car: 'Speed with silence, absence of vibration, the mysterious harnessing of great energy, a beautiful, moving, living organism of superb grace.'

SPIRIT OF ECSTASY

The Silver Lady, known as the Spirit of Ecstasy, symbolised the style of Rolls-Royce cars. Eleanor Thornton, on whom the figure was probably modelled, became Lord Montagu's secretary and the mother of his child, whose existence was kept secret. In 1916 Montagu was travelling to Egypt with Nelly when their ship was torpedoed. He was rescued after three days in an open boat. But 'the most wonderful and lovable woman' he had ever met perished.

The spiritual qualities of the statuette were not those which immediately appealed to Lord Northcliffe, who was neither the first nor the last to discover erotic connotations in motors and motoring. After a round of ninety-eight on the golf course at Fontainebleau, he told Johnson, 'I found your sweet little lady waiting to console me. Alas that she is bronze; if it were otherwise ….' Northcliffe hoped to build up a 'harem' of these mascots but amused himself meanwhile with the 'lively little Hungarian' baroness to whom Johnson had introduced him.

As this suggests, the heyday of Edwardian hedonism was about to dawn and Johnson's occupation was to attend to the pleasure as well as the business of the Automobile Club. Its members were devoted to both. At the meetings which preceded house dinners papers were read on weighty subjects such as 'What positions are likely to be occupied by steam, electricity and oil in modern mechanical locomotion?' Or 'What is likely to be the position of the Motor Car in relation to railways?' Information was disseminated about repairers, 'stables' (i.e. garages), charging stations for electric cars, and suppliers of petrol. Chemists, ironmongers and hotels were among the establishments selling two-gallon cans filled with this vital fluid which, Shrapnell-Smith recorded, 'was styled deodorised naphtha, and was often malodorous and incompletely combustible'. The intricacies of differential gears and steering cogs were discussed. So were the needs of those who wanted to go abroad with cars and those at home who were attracting the attention of the police. Worby Beaumont spoke sonorously about the Club's being the representative of 'the whole motor-vehicle constituency', whose task it was to dispel the 'misguided prejudices of a very small turbulent minority'. But a certain Mr Petter (probably Ernest or his brother Percy, who together built one of the first motor cars and later founded Westland Aircraft) punctured the pomposity by hoping that the Club would remove 'the prejudice of ladies against autocars, since that prejudice was a matter of great pain and concern to himself'.

In fact ladies were permitted to enter 4 Whitehall Court only between three and six o'clock in the afternoon. And even then they were confined to the General Reception Room. But the Club did not become a barracks as a result of their exclusion. On the contrary, the burden of formality between the sexes was so onerous that the absence of ladies added to the ease of gentlemen. As a member later said, he disliked 'cock and hen' clubs because there he had to put on 'company manners'. If admitted to the Automobile Club, he added misogynistically, ladies would 'stand and chatter on the stairs … monopolise the best seats in the dining and reading rooms … [and] demolish any barrier of rules which the mere man may erect to guard some private retreats for himself'. By themselves, therefore, the gentlemen relaxed in the lap of luxury. The lounges were comfortably furnished; many journals were provided; the card room was elaborately equipped; a billiard-table was purchased; ample meals were served in the dining room; the servants were smartly uniformed and smoothly efficient.

Later generations have been amused and puzzled by an inventory which shows that on 12 February 1898 the Club possessed only 88 glasses, 48 knives and forks and 24 spoons, while managing to cater for a hundred guests at the first house dinner. It is further known that the steward, Robert Burrows, was allowed only one pail, one flannel, one dustpan and one swab. More piquant still is the fact that Burrows possessed but two pairs of under-drawers, both of which were 'at tailors'. However, 'the silent but terribly efficient Claude' (as an MP called Johnson) was hardly the man to be nonplussed by these little local difficulties. Burrows, too, rose

"W'y, I remembers the time w'en I'd 'ave stopped *that* for furious drivin', an' I reckon it 's only goin about a paltry fifteen mile an hour!"

" .*I r!* Now them cyclists is puttin' on a fairish pace! Summat about twenty mile an hour, I s'pose. But 'tain't no business o' mine. *I'm* 'ere to stop *Motor-caws.* Wot ho!"

" 'Tain't no use tellin' me you've broke down! Stands to reason a Motor-caw goin' down 'ill 's *bound* to be goin' too fast. So we'll put it down at about thirty mile an hour! Your name and address, Sir, *hif* you please."

PUNCH ON SPEED

Early cartoons – this one is from Punch *in 1902 – mocked the standard notion of slow coaches and fast cars. In 1898 the bodyguard of bicyclists which accompanied Club tours kept up with the motorists over long distances.*

magnificently above them. He appeared in 'a gorgeous livery consisting of a blue velvet tailed coat, trimmed with gold lace, the lapels of which bore the Club monogram; yellow and black striped waistcoat, and crimson velvet breeches, white silk stockings, and patent buckle shoes'. Whatever the state of his unmentionables, he looked from the outside like 'a cross between a sergeant major in the French army in full dress and the Lord Mayor's coachman'.

MOTORING, THOUGH, was the *raison d'être* of the Club and one of Johnson's main tasks was to arrange the initial 'runs'. The first was scheduled for Easter 1898. Well advised by Simms that the cars should not attempt more than forty miles a day, Johnson planned a route through the southern counties of England. He then inspected it aboard Frank Butler's Benz. Their journey was full of incident: the car shed tyres, belts and chains; its owner had much recourse to Bath Olivers, sherry and cigars; and the two men finished their tour by train. The run itself was also eventful. There were many breakdowns. One member hit a cow. Two others severed a long-standing friendship over a dispute about whether it 'would be better for the prestige of automobilism generally' to turn an eight o'clock dinner into a ten o'clock supper. White tie and tails, incidentally, were worn for evening meals at hotels and transported in the Club's luggage van. Over the years the motor car, too small to take the trunks full of clothes which had accompanied smart Victorian rail travellers, helped to relax traditional dress codes.

Another foretaste of the future was provided on the Hog's Back by Colonel Crompton, who 'kinematographed' the Daimlers, Benzes, Bollées and de Dions. These behemoths were attended by shoals of bicyclist pilot fish; though an unkind critic used a different image, likening automobiles to dung beetles embraced by a host of parasites. Most people still regarded the cars as marvels. They had to push through 'masses' of 'enquiring humanity' in Winchester, Chichester and Tunbridge Wells. Club members talked earnestly about the 'educational' and 'proselytising' work they accomplished on the Easter tour. No doubt they were keen to gain converts. After its second tour a member deplored 'the reckless scattering of crowds and general bad form which go so far to check popular admiration for motor-carriages and their patrons'. Yet the prime purpose of these 'Pickwickian sprees' was not propaganda. It was pleasure.

In the words of Filson Young, who devoted a whole book to the joy of the road, the fact that the car 'is there – alluring and fascinating in its magical power of carrying us so quickly in the wake of our wishes – secures for it without a struggle the allegiance that used to be given to more sober pleasures'. Especially intoxicating was the novel sense of freedom. About this other Club members waxed lyrical on subsequent odysseys, both organised and disorganised. Man was liberated from the animals which had propelled him, as Claude Johnson liked to say, since the time of Noah. Unshackled from the iron grid of railways, he was emancipated as an independent traveller. He had easier access to culture. 'The motor-car enriched life like the discovery of two or three new poets,' declared Frank Harris, who said in *My Life and Loves* that he was probably the first person to have seen in one day, courtesy of the 'magical' vehicle, the four great cathedrals of France (Amiens, Beauvais, Notre-Dame and Chartres). Like a bird, man could escape from the narrow confines of time and space. He could acquaint himself once more with the distant countryside and forge fresh links with nature. Breasting hills and dancing down dales

JOINT JOURNEY

Club members toured through the eastern counties at Whitsun 1898. Here they are at the famous Arc Works in Chelmsford, developed by the distinguished engineer Colonel Crompton (seated on the right in the middle car). Also present are Charles Cordingley (seated on the right in the right-hand car) and Claude Johnson (standing at the front, second from the right), who organised the journey.

OVER THE HOG'S BACK

One can almost hear this Daimler puffing over the Hog's Back in Surrey on the Club's first tour, through southern England, at Easter 1898. Such hills presented a challenge to early motorists. But the car, driven by Ernest Instone, Secretary of the Daimler Company, carries a heavy load, including the bowler-hatted Sir J. R. Somers Vine.

in his horseless carriage, the Hon. Leopold Canning felt imbued with raw life, spirit and vigour: 'the next morning you awake refreshed and strong like a young eagle'.

The car itself became an extension of the motorist, endowing him with new capacities and inspiring him with new challenges. Rudyard Kipling was one of many Club members to revel in his mastery of complicated and intractable machinery through skill of eye, hand and brain. He compared the 'snapping levers and quivering accelerators' of a steam car to organ keys on which 'marvellous variations' were improvised, 'so that our progress was sometimes a fugue and sometimes a barn dance, varied on open greens by weaving fairy rings'.

Such raptures notwithstanding, progress on the Club's first tours was always painfully slow. Starting cars in the first place was a difficult and sometimes a dangerous business – if the motor backfired the handle could recoil and break a thumb or wrist. Drivers had to undertake a complicated ritual involving lubrication, shutting drain cocks and opening petrol valves. Bollées, which seemed to be made of 'tin biscuit boxes and wire', were particularly intransigent: 'if you wished to start out at ten you had to be up at six' and when the engine did fire (rather than *catch* fire) it sounded like 'a cross-Channel steamer blowing off'. Once going, cars deserved their popular epithet of 'hearses' and drivers got tired of hearing that they would be faster on stilts. In 1896 the highest average speed attained over a long course was no more than 16mph. Many horseless carriages simply refused to climb steep hills. Sometimes they even slid backwards to the bottom: their brakes hardly functioned in reverse and the steel anchors intended to stop them from rolling back, known as 'sprags' or 'devils', did not always hold. Going downhill forwards with inadequate stopping power could prove even more terrifying. This was especially the case in a Bollée, whose tail swayed from side to side during descents and 'would sometimes come round and look at you'.

'Stoppages,' as Baron Henri de Rothschild said, 'were as frequent as milestones on the roadside.' They were caused by every kind of mechanical defect, assisted by vibration so fierce that it was known as 'automobile ague'. Mark Mayhew recalled a journey to Wales which took a week because of faults with, or accidents to, almost every component in the car – oil and petrol pipes, ignition plugs, brakes, chain, induction valve, battery, steering gear and tyres. It was said to be possible to follow the course of a Club run by the nuts, bolts, belts, chains and other spare parts scattered over the road. Charles Jarrott maintained that on a hundred-mile tour 'one took out enough parts to make a new car, and generally made it before one got back'. Delays were so much the rule that passengers equipped themselves with books, knitting and 'Motoring Chocolate'. Drivers, who had to mend multitudinous punctures before detachable rims were introduced (in 1906), referred to pneumatic tyres as 'rheumatic'. They tried various solutions, including filling the inner tubes with straw, feathers and sticky paste. None worked and tyres were often reduced to ribbons after a thousand miles. Tempers also frayed, though happiness outweighed hard feelings.

Club members got intense satisfaction from victories of mind over machinery. They enjoyed the 'feeling of brotherhood', the sporting camaraderie which ensured mutual aid and comfort during setbacks. But they were often maddened by the cussedness of the inanimate. Towards the end of one Club tour on his suitably named Locomobile, Hubert Egerton got so furious with a recalcitrant oil lamp, which was necessary after dark to ascertain the amount of water

DECAUVILLE, 1899

The Decauville (right), called a voiturelle *in order to avoid conflict with the Bollée (below), was powered by a two-cylinder, air-cooled engine at the rear. It could be started by winding the side-wheel next to the driver's seat. The Decauville was the first petrol-driven production car to have independent front suspension.*

BOLLÉE, 1898

Léon Bollée patented the design for his three-wheeled voiturette *in 1895. Powered by a single-cylinder engine with hot-tube ignition and a three-speed gearbox, it was an idiosyncratic machine. But it worked and it introduced many to the pleasures (and pains) of motoring. The Bollée was the first vehicle specifically intended to have pneumatic tyres.*

needed to top up the boiler, that he hurled it into the River Thames at Surbiton with horrid imprecations: 'There goes three-and-sixpence to Hell!'

Cars themselves were often regarded as infernal machines by those accustomed to what Thomas Hardy called the 'tomb-like stillness' of Britain's deserted highways, where little stirred save 'a wan procession of coaching ghosts'. The English press condemned the early Club tours, which sent a 'train of fiends' scampering about the countryside. When the dirty-dungareed Duke of Sutherland, sometime President of the Automobile Club, thundered up to a Scottish toll-gate and asked how much he had to pay, the frightened keeper replied: 'Naething, Mr. De'il, to *you*.' Driving his 'fiery chariot' in Ireland another stalwart of the Club, R. J. Mecredy, was 'seriously mistaken for "Anti-Christ"'. Catholics often crossed themselves. Terror was the first response to the incursion of 'an evil-smelling, noisy monster, let loose to carry havoc among quiet folks'. In rural areas, as Charles Rolls recalled,

> every other man climbed up a tree or a telegraph pole to get out of your way; every woman ran away across the fields; every horse jumped over the garden wall as a matter of course; and every butcher's cart … bolted off, scattering various spare parts of animals about the road.

The car administered a shock to the nation's system. Since the coming of the railways Britain's roads had grown sclerotic from lack of use. Now new blood pulsed through arteries and veins accustomed only to the farmer's wagon, the carrier's cart, the brewer's dray, the beanfeaster's char-à-banc, the doctor's trap, the squire's carriage and, of course, to Shanks's pony. Traffic had been little, local and slow. The first passage of motor cars, however palsied, through any country district was so dramatic that it was recorded in every neighbourhood newspaper. Some reporters seemed surprised, according to Rolls, that the horseless carriage had occupants at all.

Familiarity bred contempt and – with it – hostility. As cars multiplied from the seventy-five-odd vehicles which the Club could muster at the time of its foundation into hundreds and then into thousands by the end of the Victorian age, so complaints against them increased. The automobile was denounced because it 'barked like a dog and stank like a cat'. 'Stinkpot', indeed, was the epithet generally hurled after what Kipling called 'the petrol-piddling monster'. It was ridiculed for sounding like 'an avalanche of tea trays'. People mocked it for being thirstier than a horse, slower than a coach and infinitely less reliable than a train. Its foreign provenance was also a handicap: nothing good, surely, could come out of bombastic Germany or degenerate France. Most Britons in 1898 regarded motoring as 'madness'. In the words of a typical provincial newspaper: 'The more one sees of these ugly, cumbersome, and noisy vehicles the less one hopes they will ever become popular.'

That this was not an absurd hope is demonstrated by the Club's exhibition at Richmond Park in June 1899. Johnson, rapping out staccato orders, went to immense trouble and expense to make it a success. He organised enclosures, marquees and grandstands. He obtained royal and aristocratic patrons, despite Sir David Salomons' protest that social toadyism smacked of

MOTOR
MISCARRIAGE

Great hopes and ambitious plans for the Richmond Show, expressed in the cheerful cover of its catalogue, badly miscarried. It attracted too few spectators and the resulting financial loss threw the Automobile Club into serious disarray.

'snobbishness and weakness'. Johnson arranged trials, hill-climbs, races and demonstrations. However, the initial procession of vehicles from Whitehall Court was badly 'stage-managed', with some breakdowns and much straggling. Many cars did not pass their official tests. The gymkhana failed to establish that petrol was a better fuel than hay: in various contests the trotter 'Gold Ring' proved at least a match for Edge on his de Dion tricycle. Two single-cylinder Decauville *voiturelles* escaped from the control of their conductors during a trick-driving display and knocked down a couple of dummy policemen. Some of the inventions displayed, such as the French 'vibrationless car', F. R. Simms's puncture-proof tyre and C. R. Hutchings's trigger-fired car bell (in lieu of a horn), were unconvincing. Attendances were poor and, as Johnson disgustedly said, the public showed that it 'didn't care a button about motor cars'. The Club lost £1,600. It could have collapsed had it not been bailed out by members such as Alfred Harmsworth and Charles Cordingley – the latter earned the right to make a private enterprise out of future Club exhibitions. Taking full responsibility for the failure, Johnson tendered his resignation. But, according to St John Nixon, Simms persuaded him to withdraw it.

If so, it was not the least of Simms's services to motordom. For at that very moment, despite appearances to the contrary at the Richmond Show, the horseless carriage was changing into the motor car. And Johnson was to be its leading impresario. Of course, the transformation did not occur overnight. The car was not a butterfly emerging from a chrysalis. It evolved, remaining for years excessively primitive and prone to breakdown. Much of the equine vocabulary remained – 'dashboard', 'boot', 'hind wheels' and so on. Improvements were not universally adopted. The controls were not standardised: in Lanchesters the driver operated the accelerator with his left foot and the horn bulb with his right; in Delahayes he pressed down the left-footed accelerator to go more slowly, released it to go faster. Even the contest between petrol, steam and electric power had yet to be resolved. But the expression 'horsepower' was beginning to evoke cylinders rather than sinews; and most vehicles had ceased to look like phaetons without shafts. They had lost the small front wheels and the high ground clearance which were legacies of coaching days. Mudguards were being incorporated into bodywork. Tillers were giving way to steering wheels. Electrical ignition was superseding platinum tubes heated by burners. Solid tyres were obsolescent and pneumatic ones were being refined. So were radiators and suspension systems. Above all internal combustion engines were becoming more efficient. Belt transmission had had its day and four cylinders were proving their worth. Club members rightly hailed the automobile's progress between 1897 and 1900 as 'marvellous'. Independent observers reckoned its usefulness to be 'so incontestable that it is certain ere long to conquer all prejudice'. This was far from being the case. In fact, what chiefly alienated the general public was the great new feature which recommended cars to their owners – power.

At the dawn of the twentieth century motorists realised the dream of the nineteenth: the sensation of autonomous speed. By 1900 they could complete long journeys at an average rate of more than 25mph. As cars got faster so their drivers succumbed to 'the fascination and the frenzy of speed for speed's sake: the rush through the air, mocking the bird in its flight'. Hearts throbbing to the beat of pistons, motorists tasted the exhilaration of acceleration. Skin tingling in the vortex of motion, they revelled in the quickened pace of existence. Danger added spice to life. Speed was a drug, to be evoked in the vocabulary of the addict. It was an

MOTOR STABLES

*The Hon. Evelyn Ellis was typical in keeping his 'stud' of cars
– looked after by 'motor grooms' – almost as though they were
horses. The words 'garage' and 'motorist' were just being
introduced in 1900, when this photograph was taken. But
Ellis still rode 'on' his Daimlers and Panhard-Levassors, not
'in' them. Edwardian automobilists retained equestrian
attitudes as well as terminology.*

'ineffable thrill', 'the exaltation of the dreamer, the drunkard, a thousand times purified and magnified'. To one's 'expanded senses the noise of movement is heavenly music, the wind like the wine of the gods.' Moderate, steady men, once behind the wheel of a powerful car, observed Charles Jarrott, seemed to become 'possessed by the concentrated energy of a thousand fiends'. One Club member compared travelling through the Lake District at 48mph aboard a twenty-four-horsepower Darracq to 'floating on a feather-bed between heaven and earth'. Club members often cocked a snook at the speed limit. It was, indeed, so unrealistic that it would have put a brake on mail coaches, which had been able to maintain averages of 14mph. Moreover, drivers argued, the roads were empty and they had their vehicles under 'perfect control'. So the legal restriction became a matter for levity. One swift-driving clergyman quipped that he 'brought more people to God by giving them a lift' than he ever did in other ways. The Club Chairman, Roger Wallace QC, advised a gathering of motorists in Lincolnshire that 'if they were going faster than they knew they were – (laughter) – never to go to the danger of passers-by'. Harrington Moore, who was himself apt to treat the Queen's highway as a racetrack, was more equivocal. 'While nearly all of us express publicly, and with great demureness, the utmost deprecation of high speeds, especially through towns and villages, and crowded traffic, I am afraid that a good many of us "wink the other eye".' It soon became plain, however, that this cavalier attitude was likely to discredit the entire automobile movement.

As a boneshaker the car could be disdained; as a bone-breaker it would be condemned. As speeds rose and accidents increased, the chorus of opprobrium swelled. The car was excoriated as a murderous 'Moloch'. It was, in the phrase of that inimitable Irish-American character Mr Dooley, a '40 horse-power Suffer Little Children'. Eminent persons pronounced that 'the excessive speed of motor cars could be and should be prevented'. The police initiated speed traps in 1898 and magistrates fined those who were caught by them. Motorists complained of persecution, sometimes justifiably. When one of Edge's friends proved that he had not been in the place where he was charged with speeding, the magistrate retorted that 'even if he were not driving at excessive speed at the place in question, he was doubtless doing so somewhere else!'

The Automobile Club, which boasted over 540 members by the end of the century, defended them in cases of 'vexatious prosecution'. Its fiery lawyer, Staplee Firth, won some such cases. On 8 November 1899 the first edition of the Club *Journal*, then known as *Automobile Notes & Notices*, crowed: 'These victories will teach motor-haters that they cannot take advantage of the prejudice which exists against motors; for motorists mean to fight for their rights.' Actually, as appears from this and subsequent issues of the *Journal*, the Club was on the defensive. It went to great lengths to discourage 'scorchers'. It advised members to avoid undue acceleration, hazardous overtaking, sudden turns, abrupt stops and driving at speed into hotel courtyards. At the beginning of 1900 the Club passed a new rule providing for the reprimand, suspension or, in aggravated cases, expulsion of members guilty of reckless driving. This was defined as anything 'ungentlemanly, unsportsmanlike, or prejudicial to the interests of automobilism'. The Committee assumed that 'larrikinism' was likely to increase as cars multiplied and fell into the hands of the 'first class "motor bounder"'.

The Club was already on the horns of what was to become a permanent dilemma. It was the arbiter of automobilism, committed to its expansion; but the larger the movement grew the less

AUTOMOBILE INSIGNIA

Designed by one of Simms's draughtsmen, this was the Club's badge from 1898 until royal patronage was bestowed in 1907. Rose, thistle and clover leaf entwine inside the diamond; but the leek is mysteriously missing. Members wore the badge on their cars and after 1900 hotels approved by the Club displayed it on large enamelled plaques.

the Club could govern it. A major part of the problem stemmed from the nature of the Club itself. By definition it was exclusive: so motor bounders and their ilk were ineligible for membership. But that increasingly tended to invalidate the Club as a representative organisation. In an important letter to the Club *Journal* S. F. Edge made the point:

> we say we are the leading and controlling body in the automobile world, but to remain in that position it seems to me that it is absolutely necessary for us to have everyone in as members who are willing to join, providing there is nothing to be said against their character, and that their social position in life should have little or nothing to do with their joining.

This was as logical as it was trenchant. But Edge at once conceded that his *omnium gatherum* was an impossible ideal. The 'Club must have class distinction if it is to in any way retain and increase its social side, and it is to be hoped that it will'. This meant, as Edge prophesied, that 'there must be quite a large and growing body of Automobilists who will be outside our ranks, and who will then sooner or later wish to found an opposition organisation'.

Edge was not alone in urging the Club to avoid this eventuality by forming its own umbrella organisation for all motorists. From the first Simms himself had proposed that the Club should act in conjunction with a Motor Union, open to every class of automobilist, though nothing had come of the scheme. In 1898 Salomons and Wallace had taken a significant step towards motoring unity by amalgamating the Self-Propelled Traffic Association with the Club, though the irreconcilable Simms opposed the move as 'likely to cause dissension'. In the same year the Scottish Automobile Club was founded (to pursue the 'new and pleasurable' sport of motoring) and affiliated to the English Club. Whitehall Court also gave its blessing to English branches which sprang up in response to provincial enthusiasm. Opening a branch in Lincolnshire, the white-moustached, smooth-tongued Roger Wallace said that 'it should be for all classes, and so long as there was good fellowship it did not matter whether they were Dukes or mechanics'. Finally, in 1901, the Club merged its Motor Vehicle Users' Defence Association, founded the previous year, into the embryonic Motor Union, forming a body which any automobilist could join. This was the Automobile Club's first (but not last) serious attempt to reconcile its wish to remain an élite with its aspiration to become a popular organisation.

Despite this democratic initiative the Club remained unconscionably grand. That was its principal strength: only its members combined the wealth, prestige, expertise and sporting spirit that were necessary to promote automobilism at that time. However, as Edge had indicated, being a club – dignified and preoccupied with its own social activities – was a definite weakness when it came to leading a mass movement. Members became increasingly aware of this handicap. Some believed that local clubs should be called 'Societies for Encouragement'. Johnson said that the Club itself, but for following the French example, might well have been named 'The Automobile Institute', modelling itself on the Institute of Civil Engineers. He did his best to broaden the Club's scope, seeing a 'great future' for it as an administrative, more than a social, body. Already, in 1899, it had beaten off a challenge from the National Cyclists' Union and constituted itself as 'the recognised authority to regulate and control all Automobile Races, Competitions and Time Trials in Great Britain and

No. 1. WEDNESDAY, 8th NOVEMBER, 1899. VOL. I.

AUTOMOBILE CLUB NOTES & NOTICES.

PUBLISHED BY
THE AUTOMOBILE CLUB OF GREAT BRITAIN AND IRELAND,
WITH WHICH IS INCORPORATED
THE SELF-PROPELLED TRAFFIC ASSOCIATION.
FOR THE INFORMATION AND USE OF MEMBERS OF THE CLUB ONLY.
Edited by a Committee of the Club.
4, WHITEHALL COURT, LONDON, S.W.

PLEASE NOTICE

This publication is intended :—

(i.) To take the place of the many notices which are from time to time issued to Members ;

(ii.) To afford to Country Members and others, who cannot visit the Club frequently, information concerning the doings of and at the Club ;

(iii.) To be a means of intercommunication between Members ; and

(iv.) Generally to keep Members in touch with the important work which the Club has in hand in the interests of the Automobile Movement.

These notes should have the effect of increasing the practical value of membership, especially to Country Members.

Members are requested to note that, in future, no notices will be sent to them other than those contained in the issues of this publication. They are therefore asked to kindly peruse carefully the weekly "Notes and Notices," and to file them for reference. By so doing they will assist to reduce the heavy work of the Club office.

The Committee of the Club desire to express to the Editors of the "AUTOCAR," "AUTOMOTOR" and "MOTOR CAR JOURNAL," and to other Editors, their sincere appreciation and cordial thanks for the courtesy and support extended to the Club by the publication of its notices and proceedings ; and the Committee hope that the Editors will continue, through the valuable medium of their respective journals, to make known to the public the purposes and proceedings of the Club.

Correspondence is invited.
The space, however, is limited, as the Committee in undertaking the very considerable expenditure involved by the publication and circulation of the "Club Notes and Notices" have decided, for the present, to confine it to four pages.

The Committee will insert as much correspondence as possible, but Members are begged to bear in mind that all correspondence, whether it be published or not, will receive the careful and unbiassed consideration of the Committee.

The "Club Notes and Notices" will be published as often as occasion may demand. Probably, except during vacations, the issue will be weekly, for a young and vigorous movement requires unremitting attention on the part of Committees, and therefore there will be much to record.

This publication does not deal with technical matters in its editorial columns, although technical matters may form the subject of correspondence between Members who are seeking co-operation or advice from fellow Members.

The Rules laid down in the conduct of this publication are briefly :—

(i.) Correspondence must be signed.

(ii.) Members writing concerning motors or accessories in which they may be financially interested will—as a point of honour between Members—declare the fact of their interest in their letters.

Coming Events.—A diary of coming events in connection with the Club will be printed at the right-hand lower corner of the front page of each issue in such a form that it may be cut out and placed in the pocket without mutilating any other part of the matter. The notices are continued on the back of this special slip.

A List of Members of the Club will be occasionally issued with this publication for the information of Members.

Records of Trials of Motor Vehicles made by the Club will be published.

Letters should be addressed to the **Editing Committee, Automobile Club, 4, Whitehall Court, London, S.W.**

To be Cut Out for Pocket-Book.

DIARY.

1899.

Friday, 10th Nov., 5 *p.m.* Meeting of Manufacturers and Members at the Club to discuss Trials and Exhibitions for 1900.

Tuesday, 14th Nov. Meet at Club, 11.45. Annual Banquet at Club 7.45 *p.m.*

Wednesday, 15th Nov., 12.30 *p.m.* Conference between Club Committee, Deputation of Liverpool Branch, and Manufacturers of Heavy Vehicles *re* TARE LIMIT.

Wednesday, 15th Nov., 5 *to* 7 *p.m.* (*and every Wednesday*). Special Evening for Meeting of Members for intercommunication and introduction.

Thursday, 23rd Nov., 8 *p.m.* At Queen's Hotel, Manchester. Meeting to inaugurate Manchester Branch of the A.C.G.B.

Thursday, 30th Nov., 8 *p.m.* At Glasgow. Meeting to inaugurate the Scottish Branch of the A.C.G.B.

[P.T.O.

CLUB CHRONICLE

The first edition of the Automobile Club's journal. The content was seldom more exciting than the typography, members often complained, but they read it like holy writ. Moreover the journal was not far wrong to say that in its pages 'must be found all the material that the future historian of the automobile movement will require'.

Ireland'. Now Johnson wanted it to do more in the way of advising governments, granting licences, organising trade exhibitions, helping the industry and disseminating information.

For publicity purposes he exploited his friendship with Harmsworth, who made 'a special feature of Automobilism in the "Daily Mail"'. It ran a series of articles extolling motors as 'vehicles of the future'. Johnson could have doubled his income by contributing to them himself but he thought the independence of the Club and its executive officers should be strictly observed. So he fed the *Mail* general information and it responded by puffing the Club, only noticing cars, for example, that were submitted to its tests. Harmsworth also helped manfully with Johnson's ambitious scheme to 'remove feelings of distrust and dislike' for cars by staging a Thousand Mile Trial throughout the United Kingdom. He not only guaranteed it financially but also offered some £450 in prizes. Years later the newspaper proprietor recalled vividly how the Club Secretary, 'always modest, never seeking the limelight', had 'worked untiringly' to organise 'the first great tour of Great Britain, which did so much to prove to the public what a change was soon coming over the deserted state of our roads'.

Johnson told Simms that he hoped the Trial would be 'the biggest and most important thing done in this country'. Once again he scouted the course, which stretched from London, via Bristol, to Edinburgh and back. It was a hazardous winter venture, including an ascent of icy Shap Fell in the Lake District with 'considerable muscular assistance' and a 'weird drive in the dark' beside Thirlmere which ended with a bent axle. Johnson secured the co-operation of local newspapers, police and surveyors, who promised to suspend road works in the cars' path. He arranged exhibitions of the automobiles *en route*. And he persuaded manufacturers to enter the Trial. It would be 'one long advertisement for the motor vehicles taking part', he urged, giving them a chance to demonstrate their reliability. In the event manufacturers were willing to pay for the privilege, so the Club was put to no expense. They also submitted to the elaborate tests which Johnson set. To ensure adherence to the rules, including that which forbade speeding, each car had to carry an observer. This did not stop the Trial from becoming a race, with the connivance of the police, in some sections of the journey. Nor did it prevent one company from surreptitiously changing engines during the Trial and then claiming a £10 prize.

Anyway, early on a cold, grey April morning in 1900, a crocodile of motor cars (accompanied by a legion of bicyclists) set off from Grosvenor Place. They were a mixed lot. On display were spanking new models of Panhard, Peugeot, Daimler, Wolseley and Napier. But there were also old-fashioned rattletraps, wheezing Benzes, clattering Decauvilles and chattering Eurekas. Some dropped out quickly, including an 'imposing-looking French vehicle with a gigantic ornamental bonnet like a great blossom, but the inner petals of which consisted of a scattered collection of oil cans and spanners, jacks and waste'. Also soon to vanish was a lady in knickerbockers called Miss Bacon riding on a Werner motor-bicycle, a vehicle which even Leopold Canning considered very dangerous, though it was capable of providing 'splendid exercise for a professional acrobat'. Once again the spectators gathered in huge numbers. The future Lord Brabazon of Tara was punished for cutting lessons at Harrow to watch 'these heroic figures on their fascinating machines'. The crowd applauded indiscriminately. Maidenhead was swathed in bunting. Twyford schoolchildren waved flags. In some places the cars' progress 'almost rivalled a royal procession'. They were greeted royally, too, at their first stop. This was Calcot

THOUSAND MILE TRIAL, 1900

Some of the sixty-five starters gather at Hyde Park Corner for a journey round Britain organised by the Automobile Club to counter hostility to the car and to demonstrate its revolutionary capacities. The first car is a six-horsepower Panhard-Levassor driven by Frank Butler, accompanied by his daughter Vera. The third is a Daimler belonging to Alfred Harmsworth (in the passenger seat) and driven by Captain Hercules ('Herky') Langrishe.

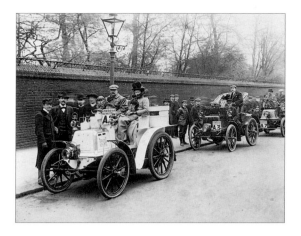

HARMSWORTHIAN HOSPITALITY

Harmsworth gives Trial participants a champagne breakfast at his country mansion, Calcot Park, near Reading. This picture was probably taken by the photographer who infuriated the founder of the popular press by intruding into his guests' privacy from the vantage point of the stable roof.

Park, near Reading, where Harmsworth had laid on a sumptuous breakfast. Inside two red-carpeted marquees white-waistcoated waiters served the motorists with salmon and quails, York ham and *pâté de foie gras*, which was washed down with 'bounteous beakers of champagne'. Harmsworth was furious when a photographer climbed a ladder onto the roof of his stables to get a picture of this feast. But when asked what he would have done in the photographer's shoes, the press magnate promptly replied: 'I should have dragged up the ladder after me.'

Thereafter the vehicles made steady, if bumpy, progress round the country. 'Stinks,' wrote that distinguished Scottish member of the Club Sir John Macdonald, 'by no means resembling the spices of Araby, floated back to us on the road, and bangs, in a succession that recalled a *feu de joie*, made us jump or laugh.' Sometimes drivers jolted along quite unconscious of the fact that the entrails of their cars were trailing on the ground. They left a jetsam of grease caps, nuts, spanners and crank handles to guide the stragglers. Hills were still a challenge: occasionally all the passengers *and* the driver had to run up steep ones beside their puffing vehicles. The cobblestones between Manchester and Preston slowed down many cars and outside Newcastle a gale blew some to a complete halt. Mechanical breakdowns were frequent. Cars could sometimes be seen with legs protruding from under them 'like the antennae of some gigantic beetle, and anon a belt would fly off in front of us, curling on the road like a boa-constrictor'. Ingenious repairs were effected. Monty Grahame-White constructed an additional casing for his vulnerable burners out of a Huntley & Palmer's biscuit tin. When his steering gear broke, he directed the car for fifty-two miles by applying pressure to the hub-cap with his foot.

Accidents also occurred. On his six-horsepower Daimler, J. D. Siddeley (later Lord Kenilworth, one of the great figures in automobiles and aircraft) collided with a 'noble quadruped'. The 'bag' of 'smaller game' consisted of seven or eight dogs, one sheep, a cat and a sparrow. The Simms tricar 'turned two complete somersaults through incautious driving on the Bristol tramlines'. When the clutch of his Napier failed S. F. Edge drove backwards down Dunmail Rise at a record 20mph, before coolly bringing it to a stop. Driving forwards down the hill into Macclesfield 'at *something* over five miles an hour', Charles Rolls lightened his Panhard of attendants and baggage at an 'unusually sharp turn'. Later his car caught fire and later still he achieved a dead heat with an express train of the North Eastern Railway when racing between Otley and Guisely, and lost his famous black hat. The unorthodox garb of the drivers, incidentally, seems to have caused more offence than their new-fangled machines. Wearing a cap that covered his whole head, the white-bearded Colonel Magrath attracted urchin cries of 'Kruger! Kruger!' Henry Sturmey, who resembled a Choctaw Indian in the region of his moccasined feet, above which he might have passed for an Eskimo, was among those who provoked an emphatic response from a lady in one market town. '"Well, now, we have seen the creatures,"' she remarked to her party, 'giving an expressive feminine gesture of disgust which said plainly, "We won't have anything to do with these motor cars."' But no disapproval could quell the exuberance of the pioneers, or onlookers, during this momentous Trial. Captain Hercules Langrishe slung a horse's nosebag from a broomstick and attached it to the bonnet of his car. Someone retaliated by fixing a placard to its rear proclaiming, 'What an ASS!'

This by no means expressed the public view of the automobile, or of the Automobile Club, in the wake of the Thousand Mile Trial. On the contrary, the whole venture was a triumph of

PLEASE DRIVE CAREFULLY

Trial cars were timed at the Maidenhead toll-gate to prevent speeding in the town. Here a Blake voiturette, *driven by its maker, accompanies competitors.*

CIVIC DIGNITY

The mayor of Reading, wearing the top hat, is taken for a spin in a seven-horsepower Georges-Richard during the Trial. The Club strove to persuade influential people that cars were safe.

what would today be called public relations. It was, indeed, the greatest such coup ever achieved by the Club. It put motoring on the map. It introduced the car to tens of thousands of people who had never before seen one. The 'motoring missionaries', as John Montagu called his fellow drivers, made instant converts. Speaking for most contemporaries, *The Times* pronounced that the Trial had achieved its object of proving the car

> a serious and trustworthy means of locomotion; not a toy, dangerous and troublesome alike to the public and its owner, but a vehicle under as perfect control as a Bath chair, capable of accomplishing long journeys, in all weathers and over every kind of road, with ease and safety, destined to take its place with the train and the bicycle as a common object of daily life, and as superior to them in many respects, as they are superior to the horse and cart.

In the Club's scrapbooks the newspaper notices of the Trial measured 504 feet in length and nearly all the coverage was favourable. Even *The Field* concluded, with a sigh of regret, that 'the roadster of the future will not be fed with oats'.

But the motor car was hardly secure in public affections. *The Field* was happy to expatiate on the kind of prejudice that was destined to grow. 'As the bicycle was described as a roving circular saw, whose mission was to wound and maim the liege subjects of Her Majesty, so the motor car is regarded as a malodorous, noisy monster, with the same malevolent intentions.' However, the Trial had for the first time presented the vehicle as a true, and attractive, reality. Before April 1900 critics could reasonably dismiss it as a piece of Wellsian science fiction, the plaything of 'visionaries and lunatics'. Giving evidence to a Royal Commission in 1899, John Major, a Yorkshire breeder, had said: 'I don't think for one moment that all the cycles and motor cars in the world, after the novelty is gone, will ever cause our English gentry, or their sons and daughters, to turn their backs on a beautiful typical riding or driving horse.'

After the Trial, as Sir John Macdonald observed, sceptics sounded like those who had preferred the semaphore to the electric telegraph and messenger boys to telephones. They resembled Dr Dionysius Lardner, who had expressed his willingness to eat the steamship which could cross the Atlantic. They were tarred with the same brush as that other scientist, supposedly Faraday, who had stated that it would be as practicable to light the streets of London with slices of the moon as to do so with gas carried in pipes. The Thousand Mile Trial, as Macdonald said, 'was the kindling of the real fire never again to cease glowing'.

The Trial achieved more still. It was, as Frederick Simms noted, the 'first milestone of the British motor industry'. Virtually all the cars which had taken part in the Emancipation Run were foreign and most were prototypes, experiments on wheels. The Thousand Mile Trial was the proving ground for new and better models. Admittedly foreign cars were still in the ascendant. And only twenty-three out of sixty-five vehicles satisfied all tests, some of which were carried out by the Club with signal lack of precision. But the Trial marked the superiority of the internal combustion engine. It demonstrated that the car, when fitted with equipment like pneumatic tyres, a steering wheel, a water cooling system and electric ignition, had decisively overtaken the horseless carriage. British manufacturers who adopted such innovations, consigning their 'antediluvian' models to the South Kensington Museum with the 'Rocket', said

EDINBURGH EXHIBITION

Nine one-day exhibitions were held in major cities en route *to advertise the virtues of the competing cars. This one is at Edinburgh's Waverley Market. The bearded man on the right of the platform is Henry Sturmey, editor of* The Autocar. *Sitting on the rail is John Montagu.*

TRIAL'S END AT WHITEHALL

A triumphant conclusion, especially for Charles Rolls, whose twelve-horsepower Panhard-Levassor (at the front) was the only car to take a gold medal. Behind is Edge's Napier (in which sits the fourteen-year-old St John Nixon), winner of a bronze.

John Montagu, would end 'the pitiable spectacle of a "four-wheeler" passing a panting motor car on Savoy Hill'. The Trial did indeed accomplish 'wonders' towards restoring public confidence in British machines after the financial fiascos of the Lawson era. It led to a surge of purchases which boosted the domestic car industry. As Montagu told Winston Churchill in 1904, automobile production 'has gone ahead by leaps and bounds, and there is a vast improvement in the quality as well as the quantity of the output during the last three or four years'. Stimulated by foreign competition, Montagu thought, manufacturers of the best British cars – Napier, Daimler, Argyll, Wolseley – were making money. In their turn, as Henry Sturmey said, garages and motor depots sprang up like mushrooms.

Last but not least, the Trial increased membership of the Automobile Club and established it, beyond a peradventure, 'at the head of the movement' for motoring in Britain. In the words of the *Automotor Journal*:

> If there is one matter more than another upon which automobilists have cause to congratulate themselves it is upon the excellent work which is being done for them by the Automobile Club. Were it not that this body, backed by the indomitable energy and perseverance of Mr. Claude Johnson, the Secretary, had stepped into the breach at a time when reckless company promoters were bidding fair to ruin the prospects of the industry in England, many years would, without doubt, have elapsed before automobilists could have expected such a cordial welcome in the country as they have received during the recent 1,000-Mile Trial.

It was a fine irony that some of these self-same company promoters, notably Simms himself, were now pillars of the Club. The buccaneering Edge was already taking advantage of it to help promote his business concerns. He later confessed that as a motor trader he had 'made very good use of the Club's facilities for demonstrating the merits of the goods I had to sell'. Edge had also driven his Napier in the private section of the Trial despite having a financial interest in its manufacture, escaping censure only because a protest against this breach of the rules was entered too late. Nevertheless, the *Automotor Journal*'s plaudits were well merited. The Club had rescued the reputation of motordom and organised the greatest automobile event which had so far taken place in Britain.

THOUSAND-MILE TRIER

A New Orleans, a trade entry driven by a certain Mr Askell, arrives at Maidenhead in 'the greatest trial ever run by the Club'.

CHAPTER THREE

THE PARLIAMENT OF MOTORING

*As Edwardian cars went further and faster they
provoked attacks from horse-riding aristocrats, bourgeois bicyclists
and plodding proletarians. The Automobile Club used all its
authority to try to quell 'motorphobia'. But it was hampered by
private feuds and public fears of death on the road.*

GRAND TOURISTS

*John Montagu's
magazine was founded
in 1902. It appealed to
the aristocracy of
automobilism during
the Edwardian period
but later moved
down market.*

FOR A TIME THE AUTOMOBILE CLUB shone with the reflected glory of the Thousand Mile Trial, and the highest in the land smiled on motordom. On 17 May 1900 Arthur Balfour, who was soon to become Prime Minister, told the House of Commons that he sometimes looked forward to a time when 'great highways for motor traffic might be constructed'. A month later Edward Prince of Wales, soon to be King, took delivery of his first car – a chocolate-and-black Daimler phaeton – and set the royal seal of approval on the marque and the movement. In the same year Kipling, who had already refused the poet laureateship, began to 'Muse among Motors' for Harmsworth's *Daily Mail*, hymning cars in various styles of verse borrowed from the past. The tributes were generous in view of the writer's own experiences with cars. His first machine, a 'heart-breaking Locomobile' acquired in 1901, had a record of 'eternal and continuous breakdown'. True, she was silent 'but so is a corpse'. During her brief flurries of animation this 'hell and a half of a motor' paved the road with her fittings and spat boiling water into Kipling's lap. He called her 'a Holy Terror' and said that she had converted him to belief in 'a personal devil'. However, despite his motoring travails, a catalogue of 'agonies, shames, delays, rages, chills, parboilings, road-walkings, water-drawings, burns and starvations', Kipling remained a staunch devotee of the automobile. It was a 'time machine' which travelled down the centuries in a land where 'the dead, twelve coffin deep, clutch hold of my wheels at every turn'. Moreover it enabled him to live in the country while enjoying the amenities of the city. The car, he declared, was a 'civilising agent, a moral force, one of the dynamic factors of the great march of progress'.

The gospel that 'transportation was civilisation' had been preached by the Club, as Kipling said, from the start. Its message, rapidly gaining ground, was that the internal combustion engine could improve the quality of life for everyone. Part of this process would be the elimination of that noxious locomotive anachronism, the horse. In the words of Worby Beaumont:

> As early as possible motor cabs and omnibuses must displace horses so as to save the space now occupied by them, avoid the spreading all over the streets of that which renders them dirty and unhealthy, and avoid the pounding to pieces of wood, asphalt and others of the best paving with the three-cwt hammer of iron-shod feet.

Beaumont's view that the motor car would ease congestion and reduce pollution in city streets may cause astonishment today. But it was an Edwardian truism, repeated by leading figures like Balfour and H. G. Wells, and trotted out by others at the drop of a top hat. This was not surprising for, in the short run at least, it was true.

The horse and cart was larger, slower and clumsier than the motor vehicle. The horse, as one Club member lamented, was 'a most imperfect machine. Its principles are horrible to the engineer. It moves in unstable equilibrium.' Surprisingly, it often made more din than its mechanical rival. Colonel Crompton was one of many who was struck by 'the extraordinary thunderous noise of the streets of London', when they were crammed with steel-wheeled, horse-drawn vehicles rumbling and clattering over granite-block paving. The horse was also far messier than the motor car. Each of Britain's three million horses, most of them urban beasts, produced between three and four tons of dung a year. 'A large town is really a colossal midden with houses dotted about in it,' wrote a journalist in 1900. Despite an army of sweepers and scavengers, the streets were in a state of perpetual filth. After rain they became manure-filled morasses and pedestrians could not go far without fouling their clothes. When the dung dried its dust blew everywhere and was stirred up in little eddies by the long skirts of Edwardian ladies. Farmyard insects abounded and 'great cities had a country air'. Confident in their mission to substitute 'the sweet, clean motor for the dirty horse', automobilists claimed their Club 'as distinctly belonging to the Progressive Party'.

Kipling described the horse as their 'hairy enemy'. Leopold Canning called for its 'total abolition', though he said that he did everything to keep out of the animal's way when driving, 'short of climbing a tree or burying the car in a neighbouring field'. But other Club members, notably Sir David Salomons, claimed that the motor was the horse's friend. Mechanical conveyances would deliver spavined nags from enslavement to the harsh hansom and the 'cruel omnibus'. On this issue alone Salomons was at one with Harry Lawson, who had hurled some of his choicest abuse at the official 'friends of the horse'. They

> blindfold him with blinkers, strap him up in shafts, gag him with iron bits and bearing reins, and sit over him with whips, putting him under the lash as a reward for his hard work. I can imagine the horse saying, 'If ye are my friends, thank God you are not my relations.'

Lawson's rhetoric rang hollow. So did expressions of compassion from motorists who were keen to get rid of 'the five-pound ten "work-him-till-he-drops-down-dead" animal'. Yet they could

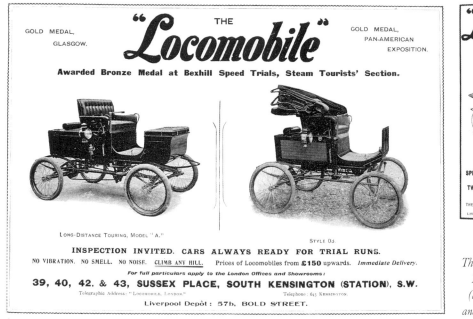

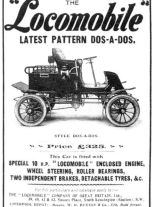

GOLD MEDAL,
GLASGOW.

THE "Locomobile"

GOLD MEDAL,
PAN-AMERICAN
EXPOSITION.

Awarded Bronze Medal at Bexhill Speed Trials, Steam Tourists' Section.

LONG-DISTANCE TOURING, MODEL "A."

STYLE O3.

INSPECTION INVITED. CARS ALWAYS READY FOR TRIAL RUNS.

NO VIBRATION. NO SMELL. NO NOISE. CLIMB ANY HILL.   Prices of Locomobiles from **£150** upwards.   *Immediate Delivery.*

For full particulars apply to the London Offices and Showrooms:

39, 40, 42, & 43, SUSSEX PLACE, SOUTH KENSINGTON (STATION), S.W.

Telegraphic Address: "LOCOMOBILE, LONDON."   Telephone: 615 KENSINGTON.

Liverpool Depôt : 57b, BOLD STREET.

THE "Locomobile"
LATEST PATTERN DOS-A-DOS.

STYLE DOS-A-DOS.

Price £325.

This Car is fitted with
**SPECIAL 10 H.P. "LOCOMOBILE" ENCLOSED ENGINE,
WHEEL STEERING, ROLLER BEARINGS,
TWO INDEPENDENT BRAKES, DETACHABLE TYRES, &c.**

For full particulars and catalogue apply to :—
THE "LOCOMOBILE" COMPANY OF GREAT BRITAIN, Ltd.,
39, 40, 42 & 43, Sussex Place, South Kensington (Station), S.W.
LIVERPOOL DEPOT : Messrs. W. H. BUXTON & Co., 57b, Bold Street.

LOCOMOBILITY

These advertisements from 1902 (left) and 1903 (above) reveal the pace and the price of change, as the Locomobile evolves from modest horseless buckboard to expensive motor carriage. Yet even as Locomobiles became more sophisticated it was clear that steam propulsion was obsolescent.

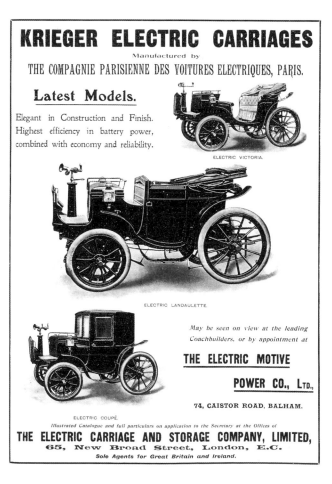

KRIEGER ELECTRIC CARRIAGES
Manufactured by
THE COMPAGNIE PARISIENNE DES VOITURES ELECTRIQUES, PARIS.

Latest Models.

Elegant in Construction and Finish.
Highest efficiency in battery power,
combined with economy and reliability.

ELECTRIC VICTORIA.

ELECTRIC LANDAULETTE.

May be seen on view at the leading
Coachbuilders, or by appointment at

THE ELECTRIC MOTIVE

POWER CO., Ltd.,

74, CAISTOR ROAD, BALHAM.

ELECTRIC COUPÉ.

Illustrated Catalogue and full particulars on application to the Secretary at the Offices of

THE ELECTRIC CARRIAGE AND STORAGE COMPANY, LIMITED,
65, New Broad Street, London, E.C.
Sole Agents for Great Britain and Ireland.

ELECTRIC ENERGY

These 1902 electric carriages still belong, in both style and name, to the horse-and-buggy age. Despite their potential, realised best in taxis, electric-powered vehicles were virtually extinct in Britain (though not in America) by 1914.

congratulate themselves on solving a problem which had been growing more acute since the time when Adam Smith had propounded his celebrated maxim that each horse consumed the food of eight people. In other words, it devoured the product of some five acres – over five tons of hay – every year. Like sheep in medieval times, horses were eating up men. During the nineteenth century the equine population had increased to cope with local traffic generated by railways – the Victorian horse was, in a sense, sired by the iron horse. Pressure on land was eased when the Edwardian horse became 'the victim of internal combustion'.

Cheaper food, better health, swifter pace, wider horizons – there seemed no limit to what could be accomplished by this powerful engine of change. The upper class could use the car to escape from insalubrious cities into the fresh air of the countryside. 'It is a case,' pronounced the motoring judge Sir Francis Jeune, 'of civilisation providing an antidote to its own poison.' The middle class would benefit from the improved delivery of goods and, gradually, an extended radius of action. The motor bus would enable workers to commute to their place of employment, liberating themselves from central slums and, Arthur Balfour hoped, providing a means of solving 'the problem of the housing of the working class'. It was exciting to contemplate physical improvements like the much-discussed 'Haussmannising' of London whereby, as H. G. Wells wrote, Piccadilly Circus might be reconstructed 'on the scale of the Place de la Concorde'. But these were as nothing compared with the more profound transformation that the motor vehicle was expected to achieve. Its English champions would have agreed with the Parisian who said in 1900: 'What alters our lives alters our thoughts; what alters our thoughts alters our characters; what alters our characters alters our ideals; and what alters our ideals alters our morals.' The 'metal demon', the Frenchman concluded, would banish restfulness from life. The 'quiet world is ending for ever'.

This revolution put paid to a rural form of existence, perhaps best evoked in Flora Thompson's *Lark Rise to Candleford* (1945), which had been trudging on since time immemorial. Beyond the iron tracery of railways motorists could enter districts which were, as one Edwardian observed, 'the very abode of loneliness, where the centuries come and go with little outward change, and the country looks much the same as it did in the days of the Stuarts, or even before their time'. Country carriers, whose pace was well suited to rolling English roads, were sometimes the only link between the village and the outside world. Archaic customs persisted: labourers still attended hiring fairs with the signs of their calling (the shepherd with his crook, the carter with his whip) to strike bargains with farmers for their next year's employment. Local dialects flourished. As the writer George Bourne said, men knew the names of potatoes better than those of politicians. Self-contained and self-sufficient, country people seldom saw strangers or ventured far afield. In *Jude the Obscure* (1895) Hardy depicted a rustic living only twenty miles from Oxford who had never visited the city and did not know its exact whereabouts. Isolation had advantages. So did the organic community, though it has been woven into myths about honeysuckle-covered cottages full of apple-cheeked peasants. But in the main rural life was harsh, narrow, inbred, backward and sluggish. No one observed it more closely than Richard Jefferies, who was struck, above all, by its stultifying *'vis inertiae'* (force of inertia).

The motor vehicle, asserted its partisans, would quicken 'the life of the countryside'. It would ramble beyond railways and penetrate secret places. Nothing would so speedily help the

HORSE-DRAWN LONDON

At the end of the nineteenth century Eros overlooks a circus dominated by equine transport. No wonder progressive thinkers expected automobiles to reduce urban traffic and dirt.

CHANGE AT PICCADILLY

Just before the outbreak of the First World War, the scene is being transformed by motor vehicles.

MOTORISED METROPOLIS

By the early 1920s the capital has become the domain of the internal combustion engine. But it is subject to new forms of congestion and pollution.

decaying village, predicted St Loe Strachey, proprietor of the *Spectator* and member of the Club, as 'the resurrection of the road'. *The Times* went so far as to forecast: 'We shall see our roads busy again, busier, perhaps, than they ever were in the old posting days.' This might diminish romance but it would increase convenience. Motor transport could supply country cousins with everything from fresh herrings to light bulbs. It would raise the value of land distant from railway stations. Above all, it would shake up dry bones and breathe new vitality into ossified communities. Asserting that the inhabitants of Lincolnshire were getting to know one another thanks to the internal combustion engine, the Club *Journal* said in 1902:

> In the days of long ago – say in 1896 – the people who lived in the villages ... dwelt
> in a small world of their own. A neighbour five miles away was seldom seen, one at a
> far cry of 10 miles never, except, perhaps, at the annual militia training or agricultural
> show ... now the big county of Lincoln is becoming very small.

It was shrinking, of course, only for the handful of people who could avail themselves of motor transport. But, as their numbers grew, they had a seismic impact on rural society. The Candleford blacksmith was one of many who decided to make 'Motor Repairs a Speciality'.

Far from trotting meekly into oblivion, however, auxiliaries of the horse often kicked up a fuss. The Marquess of Granby was typical of peers who protested because 'motor-carists' frightened the horses. When John Montagu bought an automobile some of his relations regarded him as a 'dangerous revolutionary'. The greater the success of the motor vehicle, the more it provoked resentment – establishing a pattern that was to be endlessly repeated. Those who enjoyed Arcadian seclusion and traditional pursuits like fox-hunting felt increasingly imperilled by the automotive invasion. They saw it not only as an urban, industrial assault on the natural, wholesome life of the countryside, but as an attack on the entire social order. For, as David Cannadine has said, if the horse was the 'symbol of landed supremacy, then the motor-car was the sure and certain sign that that supremacy was coming to an end'. The vehicle was a potent emblem of 'the irresponsible and corrosive plutocracy by which the patricians felt themselves threatened'. Those ensconced in the seats of power had always deemed mobility a menace: the Duke of Wellington had thought that railways would encourage 'the lower orders to go uselessly wandering about the country'. Now *arrivistes* on wheels of fortune were driving above their station. The *Pall Mall Gazette* was prompted to rhyme:

> 'Twas said by a Whig,
> That a man in a gig
> Enjoyed a clear claim to gentility.
> But a man who would now
> Win the parvenu's bow
> Must belong to automobility.

Thus by the turn of the century the motor car was replete with class connotations. It had already established itself as what would become known as a status symbol.

Members of the Automobile Club naturally disliked being identified as newly rich vulgarians. In the face of hostility from what Lord Brabazon called the 'horsey element', they were

OCTOBER CLUB RUN
Automobile Club members gather outside The Hendre, the home of Charles Rolls's father, Lord Llangattock, in October 1900. The car on the right (left) is Frank Butler's six-horsepower Panhard-Levassor. Club Runs often became races and members were urged to follow their leader. In this case (below) it is Charles Rolls himself.

obliged to 'stick together'. They also retaliated. One declared that the 'insanitary and death-dealing horse' was a 'relic of savagery' which should be banished from the streets of civilised cities. Others attributed the aristocracy's ill-will to its 'natural conservatism' and engrained hauteur. With some relish the Club *Journal* reprinted an article which said that the horse, 'though not a snob himself, is intimately connected with snobbery in some occult way'. This was partly because riding was expensive. But it was mainly because the well-bred steed occupied a central place in an old-fashioned cult of virility. The horse was a key element in the 'England's greatness due to the hunting field – *Westward Ho* – Waterloo won on the playing fields of Eton – "Broke the ice in my tub this morning" – classical education makes a gentleman – thoroughly manly and English – noble sport of horse race gambling' sort of cant. To make the car acceptable to High Society the Club would have to overcome some deep-seated prejudices.

Motorists were also under attack from the other end of the social scale. Proletarians were pedestrians. They understandably objected to being deprived of the highway, common land which seemed part of their birthright, by people who were literally rolling in wealth. The motor horn may have been, as Kipling said, the 'Note of the Age'; but it sounded a note of class discord. Its braying reminded the villager that 'the rich who are his masters are on the road'. The poor resented the reminder still more when 'the rich ruffian' not only misbehaved but was haughty and overbearing to boot. The moderately well-to-do were for the first time compelled to identify with the have-nots. One bicyclist wrote:

> It is only since the coming of the automobile that I have known what it is to be poor, only since the coming of the motor car that class distinctions have been set up all over the earth; only within the last two or three years that most of us have found that we belong to the submerged nine-tenths, the exposed tenth being composed mostly of motor makers and millionaires.

President Woodrow Wilson's well-known observation that nothing had spread Socialistic feeling through America faster than the automobile, which was 'a picture of the arrogance of wealth', applied equally well to Britain.

The issue was debated in the press. Thus when *The Times* argued that it was 'absurd and impracticable' to compel powerful cars to crawl along 'unfrequented roads' at 12mph, other papers raised the standard of the foot-slogging masses. It was astounding, proclaimed the *Yorkshire Post*, to 'demand, for what must always be a small class of people, a privilege of the magnitude claimed for motor cars ... which would amount in time to the virtual closing of the roads to the great bulk of the people'. Social antagonism was intensified by several well-publicised instances of roadhoggery, such as a two-day spree by a party of Oxford under-graduates who tore through towns and villages stampeding people and livestock and nearly killing a policeman. Roger Wallace wrote to *The Times* saying that their behaviour had 'aroused the anger of every gentleman who drives an automobile'. Privately, Club members acknowledged to one another that motorists were 'creating a very sore feeling, especially among the poorer classes'. Fear of cars was actually keeping some humble folk indoors.

The Club therefore had to defend motorists on two fronts: to show the élite that they were respectable; and to prove to the masses that they were responsible. So members spent much time

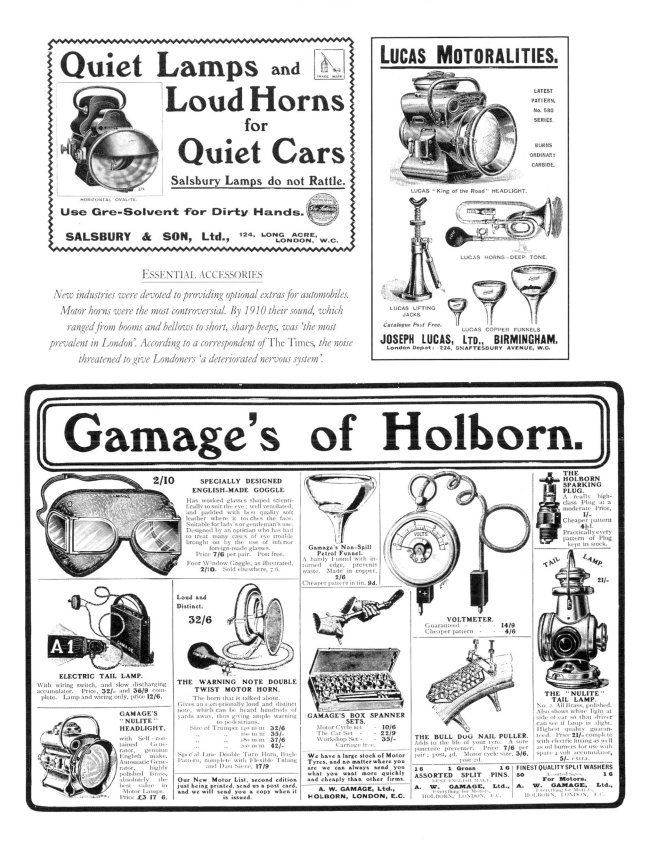

ESSENTIAL ACCESSORIES

New industries were devoted to providing optional extras for automobiles. Motor horns were the most controversial. By 1910 their sound, which ranged from booms and bellows to short, sharp beeps, was 'the most prevalent in London'. According to a correspondent of The Times, *the noise threatened to give Londoners 'a deteriorated nervous system'.*

at the dawn of the new century trying to exert influence. Understandably, they concentrated on people in positions of power. They gave government officials, county councillors and chief constables rides in their vehicles. This experience proved a 'revelation' to many, who had no conception of the steering and stopping powers of these machines. One senior policeman, who had never before 'been privileged to drive in a motor car', said that he had been conducted by a 'perfect charioteer'. But occasionally these efforts backfired. The Irish motoring pioneer R. J. Mecredy took a critic for a spin and convinced him of the motor car's merits so thoroughly that on their return journey he started to roar at plodding peasants, 'Get off the earth!'

Club members also made themselves useful to the War Office, notably by supplying cars as transport for senior officers on manoeuvres. In 1901 the portly, rubicund General Sir Redvers Buller pronounced himself 'delighted' by a motor trip across Salisbury Plain, though his ADC remained standing most of the time, saying that 'he had a few loose teeth and wanted to keep them in his head'. The following year members took Lord Roberts and his staff on an inspection tour through Kent. W. J. Crampton was so thrilled to meet Roberts and other generals who had won fame in the Boer War that he kept a record of the expedition. He noted that if the gallant soldiers had not been constrained by the out-of-date speed limit they would undoubtedly have 'made some sporting suggestions and tried to get up a race or two on the King's Highway'. Roberts himself was much impressed by the motor car's 'extraordinary facility for ... rushing hither and thither in an incredibly short space of time', thus enabling commanders to do more than they could have done on horseback.

Actually, as disillusioned Club drivers observed, the commanders had little idea of how to employ the cars to advantage except as baggage carriers. Still, in 1903 the War Office did sanction the formation of the Motor Volunteer Corps. Its Colonel was Mark Mayhew. Its most junior recruit was Private the Earl Russell, whose chauffeur drove him around in a large steam-brougham with an insatiable thirst for water and an incredible capacity to overheat – it was nicknamed the 'Hot Potato Can'. MVC officers were fitted out in a uniform consisting of khaki serge tunic with embossed silver buttons, dark green collar and cuffs, Sam Browne belt and knickerbocker breeches with red piping down the seams. Their cap badge was a wheel intersected by an arrow and the motto 'Subito' (Instantly). Officers were also supposed to wear spurs, which they called 'sparking plugs' and surreptitiously dispensed with when driving.

Such was the versatility of the motor car, which aficionados called 'the poor man's yacht', that the Club was soon winning other victories in its struggle for prestige. It was assisted by gentlemen of the press who, shortly before, had been wont to assert that motoring was 'infinitely more dangerous than performing on a tight-rope over Niagara Falls'. *Punch* shifted its ground, now satirising anti-motorists for their absurd caution. The *Tatler* began to devote a weekly page to the doings of automobilists like Lady Robert Manners, who drove to her wedding in a car. The *Daily Express* noticed that 'the automobilist is becoming legion at race meetings'. *Country Life* suggested that inconsiderate drivers were mainly motor servants, i.e. chauffeurs, probably of foreign origin. *M.A.P.* ('Mainly About People') wondered how soon a lover of the vehicle would give orders to be conveyed to the tomb by motor – in fact, the first automobile funeral had occurred in August 1901, when a Coventry employee of Daimler was taken to the cemetery in one of the firm's cars which had been converted into a hearse.

MOTOR VOLUNTEERS

Club members mustered at short notice to take senior officers to Kent on an inspection tour in August 1902. On the far left Mark Mayhew drives Lord Roberts in a Mors, while Lord Kitchener is the front-seat passenger in a Panhard-Levassor on the extreme right. One advantage of acting as chauffeur to top brass, recorded W. J. Crampton (thought to be driving the third car from the left, at the rear), was that policemen saluted instead of handing drivers a blue envelope 'for exceeding the crawling "limit of the law"'. Most soldiers continued to put more trust in horses than in cars, but in 1903 the Motor Volunteer Corps was founded.

The founder of *M.A.P.*, the ebullient Irish politician T. P. O'Connor, was an important convert to the motoring cause. He wrote a glowing account of the King's 1902 motor tour with the Prime Minister – Arthur Balfour was already a member of the Club and Edward VII became its patron the following year. O'Connor went so far as to say that people were buying cars in order to improve their position in society. 'It is almost as much as a man's social life is worth nowadays to remain without a motor car. There is a certain scornful uplifting of the eyebrows in the well-to-do if you confess to not having a motor.' The grateful Club gave him a dinner at which he proclaimed it 'the sponsor and the father adviser and spiritual director ... [of] a great, peaceful and beneficent revolution'.

To reflect its enhanced influence the Club sought larger and grander premises in 1902, and found them at 119 Piccadilly. Whitehall Court had never been entirely suitable because it was not central and lacked garage space. Also there were no bedrooms or big meeting rooms, and the food service was poor – it took half an hour to get a cup of tea. Nevertheless, as Roger Wallace said, many 'croaking prophets' forecast that a costly migration would spell 'the ruin of the Club'. Seventy-four members even threatened to resign over the issue. The crisis was averted when the rent was guaranteed by a few rich members, among them Alfred Harmsworth, who promised £300 a year for life with the words: 'I am healthy and drive nothing worse than a 20 h.p. Panhard at present.' Subsequently 288 members subscribed for £16,220 worth of debentures to finance the move.

The Piccadilly clubhouse overlooked Green Park and had once been the mansion of Lord Palmerston. It provided splendid accommodation. The premises boasted a library, reading room, dining room, balcony, card room, billiard room, smoking room, a small gymnasium and ten bedrooms. The decoration was lavish. The furnishings were sumptuous: morocco armchairs upholstered in apple green or sealing-wax red, polished mahogany tables, rich tapestry curtains, plush Turkey carpets, heavy brass stair rods. A first-class chef, lately serving 'the mess of a crack regiment', was engaged. Responding to members' requests, he soon added steak and oyster pudding, Irish stew and Lancashire hotpot to the winter menu. Several thousand pounds were spent to convert the livery stables behind the building into a garage – an amenity then unique in Clubland. Yet by the beginning of 1903 the Club was for the first time, as Salomons remarked with pleasure, 'absolutely solvent'. In the words of a contemporary, it had 'advanced in an incredibly short space of time to the dignity of a powerful, well-equipped and luxuriously appointed West-End club', to which 'every automobilist of good social standing considers it a duty to his cult to belong'. It was now, indeed, the largest Automobile Club in the world; and among its 2,180 members were forty peers and thirty MPs. On one occasion when the House of Commons found itself without a quorum, a Club member quipped: 'They were all coming here.' The Automobile Club was established as 'The Parliament of Motoring'.

As such its badge added distinction to any motor car, a mark of kudos at home, a passport abroad. But the owner of that car would lose caste sadly, in the opinion of the Club, if the government were to insist that it also bore a licence number. So, in a futile attempt to uphold the dignity of automobilism, the Club resisted the growing pressure to identify vehicles with number-plates. Its case was quaint, but it reveals much about the contemporary spread of cars as well as the nuances of Edwardian snobbery. The Club argued that the few thousand

PICCADILLY CLUBHOUSE

The Club's new headquarters had royal and aristocratic connections and was close to
Piccadilly Circus, 'the hub of automobilism'. The Yorkshire Post *said that the Automobile*
Club was now 'housed in a manner worthy of the important new industry it represents'.

THE PARLIAMENT OF MOTORING

automobiles on the road did not need numbers since they were used locally and 'they will be perfectly well known by sight, and by the liveries of the servants, and by the faces of the occupants, to nine people out of every ten who encounter them'. If motor cars were 'disfigured by labels' their owners would thereby be 'placed on a level with the drivers of hackney carriages'. Worse, they would be virtually branded as criminals. They would be at the mercy of every 'jaundiced idler' and 'unemployed county councillor' who cared to indulge in the game of reporting them for speeding. Numbering was a sinister invasion of privacy and a disgraceful infringement of the liberty of the subject, putting him on a par with the benighted foreigner who had to carry identity papers. It would lead to the decay of automobilism and (a point stressed by Harmsworth) to the death of a great industry. To inscribe names on cars, as though they were boats, might be an acceptable alternative. But if they were to bear a numerical stigma so too should carriages, bicycles, perambulators, vagrants, dogs and chief constables.

Critics of the Club hit back. Motorists were too dangerous to remain anonymous. They were a particular menace when drunk, whereas, remarked a sardonic commentator, it was unusual outside big towns for a horse and its driver to be inebriated at one and the same time. Privileged hooligans wanted to be unaccountable, above the law. Often, wrote Goldsworthy Lowes Dickinson, a disapproving Cambridge don, motorists were 'so disguised by masks and head-gear, so begoggled, swathed and mummified that one might be pardoned for mistaking them for inhabitants of another planet'. When they put on such garb it was obvious, according to Lord Wemyss, that they meant to break the law. Sometimes they refused to halt when signalled to do so by the police. Occasionally they drove their cars at constables, threatening to run them over. When motorists were stopped they might make the air blue with bad language. And they sometimes engaged in the 'ungentlemanly subterfuge' of giving a false name and address.

Anyone doing this should have 'boiling oil poured over him' opined one member of the Club, which officially condemned such 'motor blackguards'. But, it claimed, most motorists drove safely, only committing technical offences. Mark Mayhew defended them at a meeting of the London County Council Highways Committee, holding up a placard displaying figures provided by the *Motor Car Journal* which demonstrated that railways caused more accidents than cars. The radical John Burns retorted that he would 'prefer to rely on the *Undertaker's Gazette* for statistics in the matter'. Towards the end of the meeting a prankster pinned Mayhew's placard to his back and it was some time before he discovered it.

As this confrontation suggests, the Club's campaign to convince the wider public of the moral worth of the motor car was a failure. Indeed, the harder it tried – by means of 'meets', exhibitions, automobile gymkhanas, motor races, dust-laying experiments, charity rides and so on – the more hostility seemed to grow. Its efforts could have been greater, and more genuine. On occasion the speed limit officially imposed during reliability trials was nothing more than humbug. As *The Autocar* later recorded, 'The trials rules said that anyone who exceeded twelve miles an hour would be disqualified, but just before the start the observers were called to a most private meeting and told that they must not let their cars average more than twenty.' In a letter advising the Club not to hold further demonstrations of cars on the road, the Chairman of Buckinghamshire County Council wrote: 'The advertisement has been dearly purchased by the unpopularity you have gained.' In 1902 the Club did discourage members from travelling in

BEXHILL RACES

Arguably Britain's first proper motor racing event took place at Whitsun 1902 over a course along the sea front at Bexhill made available to the Automobile Club by the local landowner, Earl de la Warr. Crowds were attracted by the novel spectacle. Léon Serpollet recorded the fastest time of the day, doing the flying kilometre in 41.2 seconds aboard his streamlined car 'Easter Egg'.

CRITICAL TIMING

In front of the bow-tied Herbert Burrows, the Club's first steward, sits Colonel Crompton, in glasses, supervising the primitive electric timing device.

convoys; but, as one wrote early the following year, 'hatred of motor cars is increasing to an alarming extent'.

The public mood was exacerbated by a series of appalling accidents which occurred during the 1903 Paris–Madrid Race. Mayhew himself was injured, though Club daredevils like the monocled Lieutenant Mansfield Cumming (the original 'C' of the Secret Intelligence Service, which he set up in Whitehall Court) thought the race 'glorious sport'. According to his own account he skimmed along 'at a cracking pace' in a Wolseley that seemed far more human 'than many folks of my acquaintance'. However, as another member acknowledged, not since the days of the Roman arena had men taken such risks. Shocked by the deaths of spectators and well-known drivers such as Marcel Renault, the British press agreed. It printed headlines like 'Motor Massacre', 'Race to Death' and 'The Social Juggernaut'. Anticipating a similar slaughter on British roads, *The Times* suggested that car owners should be held responsible for the crimes of their chauffeurs. Automobiles came straight from the lower regions, said the labour leader Henry Broadhurst. Others recommended that the drivers of 'these damnable engines of Satan' should be shot on sight. For the first time there was talk of 'motorphobia'.

In June 1903 some thirty MPs signed a circular complaining of the 'gross abuse' of public roads by unidentifiable drivers travelling at 'furious speeds'. This raised the twin issues – car numbering and the speed limit – which vitally concerned the Club. Its leading parliamentary representative, John Montagu, had summed up members' gut feelings admirably in the course of a meeting at 119 Piccadilly: 'My private opinion is that I should like to go as fast as I can and never be identified.' Certainly the stocky, auburn-haired, bright-eyed Montagu revelled in speed (though he also enjoyed sedate rural pursuits and was said to be almost the only gentle-man in England who could still scull a gunning punt). A future Chairman of the Club would describe him as a 'benevolent whirlwind'. Montagu was not even ashamed to admit that he had early lost his 'automobile virginity' in a police trap. However, he recognised that Walter Long, President of the Local Government Board, was bound to bring forward a palliative measure. In the face of nascent socialism, Long wanted to quell class conflict. This was 'perhaps with-out parallel in modern times', Long told the Club, anxious to win over that influential body on which he relied, among other things, for technical information. Montagu therefore urged his fellows to agree to numbering in return for the abolition of the speed limit. This was acceptable to many members including Wallace, Harmsworth, Alfred Bird and Lord Onslow, who said that he had displayed a number when bicycling in Germany without the least injury to his pride. For those who feared that their movements would become public knowledge once cars were numbered, Onslow had this sage advice: 'if you wish to go to shady places in shady company you had better use a hansom cab'.

However, a vociferous group of motoring militants opposed all compromise. Its leader, Earl Russell, professed to be thunderstruck by the proposal that Montagu was trying to ram down their throats. The rancorous character of the diehard party is wonderfully conveyed in Kipling's short story 'The Village that Voted the Earth was Flat'. It recounts the comic-cruel revenge which motorists took on a magistrate who had fined them and called them 'cads'. Russell, Jarrott, Canning and others felt themselves to be martyrs to the prejudice of their natural allies. They had been accustomed to think of the law as their law, pronounced by social

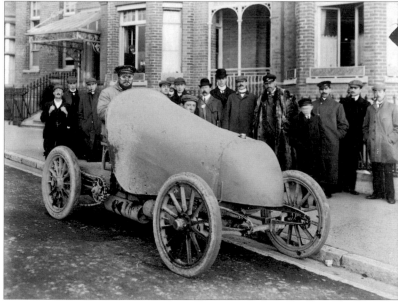

TROPHY FOR ELEGANCE

*S. F. Edge, driving a sixteen-
horsepower Napier at
Bexhill, wins the House of
Commons Cup for the
appearance of his equipage.
Evidently, in 1902, it was
deemed smarter to wear a
cap than a bowler hat in
an open car.*

RACING BARON

*Henri de Rothschild, driving
a 1902 forty-horsepower
Mercédès, so adored cars that
he built his own factory. His
cousin Lionel thought the new
shock-absorbers took the fun
out of motoring.*

equals in the courts, enforced by deferential guardians in the streets. Their view was sustained by two prison sentences which the Club *Journal* recorded (without comment) in 1903: a reckless driver got three months for killing a boy, while a young man got a year for stealing a car. But now the judicial worm had begun to turn. Magistrates were handing out fines and damning members of the Club for 'tearing madly about the country at breakneck speed' in 'noisy, dangerous abominations'. Policemen saw motorised 'toffs' as potential malefactors and adopted the 'un-English and unsportsmanlike' practice of setting traps for them. This was an inversion of the cosmic order. More galling still, the law at issue was an ass. Even its author, former President of the Local Government Board 'Squire' Henry Chaplin, confessed that *en route* to fox hunts he always drove much faster than 14mph. Chaplin, whose complete lack of humour blinded him to the amusement he provoked in others, told the House of Commons that the speed regulations were 'absurd', adding that as he himself was 'largely responsible for them … there was very good reason why that should be the case'. When Kenneth Balfour MP condemned inconsiderate drivers soon after his namesake Arthur, the Prime Minister, had been caught 'scorching', the House was 'completely submerged by the spirit of burlesque'.

Since everyone flouted the law, Russell and his band of irreconcilables felt entitled to thwart it. They tried to persuade motorists to indicate the presence of hidden constables by scattering confetti or red dye on the highway. They also wanted the Club to publish a trap map and to establish 'a code of private signals' by which drivers could warn one another of ambushes. The Executive Committee, staid and temperate, rejected both schemes. But when the law was changed, in the summer of 1903, many of the Club's moderates joined the extremists. For the Motor Car Act reflected the current hostility towards those whom one MP called 'flying millionaires'. After a debate in which other legislators demanded that 'trespassers on the public roads' who drove a 'ton of iron' at 60mph should be flogged, the Commons voted that cars should not only bear licence numbers but be subject to a speed limit of 20mph. Even the emollient Roger Wallace was outraged. Claude Johnson said that Long, a 'punctured windbag', had 'betrayed' them. The Club officially rebuked Montagu, who had seen the inevitability of a speed limit and tried to get it fixed at 25mph, for acting without its sanction. It declared that the Act would be 'fatal to motoring' and should be met with 'uncompromising opposition'.

This took various forms. Earl Russell demanded that political candidates should be threatened, the public educated, loopholes in the law exploited, appeals made and amendments sought. The Dorset magnate Lord Alington 'so strongly objected' to his county's being allotted the letters BF that he got them changed to FX. The Hon. Leopold Canning, who believed that road hogs were rare if not mythical beasts, frothed with fury. He issued a fearful denunciation of the legislature in this 'year of disgrace, 1903':

> To think that the motor car, that superb creation, that glorious outcome of science, the grandest invention of the age, should be so set upon, howled against, and torn to pieces by a lot of hyenas in Parliament, whose language and behaviour was equal to that of yelling Dervishes massacring their victims!

Motorphobia had provoked an equal and opposite reaction among 'philomobiles'. However, the hysteria ebbed as quickly as it had flowed. Canningite excesses were obviously ill-judged at a

LIMIT OF THE LAW

J. M. Hulton takes out his Aunt Alyne on a Singer motor tricycle in 1902. Presumably she was not a passenger when he was summonsed for furious driving the following year. Punch *satirised the speed limit by suggesting that 'No motor car is to pass any cart, carriage, van, bath-chair, perambulator, or other vehicle, unless the same is motionless. In the latter case the motor car shall be allowed to pass the standing vehicle at the pace of one furlong an hour; providing that all the passengers alight from the motor car, and walk past ringing hand-bells.'*

In the Metropolitan Police District.

Police Court__*Marlborough Street*

To *John Hulton*
72 Seymour Street Bryanston Square Paddington

INFORMATION has been *laid*
this day by *Henry Brown Inspector of Police*
for that you, on the *13th* Day of *March*
in the Year One Thousand Nine Hundred and *three*
at *Hyde Park*

within the District aforesaid, did *unlawfully ride a motor cycle furiously so as to endanger the safety or convenience of other persons using the said Park*

contrary to the Statute &c

YOU ARE THEREFORE hereby summoned to appear before the Court of Summary Jurisdiction, sitting at the *Marlborough Street* Police Court on *Tues* day the *31st* day of *March 1903* at the hour of *two* in the *after* noon, to answer to the said *Information*.

Given under my Hand and Seal this *17th* day of *March* One Thousand Nine Hundred and *three*

SCH. I.—2.
SUMMONS.
—
GENERAL FORM INDICTABLE
AND SUMMARY CASES.

10000-11-02. M.P. 96

(Sgd) G. L. Denman

One of the Magistrates of the Police Courts of the Metropolis.

time when many people regarded the Motor Car Act as a measure passed by the rich for the rich. As one of Montagu's supporters exclaimed: 'Motorists seem to be absolutely blind to the force of public opinion against them.' Actually, most Club members realised that they had gone too far. For they were not mere motorists. They did not see everything 'from religion to mixed bathing' (as one member put it) purely from the viewpoint of auto-mobilism. They recognised that their privileged social position could only be sustained if they acted responsibly. So, in the name of *noblesse oblige*, many heeded Montagu's plea for loyal acceptance of the Motor Car Act. They sacrificed liberty to order. Hard-line critics interpreted this as weakness, even decadence. They said that the appeasers were so 'dazzled by the effulgence of their exalted position', so emasculated by gentility, that they could not defend automobile interests with sufficient vigour. Here was a prime source of future discord. But in the short term it seemed that fears about the

BALLOONACY, 1902

This sport strongly appealed to more daring members of the Club, who saw themselves less as aviators than as automobilists aloft. One of them, the future Lord Brabazon, said in his memoirs that ballooning 'is the only way to go into the air like a gentleman'.

new Act had been exaggerated. Within a few months Montagu was being officially thanked for his parliamentary efforts and, said the *Journal*, 'old bonds of friendship' were re-established.

This was unduly optimistic. In fact, as motordom grew it became increasingly prone to divisions and disputes. Montagu himself was at odds with the Club because its *Journal* was in competition with his own motoring magazine, *The Car*. The heavily subsidised *Journal* was, in fact, a frequent bone of contention, much fought over by other members with interests in the motoring press. As the official organ of the Club, it had to ignore commercial pressures and speak *ex cathedra*. This had the effect of exposing the activities of magazines which were less scrupulous and of costing the Club money. Even the *Journal*'s business manager made the point that 'No paper run on commercial lines can to-day ignore the legitimate editorial claims of its advertisers.' He suggested that it could only remain 'a class paper of the very first order' by including, say, 'judicious' descriptions of goods on the market. Speaking for the majority on the Competitions Committee, Earl Russell entered an 'emphatic no'. 'It must never be possible to suggest that any advertisement in the *Journal* has any influence on the matter which appears in its columns.'

In the same spirit, the sporting gentlemen were intermittently hostile to members in the car business, especially those who tried to get the Club's backing for commercial ventures like exhibitions. The founding of the Society of Motor Manufacturers and Traders in 1902, by the ubiquitous Simms, did nothing to stop dissension between amateurs and professionals in the Club. There were also tensions between the parent organisation and provincial clubs, whose members resented paying their half-guinea affiliation fee to Piccadilly, though many of them acknowledged that 'the idea of splitting automobilism into factions would be exceedingly foolish'. This was a general view: the motoring press encouraged its readers to 'join the Motor Union and present a firm and powerful face to our foes'. But the growing Motor Union, though a child of the Club, was inclined to go its own way. Under the direction of its assertive Secretary, Rees Jeffreys, the so-called 'body politic of automobilism' would challenge the authority of the Parliament of Motoring. In fact, as will become apparent in the next chapter, the Automobile Club's ambition to keep the whole movement under a single banner was doomed.

One reason for this was that the man who had kept the banner flying, Claude Johnson, resigned from the secretaryship in 1903 to pursue a more lucrative career, eventually, with Rolls-Royce. His powerful hand had not only held the Club together, but had driven it forward into new areas of endeavour. Johnson had negotiated agreements with foreign countries whereby members who obtained 'triptyche' forms could avoid complex customs formalities. He had secured the Irish Automobile Club as 'an affiliated branch' in 1901. He had instituted a system of vetting and licensing hotels suitable for motorists, which could display the Automobile Club sign. He had set up an Engineer's Department to give help to members, especially those buying cars or falling victim to the new breed of 'repairing sharks', and to turn coachmen into chauffeurs. In 1903, too, the Touring Department was instituted to give members information about routes and places of interest. Finally, the dynamic Secretary had begun a programme (towards which Harmsworth, preoccupied by the hazard of 'side-slips', i.e. skids, contributed £100) of erecting green and white, diamond-shaped Control Boards at danger spots.

Johnson had also got a grip on associated activities such as 'aerial motoring', sometimes known as 'balloonacy'. This had long been an enthusiasm of Club members. Leading 'balloonatics' were Charles Rolls, Frank Butler and his intrepid daughter Vera, the first woman in Britain to be fined for speeding, who forecast that people might soon be constructing sheds on the roofs of their houses to store 'huge mechanical birds of passage'. In 1901 Rolls and Butler proposed to form an Aero Club under the auspices of the Automobile Club. Predictably, Frederick Simms claimed priority, telling Johnson: 'it has been pretty well an open secret for some time past that I intended to form an Aero Club'. But Johnson prevailed on Simms to back down and the Rolls/Butler plan was realised.

Johnson also rejected charges that Piccadilly Johnnies were too effete to ride motor-bikes. Actually some preferred motor-bicycling to steeplechasing and in 1903 the Automobile Club created the Auto-Cycle Club (later Auto-Cycle Union). In the same year it founded the Commercial Motor Users' Association. Equally satisfactory to Johnson, an old-fashioned male supremacist, was the formation of the Ladies' Automobile Club. This was affiliated to the gentlemen's but separate from it and distinguished by a solid silver badge enamelled in Lincoln green or deep red, which could also take the form of a brooch. It was better, Johnson felt, to satisfy in this way the 'almost frenzied enjoyment' which cars gave to 'motorinas' – one said that she would 'willingly give up a house and live in lodgings, and do without fashionable restaurants, and even a fashionable dressmaker and fine clothes, rather than abandon her motor'.

So, deferred to by the ladies and busy expanding its own sphere of action, the Automobile Club reached new heights of prestige during Johnson's last year as Secretary. Nothing helped more than its pre-eminent role in motor sport. As Earl Russell crowed in 1903, 'we have now acquired a power equivalent to that exercised in another department of sport by the Jockey Club'. This was partly Johnson's doing. He had 'hammered' away at the proposition that motor racing was a vital stimulus to British manufacturers in the 'splendid strenuous struggle of brain, material and money' with their foreign competitors. The argument appealed to members with commercial interests in cars, while the gentlemen-amateurs relished competition of a still more red-blooded kind. They agreed with Charles Jarrott that motor racing was the most exciting joust ever devised by man. They would also have endorsed his saying, 'If a Briton is

'MOTORINAS'

Far from being 'Everywhere', as the Latin motto on their badge suggests, Edwardian members of the Ladies' Automobile Club were a rare species of surpassing gentility. The chic trio in the 1906 open Cadillac are probably posing, not driving. Montagu recommended covered motors for country journeys.

WOMEN DRIVERS

Some women took driving seriously, such as Madame du Gast in France (here at the wheel of the 1903 de Dietrich which she drove in the Paris–Madrid Race) and Dorothy Levitt in Britain. The latter insisted that engines and road maps were 'not beyond the capacity of a woman's brain'. But she also stressed that ladies remained ladies even when they donned the overalls of the 'automobiliste'. She herself was not 'a big strapping Amazon', wrote her publisher reassuringly, but 'the most girlish of womanly women'.

not sporting he is nothing.' Thus the two most influential coteries in the Club united around motor sport.

As it happened, a couple of Club members had already scored notable triumphs for Britain on the Continent. In 1902 Charles Jarrott himself had won the Circuit des Ardennes race on a 13.6-litre, seventy-horsepower Panhard. 'Quite fearless', he had travelled at an average speed of 54mph, often almost blinded by a pall of dust as thick as a London pea-souper. Hailed as the 'darling of the gods', Jarrott also took part in the 1902 Paris–Vienna marathon, which was run concurrently with the third of the great international races sponsored by James Gordon Bennett Jnr. Bennett was an eccentric American press magnate who liked to make the news as well as to print it – he had sent Stanley to find Livingstone and raised no objection to 'Stanley's starting small wars in Africa in order to report them'. Motor races were stunts which attracted readers and Jarrott's own experiences between Paris and Vienna would have filled a book, let alone a newspaper. He denied stories that he had drunk champagne *en route*: if true, 'they would have given me a capacity equal to the petrol tank of my car' (which some people thought not impossible). But Jarrott did confess to having patched up his Panhard-Levassor with four legs surreptitiously sawn off a hotel tray stand. His mechanic, George du Cros, had been obliged to lie full length along the bonnet keeping the water in a leaky radiator with a towel. Jarrott had completed the course with

> my governor broken, my throttle gone, no exhaust-box, running in low gear, unable to change speed through the impossibility of taking out my cone, regulating my speed by the ignition, the frame of my car practically in half, no cap, no coat, no goggles.

However, astonishingly enough, all but one of the cars in the Gordon Bennett Race had fared even worse than Jarrott's. The exception was the thirty-horsepower Napier driven by S. F. Edge. He became even more of a popular hero than Jarrott, not least because of his flagrantly handsome features and his fiercely tumescent moustache. His victory meant that the next contest for the Gordon Bennett international challenge cup would have to be held in Britain.

This posed a problem since racing on British highways was against the law. Edge complained about legislative 'throttling' in London which meant that Paris would remain the 'centre of automobilism'. But the authorities continued to dither. England's hesitancy became Ireland's opportunity. Edge himself may have suggested that John Bull's other island, with its sparse, poverty-stricken population, was an ideal locale for the race. He certainly thought it offered 'great advantage to the English trade', a view not shared by Herbert Austin, who considered that the risk of accidents was 'too great' in Ireland and wanted the race held in the Ardennes. However, Johnson worked out a viable route. After travelling for hundreds of miles with Count Zborowski in the latter's Mercédès, he selected a kite-shaped circuit south-west of Dublin which passed through Kildare, Stradbally, Athy, Carlow and Castledermot.

The Club canvassed local opinion, stirred up commercial interests on both sides of the Irish Sea, promised that the race would not be held on a holy day and lobbied MPs of all persuasions.

DASHING STYLE
Outfitters like Dunhill's soon saw the possibilities of adapting specialised clothes designed for hunting or golf to the needs of motoring ladies. Less formal and more comfortable than ordinary Edwardian dress, this garb anticipated other sartorial changes encouraged by automobilism. The car also fostered new fashions in behaviour and aided female emancipation.

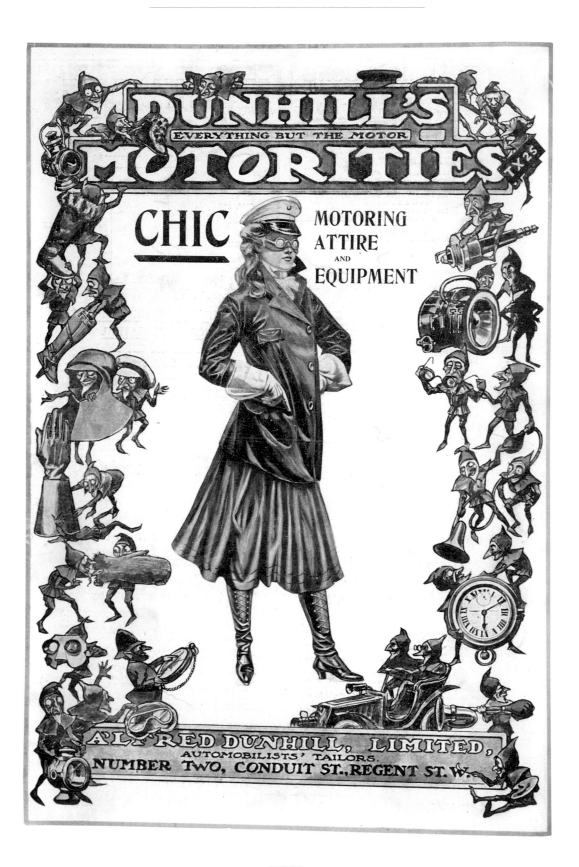

According to the *Northern Whig*, it achieved a 'unanimity of which some people consider Irishmen incapable …. When we look at the list of persons in Ireland who have offered a cordial welcome to the Club we see a wonderful blending of orange and green.' The *Irish Times* concurred. The race was a major topic of conversation in Dublin and everyone wanted to see 'modern marvels perform their wonderful feats of speed'. From this 'magnificent carnival' the country would draw immediate profit. (So it did: prices soared and *The Autocar* grumbled that 'jarveys unblushingly asked for ten shillings a seat from Athy to Ardscule, while twopenny mineral waters cost sixpence in the meanest shebeen'.) Furthermore, continued the *Irish Times*, the nation's 'sporting spirit would have a world-wide advertisement and the people themselves would have a lesson in progressive methods'. Persuaded that it was a matter of national importance, parliament rushed through a special act to sanction the race.

A few weeks later it almost succumbed to panic as a result of the lethal Paris–Madrid contest – the French government itself not only called off the race, but decreed that surviving cars should be brought back to Paris by train after being dragged to Bordeaux railway station by horses. In Piccadilly the Automobile Club held anxious meetings. Roger Wallace refused to be frightened by 'the general outcry in the press'. If they abandoned the Gordon Bennett competition there would be 'a general outcry against the Club' and 'the whole of the automobile movement would be set back ten or twenty years'. The Club took the line that the Irish race would be better conducted than the Paris–Madrid one, during which spectators had stood in the middle of the road taking photographs and jumping aside just before cars flashed past at 70mph. The Club contributed £1,500 to fence and repair Irish roads, treating some with 'Westrumite', a mixture of tallow, turpentine and water, to keep down the dust. Another £1,000 was guaranteed to pay for 7,000 policemen, who were warned that the Club would withdraw if they proved too greedy or obstructive. The stewards arranged to impose stringent safety measures in Ireland and to advertise them in England. The public might have been less reassured if it had been aware of the high-speed eliminating trials which the Club held at home before the race. But Johnson 'maintained great secrecy', issuing sealed orders and requiring early-morning starts in order to elude the vigilance of the constabulary. Meanwhile, in the privacy of Piccadilly, Edge bluntly dismissed most of the Club's precautions. Trying to minimise the danger for onlookers and officials was all very well, he said, but 'they were simply wasting their time' attempting 'to make the race safe for competitors'. Anyone who intended to win would be 'compelled to risk something'.

Seeing Edge at speed for the first time as his shock-absorberless Napier bounced as much as a foot off Irish roads, one of his friends burst into tears: he was convinced that Edge would kill himself. In fact, only his pride and his pocket were wounded. The British Napier, in which Edge had such a strong stake, was eclipsed by the German Mercédès. This car, ever since the revolutionary thirty-five-horsepower prototype had been built in 1901, was so far ahead of its time that even patriotic Frenchmen talked about entering *'l'ère Mercédès'*. Admittedly some of the car's innovations, such as the pressed-steel chassis, the honeycomb radiator and the 'gate' gear change, had been anticipated. But Mercédès pioneered the use of mechanically operated inlet valves. Previously these valves had been opened by suction as the piston went down and the improvement vastly increased the engine's efficiency. With its low profile and raked

PARIS–VIENNA RACE, 1902

Drivers (like Pinson, who came fifth in this seventy-horsepower Panhard) took part because hazards like dust clouds made motor racing more exciting than steeplechasing. But races also promoted mechanical improvements. More important still, victories advertised cars and the financial rewards could be great. Charles Jarrott complained that motor sport had been blighted from the start by 'the curse of commercialism'.

PARIS–MADRID RACE, 1903

Here being tested before the race, Lorraine Barrow's de Dietrich was, like most other cars taking part, a potential death trap. It was too heavy and powerful to be properly controlled by steering or brakes. Its thin tyres were vulnerable. The ill-protected driver and mechanic were among at least ten people killed during this contest, which prompted the move to racing on closed circuits.

steering wheel, its coil spring clutch and internal expanding back brakes, the new Mercédès was a world away from the horseless carriage. It was the very model of a modern motor car. German social attitudes, however, were less progressive than German engineering techniques. Before the race there was a nasty row about whether works drivers, not sufficiently '*hochwohlgeboren*' [high-born] to join the German automobile club, should be allowed to compete. One was excluded. But the Belgian, Camille Jenatzy, although engaged in trade, just gained acceptance. Mild and unassuming outside the car, he was known as the 'Red Devil' because of his fiery hair, moustache and pointed beard, and because he drove like 'the demon of speed incarnate'. During the 1902 Circuit des Ardennes he had crashed so badly that the body of his car came to a halt in one ditch and all four wheels ended up in another.

Shortly before the start of the Irish Gordon Bennett Race a fire at the Cannstatt factory destroyed the three racing Mercédès and Jenatzy had to drive a stripped-down version of the sixty-horsepower touring model. Nevertheless, Mercédès won the lap record at an average speed of 52.2mph and Jenatzy's car suggested 'a condensed edition of "The Inferno"'. Yellow flames shot out of its exhaust as he hurled the great white machine forward like a projectile ricocheting along the ground. Wild-eyed, his sun-burned face covered in oil and dust, his body rigid to resist the air pressure, Jenatzy drove over the 370-mile course with a recklessness that astonished even Jarrott. The spectators, some sitting in a beflagged and buntinged grandstand which the Club had erected over the course at the Ballyshannon starting-point, were thrilled by this exhibition of daredevilry. Jenatzy gave his own account of it:

> When in the distance a cloud of dust proclaims that another car is being overtaken, a delightful feeling of triumph comes over you. This is the time when you need to recall all that you know of the features of the landscape, for then begins a real journey into darkness. The cloud of dust ... thickens gradually till the only objects which can be distinguished are the treetops on the edge of the road. When you finally emerge, you see the rival car only a few yards ahead, and the dust cloud changes into a hail of flints and pebbles. If the other competitor sees you he will draw aside, but usually he does not heed your signals. There seems to be no room to pass, but you pass all the same ....

Jenatzy did pass, to the chagrin of the drivers whose Napiers were green – this being the racing colour of Britain, newly selected as a tribute to the Emerald Isle. Edge was delayed by tyre troubles. Jarrott's steering-gear failed, whereupon he careered into a wall, turned the car over and broke his collar-bone. When he heard that Jenatzy had won the race 'the misery of abject despair took possession of me, and I wished, in my wretchedness, that the smash had been complete and that I had not been left to live'. It was scant recompense to be told that the whole event had been an 'unparalleled success'. Still, for most members this was a moment to savour. Only a year before the Club had been criticised for not having learnt 'the A B C of sport promotion'. Now it had organised the major international motoring competition of the day without a single serious mishap.

Scudding stylishly back to Dublin, the Gordon Bennett drivers hardly noticed the vile country roads and the 'miserable cottages which the peasantry shared with their livestock'. For the atmosphere was one of euphoria. James Joyce, who observed the cars running like pellets

GORDON BENNETT VICTORS

*S. F. Edge won the 1902 Gordon Bennett Race in his Napier (above).
Thus the 1903 Race was held in Ireland, where victory went to the
Mercédès of Camille Jenatzy (below). He was 'meek and mild' out of the
car but 'daring and excitable to the utmost degree when actually racing'.*

down the Naas Road, which was lined with onlookers eager to pay homage to their heroes, sensed the elation afforded by rapid motion through space. In his short story 'After the Race', published in *Dubliners*, he wrote: 'The journey laid a magical finger on the genuine pulse of life and gallantly the machinery of human nerves strove to answer the bounding courses of the swift blue animal.' Blue was the French racing colour and the two Panhards, which had come second and third, drew the loudest cheers from the crowd – which might have been less enthusiastic had it known how disgusted the Frenchmen were by Irish food and how they refused to touch Irish whiskey unless they saw the bottle being opened. There was more rejoicing, as well as speechifying, at the Shelbourne hotel, followed by record-breaking speed trials in Phoenix Park watched by 30,000 people. 'For the nonce,' wrote one journalist, 'the capital of Ireland had become an annexe of the Automobile Club.' The Parliament of Motoring, incorporating the Jockey Club of motor sport, enjoyed its hour of self-congratulation. Back in England, however, more trouble was brewing. Earl Russell declared that 'the Committee is manned, and the whole Club is run, entirely in the interests of wealthy owners of racing cars'. The maverick peer had now become the self-appointed spokesman for ordinary motorists. And increasing numbers of them felt that the Automobile Club was not representing them properly.

INTERESTED PARTIES

*The Automobile Club's Secretary,
Claude Johnson, drives its Chairman,
Roger Wallace, in the former's twelve-
horsepower New Orleans at the
Bexhill race meeting, 1902.*

CHAPTER FOUR

RAC
&
AA

As the car cult grew, the Automobile Club could no longer control it. In 1905 militant motorists, bent on resisting police 'persecution', set up the rival AA. The moderate Club won its royal title and tried to attract a popular following – Associate members.

THE RIVAL BODY

When motorists founded the AA in order 'to circumvent police traps', critics denounced this as the 'badge of the law-breaker'.

THE SHEER SIZE OF THE AUTOMOBILE CLUB, which by 1904 had 2,500 members, meant that individual interests were bound to diverge. Conflicts were legion, giving Earl Russell ample scope to pursue his favourite hobby of fishing in troubled waters. But the central rift, which had never healed, was the original one between moderates for whom the Club was primarily a social and sporting body and militants who thought it should act as a Praetorian Guard to protect motorists against 'insane persecution'. This explains the ill feeling caused by Rees Jeffreys' letter to *The Times* in December 1903 which suggested that motorists, who were at liberty to pay the new £1 car registration fee into the coffers of the county borough of their choice, should vote with their money to benefit counties which favoured them. John Montagu said that Jeffreys' attempt to dictate to local authorities was worthy of the Tsar of all the Russias. Equally offensive to gentlemen amateurs was the Committee's decision that the Club should abandon its commercial neutrality and become patron of Charles Cordingley's annual motor exhibition at the Royal Agricultural Hall for a fee of £500. The decision also infuriated many members involved in the car business, who supported the SMMT's rival show at the Crystal Palace and accused the Club of having sold its soul for lucre. Thus the Parliament of Motoring was not only divided into two major parties, but these in turn were split into factions. When Edgar Jepson became editor of the *Journal* in 1904 he found himself plunged into 'a new world, a world of feuds, intrigues and jealousies'.

The truth was that Claude Johnson had left a vacuum. Attempting to explain what it called 'the decadence of the Club' at the beginning of 1904, *The Autocar* lamented that there was no 'managing director', 'no master brain'. This was because a single leader had been replaced by a triumvirate. The unpopular, domineering Rees Jeffreys was in charge of administration; Basil Joy, once a manager at the Simms Manufacturing Company, took control of technical matters; and Julian Orde, first among equals, tried to fill Johnson's shoes. Born in 1861, the son of an East Anglian banker, Orde had gone to school at Haileybury and spent twelve years ranching in America. On returning to Europe he had worked in business and attracted the attention of John Montagu, who recommended him to the Club. Orde lacked Johnson's vision and drive: Russell was to complain about the 'slackness' of his administration. But Orde was no cipher. Indeed a future chairman, Arthur Stanley, paid extravagant tribute to his 'genius for the work of the Club' and said he was just the man to solve the Irish problem. With him in charge, 'Ireland would become peaceful for the inhabitants and a paradise for motorists'.

Elegant and imposing, Orde was a 'stickler for discipline', especially where motor sport was concerned. 'We used to call him Orde God Almighty,' recollected the 100-year-old Sir Thomas Sopwith in 1988. Even when giving orders, however, Orde had a light touch. He sealed his popularity at one hill-climb, where it was forbidden to leave the 'cut-out' open (the open 'cut-out' allowed noisy exhaust gases free passage), by shouting above the din: 'Have any of you cut-out?' There was a roar of 'Noes'. After a pause, Orde bellowed: 'Then shut 'em!' Members saluted him as a 'gentleman' who did not treat them as 'chattels' and as a wit who kept them entertained. He once explained that French cab drivers, unlike English ones, took deliberate aim at pedestrians: 'one got heavily fined for being run over, and the cabman got half the fine, which was a distinct inducement to him to have a shot at one again'. But 'Lord Orde' (to give him his other nickname) was also a peerless champion to be invoked at moments of trial. 'When a motorist is in trouble, when, for example, he is being haled away to the *oubliettes* of the Surrey magistrates,' wrote a journalist, 'it has been remarked that the last intelligible words he has been heard to utter are "Orde! Orde!"' So, at the end of 1904, Orde became sole secretary, Jeffreys being confined to legal matters and Joy to technical ones. The Club hoped thus to gain what had previously been lacking – 'unity of control and convenience of administration'.

While the triumvirate was still in operation, however, there was a coup at the top. Hostile factions coalesced against the Chairman, Roger Wallace, and his Committee. The 'Old Guard', as Montagu called them, were variously accused of supporting specific trade interests, ignoring ordinary motorists and displaying such feebleness that the Club had lost 'influence and prestige'. There were even hints of financial irregularity. Wallace apparently owed the Club £152 8s, a debt which elicited from him a plea worthy of a browbeaten barrister and recorded in the Club's Minute Book, on 12 July 1904, as follows: 'Whilst on the one hand denying the liability, on the other hand he stated that considering the amount of work he had done for the Club this amount might be remitted.' Describing the Club as 'appallingly weak and rotten', one member urged Montagu to start another motoring organisation. The plan was seriously discussed by a 'good many influential men', some of whom resigned their membership. But Montagu was determined to mend rather than to split. According to his diary, he told another member, Roger Fuller, that he 'wanted reformation and meant to have it'. After their talk, he continued, '[Fuller] leaves far more convinced and reasonable, also probably realising that J. M. [John Montagu] is a far stronger man than most take him for – he may be regarded by the old 'uns and cranks of the Club as a "young enthusiast" but his ideas are sounder

DUKE OF SUTHERLAND

A patrician President at the time when the Automobile Club became royal, the 4th Duke was immensely rich and passionately keen on cars. His elegant Duchess, Millicent, presided over the Ladies' Automobile Club.

BRIG-GEN. SIR H. C. L. HOLDEN

A founder member of the Automobile Club, Holden became its second Chairman in 1904. But he was too busy to remain for more than a year, being not only an artilleryman but a mechanic, electrician, inventor, designer and FRS.

SIR ARTHUR STANLEY

The only man to have been the Club's Chairman twice (1905–7 and 1912–36), Stanley was no great administrator. But, said Northcliffe, he deserved the 'blue ribbon' for diplomacy.

SIR JULIAN ORDE

Secretary of the Club for two decades, Orde is pictured by Junior Ape in Vanity Fair. *Sir Julian, as he became in 1919, always looked worthy to be called 'His Ordeship'.*

than one might think.' Montagu's self-esteem was matched by his outspokenness. Over a lunch he brusquely told Wallace that he was 'most unpopular and must resign'. When Wallace accepted this advice, Montagu conspired with Johnson to elect a reforming Committee.

Reform covered a multitude of issues. They included matters of principle, such as the extent to which the Club should help the police by trying to suppress dangerous driving. They also included matters of business. Montagu himself, for example, pressed for the improvement of the Club *Journal*; but he was obviously intent on diverting its advertisements to his own magazine, *The Car*. Staplee Firth said that Montagu's judgement was warped by 'self-interest'. Harrington Moore also had a commercial axe to grind: his garage had lost business when the Club established one of its own. Most members, who simply owned and drove cars, were resentful of 'the clique of makers and agents' who supposedly ran the Club for their own gain. But when Lord Shrewsbury proposed that they should be excluded from the Committee, he stirred up a hornet's nest.

Claude Johnson and others furiously declared that never 'had any member of the Committee interested in the trade used that connection in a prejudicial manner'. They protested too much. Even Roger Wallace, who himself dabbled in the trade, admitted that those involved sometimes 'pressed their views rather too hardly in their own interests'. Johnson was on stronger ground when he argued that horse owners were not excluded from the Jockey Club and that the money, energy and technical expertise provided by the trade were vital to the Club. Simms concurred. 'If the Automobile Club shall be reduced to a club of amateurs pure and simple,' he said, 'we can hardly expect any public body to continue to recognise it as a practical authority governing automobilism in this country.' Simms recommended a division of labour between different sections of the organisation. The Club, with high entrance and subscription fees 'eliminating all elements socially ineligible', should deal with matters of automobilism as a sport and pastime. Meanwhile the subordinate Motor Union, open to anyone at a modest charge and already (with over 5,000 members, some of them women) the largest motoring organisation in the world, should be 'the practical body governing automobilism as a society of encouragement'.

The reform controversy raged through the columns of the motoring press and stirred up enormous excitement. Montagu printed the details because 'the future of automobilism is largely bound up with the management of the Automobile Club'. But the debate was also a matter of general concern: the Club's pursuit of 'a policy of provocation instead of a policy of conciliation had alienated a large body of the public'. Propaganda, intrigue and even perhaps some sharp practice by the Old Guard over the proxy voting papers, preceded the Club's annual general meeting in March 1904. It was, said *The Autocar*, the 'most momentous' gathering since the Club's foundation seven years before. The drama was heightened when Wallace arrived bruised and shaken after a road accident during which, he reported, 'a determined attack was made upon me by a hansom cab horse'. Despite his appeal for 'good feeling' and Salomons' plea to end 'pin-pricking and bickering', Wallace was further assailed during the meeting itself. The dispute became general. Members exchanged insults. Montagu was accused of

MOTORING VOGUE

The Car *was the arbiter of motoring fashion during the Edwardian period. However, its hard-pressed owner, who became Lord Montagu of Beaulieu the year after this number appeared, complained that the* Automobile Club Journal *'takes some £5000 a year from the trade in advertisements'. In 1915 Lord Montagu's magazine eventually absorbed the* Journal.

PRICE ONE SHILLING. By Inland Post, 1s. o½d.

THE CAR
ILLUSTRATED.

A JOURNAL OF TRAVEL
BY LAND, SEA, AND AIR.

Vol. XI., No. 134.   Edited by the Hon. JOHN SCOTT MONTAGU, M.P.   December 14, 1904.

XMAS 1904.

CHRISTMAS GREETINGS.

dishonourable conduct. There were cries of 'Shame' and 'Order'. Finally a new Committee was elected, 49 out of 50 of Montagu's candidates being successful. This represented a victory for the trade: as Colonel Crompton noted, over a third of the new Committee was drawn from that five per cent of the membership which had a stake in the car business. But it was also a victory for conciliation, as opposed to 'pugnacity and brickbats'. Wallace's successor as Chairman, Lieutenant-Colonel H. C. L. Holden, was not only a distinguished inventor but also a noted moderate. Holden promised that his Committee would resolutely set their 'face against dangerous and inconsiderate driving' and would put their 'house in order'.

It was a serious pledge. In 1904 the Club issued the first edition of the *Automobile Handbook*, which not only contained information about routes, hotels, signs, engines, law and taxation (the duty charged for putting armorial bearings on a car, it noted, was two guineas), but also laid down 'the understood etiquette of the road'. The Club improved its course of instruction, which the *Tatler* had denounced as 'a mere farce'. In 1905 it instituted an examination and awarded a certificate to successful chauffeurs and owner-drivers. According to the *Journal*, used cars were now falling into 'undesirable' hands. The Club stationed paid watchers around London to take the numbers of ramshackle jalopies emitting noxious fumes, though it could do no more than issue a warning and it blamed the worst motoring offences on 'the cheap scorcher … [with an] ingrained tendency to underbred caddishness'. Earl Russell wrote to *The Times*: 'the AUTO-MOBILE CLUB, backed by … all decent motorists, is ready to do everything in its power to stamp out genuine cases of hooliganism'. But early in 1905 the Club acknowledged that its members broke the law and set up a new tribunal, quaintly named the Inconsiderate Driving Committee. This had the power to expel miscreants. 'As the Club is almost as representative of the road as the Jockey Club is of the Turf,' wrote the *Daily Mail*, 'the penalty from a social point of view is a severe one.' Though seldom imposed, it was an earnest of good intentions.

Some members went still further, questioning whether the Club should back hazardous 'speed contests'. These could be 'harmful to the interests of automobilism' at a time when its very existence was threatened by further parliamentary hostility. Johnson took that view. It was shared by manufacturers who dwelt more on the actual costs of racing than the possible financial rewards. At this stage, though, most makers believed in the advertising value of competitions. One of them, the taciturn Herbert Austin, was surprised by the number of people who 'came into the works and gloated over the racing cars'. As for Club members, many agreed with Edge that racing played a vital part in 'the evolution of the perfect car'. More took an interest in the competitions themselves. Since it was forbidden to close English roads, the Club obtained permission to conduct the trials for the 1904 Gordon Bennett Race on the Isle of Man. This was the first of many automotive contests held there. The venue was a handicap to British motor sport because of its remoteness; a boon because it was available.

The trials were a complex test of speed and reliability. To a spectator asking who had won, Earl Russell replied magisterially: 'It isn't a race, it isn't over, and, as in Alice in Wonderland, they have all won.' In fact, as usual Edge and Jarrott led the field. But in the Gordon Bennett Race itself, which was held in Germany, British cars were again outclassed. Jarrott's Wolseley suffered from a host of ills – lost chain, leaking radiator, malfunctioning governor, broken petrol pump, defective third gear – and ended up firing on only three cylinders. It could not compete

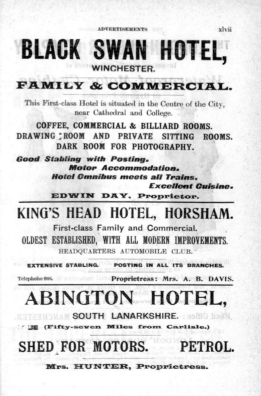

THE MOTORIST'S MANUAL

*First issued in 1904 and updated
annually, the Club's* Handbook *aimed to
provide all the information a motorist
might need. To attract the affluent new
motoring trade, hotels (sometimes
converted coaching inns which had just
taken down signs saying 'No Automobiles')
not only sought Club approval but
advertised in the* Handbook.

with Jenatzy's Mercédès, whose ninety-horsepower engine enabled the Red Devil to corner in what Jarrott facetiously called a 'Christianlike manner'. And even Jenatzy was beaten by Léon Théry, whose Richard-Brasier was fitted with shock-absorbers which gave it a marked advantage. Club members who did not attend the race ran a sweepstake on the result. They were especially fascinated by the rise of 'leviathan racing cars'. These embodiments of power presented a contrast to increasingly sybaritic touring models with their roomy saloons, six-cylinder sophistication and plush accoutrements – Morocco leather armchairs, green baize card tables, walnut veneer drinks cabinets and sash windows with oiled silk blinds. Maurice Maeterlinck was one of a number of contemporaries who celebrated the beast in the machine. To him it was a fierce, primordial creature, a 'dreadful Hippogriff': 'The soul of this monster is the electric spark; its complex heart is the carburettor, explosion chamber and piston; its body the bonnet and tonneau; its limbs the four wheels.' But though such flights of fancy appealed to those members of the Club who did not use its library as a dormitory, they were calculated to increase public suspicion of 'motor mania'. A play of the time by Israel Zangwill included a 'motor maniac' called Lord Tottenham who was also a member of the Club.

It was the growing speed of vehicles driven by the likes of Lord Tottenham which provoked further opposition in 1905. A man who had been expelled from the Club claimed that practically every member exceeded the limit and that 'plenty who are on the Committee' drove at over 70mph. The *Daily Telegraph* complained that the 'scorcher'

> becomes absorbed in his own tingling delight and selfish gratification. Proud of his cool judgement and nerves of steel, he knows to a nicety how to miss a cyclist …. And so he races by, but the unfortunate cyclist feels that it was Death which passed him close and turns sick with fear.

Yet again MPs considered imposing stiffer penalties on the motorist. One said that, for the first time since the French Revolution, the working class looked on the wealthy as 'an intolerable nuisance'. A poor man, he added artlessly, 'did not like to be run over by a man of superior social position'. Such was the strength of feeling, remarked another MP, that it might 'be necessary to stop motoring altogether'. Arthur Stanley, who succeeded the overworked Holden as Chairman of the Club in 1905, defended motorists in the Commons with all the ingenuity that might be expected from a former secretary to Arthur Balfour. There was no time, in the event, to pass a measure. Moreover, Westminster Palace Yard, to which Montagu's car had been forbidden entry only six years before, was now full of motors. As Stanley's driver remarked, there was 'not a blooming carriage in the place'. Within the lower house the motor interest was becoming increasingly powerful. When Montagu complained about members' slowness in going through the division lobbies, the Liberal leader Sir Henry Campbell-Bannerman essayed an elephantine, but apposite, joke. He hoped the government would not listen to any suggestion Montagu might make that members should *drive* through in motor cars.

Outside parliament opposition to speeding automobiles took more alarming forms. The Marquess of Queensberry announced his intention to carry a loaded revolver when in Hammersmith for the purpose of shooting dangerous drivers. Others, including Canon Greenwell, a Durham JP, endorsed the idea. The *Tatler* suggested that between March and May

ELIMINATION TRIALS

Prohibited from driving at speed on English roads, the Club went to the Isle of Man in order to select national contestants for the 1904 Gordon Bennett Race. Here Clifford Earp is seen at the Ballasalla time control in a forty-five-horsepower Napier. Earp did well but later crashed and was eliminated amid controversy. The Club's selection procedure involved conjuring with regulations and 'juggling with slide-rules'.

JARROTT ON TRIAL

Gordon Horner portrays Charles Jarrott driving a Wolseley in the 1904 trials. He was selected. But by now, Jarrott said, speeds were such that racing was less a sport than a 'positive torture'. The 'spectator gazed with horror at the sight and the driver knew that he carried his life in his hands'.

there should be a close season on motorists. Farmers, out of patience with the dust storms raised by 'scorchers', proposed that bombs should be fitted to cars in such a way that a foot pressed too hard on the accelerator would trigger an explosion. In rural districts cars were stoned. A wire was stretched across the Slough–Maidenhead road in an apparent attempt to decapitate fast drivers. Various associations added their weight to the attack. The Canine Defence League was particularly vocal, with some justification. The Automobile Club had advised its members not to stop when they hit dogs as a 'vexatious prosecution' was likely to ensue which would cost them 'time, temper and money'. Moreover, drivers tended to be somewhat cavalier in their attitude towards man's best friend. Some boasted about their 'bag'. A Club member who had squashed a mongrel quipped, 'they said it was a dog, but it looked more like a door-mat'.

Children, too, were killed. One was run over by the chauffeur of Hildebrand Harmsworth, Alfred's brother. The case stirred passions to new heights. Papers printed items like 'The Motor-Death Roll'. Motorists were greeted with shouts of 'Murderer!' Goldsworthy Lowes Dickinson declared that the citizen without a car 'has become a kind of outlaw on his own highways'. Montagu's new Considerate Drivers' League was reviled as a callous piece of hypocrisy: it was like forming a society of inebriates to promote temperance. Magistrates, known to their motorised victims as 'bench hogs', became more rigorous though not necessarily better informed. One JP, trying a man charged with having an improper silencer and being told that the noise was caused by gas passing though the exhaust, said that 'it was very important that Corporation gas should not be used in this way'. Speed traps proliferated. The police were especially active on highways that had been treated with tar to diminish the dust menace. Club members suspected a Machiavellian plot on the part of the authorities to improve road surfaces in order to encourage speeding and reap a rich harvest of fines. Motorists lived, as Earl Russell said, in 'an atmosphere of persecution'. The pressure to retaliate was intense.

The Club, though, was in the hands of a moderate majority which was committed to a policy of conciliation. Jarrott and other activists had already initiated piecemeal schemes whereby men were employed to patrol popular routes and give motorists advance warning of constables hiding behind hedges with stopwatches (though some relied on church clocks). But Shrapnell-Smith, an expert on commercial vehicles, expressed the Club's objection to this tactic. It was like 'a burglar's pal' tipping him off about the presence of the police, and 'One did not like to class oneself with burglars.' Jarrott, Edge, Mayhew and their ilk were less scrupulous. In their eyes the Club was guilty of 'tasteful posturing and elegant inertia'. Meeting at the Trocadero Restaurant, they endorsed Jarrott's view that the only way to secure fair treatment was to fight for it. They determined, in Mayhew's words, to strike 'a blow for automobilism as opposed to blind prejudice, crass ignorance, and that form of highway robbery which masquerades under the title of "fines" for so-called excessive speed'. So, in June 1905, they formed the Automobile Association. Its sole *raison d'être* was to combat police traps.

MANY CLUB MEMBERS joined the '"fighting" movement'. And at first, acting as the mailed fist of motordom, the AA seemed to complement the Club's pacific efforts. If the senior body were to employ road scouts to counteract the police, as Mayhew said, 'a great deal of

Motor Fiend. "Why don't you get out of the way?"
Victim. "What! Are you coming back?"

SO INCONSIDERATE

"Jove! Might have killed us! I must have a wire screen fixed up."

A POPULAR VIEW

Punch *caricatures Edwardian motorists as callous scorchers. But serious critics said that the Automobile Club had 'lamentably failed in one of its most important duties – namely, suppressing dangerous driving'.*

parliamentary, official, and public opinion would at once be alienated from the Club, which is trying to work in cooperation with, rather than opposition to, the "powers that be"'. This was the crucial point. The Automobile Club was already exerting significant influence on Westminster, particularly over the Royal Commission on Road Traffic. Its report, published in 1906, enshrined many of the Club's recommendations – for example, that revenue from cars should fund road improvements, that the speed limit should be abolished and that the Club itself should hold official driving tests. The Club's tactic was therefore quietly to nurture what it did not yet recognise as a cuckoo in the nest. It even saved the fledgeling AA from extinction by donating £50 towards its legal costs in a contested case. The Club was duly thanked by the Secretary of the AA, Stenson Cooke, a former life-insurance salesman with a waxed moustache and a hail-fellow-well-met manner. Cooke was more interested in fencing, dancing and philandering than in motoring – he never learnt to drive himself. But he proved to be a forceful and charismatic leader. At this stage he thought the AA was like a torpedo boat compared to the battleship of the Club. He paid tribute to its 'wisdom' and 'superior judgement'. It was 'the peerage of Automobilism'. But later, when the two bodies became clear rivals, Cooke began to harbour a paranoid hatred for the Club and all its works.

As yet, however, Club members were unaware that the long-heralded schism within their ranks had actually occurred (though Edge did note that the old 'cohesion' had gone). Their own vigorous Motor Union, with 11,000 members, dwarfed the AA and seemed quite capable of defending the interests of car owners. Meanwhile the Club itself grew in prestige as the scope of its activities widened. In 1905 it founded the Motor Yacht Club, thus establishing control over 'the marine section of automobilism'. Its headquarters were the former Admiralty yacht *Enchantress*, a thousand-ton floating clubhouse moored at Buckler's Hard, not far from Beaulieu, in Hampshire. In the same year the Touring Department arranged for 600 cars to go abroad. A clubhouse was acquired for members at 18 Rue des Pyramides in Paris, where many liked to patronise the *Folies Bergère*. The Touring Department was compared to the parrot which didn't say much but thought a lot. But it gave copious advice about the hazards awaiting motorists on the Continent: around Rome, for example, the rule of the road was to keep left in town and change to the right in the country; in Denmark no driving was permitted at night; and anyone wishing to drive in Serbia had to submit a sample of his petrol to government laboratories for analysis. Domestic information, too, was gathered assiduously. Club approval was given to more garages and hotels, though Earl Russell tried to ensure that its official blessing was withheld from establishments in districts where police 'persecution' of motorists was rife.

The work of the Club was conducted by a web of committees, a form of management to which it has remained notoriously addicted. There was even a committees committee, or at any rate an Agenda Department to monitor the work of the twenty-odd subcommittees. Edgar Jepson complained in his memoirs that the committees, as well as being part of a vast conspiracy against non-motorists, were 'dismally dull'. They usually resulted in 'a long wordy squabble about matters of astonishing triviality, between astonishingly trivial people'. At the time, though, Jepson paid tribute to 'that strenuous body of active workers in the Movement whose resourceful energy finds such valuable expression on the committees' of the Club and its affiliates. Doubtless the truth lies somewhere between these versions. Certainly much toil went

AA LEADER

Although eccentric and dictatorial, Stenson Cooke was an effective Secretary of the AA for nearly thirty years. Between the wars he broadcast often, cleverly using the BBC to win support in his 'fight' with the RAC. Cooke was knighted in 1933: it must have been the first time, he joked, that anyone had been so honoured after conspiring to defeat the ends of justice.

MODEST BEGINNINGS

Lacking the Club's resources, the AA borrowed a room in Fleet Street for its first office, which Cooke shared with a typist. Cooke liked to pop out and tread the measure at thés dansants.

into the committees: in 1906, for example, 250 separate meetings took place. But members themselves complained that the Club only seemed able to 'express itself in the terminology of a particularly stodgy Blue-book'. And when Sir David Salomons observed innocently that he found the advertisements the most interesting part of the *Journal*, which printed interminable minutes, Montagu provoked roars of sympathetic laughter with a fervent 'Hear, hear!'

Nevertheless, the committees unquestionably produced a breed of amateur specialist who could and did pronounce with authority upon all aspects of motoring, from headlight dazzle to tar consistency, from the longevity of a coupling-rod pin to the correct note of a motor horn. Often they were right, especially about technical matters. They sensibly rejected Lieutenant-Colonel A. B. Williams's scheme to make cars carry 'a telescopic staff with a small flag affixed' so that they could be seen round corners and over hedges. They also turned down a nautical member's proposal for a code of horn blasts to signal direction: one short blast for starboard; two for port; three for astern; and a single long blast for ahead. With less perception, committee members fussed about the imminent exhaustion of the world petrol supply and dismissed talk of equipping automobiles with wireless: it was 'one of the "Yankee notions" that will not add to the pleasures of life'. The Publications Committee, moreover, was inclined to confuse information with propaganda. For example, it tried to assert that motors were within the reach of men of 'moderate means'. In fact, before the Great War horse-drawn carriages were cheaper to run than cars and most people could barely afford public transport. Nothing daunted, the Club continued to preach the gospel of the automobile: 'Yesterday a plaything of the few; to-day a servant of the many; to-morrow the necessity of humanity.'

On social matters connected with the movement, though, the Club's sway was unchallenged. Orde himself acted as the final arbiter of motoring vogue. As *The World* wrote: 'Whenever a lady of fashion desires to know whether it is correct to dress her chauffeur in boots and cords, or whether it is smart to have the family crest emblazoned on his goggles, the idea that suggests itself first is to "ring up Orde".' The Secretary solved such perplexing problems with ease and grace. Thus it was established that 'the aggressive and vulgar toot on the horn' was shocking bad form. A peaked cap should never be worn by an owner-driver, who might thus be confused with a chauffeur – itself a term redolent of confusion, which the Club tried to banish in favour of 'paid driver'. (It approved the Kaiser's linguistic cleansing: he insisted on the word '*Wagen-fuehrer*'.) A man might properly drive his own dogcart, phaeton or wagonette without a top, but it would be 'social blasphemy' for him to drive a landaulette – here the chauffeur should take on the role of coachman. The mechanic at the wheel was a different species from the teamster at the reins. He was technically better qualified and could command a higher wage. Often, too, he knew more about cars than his employer, who resented his dependence and complained about any show of 'side'.

One Club member objected to the spread of Frenchified waxed moustaches among chauffeurs: 'People would not tolerate for an instant any fancy hairdressing on the part of their coachmen or grooms.' In his play *Man and Superman*, which was first performed in 1905, George Bernard Shaw introduced a sharp, superior chauffeur, 'Enry Straker, to illustrate the absurdities of the social hierarchy. 'He positively likes the car to break down,' Straker's employer says, 'because it brings out my gentlemanly helplessness and his workmanlike skill and

SPORTING OCCASIONS

*Motoring for its own sake long remained a sport. But
Club members soon used it to enjoy other sports,
organising Runs to places like Newmarket. Here Frank
Butler (standing by the front wheel of his Benz) has
taken his family on what may have been a Club outing
to Henley Regatta in about 1898.*

resource.' But most denizens of the Club (which Shaw was soon to join) saw the chauffeur, with his lounging manner, swaggering airs and esoteric abilities, as a serious challenge to the established order. In the unmistakable tones of the class warrior one member, Max Pemberton, denounced that 'terror, the professional chauffeur … [the] grinning and greasy lout who costs us so much … consorts with the local "Mary Ann" … [and smokes] the cheapest brand of cigarette'. The Club's solution was a familiar one: the chauffeur must be kept in his place. He must be uniformed in blue or green. He must be disciplined and addressed though a speaking tube. He must be exposed to the elements while his master was protected behind glass.

Needless to say, members were creatures of their class; and even in the course of the amusements which the Club existed to furnish and to foster they did not forget it. During dinners and discussions they laughed at stories about 'white-eyed Kaffirs'. Cracks about the dirty unemployed were sometimes made at smoking concerts, rumbustious events which featured Music Hall 'artistes' like Harry Lauder, Little Tich, Clara Alexandra and Vesta Tilley, to say nothing of assorted female impersonators, farmyard imitators, speakers of gibberish, telepathists, ventriloquists, contortionists, conjurers and comedians. It was not true, quipped one Club humorist, that those benefiting from cheap workmen's railway tickets gave nothing in return: they contributed 'nameless vermin'. Even lyrical accounts of touring were occasionally marred by expressions of disdain for the 'lower orders'. Describing a delightful visit to the north Cornish resort of Bude (where the railway had only arrived in 1898), one member wrote: 'I marvel that this part of the country is not better patronised. There were only a few hundred visitors, all of whom were of the better classes – the tripper, such as we know him, *non est*.' The best that can be said of such remarks is that Club members were equally blunt with one another, particularly where their own interests were concerned.

Claude Johnson, now promoting Rolls-Royce, criticised the Club for being 'to some extent in the hands of those who have large interests in the sale of foreign cars in England'. He then instructed his fellow members that there was no need for a Britisher to buy an alien vehicle 'unless he wishes deliberately and in cold blood to do an unpatriotic deed'. In the cause of motordom generally another member, a rubicund squire from the shires, was still more outspoken. Striding up to a timid, silent, solitary member in the Smoking Room, he roared:

> Don't talk to me about railways, Sir! I won't hear a word about them! The North-Western – yes, Sir – the North-Western, which is the best of them, was three hours and fifteen minutes taking me five miles! All on account of a little bit of fog! They're obsolete, Sir! Obsolete! They must be done away with! Give me a motor car! Hang your railways! Are you a shareholder? Eh? Are you, Sir? Are you?

Sporting gentry easily adapted the manners of the hunting field to the pursuit of motoring.

Few of these gentry were happy when the Club tried to tame motor sport, peril being regarded as its essence. The Club did so – to conclude its round of activities for 1905 – by holding the first Tourist Trophy Race. The intention was that this competition between touring cars should 'take the place of the Gordon-Bennett Race', a contest between racing cars which was not only dangerous but costly, restrictive, and less helpful to the trade. '"Wobble, wobble, little club," appears to be the motto of the Automobile Club,' declared *The Autocar*, which accused

MOTORING TOGS

Since most early cars were open, motorists needed protective clothes, ranging from waterproof greatcoats to all-embracing 'motor envelopes'. There was no standard kit. Gentlemen, an Edwardian remarked, 'have a horror of anything approaching a uniform'.

PAID DRIVERS

'The perfect motor servant,' said Alfred Harmsworth, 'should be a combination of gentleman and engineer.' But to make class distinctions plain, Edwardian chauffeurs had to dress correctly.

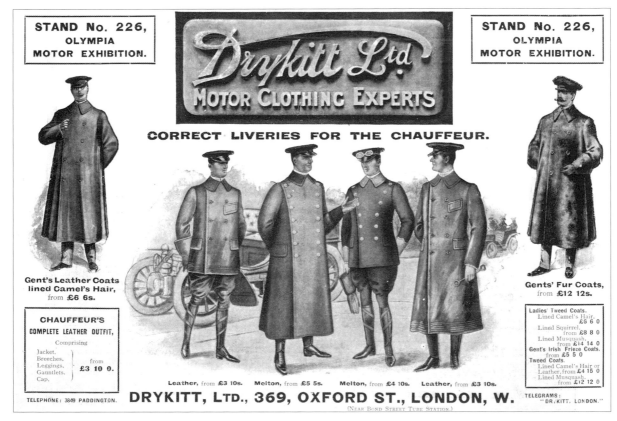

it of withdrawing its support from the Gordon Bennett Race to appease anti-motorists. The journal even demanded the formation of a new, independent sporting body strong enough to resist ostrich-like policies. As it happened, the Club's policy was far-sighted: the TT Race remains today the oldest regularly run motor competition in the world. But it began as it continued – with controversy. No one could agree about what constituted a touring car or how far the 'freaks' and 'thoroughbreds' masquerading as ordinary models were acceptable. The Club laid down complicated rules (which often changed) and set up a tented camp, gay with the flags of manufacturers and suppliers, just outside Douglas on the Isle of Man. Here its officials checked the vehicles. Some drivers attempted to evade the regulations, particularly those regarding weight, with concealed petrol tanks, hidden pipes and other 'jiggery-pokery'.

Orde supervised the investigative process, including the operation of the weighing machine, 'an instrument of vast proportions and dreadful inaccuracy' – actually it consisted of four separate machines, one for each wheel, borrowed from Manx railway stations and roughly synchronised. The Secretary was ubiquitous and omnicompetent. He was once seen driving through Douglas with scores of yard brooms, which he had just purchased from an ironmonger, protruding from every opening in his motor car, making it look like an enormous porcupine. Orde's main concern, though, was safety. He did much to improve surfaces whose undulations caused speeding cars to hop, skip and jump like so many Olympic athletes. But the task was well-nigh impossible since the hilly 52-mile circuit was full of sharp bends and narrow bridges, and flanked by dry-stone walls or kerbside lampposts. These circumstances soon prompted English abuse of the 'Isle of Manslaughter' and eventually proved fatal to motor (though not motor-cycle) racing there. Nevertheless, the only incident of note in the first race occurred at the beginning. Charles Rolls stripped the gears from his eponymous car and then suggested that someone had tampered with it. His sportsmanship was criticised but his rage was understandable. It cost £3,000 to bring a car to the starting line. The commercial rewards, however, as Rolls discovered when he won the following year, were considerable.

Sales followed victories. The Duke of Sutherland, President of the Club since Montagu's putsch, was to own four Rolls-Royces simultaneously, one of which was always kept with its engine running, ready for immediate departure. But the TT Race not only promoted trade, it stimulated fantasy. It helped to invest the ordinary car with extraordinary glamour. For some the vehicle became not so much a cherished possession as an object of worship. It was a fetish with a famous name but an individual character. Before mass production a car was tailor-made to suit a customer, built by craftsmen 'true to traditions handed down to them through the old Coachmakers' Guilds'. Sometimes a future owner visited the factory to ensure that the vehicle he had ordered was personally consecrated to him. At Napier's Acton works, for example, the nonagenarian Lord Wemyss made 'several useful suggestions' about the construction of the body of his landaulette. Colour could be as sacrosanct as design. Lord Lonsdale, later President of the AA, 'once tackled the owner of an English Daimler in St James's Street, whose primrose-coloured coachwork he claimed to be an infringement of his registered racing colours and actually told him he would have to have [it] changed immediately'.

Intellectuals also succumbed to the car cult. Joseph Conrad and Ford Madox Hueffer became devotees. Arnold Bennett recorded that the novelist Arthur Morrison 'sold his Japanese

1905

1929

1932

THE TOURIST TROPHY

Aiming to give excitement with minimal risk and to promote British motor manufacturing, the Automobile Club started a competition in 1905 for standard touring cars. But defining 'standard' is difficult and, as these programme covers show, the regulations have often changed. Still, the TT continues – the world's oldest motor race.

1994

1984

1973

1938

1953

1958

1964

prints to the British Museum' for £4,000 and bought a motor car'. Lord Berners later had a portable organ fitted into his automobile so that he could compose while on the road. Bernard Shaw became a slave to his double-cabriolet Lorraine-Dietrich, even though it was (in the words of his chauffeur) 'a proper bugger' to start. Henry James was held in thrall by that 'magical monster the touring Panhard'. Aboard this 'chariot of fire', which belonged to Edith Wharton, he found the experience of seeing France so easy and intelligible that it reconciled him to the monstrous processes of the machine. 'It's the old travelling-carriage way glorified and raised to the 100th power.' Other writers disagreed. Lowes Dickinson said that the car hermetically sealed its occupants from illuminating influences and typified the soulless society of the twentieth century. In E. M. Forster's view 'the throbbing, stinking car' not only turned the landscape into porridge, it was the supreme symbol of a detested mechanical civilisation. But the very potency and dynamism of the automobile, overcoming space and time, was what appealed to the avant-garde. As F. T. Marinetti famously wrote in the *Futurist Manifesto* of 1909:

> We say that the world's magnificence has been enriched by a new beauty, the beauty of speed. A racing car, whose bonnet is adorned with great pipes, like serpents of explosive breath – a roaring car that seems to ride on shrapnel – is more beautiful than the *Victory of Samothrace*.

Women, too, were devotees of the car, sometimes in a way that sadly confirmed Edwardian stereotypes. One lady doted on her motor because it 'outstrips our thoughts and leaves our mind a delicious, restful blank'. Another lady devised a means by which her car should emit 'a scented vapour'. Many revered the automobile as the ultimate appurtenance of fashion. Driving in open cars, ladies were naturally apt to arrive with 'their fringes out of curl, or the feathers in their hats drooping', and they could not expect to preserve the 'soft, peach-like bloom' of their skin. But they enjoyed unparalleled opportunities for display. One 'motorina' matched her car to her clothes, so that together they made 'one harmonious heliotrope whole'. Writing a weekly article entitled 'Costumes and Chatter' under the pen name 'The Goddess in the Car', Montagu's wife gave counsel about reversible tweeds and fur tartans, crêpe de Chine veils and astrakhan wraps. There was much discussion about whether the best motoring coats were made from the skins of silver baboons, blue foxes, Russian colts, wild cats, chamois, racoons, otters, wombats or opossums.

With their crank starts and their frequent breakdowns, cars still required the frequent application of brute force, so it was hardly surprising that they were not yet vehicles of female emancipation. As romantic novels of the time reveal, they could act as 'Cupid's agent'. Hearing that cars ground to a halt in lonely places, bishops (not a single one of whom had yet joined the Club) tut-tutted. But Edwardian cars generally reinforced the current image of feminine frivolity and helplessness. The *Gentlewoman*, for example, advised its readers to consult a male when buying a car – 'no woman should trust her own judgement'. Gentlewomen even seemed content to be patronised by gentlemen. One Club member wrote that although female drivers 'may not be quite so expert as members of the opposite sex, in the vast majority of cases they recognise the limits of their capabilities'. Some ladies were made of sterner stuff. Dorothy Levitt, who in 1906 broke the women's world speed record, at 96mph, advised the 'dainty motoriste' to carry

FIRST TT CHAMPION

John Napier, portrayed by Gerald Horner, rounds Ramsey's Hairpin Corner on the Isle of Man in his eighteen-horsepower flat-twin Arrol-Johnston. Napier won a hard-fought race lasting just over six hours by only a couple of minutes, driving at an average speed of 33.9mph.

DELIVERING THE GOODS

Car manufacturers were always quick to advertise their racing success but sometimes slow to meet the orders that followed. Charles Rolls, victor in the 1906 Tourist Trophy, emphasised that Rolls-Royce was 'in a position to take full advantage of the commercial value of a win'.

'a small revolver' while driving alone and unchaperoned. When an impious male hand was laid on Lillie Langtry's immaculate six-cylinder Wolseley, her face 'convulsed with rage' and she seemed about to resort to violence. Instead 'she expressed herself in language which not even a lady of her great personality could use and get away with'.

Perhaps she had learnt something from King Edward VII about defending the prerogatives of the motorist. The monarch, in the tenth year of its existence, set his seal upon the Club. Even as Prince of Wales he had had a close connection with it, though his first motoring experiences were not entirely happy. When in 1897 Evelyn Ellis's car reached the dizzying speed of 9mph, the Prince had cried: 'Evy, Evy! Don't drive so fast. I'm frightened, I'm frightened.' But Edward persevered, despite the fact that when he rode in J. S. Critchley's Daimler a year later it still had to be pushed up hills. The Club did everything possible to encourage the royal enthusiasm and to associate itself with the crown. At the time of the coronation in 1902 it illuminated the Piccadilly premises with motor car lamps which shone with such dazzling silver and white radiance that people could read newspapers everywhere in Green Park. Claude Johnson personally conducted Queen Alexandra on a nerve-racking spin in a fourteen-horsepower New Orleans. At the bottom of one hill he had to extinguish a smouldering brake lining with a glass of water from a pub. Moreover, Johnson told Harmsworth, 'the Queen being a dog lover, naturally every dog in the road attempted to commit suicide under my wheels'. By becoming its patron in 1903 the King was said to have conferred 'inestimable benefit' on the Club. He gave it copper-bottomed, gold-plated respectability.

Ironically, King Edward himself was anything but a motoring moderate. He behaved as though the speed limit did not apply to him. He was 'proud of having exceeded sixty miles an hour on the Brighton road as early as 1906'. He ordered his chauffeur to overtake everything in sight: 'Go *on*. Go *on* ... Pass him. We don't want his dust.' The sovereign liked to signal his advent with blasts on the four-key bugle which, in emulation of the Kaiser, he employed instead of a motor horn. He was so impatient that his mechanic frequently had to conduct running repairs on the engine from the wing while the vehicle was pounding along at 40mph. When Haffigan's pig got its tail stuck in the machinery of the 'monster jaunting car' in Shaw's play *John Bull's Other Island*, so that the more the brake was applied the louder the animal squealed and the faster the motor went ('as if it was enthered [sic] for the Gordon Bennett'), the King laughed so uproariously that he broke his chair. But motoring was a serious business. Directly he alighted from his car on a visit to John Montagu, the monarch began a 'recital of his drive to Newmarket' and kept everyone waiting until this important topic of conversation was exhausted.

Evidently it was not Montagu (who became the second Baron Montagu of Beaulieu on the death of his father in 1905) but Arthur Stanley, the third son of the Earl of Derby, who persuaded King Edward to imitate the crowned heads of Germany, Spain and Portugal, all of whom had granted the royal accolade to their automobile clubs. Doubtless, too, the King would have been impressed by the fact that the British Club now had over 3,000 members. Among them were leading figures from almost every walk of life, including two ex-premiers

MOTORING *A LA MODE*

These advertisements, which appeared in 1907, show some of the most extravagant female fashions called into being by the open car. As saloons multiplied, ladies adopted less heavy and elaborate styles of costume.

ALFRED DUNHILL LTD.

THE PREMIER
AUTOMOBILISTS
TAILORS

2 Conduit St
London W
And at
Manchester
& Edinburgh

1. Coloured leather, lined tweed, 12½ Gns. 2. White serge, lined to waist satin, 6½ Gns.
   3. Silk Dust Coat, 5 Gns.
4. Stone-coloured faced cloth, trimmed 5. Mackintosh in pretty-coloured gloria
   pale mauve-kid, 9½ Gns. silk, 4½ Gns.

Write for Catalogue,
No 18.

(Rosebery and Balfour) and the monarch's close friend Sir Ernest 'Windsor' Cassel. Describing the influence of the Club and the ramifications of its 'great work', the *Daily Telegraph* concluded that it was 'one of the most remarkable organisations in the world'. So in March 1907 the King decided, through the Club, to 'honour automobilism as a branch of the national life'. He marked 'his identification of the CLUB's welfare with the welfare of the motoring movement in general ... [by] graciously bestowing' on it the prefix 'Royal'. At a time when people asked to touch the King's claret-coloured Daimler as though it were a talisman, the title invested the RAC, as it may now be called, with an almost magical aura of prestige.

The RAC benefited from this in many ways. Its endeavours took on a quasi-official character. The many trials it held – of tar, tyres, exhaust emissions, headlamps, speedometers – were amply reported in the press. Even its shortcomings seemed less culpable. For example, the Club signally failed to solve the 'great question of the hour' – how to repress the dust stirred up by automobiles. Thick clouds of it, 'like the smoke from a double broadside of quick-firing guns', poisoned the lives of those who dwelt near the roadside. Conditions were far worse than anything seen in coaching days. Then the entire London–Bath road had to be watered to lay dust and now it was seriously suggested that seawater should be piped from Brighton to spray on the capital's streets. Dust stifled pedestrians, choked livestock, ruined crops, blackened clothes, wrecked typewriters, shrouded houses and lowered property prices.

The Club's efforts to eradicate this menace put the cart before the horse, or rather the car before the surface. Its Dust Committee carried out elaborate tests. It used electric timing devices and cinematograph equipment (to say nothing of a gang of labourers to supply and rake dust) in an effort to appraise – and eventually to subdue – the gritty tail of the automobile comet. But to 'exorcise the demon of dust altogether', as *The Times* noted, it was necessary to treat highways rather than to reshape motor cars. Tar might, as some lamented, put roads into 'mourning' but this was the way of the future. Yet despite its miscalculation the RAC's authority was hardly dented. Its name commanded respect. Its views on, say, the scientific regulation of traffic were heard with attention even though, as Earl Russell remarked sardonically, the 'scientific regulation of anything ... [is] naturally abhorrent to the mind of every Englishman'.

So elevated was the RAC's status that, despite further mistakes, it helped to turn Brooklands, the 'great motordrome' built near Weybridge in 1907, into 'Ascot on wheels'. Actually the Club had proposed to construct a similar racetrack of its own in Purley four years earlier but the project had foundered. It therefore supported H. F. Locke-King, a wealthy Surrey landowner (who was also responsible for Cairo's Mena House hotel), in his patriotic endeavour to provide a closed circuit where British cars could exercise at speed. Based on advice from Edge and Jarrott, as well as guidance from Holden, Brooklands was a major engineering feat – it even involved diverting the River Wey. The track consisted of a vast concrete oval, banked at the curves, 100 feet wide and 2¾ miles long. To the Club it was the fulfilment of a dream. Locke-King's neighbours regarded it as 'a perfect nightmare', a raucous 'purgatory of motor stables', stands and paddocks.

As this suggests, everything at Brooklands was 'conducted on horse-racing lines'. Bookmakers shouted the odds. Tipsters nobbled punters. Officials warned against welshers. Drivers wore coloured smocks like jockeys. The ex-starter of the Jockey Club himself gave the

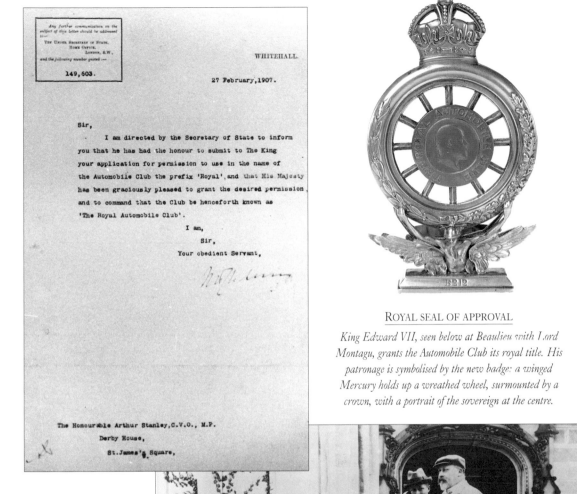

WHITEHALL.

27 February, 1907.

Sir,

I am directed by the Secretary of State to inform
you that he has had the honour to submit to The King
your application for permission to use in the name of
the Automobile Club the prefix 'Royal', and that His Majesty
has been graciously pleased to grant the desired permission,
and to command that the Club be henceforth known as
'The Royal Automobile Club'.

I am,

Sir,

Your obedient Servant,

The Honourable Arthur Stanley, C.V.O., M.P.

Derby House,

St. James's Square,

ROYAL SEAL OF APPROVAL

*King Edward VII, seen below at Beaulieu with Lord
Montagu, grants the Automobile Club its royal title. His
patronage is symbolised by the new badge: a winged
Mercury holds up a wreathed wheel, surmounted by a
crown, with a portrait of the sovereign at the centre.*

signal to go and the wire across the starting line failed to rise in time, 'nearly decapitating several drivers'. But despite this there was not enough excitement. After Edge had christened the course with his record-breaking 24-hour drive in a Napier, covering 1,581 miles at an average speed of 65.9mph, the first race meeting was an anticlimax. According to the Club *Journal*, the spectators gasped in wonder at the uncanny manoeuvrability and 'the terrific noise made by the impatient monsters'. In fact, only a dead heat between Edge and Jarrott managed to galvanise the crowd. The cars gave little impression of speed as they traversed the broad cement surface. Changes, such as the abandonment of horse-racing traditions and the introduction of handicapping, improved matters.

In 1910 the centre of the circuit was turned into an aerodrome and the Royal Aero Club (as it had become) organised flying gymkhanas, aerial Derbys, balloon steeplechases and point-to-points. But on the ground Brooklands was less successful as a racing circuit that appealed to the public than as a test-bed for speed and endurance. Here Count Louis Zborowski, his dark-brown eyes glaring through huge goggles, his black-and-white checked cap worn backwards with magnificent panache, roared around at over 100mph in the famous Chitty-bang-bang, a Mercédès chassis powered by a Benz airship engine. In the words of the French racing driver, Chevalier René de Knyff, Brooklands gave British manufacturers an 'inestimable advantage'. And what it lacked in popularity it made up for in distinction, attracting the cream of Edwardian society. This was thanks largely to the RAC, which provided many of the committee members of the Brooklands Automobile Racing Club. Its unofficial motto was 'the right crowd and no crowding'.

The Club cherished its exclusiveness, but the royal title itself was not an unalloyed blessing. Although it conferred privileges, it also imposed responsibilities. It put a premium on keeping up appearances. Above all, it inhibited the RAC from taking the kind of direct action on the roads which was not only winning the AA adherents (4,000 by 1907) but making it a 'new force in automobile politics'. Indeed, the Club felt obliged to restrain its own 'democratic' affiliate, the 19,000-strong Motor Union, when it began to compete head-on with the AA. The consequences were shattering.

There had always been friction between the élite Club in its smart premises and the popular Motor Union, which had 'no social habitat, but only offices'. Although the two organisations had worked out a theoretical division of labour, the Motor Union always seemed to be trespassing on the Club's preserves, even attempting to poach its members. Rees Jeffreys, the Motor Union's combative Secretary and the Club's over-mighty subject, felt that the bumbling amateurs of Piccadilly should confine themselves to social and sporting affairs. Meanwhile he interfered with technical matters like 'cut-outs'. He tried to get the Motor Union's name put on RAC signposts. He invaded the territory of its Touring Department. He even plagiarised large sections of the Club's *Handbook* without permission or acknowledgement. Then, in the summer of 1907, Jeffreys took on the Automobile Association. He pirated the AA's entire road programme, right down to its badge, of which he produced a passable copy.

The Motor Union announced that it was putting 'a limited number of trustworthy agents on the roads to act with the police in warning drivers of dangerous places'. These men (some of them former police constables and sergeants) were also supposed to act as the servants of

BROOKLANDS RACE TRACK

Although built for the fastest cars, Brooklands produced some spills but few thrills. On its wide circuit, said The Autocar *in 1907, 'Nothing but the rush of the wind and the bite of the concrete dust indicates speed at all.' But Brooklands was excellent for testing new vehicles.*

members. They had to protect them from assault, direct them to hotels and repairers, help in case of accident or breakdown, erect warning signs, remove nails from roads. However, this was all camouflage. The Motor Union's agents, with their bicycles, peaked caps, red-and-white armlets and white leather pouches, were mere replicas of the AA's yellow-brassarded scouts. And their transparent purpose was to warn motorists of speed traps. Like the AA, though, the Motor Union had to address its members in coded language. When a driver comes upon an agent in an unexpected place, it said, 'he realises instinctively that there must be some urgent reason for the man's presence on the spot'. The agent was even given a little red flag with which to slow down or stop the approaching vehicle. If he merely saluted it meant that the road was clear.

The AA was understandably incensed that its programme had been 'cribbed' in this 'disgraceful' fashion. Stenson Cooke refused all compromise and invited disaffected members of the Motor Union to join the AA. Its Chairman, Colonel Bosworth, announced: 'We shall fight to the finish.' The RAC's own Chairman, C. D. Rose, a retired banker and the sporting Liberal MP for Newmarket who had just taken over from Stanley, did not cover himself with glory in the subsequent 'internecine and fratricidal dispute'. Perhaps he sympathised with the Motor Union's bold initiative. Certainly he loved speed and courted danger. Wearing a Balaclava helmet which concealed his flowing white locks and luxuriant moustache, he hurtled around the Berkshire lanes in his sixteen-horsepower Argyll. Rose's family believed that Kenneth Grahame, a frequent visitor to their exquisite Tudor manor, Hardwick House, where he loved to lie on the bank of the Thames gazing into the water, 'immortalised' him as Mr Toad. Actually Toad, whose 'poop-poop' sounded the knell of the rural Elysium magically evoked in *The Wind in the Willows*, seems to have been a composite character. And he drew much of his 'colour' from that flamboyant vulgarian Horatio Bottomley.

Anyway, Rose at first tried to defend the Motor Union. In a disingenuous letter to *The Times* he averred that its purpose was to help the authorities restrain the 'small minority of motorists who are deficient in the common courtesies of the road'. However, most independent observers and many members of the RAC itself considered that the AA had a burning grievance. Montagu, for example, said that the Motor Union, jealous of its growing rival, had attempted to swallow it. The scheme had deservedly failed and Rees Jeffreys had generated nothing but 'bitter feelings' by his 'Napoleonic tactics'. 'Tammany methods', said the *Automotor Journal*, had been employed to carry out 'an overweening policy of militant self-aggrandisement'. The RAC could not become embroiled in such mud-slinging without damaging its dignity, or worse. So Rose beat a hasty retreat, saying that there had been no intention to steal the AA's thunder. Behind the scenes the Club reined in its unruly subordinate. Jeffreys was forced to negotiate a settlement. He obtained a few face-saving concessions from the AA, such as the right to superintend rural signposts. But in November 1907 he agreed to modify the Motor Union's badge and to withdraw its road patrols. This was an unmitigated defeat, and the RAC itself could not escape a degree of humiliation.

A few days later the Club responded with what Russell called a 'bombshell'. Taking the entire automobile world by surprise, it broke with the Motor Union. The RAC terminated its subsidy, relinquished control and severed relations with its errant offspring. It endeavoured to preserve a façade of unity. The Club *Journal*, for example, was to remain a joint publication until

A DAY AT THE RACES

The RAC, closely involved with creating and running Brooklands, aimed to provide a motorised version of the sport of kings. If thoroughbred cars lacked the nobility of thoroughbred horses, they continued to draw fashionable crowds.

the end of 1908 and there would be, the Committee hoped, 'a rivalry of good works'. Moreover the RAC agreed not to form another popular subsidiary and not to 'attempt directly or indirectly to detach the present individual members of the Union'. This undertaking was breached. The Motor Union scrambled to recruit members of the RAC's affiliated clubs in the provinces. As the *Automotor Journal* said, it was willing to 'see all other automobile institutions discredited and weakened if only the power of the M.U. could be made supreme'. For its own part the RAC was anxious not to lose its representative character as the 'motor parliament'. At the end of 1907 it initiated a scheme whereby local clubs could become associates of the RAC, with representation on its Committee.

Then began what one motorist called 'a fight between the officials of the two organisations for the pickings'. This 'civil war' became so vicious that members of provincial clubs held a conference in a vain attempt to end it. The RAC, meanwhile, tried to maintain the fiction of friendliness. This enraged Earl Russell: 'It seemed like the friendliness of a man who told one that he was extremely friendly while with a knife in one's thigh he was sapping one's life blood.' Russell, who had a stake in the Motor Union's insurance scheme, was characteristically outspoken. But he had a point. With its prestige and wealth, the RAC attracted more members than the Motor Union, which could not define a clear role for itself. By 1910 it was so anaemic that its chairman, William Joynson-Hicks, believed that it could not sustain an independent existence. When Rees Jeffreys left to become secretary of the new Road Board, the Motor Union (after much manoeuvring) amalgamated with the AA. The secretary of the enlarged body was nicknamed 'Extension Cooke'.

So the pattern of leading British motoring organisations was set for the rest of the twentieth century. True, the AA was already becoming more respectable, expanding its functions and growing enormously in strength. Indeed, Earl Russell actually resigned from the AA because it became too cautious as it 'waxed fat and rich'. It refused his request to placard Surrey with posters contrasting the £15 fine exacted from speeding motorists with the forty-shilling penalty which, Russell claimed, was imposed on 'a man bashing his wife to a jelly with a poker'. Nevertheless, the AA remained the so-called 'Yellow Peril', a body as prone to aggression as its new President, the 'Yellow Earl'. He was Lord Lonsdale, the Croesus-rich bruiser who was said by one of his peers to be 'almost an Emperor and not quite a gentleman'. Lonsdale bestowed his 'personal' shade of yellow on the AA. Characteristically he once 'gave orders to his grooms to attack with whips in Carlton Mews' anyone else attempting to copy the distinctive colour from his vehicles. The AA represented the militant wing of motordom, asserting its rights against all comers. Harry Graham aptly satirised its partisanship in one of his *Ruthless Rhymes*:

Once, as old Lord Gorbals motored
Round his moors near John o' Groats,
He collided with a goatherd
And a herd of forty goats.
By the time his car got through
They were all defunct but two.

The motoring organisations often imitated each other's more successful endeavours and the AA Handbook, *first issued in 1908, was clearly based on that of the RAC. The Autocar complained that there were 'too many associations', duplicating one another's efforts. But competition was productive.*

FIRST AA SCOUTS

The AA initiated regular road patrols. Their purpose was to warn members of speed traps – or, as the AA Handbook *delicately put it, 'impending danger'. The photograph dates from 1906 and these bicyclists are about to scour the Portsmouth Road for 'trappist' police.*

Roughly he addressed the goatherd:
'Dash my whiskers and my corns!
Can't you teach your goats, you dotard,
That they ought to sound their horns?
Look, my A.A. badge is bent!
I've a mind to raise your rent.'

The *Glasgow Herald* was no more jaundiced than most newspapers when it described the AA as 'guide, philosopher and friend to ... inveterate roadhogs'.

The RAC, by contrast, was inhibited from indulging in excesses of automobile chauvinism by notions of dignity, propriety and restraint. Its more militant members endorsed the AA's campaign against the 'trappist' police, 'these hedge creepers and drain crawlers'. But the moderate majority valued still more the exalted position which the Club now occupied in the Establishment. It accepted what Wallace had long laid down as one of the guiding principles of the Club: 'We should at once lose the sympathy and trust which are given to us by the Government Departments if we were to adopt a position of a body of selfish men who only seek their own ends.' This attitude was generally understood. As a motoring journal observed, the Royal Automobile Club could not do anything that might 'be taken as opposition to the actions of recognised authority' or it would 'stultify itself with the "powers that be"'. However, just as the AA was adopting the more responsible language of the RAC, so the RAC would have to borrow more assertive tactics from the AA. The RAC would also have to come to terms with the fact that it no longer represented, as had been the case until 1905, 'practically every motorist'. Being overtaken, in membership terms, by its thrusting young rival was a bitter pill for the RAC to swallow. But what it lacked in popularity, it more than made up for in status and influence. Government and people still looked on the RAC as 'the head and front of British automobilism'. It was a pre-eminence soon to be symbolised on a palatial scale – in steel, stone, stucco, bronze and marble.

DRAMATIC APPEARANCE

The actress Zena Dare in her 1907
fifteen-horsepower Coventry Humber.
She later married the future Lord
Esher and – an increasing trend – cars
played a part in their courtship.

CHAPTER FIVE

A PALACE IN PALL MALL

*In 1910 the RAC built the 'Parliament House' of motoring,
which still dominates Pall Mall. To meet the needs of
Associate members who were not privileged to belong, the Club
formed its corps of road patrols – RAC Guides to
compete with AA Scouts.*

RAC APPOINTMENT

*Only hotels and
repairers officially
approved by the RAC
could display the Club's
metal plaque, with its
patriotic motif.*

AS EARLY AS 1906 the Club had outgrown its premises at 119 Piccadilly and members were considering a move. Already several departments had been transferred elsewhere, to the extent that staff were complaining about 'decentralisation run mad'. But still members felt 'cramped'. So, at about the same time as the royal title was bestowed on the Club, its Chairman began negotiations with the Crown to purchase a tract of land on the south side of Pall Mall. The locale of the original Cocoa Tree Tavern, it was now occupied by a warren of eighteenth-century buildings which had been recently vacated by the War Office. The site was just over an acre in size, offering the RAC accommodation ten times larger than that afforded in Piccadilly. It was in the heart of Clubland, a stone's throw from the Athenaeum, the Travellers' and the Reform. At least one clubman objected to the arrival of such noisy neighbours: 'I fancy I can see them now, furred, goggled, spare-tyred and cigar-smoking, with a crowd of messenger boys and loafers sitting on the mudguards of the cars … and the background full of "well-known motorists" and elegant-looking committeemen.' Anyway, much influence was required to secure the ninety-nine-year lease. Orde said that acceptance of their bid, in December 1907, was 'entirely' due to the intervention of King Edward VII himself. But the RAC's declared intention to spend £250,000 on building 'a home worthy of the largest Automobile Club in the world' was no doubt persuasive. The new clubhouse would become the greatest of what one contemporary called 'the joint-stock palaces of Pall Mall'.

The huge capital sum was to be raised by selling £100 debentures to members. The Club would pay five per cent interest and could reacquire them when it wished at a ten per cent premium. Thus, by investing its profits in its premises, the RAC would gradually buy back the clubhouse from its members. Not everyone liked the scheme. Earl Russell, in particular, was 'most pessimistic' about the figures. He estimated that the annual cost of occupying the new building would be £25,000 (of which £7,500 would be ground rent) and that to cover it the Club would have to increase its subscriptions and double its membership. Others were more sanguine. Edward Manville assured his fellows that even if Russell's worst prognostications were realised 'they might sleep very comfortably in their beds'. His view prevailed. Over 1,500 members became shareholders in the clubhouse. The RAC had no difficulty in raising additional sums to purchase furniture (£27,218), fittings (£15,518) and china and glass (£9,380). In the end the total cost of the new clubhouse amounted to about £330,000. The investment was worthwhile, argued Colonel Holden, for it would not only 'raise the status of automobilists in this country', but would 'put us in a position of superiority even to the French Automobile Club'. Theirs, said the new Chairman, Prince Francis of Teck (who succeeded C. D. Rose in May 1908), would be the 'most up-to-date and comfortable Club ... in the world'.

Prince Francis, despite being a Serene Highness and younger brother to the future Queen Mary, was hardly a figure to imbue his fellow members with confidence. Expelled from Wellington for tossing the headmaster over a hedge, he had rapidly become the black sheep of his family. As a young subaltern Teck engaged in what he called 'heavenly' sprees; dressed extravagantly at his tailor's expense; and lost £10,000 in a single bet at Punchestown races. He was thereupon exiled to India, which he regarded as hell on earth. Soon after resigning his commission he was to be seen whizzing around London in an electric brougham 'busily occupied in doing nothing'. Nevertheless, Teck proved a surprisingly competent Chairman. Tall and handsome, with coal-black hair and china-blue eyes, he was a dignified figure (though turning to fat, doubtless as a result of undue indulgence in his favourite dishes, Irish stew and jam-roll pudding). Although pernickety about precedence and ever mindful of his rank, he was a good mixer and possessed a lively, irreverent sense of humour. Moreover, by the end of the Edwardian era he seems to have reined in his rakish tendencies. He raised money for the Middlesex Hospital and devoted himself enthusiastically to the business of the RAC. He was said to be 'no figurehead, but a man of affairs'.

He may even have had a hand in appointing the architects of the new clubhouse, Charles Mewès and Arthur Joseph Davis, who found special favour in the eyes of royalty. It was with regal 'tastes in mind' that they had designed sumptuous buildings like London's Ritz hotel. Both star pupils of the official French academy, the École des Beaux Arts, they championed the formal symmetry of Louis XV, as opposed to the sinuous lines of modish Art Nouveau. Their Anglo-French partnership embodied the spirit of Edward VII's Entente Cordiale. As Jews, they were not unacceptable to his cosmopolitan court. They became the most fashionable architects of their day because they excelled at combining Roman magnificence with Edwardian convenience. Their plan for the RAC's clubhouse, scale models of which were exhibited for the benefit of members, incorporated in equal measure classical grandeur and modern technology.

Work began on the new 'Parliament House and home of motordom' in 1908. Mewès and Davis had to employ the most advanced methods. The sixty-foot hole they dug in the London clay (unearthing seventeenth-century cesspits, fossilised mammoth teeth and the hip-bone of some huge antediluvian creature) took the foundations well below the water-table and pumps

SIR CHARLES ROSE

Chairman of the RAC (1907–8) during the crisis with the Motor Union, the popular, sporting Rose tried to maintain goodwill all round. Here seen behind the wheel of a seventy-horsepower Mercédès, he died in 1913 immediately after taking his first flight in an aeroplane.

PRINCE FRANCIS OF TECK

Brother of the future Queen Mary, Teck was Chairman of the Club from 1908 until his death in 1910. He shocked his sister by giving the famous Cambridge emeralds to an elderly mistress. But, for all his indiscretions, the Prince brought both dignity and ability to the chairmanship.

had to suck out 200,000 gallons a day. Pall Mall itself had to be propped up from below as the excavations, which looked like the aftermath of a 'mysterious earthquake', extended well under the street. The footings were embedded in a massive concrete raft, like that supporting the London Ritz. This platform, over an acre in size and reinforced with 15,000 iron rods, was encased in a vast waterproof trough. On the base huge steam cranes erected a steel frame eight storeys high, weighing 2,000 tons, which was duly clad with Portland stone. Watching the work in progress, Colonel Holden exclaimed: 'If the walls of Jericho had been built like that they would be standing today.'

Every facility which science could offer was embodied in the structure: electric and hydraulic lifts; central heating and air-conditioning; a vacuum-cleaning system; 120 telephone lines linked to a central switchboard; refrigeration machinery capable of making five tons of ice a week; gas flares to illuminate the front of the building on ceremonial occasions; fireproofing; electric lighting. The last, installed in consultation with W. J. Crampton (the Club member who had 'electrified' Sandringham), did not meet with complete approval, even in a community dedicated to progress. When the clubhouse opened one old member was heard to mutter while flicking a light switch on and off: 'That fellow Crampton! No good will come of this!'

Although 'conceived in an absolutely modern spirit', the new clubhouse resembled a Renaissance palace. Mewès and Davis drew inspiration from the Place Vendôme in Paris and Ange-Jacques Gabriel's Hôtel de Crillon, overlooking the Place de la Concorde, the home of the Automobile Club de France. The 228-foot façade which now confronts Pall Mall is a model of classical strength and simplicity. Above the deeply recessed, semicircular-headed windows of the rusticated ground floor is an Ionic colonnade crowned by a balustraded parapet. The shallow-pitched roof is tiled in Westmorland slate. A portico projects over the entrance, which is protected by elegant wrought-iron gates. Its four columns support a pediment, whose tympanum contains a many-peopled sculpture, executed by Parisian craftsmen and representing 'Science as the Inspiration of the Allied Trades'. It includes a cherub riding a motor-bike. At each end is a pylon with cartouches denoting the four elements, Earth, Air, Fire and Water, over which, it was said, the Club claimed dominion. In terms of dignity, the rear elevation equals the front: Club members boasted that they occupied a 'house without a back'. Many thought that the spacious, south-facing terrace rivalled that of the House of Commons. Certainly it commanded one of the finest views in the city, stretching from Nelson's Column across Carlton Gardens, Whitehall, Westminster and St James's Park, to Buckingham Palace. One day soon, members expected, aeroplanes would use the terrace as a landing-strip.

The interior of the clubhouse was conceived on an equally grandiose scale. The axis of the building, up the stairs from an ample entrance hall, is a large, oval vestibule. It was carpeted in red and decorated in the style of Louis XVI, but was complete with thermometers, barometers, tape-machines, a clock and a dial wind gauge (of particular interest to aeronautical members) communicating to a weather-vane on the roof. Two storeys high, the vestibule is domed and encircled on the first floor by a Doric colonnade. Behind it, opening out through French windows onto a terrace, is the Great Gallery. This superb saloon, ornamented in the manner of Louis XIV, has a ceiling painted by Marcel Boulanger. Eighty feet long, forty wide and thirty-two high, it can hold five hundred people in comfort. The Great Gallery, which has a

OLD WAR OFFICE

The old War Office (right) consisted of some thirteen rambling converted buildings on 'the sweet shady side of Pall Mall'.

STEAM ENGINEERING

The latest construction techniques, including huge steam cranes, were employed to build the clubhouse. RAC members remarked that 'the spectacle is like watching a town being brought into being'.

THE NEW ROYAL AUTOMOBILE CLUB

The Edwardian press treated the construction of a Ritz of clubs, designed by the architects of that hotel to lend dignity to one of the most prominent sites in London, as 'an event of first-class importance'. Commentators were not disappointed as the result took shape.

balcony at one end and a stage at the other, was designed for balls, concerts and other entertainments. To the left of the vestibule was the restaurant, embellished with a fine painting of the
school of Hubert Robert, imported from a French château and cut up like wallpaper to fill the
available panels. To its right is the stately club-room with ceiling and frieze modelled on the
Palladian plasterwork removed from the Secretary of State's sanctum in the old War Office.

All told, the clubhouse contained 258 rooms, including a library, photographic studio,
its own post office, barber's shop, offices, bars and lounges. Not forgotten was a ladies' dress-
ing-room where, intoned the *Journal*, those 'touches so dear to the feminine heart, but so little
understood by mere men, can be indulged in'. There were waiting rooms, assembly rooms, committee rooms, smoking rooms, writing rooms, cloakrooms and over a hundred bedrooms. The
last were soon nicknamed 'the casual wards' but they rather resembled the sleeping accommodation of 'a modern hotel with the Bath Club thrown in as an annexe'. In fact, as at their
masterpiece the London Ritz, Mewès and Davis enhanced the impression of opulence by lavishing care on detail. The treads of the stairs become broader as they go down. Wallpapers were
shunned in favour of natural surfaces – mahogany, stone, marble and bronze. Leading firms
contributed to the majestic effect: the garter-blue carpet in one reception room was produced
by the company which made the coronation carpet for Westminster Abbey. Another room, pan-
elled in antique green and old ivory in the style of William and Mary, 'reminds one of an
immense piece of Wedgwood china'. When they first saw the clubhouse, admiring journalists
were lost for superlatives. The *Daily Graphic* declared: 'It is practically impossible to convey in
print an adequate idea of the magnificence, luxury and convenience of the building.'

What impressed visitors most was the extraordinary range of recreational and sporting
facilities. They were not surprised to find a card room, billiard-saloon, fencing room and gymnasium. But in addition there was a rifle range – King George V tried it out, proving to be a
good, but not a faultless, shot. Members got ten rounds for half a crown and, in an atmosphere
of 'gun oil and cordite', they could aim at a choice of four electrically operated targets, including 'celluloid balls floating on a current of air'. Soon a bowling alley was added. The squash
courts in the basement were also a novelty, though C. D. Rose's plan to include a real tennis
court was scotched. As a result, incidentally, the brilliant tennis professional 'Oke' Johnson
changed to squash, encouraging the game to such effect that at times the Club team was to be
synonymous with the national team. Equally spacious was the Turkish bath with its douches,
its vapour and plunge baths, its rooms set at different temperatures (*frigidarium, tepidarium,
calidarium, laconicum*). It also had twenty-five couches where members could spend the night.

The *pièce de résistance* was the swimming pool. As the *Architectural Review* wrote in 1911, the
most impressive *'coup d'oeil* in the whole building – as charming as it is unexpected – is the
sudden glimpse of the mosaic columns, marble walls, and shimmering green water of the
swimming bath as seen across the lower vestibule'. The slender Doric columns were inlaid
with coloured mosaic patterns. White Sicilian marble covered the floor and bronze balconies
overlooked the pool, which was eighty-six feet long, thirty wide and eight deep. Entering the
glittering aqueous cavern, said one member, was like stepping into a picture by Alma Tadema.
Here was the 'most beautiful swimming bath in England, in the Pompeiian style'. It was the
crowning glory of a clubhouse which eclipsed old fashions and set new standards. In the words

ELEGANT INTERIORS

The splendour of the rotunda (right) and the Great Gallery (below) did much to confirm the contemporary view that the Club resembled a Renaissance palace 'fitted up with modern services'.

of *The Autocar*: 'Just as the *Dreadnought* scrapped all predecessors and made revision of every naval calculation imperative, so has this new Pall Mall palace upset all preconceived notions in the matter of clubhouse premises and comforts.'

Nevertheless, not all members were happy about the clubhouse. Thomas Sopwith actually resigned from the RAC when it moved to Pall Mall because he thought the new building looked like a 'bloody great railway station'. Other members complained about the lack of stabling for their motors, a necessity at a time when open cars abounded. (Actually, a large new motor house was available at York Street in Westminster.) Despite the initial provision of white direction posts, members got lost in the labyrinthine interior. At the opening banquet they were further bewildered by a profusion of fine wines unaccompanied by swift food service, the kitchens still not being finished – one guest became so intoxicated that he jumped into the swimming pool oblivious of the fact that it had yet to be filled with water. Since many who had shunned Piccadilly used the new clubhouse, the porters had to keep asking them to give their names. One elderly gentleman glared at his inquisitor and barked: 'Certainly not! Not in my own Club!' Others objected to the noise made by the squash players, the failures of the ventilation system, the fact that south-facing rooms were the least used, and the preponderance of foreign waiters. In short, many 'incidental minor grumbles mixed with the more general praise'.

Outside the Club, the grumbles were louder. The Lord Mayor of Liverpool suggested that a belligerent RAC had occupied the site of the old War Office with the intention of defying its 'enemies'. H. G. Wells blamed 'the new Automobile Club' for the current labour unrest because it was a blatant monument to luxury only made possible by the exploitation of workers. Others levelled 'charges of aggrandisement' at the RAC. But they cut little ice in an age when wealth was unashamedly displayed as the visible index of success. The 'palace of motordom' bore witness to the progress of automobilism, an advance so remorseless that no opposition could check it. The building was also regarded as a sign of the 'extension of power' of the Club and an earnest of 'even greater activity and wider influence' to come. This was certainly the view of the RAC itself, which argued that its officials as well as its members needed the extra space. The Pall Mall premises might supply ample accommodation, as the *Daily Telegraph* said, for 'that most crotchety epicurean – the London clubman'. But it was also the headquarters of an expanding business.

THE SCOPE OF THE RAC'S OPERATIONS was remarkable. The Touring Department, which also served visiting members of the American Automobile Association (as well as members of the British royal family), was busier than ever. In 1903 it had issued 89 foreign customs papers: by 1908 the figure was 1,397. The department employed 'a small army of clerks' and had a turnover of £50,000. Preparing members to cross the Channel involved them in mountains of complex paperwork. But the RAC examination for an international driving licence was singularly easy. David Lloyd George's son Gwilym later recalled: 'I was taken for a little ride through a pleasant square. I did not meet anything, and I did not cross the road, and I was passed as fit to drive my car. It is true that I should probably kill foreigners not Britishers, but that was the test.' It was, at least, more onerous than the test imposed by the French Ministry of Mines on

BATHING BEAUTY

*The swimming pool at the clubhouse is
pictured here soon after it was completed.
Combining Greek sophistication with Roman
splendour, it is a classic of its kind.*

British drivers who crossed the Channel. This was variously said to consist of buying petrol from the examining official's brother and being able to tell the difference between an exhaust pipe and a back axle.

The Touring Department was also occupied with domestic matters since 'some members and Associates never even go [on] a week-end trip without asking for advice'. Staff accumulated and disseminated encyclopaedic amounts of information about roads, routes, places to visit and avoid, garages, hotels and so on. To keep itself up to date the Touring Department encouraged members to submit confidential reports of their experiences. None did so more assiduously than Bernard Shaw, who has been credited with inspiring publication of the Club's *Continental Handbook*. The *Journal* could not resist printing (anonymously) his waspish account of an Irish hotel whose proprietor 'considers that three days' clear notice is not sufficient … to procure a dish of macaroni or curried eggs' and where the playwright himself was expected to write 'in the public drawing-room at such moments as the other guests happen to be in the Smoke-room or in the grounds'.

Other members were equally free with their criticism, sometimes mixing it with chauvinism. Describing a tour of Germany, conducted with 'bewitching rapidity' in their open Renault 'Maria', Mrs D. R. Cameron, a member's wife, explained that rude waiters were no match for 'the bull-dog Englishman who shows his teeth and growls at the least tampering with his dignity'. Such reports often bore fruit, for the RAC's approval was valued. The proprietor of a hotel in the south of France travelled all the way to London in an attempt to convince the Club that he was not running (as members had reported) 'a den of thieves'. Establishments which had formerly spurned motorists were now only too keen to receive the RAC's official appointment – this was restricted to 'swagger' hotels, though less expensive ones were included in the *Handbook* provided that they were clean and comfortable. As that indefatigable traveller Edith Wharton observed, 'the demands of the motorist are introducing modern plumbing and Maple furniture into the uttermost parts of France'.

The RAC also made strenuous efforts to point motorists in the right direction. Signposts were few, local and, until 1930, anything but uniform. They tended just to indicate the neighbouring village or town. Motorists constantly had to stop to ask the way. Those in search of distant destinations faced all sorts of problems. The proprietor of the Cock Inn at Wellington, in Shropshire, put up signs to Holyhead and London. He placed the signposts 'so that motorists might catch sight of the London sign first, and thus assure themselves that they were *en route* to that city'. It was immaterial to him that the sign to London pointed in the wrong direction, as did the sign to Holyhead. With some difficulty an RAC member persuaded him, in 1909, to change them. Signs came in all colours, shapes and sizes. A warning might be indicated by anything from a red triangle to a skull and crossbones. There was even a move to introduce French signs, but Britons ridiculed them: the twirly symbol indicating a 'Descent with Sharp Turns', for instance, was said to resemble 'something between a freak radish and a flash of lightning'. Signs failed to catch the motorist's eye because they were posted at random.

From the first the RAC had pleaded for comprehensiveness and standardisation. The Club set local authorities an example by signposting the London–Folkestone road (in 1905) and the Great North Road (between 1909 and 1911). But this very endeavour added to the chaotic

LICENCE TO DRIVE

From 1903 to 1934 the driving licence was, in effect, a licence to drive badly. This was because motorists could obtain it without passing an official driving test. Furthermore, the RAC's 'Driving Certificate' was initially awarded to any member who could show that he was 'a careful liver'. Still, dangerous drivers could lose their licences; and the RAC's training and examining did become more demanding.

variety of wayside notice-boards. Nor were the Club's efforts entirely disinterested. Its 'Please Drive Slowly' signs were often strategically placed to discourage the imposition of speed limits. Moreover, like Daimler and other motor manufacturers, both the RAC and the AA erected signposts for publicity purposes. As *Motor News* noted in 1910, the motoring organisations had found in direction posts a cheap and effective method of 'advertising', as evidenced by the prominent display of their own names 'to the exclusion of more useful information'. Those who took note of the signs of the time found the growing rivalry between the two bodies writ large in RAC blue and AA yellow.

There was, to be sure, some co-operation between them vis-à-vis the authorities. In 1908 Montagu even led a joint delegation to meet the police. It resulted in the AA's adoption of the more conciliatory language of the RAC – Stenson Cooke praised motorists who drove 'like gentlemen'. This pulling together was sensible at a moment when the climate of opinion had become even more hostile to the growing motoring fraternity. By 1909 there were 45,000 cars on the roads. In that year C. F. G. Masterman published his book on *The Condition of England*, which memorably inveighed against them. Travelling at incredible velocity these machines 'scramble and smash and shriek' along rural ways, park 'twenty or thirty deep outside the new popular inns' and deluge the countryside in dust. The public, concluded one Club member, thought that 'motorists were a bloodthirsty set of Bashi-Bazouks'. Still concentrating on speed traps, the AA would not collaborate with the RAC on broader issues. In particular, Cooke was as yet reluctant to become embroiled in 'motor politics'. So the RAC was left alone to patrol the corridors of power. According to Lord Montagu, it held the 'premier position which arises from being the first corporate body of motorists, and having the confidence of governments, and being the official body for foreign relations'.

Yet the RAC could not prevent motor taxation, despite efforts by which it set much store. The *Journal* even attributed the favourable budget in 1908 to the Club's 'quiet working', though the Motor Union also claimed the credit. But the RAC's tactics proved ineffective the following year. In his 'People's Budget' speech the new Chancellor of the Exchequer, David Lloyd George, declared that motorists were 'willing and even anxious [laughter] – to subscribe handsomely' towards the upkeep of roads which they tore up and converted into dust storms. Needless to say, motorists were indignant. Some attacked the Club for the futility of its endeavours. Others accused it of having betrayed them. But taxation was inevitable. In the words of a leading Club member, Henry Norman MP, 'they were not asked whether they would like to be cooked, but with what sauce they would prefer to be served up'. Furthermore, the RAC won two significant concessions. First, Lloyd George agreed to devote the revenue raised from motorists, including the tax of threepence a gallon on petrol, 'exclusively to the improvement of the roads'. Secondly, cars were to be taxed according to the horsepower formula worked out by the RAC – Holden himself had made the calculation, which was based on the internal diameter of a car's cylinders. Thus owners whose cars were under 6½ horsepower paid two guineas; three guineas were charged for those under twelve horsepower; and the scale rose to forty guineas for cars of sixty horsepower or more. The tax, which put a penalty on speed and rose in accordance with the cost of the car, was generally seen as fair. Official approval of their formula for measuring engine power, crowed Orde, was 'a feather in the cap of the Club'.

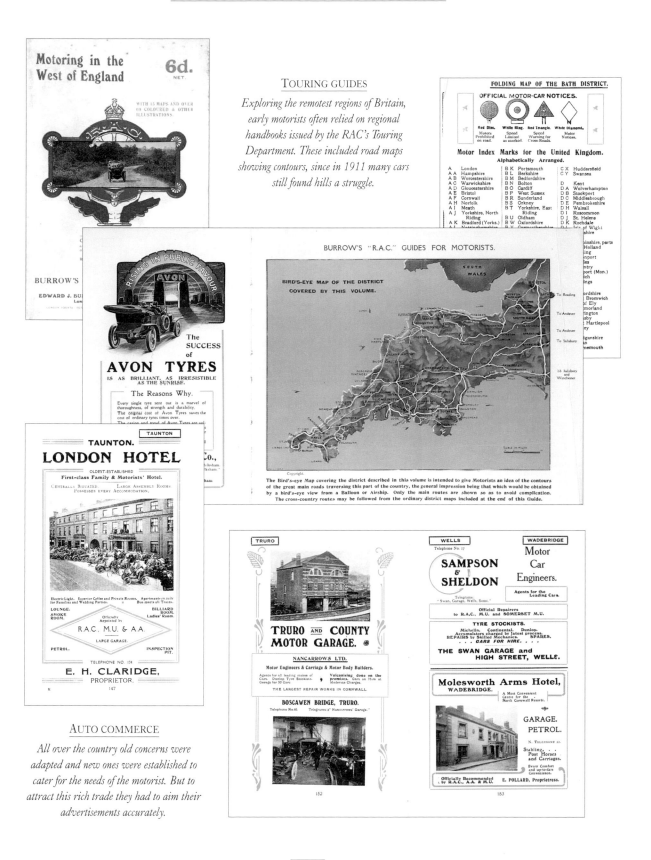

Touring guides

Exploring the remotest regions of Britain, early motorists often relied on regional handbooks issued by the RAC's Touring Department. These included road maps showing contours, since in 1911 many cars still found hills a struggle.

Auto commerce

All over the country old concerns were adapted and new ones were established to cater for the needs of the motorist. But to attract this rich trade they had to aim their advertisements accurately.

It was a somewhat bedraggled feather, however. The RAC's Technical Committee, which approved the horsepower formula, may have contained, as Orde claimed, 'the best brains in England'. But the effect of their decision was to encourage the production of long-stroke, small-bore engines. Although quiet and durable, they imposed a design that was 'tall, ungainly and expensive' when it should have been squat, light and cheap. Domestic car makers increasingly began to turn out small, low-powered models. Indeed, as the *Journal* reported at the end of 1909, this was the 'keynote of the year's mechanical development'. It remained the keynote for decades. British manufacturers, protected by a tax that was in effect a tariff on powerful, mass-produced foreign cars, could thus hold their own with the likes of Ford. This bred complacency. J. S. Critchley declared that 'the British car is ahead of any car in the world'. But British exports stagnated. Cushioned by an expanding home market, manufacturers had little incentive to pioneer new methods of engineering or construction. In 1913 Ford employed 13,000 Detroit workers to make 267,720 cars, while 800 men assembled 6,000 'Tin Lizzies' from imported parts in Manchester. In the same year the most productive and efficient British firm, Wolseley, employed 4,000 workers to make 3,000 cars. The fiscal application of the RAC's horsepower formula 'largely influenced' the design of British cars. It also signally contributed to what one authority has called the 'general backwardness' of the British motor industry.

Yet the RAC was responsible for countless improvements in British vehicles. Critchley was right to say that the Tourist Trophy competition on the Isle of Man helped to better the quality of ordinary models. Even in the 1908 'Four-inch Race', so labelled after the new limit on cylinder diameter, the cars were far less powerful than the 18-litre 'flying bedsteads' built to compete in the new French Grand Prix. The RAC shunned the Grand Prix, preferring to fight on home ground. It also wanted to encourage the manufacture of a cheap, light car through the TT. The Club even provided pits for the first time, a row of pens in front of bell tents where the drivers' families were served beef tea, jellies, chicken and oysters. At the Club members followed the race in the smoking room by means of a huge white screen on which the thirty-eight competitors' names were written in charcoal. Their progress over the nine-lap, thirty-seven-and-a-half-mile circuit was plotted with yards of red tape. Sheafs of telegrams conveyed the news: Stocks's clutch was malfunctioning; Lewis had broken his crankshaft; Moore-Brabazon was *hors de combat* with ignition trouble; George's carburettor had caught fire; 'Jack Hutton had had an argument with a wall, but nothing was damaged except the car'; and W. Watson had won in a Hutton at an average speed of 50mph.

The RAC had taken meticulous safety precautions and none of the accidents was serious. This evidently proved to be a disappointment to pressmen, who, according to *The Motor*, 'had been instructed by their journals to smother the course with blood and strew the hedges with smashed-up cars and mangled corpses'. Nevertheless, the Four-inch Race inflamed public opinion against motorists and the RAC was accused of 'pandering to savage instincts'. This gave traders like Edge the excuse to withdraw from future competitions on the grounds that they were too dangerous. In fact, at a time of economic recession it was the cost of racing, especially to the losers, which deterred those in the trade. Yet the development of light cars, as urged by the RAC, could well have broadened the appeal of motoring, spread the habit

Speeding the Parting Guest.

YOU PAY A TAX

ON YOUR CAR ACCORDING TO ITS HORSE
-POWER. BUT TO BE CERTAIN THAT YOU
ARE REALLY GETTING THE HORSE-POWER
YOU PAY FOR

USE PRATT'S

PERFECTION SPIRIT

PRATT'S MEANS MORE
MILES FOR LESS MONEY AND
GREATER POWER ON HILLS.

PETROL WITHOUT PUMPS

Lacking roadside filling stations, Edwardian motorists bought petrol from hotels, shops (including Harrod's) and other agencies. It came in two-gallon cans, coloured to indicate the brand – red for Shell and so on. The most favoured fuel was Pratt's Motor Spirit (later Esso), which was sold in green cans.

and 'hence stimulated a more rapid expansion of the industry's output.' However, no TT race was held again until 1914 and in the meantime the RAC concentrated on other tasks.

It continued to supervise trials of every kind, assessing the merits of non-skid tyres and non-dazzle headlights, front-wheel brakes and rear reflectors, patent speedometers and fuel-saving carburettors. In 1907 it conducted the most extensive tests ever held on commercial vehicles. The Club's scrutineers were described as 'sternly upright – but seemingly inhuman … trusting no one'. On their advice the Technical Committee often rejected manufacturers' claims – over dustless cars, for example – or made other damaging judgements. Sometimes this caused controversy. Occasionally the RAC's good faith was challenged. For example, the proprietor of the Victor Tyre Company alleged that his commercial rivals within the Club had denied him fair treatment. Actually, those in the trade were not permitted to sit on the Technical Committee. But there is no doubt that, as *The Autocar* said, the RAC brought certain makes of car into 'a far more prominent position' than they would otherwise have occupied. This was because manufacturers found means to exploit the Club, notably by inviting it to supervise tests of their own devising and by publicising the results which were favourable.

Thus in 1907 Claude Johnson arranged for a Rolls-Royce Silver Ghost to be observed running continuously for 15,000 miles. When it was dismantled and examined the repair bill amounted, famously, to the sum of £2 2s 7d. Soon afterwards the Rolls-Royce was advertised as 'The Best Car in the World'. Journalists were persuaded that it had 'reached the limits of perfection, and man's ingenuity can take this branch of mechanical art no further'. In 1908 (a year which also saw the 2000 Mile Trial) the RAC conducted a more significant experiment. It monitored the stripping down of three identical Cadillacs, each into its 721 separate components. All these were jumbled together and the cars were reassembled. When they were successfully driven round the track at Brooklands, this became proof positive that mass-produced parts were interchangeable. Cadillac won the RAC's coveted Dewar Trophy (presented by Sir Thomas Dewar in 1904 and awarded annually for the most outstanding technical achievement in automobiles) and adopted the slogan 'Standard of the World'. In 1909 Charles Knight's sleeve-valve Daimler engine was tested over a 2,000-mile run at Brooklands. Built, as its inventor told the RAC, to eliminate 'the annoying clatter of the poppet valves', the so-called 'Silent Knight' was the subject of much dispute. But the RAC's trial quieted its critics. Such was the rage for silence that motorists were mockingly accused of demanding noiseless horns.

In its technical appraisals the RAC remained surprisingly fallible. The 'Silent Knight' gulped oil and was unclean. The Rolls-Royce, produced by what one worker called 'the finest collection of second-hand rattleguts machinery in Manchester', was a model of engineering conservatism. It still had open tappets, valve-guides and springs, to say nothing of sixty-three grease cups that needed weekly filling. The magnificent Silver Ghost did perform with spectral smoothness, but only because it was, as a contemporary cruelly remarked, 'a triumph of workmanship over design'. Sometimes, too, the Club ignored new insights, such as the observation of one member that even at the distance of a hundred yards, the eyes of a cat had 'strong reflective power'. Not until 1934 did Percy Shaw, whose life was saved by the feline glint, invent 'cat's-eyes'. These clear glass marbles, encased in rubber and steel housings set into the roadway, not only made his fortune but rendered a signal service to motoring humanity. Yet at a time

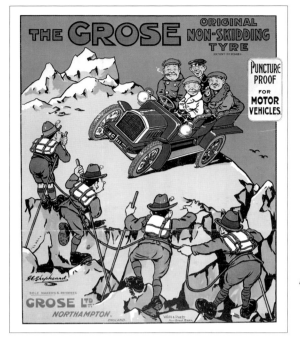

WHEELS OF FORTUNE

Tyres, said the RAC Journal, were the one blot on the Edwardian car owner's 'otherwise clean sheet of happiness'. Manufacturers tried hard to improve them and the Club tested their sometimes eccentric products rigorously. Its endorsement was of great commercial value.

MICHELIN MANIFESTO

Noting the punctures suffered by Michelin's pneumatic tyres in the Paris–Bordeaux–Paris Race of 1895, Levassor had said that tyres might be filled with hay or straw but could never succeed with air. Less than ten years later solid tyres were obsolete and by 1911 a set of Michelins might last a careful driver 10,000 miles.

when newly metalled surfaces seemed to soak up the beams of headlamps, merging roads into verges and hedges, the best the RAC could do was to 'undertake a vigorous campaign in which white paint will war with black tar'.

Nevertheless, acting as a 'society for encouragement' and lavishing so much money on trials that some members complained of paying a hidden subsidy to the trade, the RAC unquestionably promoted motoring progress. Its trials, said one early motorist, were 'of enormous value'. By the end of Edward VII's reign they had contributed to breathtaking automotive advances. The live axle had largely superseded the chain drive. Force-fed lubrication had displaced the gravity-feed method. The magneto had overtaken the coil and accumulator. Radiators, often fan-assisted, had solved cooling problems. Triplex laminated glass was invented, and soon non-splinterable windscreens were on the market. Dynamo-charged electric headlights were set to take over from oil lamps and acetylene burners. The self-starter was about to make the crank handle obsolescent. The RAC drew attention to the rapidity of automobile evolution by advertising an exhibition of historic cars which Salomons, Holden, Montagu and Claude Johnson organised at White City in 1909. Club members marvelled at the 'absolutely absurd appearance' of these tiny, 'shabby old ... crocks'. They presented an astounding contrast to the new models at the Olympia Motor Show. These were paragons of 'absolute luxury' with such 'amplitude of accommodation' that they seemed designed for giants or Martians.

On a more mundane level, the RAC's Engineering Department attended to the immediate motoring needs of its members. In particular it advised on buying new, and repairing old, cars. For example, a member might ask about the best vehicle to take two people and their luggage round India, or to carry six passengers to and from a shooting box across forty miles of rough track. The Club's engineers would also vet and test second-hand cars, whose most common fault at that time was the ill-alignment of the front wheels. They would give counsel about whether members should mend or scrap cars overtaken by accident or old age. They would pronounce on the merits of patent equipment such as 'Instanto' tyre levers, 'Shrapnel' splash-guards or even 'Dunhill's Bobby Finders', magnifying spectacles which enabled the wearer to spot a police constable at half a mile even if he were 'disguised as a respectable man'.

Similarly, since 1907 the Legal Department had been giving free advice to members. It helped them with civil claims, assisted them in criminal cases, and sometimes contributed financially where a prosecution was deemed contentious. It also resisted dozens of applications by urban and district councils to impose local speed limits of 10mph. Where these were enforced the drivers of horse-drawn barouches delighted to canter past steaming motor cars. It was an experience which red-blooded RAC members like Earl Russell found particularly hard to bear, and so more work was created for the Legal Department.

Because it was impossible to co-ordinate the work of 2,000 highway authorities, the RAC favoured what Orde called the 'nationalisation of roads'. It was even willing to learn from foreigners, deputing Montagu and Rolls to attend the first International Road Congress in Paris in 1908. Montagu's ideas were remarkably advanced, though he had long been conscious of what centralised transport planning implied: 'Straight roads and symmetrical cities betray despotic power, caring little or nothing for the rights of property.' Like other motoring organisations at the time, the RAC itself opposed the creation of motorways – 'special speedways' –

DUST DEVILS

Edwardian roads were a compound of stones, dirt and manure. In dry weather cars turned them to dust which blanketed the landscape, filling people's 'mouths with grit and their hearts with bitterness'. Here the Automobile Club records the effect of a Relyante (right – the Panhard on the left is measuring speed) on flour laid at the Crystal Palace track. Dust tests were of limited use: roads had to be adapted to cars and not vice versa. But in general the 1903 Reliability Trial, of which this test was a part, taught helpful lessons both to the Club and to manufacturers.

for fear that cars would be banished from ordinary roads. But it did support the establishment, in 1910, of the Roads Board. This was the first central organisation to administer the nation's highways since Roman times. Rees Jeffreys, who became its secretary, liked to quote John Ruskin's maxim that 'all social progress resolves itself into the making of new roads'. Ruskin's own efforts in this direction, had been notoriously flawed. So were Jeffreys' achievements, largely because he was answerable to the Treasury.

LOOKING FOR
TROUBLE

*Motoring brought the
police into regular conflict
with their social superiors
for the first time.
Constables regarded these
'Bobby Finders' as masks,
while drivers maintained
that the binoculars
revealed systematic
'police persecution'.*

The RAC did its best to support him, lobbying with facts and figures. As it pointed out, in 1910 the nation's expenditure on roads was £4 million whereas motorists' bills for tyres alone amounted to £10 million. The *Journal* further claimed that London's road system was 'practically identical' to what it had been a century before, though this was to ignore great Victorian building achievements such as the Thames embankments. Still, the capital's population was seven times larger than it had been at the start of the Regency period and the 'travelling habit' had grown enormously. Each person had undertaken 22.7 journeys in 1867; the figure had increased to 128.7 by 1901; and to 218.5 by 1910. Congestion was such that as early as 1909 the city's Planning and Housing Committee considered purchasing a strip of land a quarter of a mile wide for £7.2 million and building a ring road. This would have been a boon since by 1911 almost half London's traffic was motorised. In certain West End streets, noted the *Journal*, 'the appearance of a horse-drawn conveyance is little short of a novelty'. Horse-buses now attracted the urchin cry of 'Hearse!' Ostlers grieved and Sir Arthur Conan Doyle, a keen member of the Club, expressed the groom's lament in verse:

> I seed it in the stable yard – it fairly turned me sick –
> A greasy, wheezy engine as can neither buck nor kick.
> You've a screw to drive it forrard, and a screw to make it stop,
> For it was foaled in a smithy stove and bred in a blacksmith shop.

However, the success of automobilism, to which the labours of the Club had contributed so much, did not result in a massive addition to the associate membership of the RAC.

Nevertheless, since the break with the Motor Union, the associate section of the Club had grown stronger. The RAC had 'constituted all its associated clubs as its county and district branches'. It had thereby linked up 'the whole country with a complete organisation of responsible and representative' confederates. In the motoring metaphor of Captain A. S. V. Hume, its assistant secretary, the RAC was the chassis while the provincial clubs were the body. But the adherence of the Associates did not, as Massac Buist claimed, represent 'the unification of the motoring interests which the Royal Automobile Club has striven to attain'. On the contrary, by 1910 only one driver in three belonged to a motoring organisation. Moreover, in that year the AA finally amalgamated with the Motor Union to form a coalition 40,000 strong. Even counting everyone in its 125 provincial clubs, the RAC could not muster more than 25,000.

More awkward still, there was a palpable division between Associates and full Club members. It was given monumental emphasis in March 1911, when the new clubhouse opened its

doors. The Pall Mall palace, billed as the smart 'younger man's rendezvous', admitted Associates only to the reading and writing rooms. Naturally they grumbled about 'not having the run of the whole clubhouse'. Associates also had separate access to the Touring Department when it moved to 83 Pall Mall, which they 'looked on as only being received by the back door'. They reckoned that the Club gave 'too much attention to the purely social side of its duties, such as the housing, feeding and bathing of members, and not enough to the things that matter, such as taxation, grievances of private owners and legislation'. Many Associates belonged to the Auto-Cycle Union and held the traditional view that the 'Club looked down upon the motor cycle from such an altitude that they hardly saw it'. Since the RAC tried hard but unsuccessfully to dispel this view, it probably had some foundation. Certainly King George V, who became the Club's patron on his father's death in 1910, thought that 'only bounders rode motor bicycles'.

Eager to placate the Associate members, and to add to their numbers, Orde insisted that the RAC's Pall Mall edifice had been built 'not in any ostentatious spirit' but as a 'monument to automobilism'. Far from being purely a social and sporting body, the Club aimed to 'better the conditions of motorism and to spread the movement'. To that end Associates had been represented on its General Committee since 1907. In 1911 the RAC published a pamphlet designed to inspire old adherents and attract new ones. Entitled 'Freedom of the Road', it puffed the Club's role as champion of the ordinary motorist since pioneering days and issued an appeal couched in terms which now sound laughably dated:

> Every good Briton, and especially every good motorist, is a sportsman. 'Playing the game' is a British phrase; and is a characteristically British quality. The sportsman is loyal. In matters Imperial, he is loyal to the Empire; in Affairs, loyal to his profession; in sport, loyal to 'the game' and to the Institutions which govern it. On these grounds, many thousands of Motorists are Associate-Members of the Royal Automobile Club.

Even at that time such exhortations would probably have rung rather hollow and the RAC realised that its Associate members needed something more solid.

The situation perturbed clever Club members such as J. R. Nisbet, who were already worried about 'the growing popularity of the Automobile Association'. In November 1911 Nisbet told his fellows that, when trying to decide which motoring organisation deserved their allegiance, RAC Associates as well as unattached car owners 'would probably consider that the A.A. was doing more as it looked after the motorist on the road. In his opinion 'the man on the road in uniform was the crux of the whole position'. This was a shrewd judgement, as valid today as it was then. Nisbet went on to make a revolutionary proposal: the RAC should develop its own force of road patrols, as the Motor Union had done. They could do as much as, or even more than, the AA Scouts. But they would not be permitted to warn motorists about police traps. As it happened, the RAC already had an embryonic body which could evolve in the way that Nisbet suggested.

In 1910 the Club had recruited a handful of so-called 'Road Guides'. Their purpose was 'to accompany motorists on their cars in order that they might see interesting districts with which they are not acquainted to best advantage'. The automobile press was somewhat scornful of this innovation, which implied that motorists were sheep who had to be herded around

PICCADILLY CIRCUS, 1910

*Motor cars arrived quickly but, as this
photograph shows, people were slow to
adapt to them. Although the traffic here is
chaotic, workmen still dig up the road
without protection.*

by a personal conductor in the manner of Cook's tourists. But the RAC maintained that its Guides did a useful job. They were 'men of education' who would introduce drivers to little-known sites of interest, as opposed to the usual 'round' of churches, cathedrals and castles. They had to know about cars because conversation with motorists 'invariably reverts to the sport'. But, having leisure and independent means, they would act 'more as friends than retainers'. The first Road Guide, Charles H. Ashdown, who lived in St Albans, was an author, archaeologist and Fellow of the Royal Geographical Society. His services were recommended for the unusual reason that he had helped Oliver Wendell Holmes find a piece of human bone in a pile of earth removed from a monastic burial place. The great American jurist had exclaimed, 'Every rubbish-heap in this wonderful country teems with interest.'

From the acorn of these Guides grew a mighty oak – the RAC corps of service patrols who today glory in the title 'New Knights of the Road'. For in February 1912 the Club implemented Nisbet's plan and announced an 'extension' of the Guides scheme. The RAC would station uniformed men at home ports, selected hotels and danger spots. They would also patrol roads where inconsiderate or reckless driving had occurred. By Easter the scheme was 'well launched'. The Guides, most of them old soldiers or ex-policemen, wore caps with the RAC letters above the peak, dark-grey breeches and tunics with blue facings. They rode blue bicycles, equipped with lamps and bells and costing (together with their mackintoshes) £4 12s. 8d. Each Guide carried maps of the vicinity, a first-aid kit, telegraph forms, postcards and stamps. Each, too, was supposed to be furnished with copious local knowledge about road surfaces, alternative routes, hotels, repairers and the 'position and precise location of speed limits'. In theory the Road Guides, who numbered only a few dozen at first, were charged with assisting the police to prevent dangerous driving. There was, indeed, some co-operation. For example, the Chief Constable of Surrey, M. L. Sant, who was notoriously strict in his dealings with motorists, deputised the RAC's Guides to regulate traffic passing through Godalming, where there was a local limit of 10mph. However, it seems likely that in practice RAC Guides imitated their AA counterparts and warned badge-bearing members of the presence of speed traps. The *Journal* wrote triumphantly about the 'noticeable decrease in the number of "captures"' in Godalming.

Fearing the effects of such a direct challenge, Stenson Cooke reacted angrily. In letters to the motoring press he declared that the RAC's 'deliberate piracy of ideas' amounted to an act of 'aggression'. Most who wrote on automobile matters took his side, saying that the RAC's extravagant 'plagiarism' was neither 'dignified' nor 'sportsmanlike'. But some opposed Cooke. They argued that the AA, which had itself copied much from the RAC (notably its successful Touring Department), 'holds no letters patent' on the road service. Since the AA had only 250 Scouts to monitor 230,000 miles of British highway, there could be little duplication of effort. In any case, competition would improve the AA's performance: motorists suspected that its Scouts 'deliberately "manufacture" traps in order to justify their existence'. A few commentators pronounced a plague on both motoring organisations. *The Autocar*'s effervescent columnist O. J. Llewellyn, who wrote under the pen-name 'Owen John', described their struggle as being of 'the most paltry, stupid, evanescent, feminine, and two-penny-halfpenny importance'.

It was important to Orde, whose salary had risen to £2,500 a year. He had to defend a weak position against a tenacious opponent. Hysterical though Stenson Cooke may have been, he was

BRADFORD
AUTOMOBILE CLUB

COVENTRY &
WARWICKSHIRE
MOTOR CLUB

DERBYSHIRE &
NORTH STAFFORD
AUTOMOBILE CLUB

ESSEX COUNTY
AUTOMOBILE CLUB

HERTS. COUNTY
AUTOMOBILE &
AERO CLUB

HULL & DISTRICT
AUTOMOBILE CLUB

AUTO-CYCLE UNION

KENSINGTON
AUTOMOBILE CLUB

YORKSHIRE
AUTOMOBILE CLUB

LANCASHIRE
AUTOMOBILE CLUB

WOLVERHAMPTON &
DISTRICT
AUTOMOBILE CLUB

MANCHESTER
AUTOMOBILE CLUB

SUSSEX MOTOR
YACHT CLUB
(AUTOMOBILE
SECTION)

MANCHESTER
MOTOR CLUB

HERALDRY OF MOTORDOM

After the Club broke with the Motor Union in 1907 most provincial automobile clubs associated themselves with the RAC, showing their loyalty with a composite badge. Local centrepieces, such as those which form the frieze of this page, were surrounded by the national emblems and surmounted by the crown. But the design of badges often changed, as the three complete national ones (dating from the early 1920s) indicate.

SOUTH WALES
AUTOMOBILE CLUB

MIDDLESEX COUNTY
AUTOMOBILE CLUB

SOMERSET
AUTOMOBILE CLUB

NOTTINGHAMSHIRE
AUTOMOBILE CLUB

NORTHAMPTONSHIRE
AUTOMOBILE CLUB

NORTH-EASTERN
AUTOMOBILE ASSOCIATION

MONMOUTHSHIRE
AUTOMOBILE CLUB

MIDLAND
AUTOMOBILE CLUB

plainly right to say that the RAC's new Road Guides had more in common with his own cohorts than with the band of genteel antiquaries headed by Charles H. Ashdown. Orde could only maintain that the RAC was entitled to do what it liked for its members. But he did emphasise that its patrolmen, unlike those of the AA, would not only serve every motorist but would salute every car. This all-embracing pledge proved an embarrassment. The RAC needed to take another initiative which would give specific benefits to its own constituency. So, on 1 September 1912, Orde inaugurated the momentous 'Get-you-Home' scheme. Its 'talisman' was an oval metal token, soon superseded by a voucher, which guaranteed that the RAC would meet the cost of any assistance given to the holder. Club members and Associates could apply for the 'magic disc', attach it to their key-rings and hand it to a rescuer and repairer, who would return it to the RAC for payment. The 'Get-you-Home' scheme was a masterstroke. It provided a unique and valuable service to the motorist. And since Cooke declined to imitate it on grounds of expense, it gave the RAC a significant advantage over the AA until after the Second World War.

So the Club provided its Associate members with something 'tangible' in return for their guinea subscription. The RAC acquired its best recruiting agents, mobile advertisements in uniform. By their exertions on the road the Guides attracted new members and, working on commission, they swiftly mastered the art of enrolling them. Their very success disquieted the RAC's provincial clubs; middlemen who found themselves cut out as new members were put directly in touch with Pall Mall. The trunk was destined to grow at the expense of the branches. Leading figures in the RAC were unapologetic about its self-assertion. As one said, only by introducing the Road Guides in their present form could the Club's Committee 'remain the power in the land that it ought to be'. The new policy also made it easier to refute critics like the 'automobilious' (his word) Owen John. He argued that the RAC should restrict itself to motor sport, technical matters and social recreation. The AA, lacking palatial premises, should reign over the high roads. The division of labour made sense, John suggested, because the RAC's original mission to help the motorist had been 'lost sight of behind a mountain of concerts, squash racquets, restaurants and non-motoring members'. However, there was no escaping the 'unqualified success' of the Road Guides and John himself later acknowledged that the Pall Mall clubhouse also served a general purpose. It proved to the world that 'automobilism is a very big thing indeed'.

Certainly it was the most conspicuous of the three main elements which have ever since comprised the RAC (the other two being, of course, road services and motor sport). But the clubhouse, too, was a curious hybrid. It was partly an office block, partly a 'leisure centre' (to use the modern term) and partly (as one contemporary said) a 'glorified hotel'. It was also the headquarters of 'a national institution'. And it was a 'great cosmopolitan rendezvous' attracting the representatives of motoring interests from all over the world. There was, furthermore, substance in Arthur Stanley's claim that 'we are to a certain extent revolutionising the idea of clubs in this country'. The new building was designed to be the 'apotheosis of the West End Club'. This meant that, in the traditional sense of the word, it was hardly a club at all. It would not, at any rate, have been recognised as such by the Restoration blades, Georgian dandies and Regency bucks who had once haunted Pall Mall. It was too large, just as the RAC itself was too large for all the members to know one another. They might just as well have been clubbable

GETTING HOME FOR A GUINEA

The RAC's 'Get-you-Home' disc was a passport to the 'freedom of the road', given to Associate members in return for their guinea-a-year subscription.

ADVANTAGES OF ASSOCIATESHIP OF THE ROYAL AUTOMOBILE CLUB.

The Royal Automobile Club is the premier association of motorists in the United Kingdom, and, with its immediately associated bodies, is the most influential and powerful automobile organisation in the world, claiming the allegiance of over 40,000 automobilists.

The R.A.C. scheme of benefits is framed to meet the requirements of the owner of the 60-h.p. car *de luxe* as well as the user of the low-powered motor-cycle; offering to everyone tangible benefits.

R.A.C. TOURING GUIDES ON THE ROAD.

The Royal Automobile and Associated Clubs maintain the corps of R.A.C. Touring Guides to assist you on the road. These men, any one of whom may be readily recognised by his smart blue-grey uniform, the badge on his arm, the initials of the Club on his cap, or the bicycle painted in royal blue, are stationed throughout Great Britain at particularly dangerous corners to ensure your safety, at great road junctions to advise you as to choice of routes, in the principal touring centres to direct you to the places of interest, on the outskirts of large towns to show you the way through them, at certain ports to help you when entering or leaving the country with your car, and at those places where you are likely to require special information when touring.

Every guide has an intimate knowledge of the district in which he is posted. He is able to tell you exactly what the condition of the roads ahead is, and to recommend alternative roads when necessary. He knows the precise position of all speed limits, and will warn you of any dangerous corners or cross roads. His equipment includes large scale reference maps of the immediate district and maps on a smaller scale covering a considerable area beyond, telegraph forms, letter paper, postcards, stamps, and a first-aid outfit for use in case of emergency. The majority of the men are skilled in tyre manipulation, and are capable of rendering you intelligent assistance if you are unfortunate enough to be stopped on the roadside.

In short, the R.A.C. Guides are, as indeed every part of the R.A.C. organisation is, always ready to your command.

ASSISTANCE IN CASE OF BREAKDOWN.

If you carry the R.A.C. Associate Badge on your car, you may obtain, by application, a brass Disc, reproduced here, which will be of service to you if you have the misfortune to be stranded on the roadside by a breakdown of your car. The presentation of the Disc to an R.A.C. Repairer or other person will bring the necessary assistance and will indemnify you as the owner of the Disc against the cost of hiring another car to get you and party home.

On the occurrence of a breakdown, you send this Talisman by an R.A.C. Touring Guide, or by the first available messenger, to the nearest R.A.C. Repairer, who will, in accordance with his agreement with the Club, at once send a relief car either to convey your party to your home or destination, or to the nearest point from which you can reach home (within a distance of 20 miles of the place where you were stranded), or alternatively, to tow the brokendown car with its passengers to your home or destination (within a distance of 10 miles.)

THE DISC THAT BRINGS ASSISTANCE

The Disc will not only ensure the immediate attention of the Repairer, but it will provide a relief car **free of cost** for the purposes mentioned.

In the event of assistance which is not covered by the scheme being required, you are recommended to send your Disc to the Repairer, or other person from whom assistance is demanded, as evidence of your *bona fides*.

2

3

in a cathedral. Like other late-Victorian clubs, as described by *The Times*, the RAC was not a little individual society but a vast impersonal mass, 'a sort of congealed interest … a machine for providing the Members with a certain amount of comfort and luxury'.

Yet the sheer size of the Pall Mall clubhouse and the corresponding splendour of its amenities were what made it popular with the *beau monde*. The Club's turnover rose from £385,000 in 1910 to £970,000 the following year. This was partly due to the large influx of new members, who paid 25 guineas a head to join and an annual subscription of ten guineas, before the First World War. Among them was Winston Churchill, then Home Secretary, an early champion of motoring. In late afternoons during the summer of 1911, at the height of the Agadir Crisis with Germany, Churchill made a habit of bringing Sir Edward Grey to the Club, where (the Foreign Secretary later recalled) 'he would cool his ardour and I revive my spirits in the swimming-bath'. Lord Curzon, who lived nearby at 1 Carlton House Terrace, also found the Club useful. He arranged his first assignation with his future wife Grace, who was then married to someone else, in the anonymous surroundings of the Club dining room because 'the location would excite less gossip than a rendezvous in a restaurant'.

The Club's echoing amplitude was often the subject of satire, connoisseurs of snobbery regarding size as being incompatible with smartness. In Harold Nicolson's *Some People*, mischievous Oxford undergraduates easily convinced the social-climbing Marquis de Chaumont that 'the most exclusive club in England was not, as he had heard, the Royal Yacht Squadron but the equally Royal Automobile Club in Pall Mall. He had thereupon pulled endless strings to secure election.' Rudely shocked by 'the Byzantine vestibule and Sassanian lounge' of Lord Copper's Fleet Street headquarters, William Boot, the central character in Evelyn Waugh's *Scoop*, 'thought at first that he must have arrived at some new and less exclusive rival to the R.A.C.' A less sardonic view of the Club was penned in 1914 by another writer of fiction, Ian Hay, who provided the most vivid evocation of its pharaonic scale and gargantuan energy.

The hero of his novel *A Knight on Wheels*, a young motor engineer called Philip, is taken there one evening by his ebullient friend Timothy.

> Members swarmed in the great central hall, upon the staircase, and in all the lofty apartments opening therefrom. There appeared to be at least six hall-porters, and there were page-boys innumerable, who drifted about in all directions, wearing worried expressions and chanting a mysterious dirge which sounded like 'Mr. Hah-Hah, please!' There was a real post-office in one corner, and a theatre ticket office in another. There were racquet courts, and a swimming-bath, and a shooting-gallery, and a gymnasium, and a bowling-alley, and a fencing school. Timothy confidently announced that there was a golf-course somewhere, but that he had not yet found time to play a round owing to the excessive length of the holes.

The pair shun the downstairs dining room where ladies and gentlemen eat together to the sound of music. Instead they take the lift to the sexually segregated first floor. Here they sit down in a 'vast refectory' and are served by a legion of waiters, themselves supplied by seventeen cooks. Afterwards the friends drink coffee and liqueurs in an apartment which reminds Philip of Victoria terminus, as recently rebuilt. Then, failing to find a tube station in the Club, the young

CROWNING GLORY

The new clubhouse is en fête *to
celebrate the coronation of the second
sovereign patron of the RAC, King
George V, on 24 June 1911.*

men take a taxi to the Empire, in Leicester Square – a favourite resort of members who enjoyed being entertained by scantily clad young women.

Robert Surtees had said that the comfortable Victorian club completed the luxury of railway travel, as a coaching-house, with 'its large cabbage-smelling coffee-room', could never do. The RAC's great caravanserai in Pall Mall completed the luxury of motor travel. It provided wealthy Edwardian car owners with premises which complemented their vehicles – plush, exclusive and, above all, modern. Members had the further satisfaction of being able to regard themselves as the leaders of a powerful new movement with a nationwide following. But the clubhouse's most obvious purpose was to give pleasure. Its revenue account for 1913 reveals that members spent £3,441 on cigars and £13,800 on wines – its cellar was enormous, containing Madeira dating from the year of Waterloo and brandy dating from the year of Trafalgar. The entertainments were lavish, especially those connected with royal events: the Club made £5,000 from celebrations connected with George V's coronation and the 1911 Durbar Ball was a glittering festivity for which an annexe was specially constructed on the terrace. At it one member got so drunk that he was hauled before the Committee, which decided to pardon him on the grounds of his youth.

The clubhouse was an increasingly frequent starting-point for social life outside London. The 'week-end' habit was growing thanks to the car. Members could easily drive to the countryside for a couple of nights. Many liked to stay aboard the *Enchantress*, shooting teal, widgeon and mallard in the Solent marshes during the day and dancing at night in her eighty-foot ballroom. Others joined the RAC's Golf Club (formed, like the Fencing Club, in 1910) or Fishing Association (1914) and made shorter excursions. Some engaged in even more recherché sports such as 'motor polo' at Ranelagh. The RAC took a dim view of this game, describing it as 'dangerous to the players … wearisome to the spectators … [and an] irreverent profanation of a cherished national institution'. The car was built for nobler purposes. As Montagu said, it was 'a great force which was silently and slowly altering our habits and altering the relations of mankind'. Like the automobile to which it was an adjunct, the RAC's palace in Pall Mall contributed notably to the *douceur de vivre* which affluent Britons enjoyed before the Great War.

SUNBEAM

One of the many bicycle makers who became car manufacturers, Thomas Cureton, pictured above in 1910, created the Sunbeam.

CHAPTER SIX

PEACE
AND WAR

*Before 1914 motor vehicles had come to play a major role in
British life, with the RAC acting as an important impresario.
The First World War threatened the existence of the Club. But
it forged new engines of conflict and spread mechanical
knowledge to millions.*

BADGE OF
COMPETENCE

*Drivers wishing to sport
this badge had to take a
written test in which
they answered ten
questions in two hours.*

AS A CENTURY OF ALMOST UNBROKEN PEACE in Europe drew to its close,
something akin to a motoring culture began to emerge in Britain. Seldom
were heard the kind of apocalyptic words about the automobile so often
uttered during the reign of Edward VII. Then, for example, Prince Albert's
biographer, Sir Theodore Martin, had denounced the motor car as 'a curse
on the community' which stank 'worse than the infernal regions' – though,
an RAC member slyly riposted, it was hard to understand how Sir
Theodore could know this *yet*. George V's subjects laughed such jeremiads
to scorn. They, in contrast, were struck by the healthy progress and
ubiquitous influence of the motor car. By 1914 cars were beginning to
dominate roads which had increasingly been tarred to give smooth, dust-
free surfaces. A prophetic article, by Massac Buist, was entitled 'From
Motoring for the Few to Automobilism for the Many'. At a time when
four per cent of the population owned ninety per cent of the wealth and the masses could not
aspire to car ownership, Buist was indulging in something of a pipedream. But Claude Johnson's
eulogy of the automobile movement did not seem extravagant:

> the genius and foresight of the fathers of motorism, the enthusiastic and sweeping
> methods of their apostles, the passionate and fiery onslaught of their opposers, the
> rapid development, and, in an astonishingly short period, the triumphant victory of
> the newcomer, go to make a history of which it would be difficult to find a parallel.

Suddenly, it seemed, motoring had matured from 'weakling infant into lusty giant'.

By American standards, of course, Britain's giant was a pygmy. John Montagu, who crossed
the Atlantic in 1912, was amazed by the industrial capacity he found. The United States

contained more than half the cars in the world. Most of them were uniform types like the Model T Ford, whose manufacture was about to be revolutionised by the moving assembly line, which cut construction time from 12½ to 1½ man hours. Ford turned out 75,000 Tin Lizzies in 1912, whereas no single British model was produced in numbers larger than 200. British cars were built like cathedrals. They took ages to craft and were made to last. They were therefore expensive and, significantly for the future of the industry, already lagged behind their rivals in terms of technology. Some 'cramped, ill-lit, draughty, heavily-built vehicles' still provided a motoring experience which was like being 'on board ship in a storm'.

Nevertheless Britain was more motorised than her European neighbours. By 1913 the United Kingdom contained 426,000 motor vehicles all told, including 140,00 cars and 180,000 motor-bikes as well as lorries, vans, buses and so on. France did not equal this total until well after the First World War, though her motor industry remained larger than Britain's until the onset of the Depression. Ninety-four per cent of London's passenger vehicles were motorised by 1913, whereas Berlin had 460 horse-buses as against only 300 motor buses. Paris boasted 5,000 motor-cabs while London had 8,400. In fact, the hansom cab driver was 'quickly fading into oblivion'. This familiar Cockney character, with his bowler hat, his weathered face, his harsh refrain of 'Keb, sir?' and his 'apparently limitless and certainly instinctive' additional vocabulary, was being replaced by the peak-capped, brass-buttoned taxi-driver. His more respectable presence helped to make chaperones seem outmoded and thus unwittingly encouraged novel freedoms in behaviour. In 1912 the play *A Girl in a Taxi* brought a new catch-phrase into the language: 'If you can't be good – be careful.'

On every side there were signs that the motor culture was becoming established. Smart houses were increasingly being built with garages, which no longer needed 'pits' (because cars were more reliable) but were still, like stables, placed at a distance from living quarters. Railway stations, thanks in part to representations by the RAC, were also beginning to provide garages for their passengers. The Club was less effective, though, in quelling motoring manifestations of which it disapproved. Wayside billboards proliferated and RAC objections to these 'ugly eyesores' were largely ignored. The Club could do nothing to stem the novel habit of hitchhiking, though it advised members not to give lifts to itinerants who so 'impudently' signalled them to stop. Some hitchhikers were picked up by motor-cyclists and the RAC warned in vain against the hazardous 'new fashion of pillion riding'.

The Club was also unsuccessful in preventing the promiscuous use of noisy horns, the 'loud, dictatorial, screeching notes, ear-splitting whistles, and all the new-fangled rows that on holidays and Sundays make some places an inferno'. Snootier denizens of Pall Mall were apt to blame this cacophony on the emergence of a vulgar class of motorists typified by 'Mr Newrich'. He was to be seen any Sunday on the Brighton road 'accompanied by two or three over-dressed, painted, powdered, scented, feathered females'. Mr Newrich was doubtless the sort of man who embellished his house with Gamages novelty items such as the clock which sported a motor car instead of a cuckoo: on the hour it emerged from its garage and gave 'the appropriate number of toots on its horn before driving into another garage'. Perhaps, too, he would have decorated his car with 'motoring mascots' such as toy cats, dogs and golliwogs, stickers, medallions and badges – the last being the automotive equivalent of horse brasses.

FORDISM

*By 1914 Henry Ford made almost half the cars
produced in America, thanks to the moving
assembly line. This employed, he said, 'the
principles of power, accuracy, economy, system,
continuity, speed and repetition'. Above, workers
fit petrol tanks to Model Ts. Right, magnetos are
assembled. Below, Ford's 1920 Rouge River
plant at Detroit has 27 miles of conveyors.
Everything practicable was done to increase
manufacturing speed.*

To instruct the likes of Mr Newrich, schools of motoring multiplied. The worst were incompetent, extortionate and unscrupulous, having a vested interest in the failure of at least some of their pupils to pass the RAC's driving test. The Club's experts inspected the British School of Motoring, for example, and discovered that it operated from a small, dirty garage in Peckham with a fleet of five dilapidated cars. The RAC campaigned in the press against Do-the-Motorist academies and advised aspirant drivers to patronise only the handful which it licensed. Better still, they should make use of its own Instruction Department, which had begun in 1902 and gave 1,200 lessons in 1911. Not everyone was convinced by the efficacy of tuition, let alone of driving tests. Winston Churchill amused a deputation of trade unionists in 1911 by asserting that 'Few accidents arise ... from ignorance of how to drive, and a much more frequent cause of disaster is undue proficiency, leading to excessive adventure.'

In fact, traffic accidents were increasing at an alarming rate: 155 Londoners had been killed on the roads in 1904; by 1912 the number had risen to 537. But there was no agreement about the cause. Indeed, in 1912 the Home Secretary issued a circular stating that exceeding the 20mph limit on clear, open roads was not dangerous and advising local police authorities to set traps only in places where high speed was an obvious hazard. This tacitly conceded the case long argued by the RAC and the AA, who now engaged in some limited political co-operation through a newly founded forum called the National Automobile Council. It offered only a feeble response to the growing carnage on the nation's highways and opposed most forms of compulsion on the motorist. The RAC in particular pleaded for better road manners. Drivers should have a 'recognised code of signals'. Slow vehicles should keep to the left. Closed cars should be fitted with rear-view mirrors, which were then optional extras. Finally, after first maintaining that motor-bikes were honorary bicycles and could therefore make do with rear reflectors only, the RAC concluded in 1914 that they were quasi-cars and needed red rear lights.

The pre-Great War generation, like all subsequent generations, felt both that the roads had become unhealthily crowded and that self-propelled vehicles were, in Massac Buist's words, 'an indispensable convenience of modern life'. Or, to quote Henry Norman MP, owning an automobile was like having a wife: it increased expenses and responsibilities but 'broadened sympathies and made life vastly more worth living'. The role that motor vehicles were beginning to play in the life of the nation was dramatically illustrated by the dockers' strike in 1911. By interrupting the distribution of fuel and lubrication oil it threatened to paralyse London. The strike showed for the first time the extent of the capital's 'dependence ... on the internal combustion engine'. London's motor buses, now being praised by the *Pall Mall Gazette* after 'years of contumely', carried over 250 million passengers in 1911.

In the spreading suburbs 'the struggling professional man' was ever more likely to be reliant on the diminutive light car, 'the dog-cart of the motoring world'. The countryside was being invaded not only by automobiles but by 'tourist-laden char-à-bancs'. Fire engines were being motorised. Small boys had taken up the hobby of collecting car numbers and it was rumoured among them, said Henry Williamson, later the author of *Tarka the Otter*, that some day 'a big prize' would be given for the longest list. In 1912 well over a million Britons (the vast majority of them train travellers) crossed to the Continent and the Club *Journal* opined that a Channel Tunnel, after a century of 'spasmodic consideration', was soon bound to become an 'accom-

CALAMITIES AND MISADVENTURES

The growing number of fatal car accidents stimulated 'motorphobia'. The RAC publicised reports of accidents caused by horses and criticised trams, which had priority over all other traffic in most towns (a circumstance of which their drivers took full advantage). The Club also put forward safety measures and condemned 'scorching'. But many members continued to regard motoring as a sport and speeding as an adventure.

plished fact' – but the RAC advocated a road, not a rail, link. Walter Long, an honorary life member of the Club, was one of many who harped on the palpable transformation being wrought by the car. Its effects were to be seen in everything from revitalised villages to cleaner city streets – between 1905 and 1913 the amount of horse dung carted away from Battersea halved. The automobile had 'done more to revolutionise the conditions of life within the country than anything,' Long said, 'far more than the development of railways'.

The RAC was often hailed as the midwife of the revolution, not least because of the sporting enterprises it masterminded. These were thought vital to the development of motor cars. So, although by 1914 the AA had about twice as many members as its rival, *The Standard* could still refer to the RAC as 'the big dog of the motor world, with a lot of little dogs forever yapping at its heels'. The most spectacular event which the Club organised before the Great War was a friendly, amateur competition with the Imperial Automobile Club of Germany. It was designed to bring the two nations 'closer together' and to mark the coronation of King George V. The intention was also to provide 'sport without speed'. Thus the Prince Henry Tour, as it was called, after the Kaiser's brother, was purely a test of reliability. In fact, it turned out to be little more than a glittering procession punctuated by grand receptions and elaborate banquets. The Duke of Connaught, who had just succeeded the Duke of Sutherland as President of the RAC, led the twenty-six-strong British team. It included notables like Conan Doyle and Lionel de Rothschild, and it was fêted enthusiastically throughout the German leg of the Tour. In Britain the Tour 'roused the countryside in a way that has never been witnessed since the Thousand Mile Trial' of 1900. Prince Henry observed that the spectators cheered even though they 'swallowed dust by the ton'. The RAC won the Trophy donated by Prince Henry. Club members saluted him as 'a veritable *preux chevalier* among sportsmen' – a tribute they were soon anxious to forget. When war broke out his name was struck off the Club roll.

Other contests, such as the standard car race at Brooklands in 1912 (won by a Singer) and the revived Tourist Trophy Race on the Isle of Man in 1914 (won by a Sunbeam), probably did more than this princely progress to improve the quality of ordinary cars. The Club even hoped that the TT Race might rival the Grand Prix, 'the "blue riband" of motordom'. But by 1914 the Grand Prix authorities had attracted English entries and eliminated monster engines, which helped to foster automotive advance. More blasé members of the RAC were apt to say that motoring had now 'become so monotonously reliable and luxurious that half the fun has lapsed' and they now had to look to aeroplanes for excitement.

Certainly they took a keen interest in what was still thought of as aerial automobilism. Prominent aviators like Charles Rolls and Frank Butler now found balloonacy too tame, though it still flabbergasted most of their countrymen. (Hovering low over the ground, Rolls had once shouted to a rustic, 'Where are we?' The man replied, 'Why, you are up in a balloon.') Rolls was quick to cultivate the Wright brothers and he flew with Wilbur in 1908. So did the bulky Frank Butler, solid proof, in Rolls's view, that powered flight was a practical proposition. It was also, he told an RAC audience, an unparalleled thrill. There was 'nothing so fascinating or exhilarating as flying. It gives one an entirely new sense of life.' In July 1910 it brought Rolls's life to a premature end. His aircraft, in which he had earlier crossed and recrossed the English Channel, crashed at Bournemouth. Rolls had fitted a redesigned tailplane which collapsed while

INTERNAL COMBUSTION

In August 1913 the last horse-bus ran through the City of London. By then the capital was almost entirely dependent on motor buses, which carried nearly 500 million passengers in the final year of peace. Advanced vehicles such as the 1914 Dennis fire engine were now generally accepted.

he was making a steep descent. Somewhat unfeelingly, Henry Norman remarked on Rolls's 'crankiness' – he had been a 'rabid teetotaller' and non-smoker – and claimed that a perverse 'bit of trick-flying' had caused the accident. Fellow members of the RAC continued to regard the aeroplane as they had once regarded the automobile. It was a sporting machine, though some day it might 'even rival the car in progression along utilitarian lines'.

Meanwhile record-breaking feats of aviation were celebrated in Pall Mall with unabashed gusto. One of the most memorable was achieved by Benfield Hucks, who in 1913 became the first Englishman to loop the loop. RAC members rewarded him and his fellow pilot Gustav Hamel with an 'Upside-down Dinner', which attracted much publicity at the time and has since become part of the Club's folklore. The invitation cards showed the flyers with their heels in the air. The usual order of the meal was reversed. It began with cigars and concluded with hors-d'oeuvres. Everything else was topsy-turvy. The guests of honour sat in front of large distorting mirrors at a loop-shaped table with a set of legs pointing upwards. Charles Coborn sang a song while standing on his head. In his speech Hucks started with 'Lastly', went on with 'Thirdly' and finished with a sentence which began 'Firstly'. Curiously, most of the diners felt hungry after the banquet and some seriously suggested that they should now embark on a 'right-side-up' repast. One of the aviators wrote on his menu, 'The dinner requires even more practice to enjoy than flying.' The humour does not travel well, but the episode reveals much about how members of the Club amused themselves in the last months of peace.

They enjoyed further recreation at Woodcote Park, an estate near Epsom which the RAC purchased in 1913 as its 'country headquarters'. The park consisted of 338 acres adjoining Lord Rosebery's famous estate, The Durdans, and contained beautiful spinneys, picturesque gardens and magnificent century-old cedars. The original manor house had belonged to the Abbey of Chertsey but the property had eventually passed to Richard Evelyn, brother of the Restoration diarist John, who built a splendid house on the spot. During the eighteenth century it was extensively restored by a new owner, the sixth Earl of Baltimore. Thus the RAC acquired a noble Palladian building with exquisite interior work by Antonio Verrio, Grinling Gibbons and Sir Henry Cheere. But art was subordinated to comfort. Many of the finest features – rococo mantelpieces, carved panelling, painted ceilings – were torn out and sold so that electric light and modern plumbing could be installed. As it happened, the Club's philistinism proved to be a blessing in disguise. The Boston Museum acquired some of the décor and preserved it as part of its superb 'Chippendale Room'. Some years later Woodcote was completely gutted by fire.

The purpose of Woodcote Park was to provide members with a spacious sports complex only sixteen miles from Pall Mall. In particular, the Club's Golfing Society, described as a 'cuckoo' because it kept laying its eggs in others' nests, would now have a home of its own. Golf was a passion with many members and to satisfy it the RAC planned to lay out two eighteen-hole courses. It also proposed to create facilities for cricket, tennis, polo, shooting, archery and other sports. The cost was £50,000 for the purchase and £25,000 for the refurbishment. Such was members' enthusiasm for the scheme that they eagerly bought £100 debentures and the purchase was completed on the same lines as that of the Pall Mall clubhouse. The motoring press was less keen on the enterprise. It accused the RAC of wasting time, money and energy on an 'unwarrantable' luxury for full members while neglecting the interests of its Associates.

BOTTOMS UP

The RAC enjoys skylarks and salutes a spectacular automotive achievement. Looping the loop soon became a standard stunt: performing it at Brooklands in October 1913, the pilot Adolphe Pegoud said that he felt 'as comfortable as sitting at home in his armchair'.

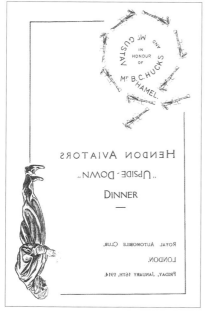

The *Journal* replied, correctly, that not a farthing of the RAC's funds had been spent on Woodcote. However, because of its composite character the Club was always vulnerable to such charges. Columnists like Owen John harped on the unsatisfactoriness of having 'two grades of members … people in the stalls and those in the pit'. Increasingly the Club maintained a dignified silence about its internal affairs, while not hesitating to damn its critics for ignorance. It was apparently so anxious to suppress any idea that Associates were second-class citizens that the *Journal* kept quiet about the progress of refurbishing Woodcote Park. But it could hardly disguise the fact that full members had lavishly enhanced their already privileged position.

WOODCOTE PARK

The RAC's Epsom country club, shortly before it was ravaged by fire in 1934. Its façade then reverted to the original red brick, which had been overlaid with stone in the nineteenth century. Members pioneered the habit of taking a Sunday spin to play golf.

The new Chairman of the Club, Arthur Stanley, was unconcerned. Prince Francis of Teck had died unexpectedly in October 1910 – RAC members swathed their badges in mourning crêpe for a month – and he was briefly succeeded by his elder brother, Adolphus ('Dolly'), Duke of Teck. He stood down early in 1912 to become personal ADC to his brother-in-law, King George V. So Stanley, who had already occupied the post of Chairman between 1905 and 1907, now began a second stint that was to last until 1936. As the third son of the sixteenth Earl of Derby, Stanley was not quite royalty; but his family was the next best thing. It was said of his eldest brother, who in 1908 inherited the earldom and became the uncrowned 'King of Lancashire', that if some catastrophe annihilated the royal family and people called for a new monarch, 'their first choice would be Lord Derby'. Arthur Stanley had been educated at Wellington. He was an ardent sportsman, doing much to popularise the sport of ice hockey when his father (whom he persuaded to present the Stanley Cup) was Governor-General of Canada. Stanley had served as a diplomat, acted as private secretary to Balfour and become an MP. As a parliamentary spokesman for the Club he had, according to the *Morning Post*, stated its principles 'admirably and moderately'. But he did not take his role with undue solemnity: he told Club members that the Commons' carburetion was wrong – 'too much gas'.

Stanley was a popular figure in Pall Mall. He was not strong physically and he lacked a powerful personality. Indeed, during his long second term as Chairman, he allowed himself to be dominated by what Monty Grahame-White called the 'Secretarial Bodyguard'. But Stanley was distinguished by an 'imperturbable good humour'. He promised to ensure that the temperature in the Club's library was 'conducive to sleep'. He jested that if mothers had as much trouble with their first child 'as I have with my car we younger sons would never be born'. In 1913 he told members that the performance of almost every department in the Club had improved on the previous year's except that of the shooting range. This would be better patronised, he remarked, if 'Germany goes on adding to her aerial fleet'.

ALTHOUGH STANLEY MADE A JOKE OF IT, the RAC had for years been seriously concerned about the dangers of a mechanised war with Germany. In part this reflected the motoring rivalry which the Prince Henry Tour had been designed to assuage. Claude Johnson revealed the essence of the competition between the two nations when pleading with Lady Northcliffe to

substitute a Rolls-Royce for a Mercédès: 'Please forgive my greed, but I shall never be happy until you give up using cars made by our natural enemy, the German.' More important was the Club's realisation that the War Office had largely failed to grasp the military implications of the internal combustion engine. Regular meetings were held both in Piccadilly and in Pall Mall to discuss this issue. Members deplored the fact that the cavalry charge, so plainly an anachronism, was 'still the delight of the organisers of spectacular performances'.

Other Club stalwarts contributed specific criticisms and suggestions. Conan Doyle put forward a scheme to repel any German invasion with a motor-borne 'swarm of sharpshooters'. Mark Mayhew wanted the government to commission British factories to duplicate Krupp's experiments with armoured cars, even though these conveyances might savour of 'the dreams of the romancer'. Shrapnell-Smith denounced the dilatoriness of the War Office in registering commercial vehicles for war service and said that some of its own motor transport, as used on manoeuvres, 'would have disgraced a third-class engineering shop'. Actually, thanks in part to persistent RAC nagging, the army had shown some appreciation of the benefits of automation. In 1911 it had begun to subsidise those who kept their vehicles up to set standards and agreed to make them available in time of war. It had also adopted the Maudslay lorry after seeing 'an impressive display' at RAC trials. But Shrapnell-Smith was not far wide of the mark. The Straker-Squire lorries (known as 'Squeaker-Squags') used by the military in 1914 were said, in a promiscuous phrase of the time, to be unable 'to pull the skin off a rice pudding'.

As early as 1908 Frank Butler had warned that 'future battles will be fought in the air and a new aërial force, different from the army and navy, will be formed'. The RAC worried that Britain was ignoring the peril of bombing from the air and 'lagging behind foreign countries in introducing aeroplanes'. Yet as late as 1911 the Secretary of War, R. B. Haldane, dismissed aeroplanes as 'costly and dangerous toys'. In the same year Claude Grahame-White (Monty's brother) gave a demonstration of how dangerous they could be by dropping a bag of sand onto a battleship from a height of 250 feet – a lesson the Admiralty did not take to heart until well into the Second World War. Also in that year a competition took place in which eleven aeroplanes, mostly French, crossed from Calais to Hendon. It prompted George Holt Thomas, an enterprising member of the RAC with a keen interest in aviation, to conjure up the prospect of airborne armadas and thousand-bomber raids on Britain. 'We *must* wake up,' he said: no empty words since, employing Geoffrey de Havilland as his chief designer, Thomas went on to produce nearly a third of the aeroplanes used by Allied forces during the First World War. But before its outbreak, despite the Club's prescient counsel and its influence in high places, the War Office as a whole remained lethargic. By 1914 it was making elaborate plans to win the Boer War and 'the generals were still horse-minded to a degree'.

None of this is to suggest that members of the RAC had a monopoly of wisdom about the coming conflict. Some believed that it would never happen because no country could face the horrors of mechanised slaughter. Montagu forecast that improved locomotion would 'make war more terrible, rapid and destructive' and that it would therefore also 'bind nations together with bonds of peace'. Other members thought that the next war would be between capital and labour, in which case motor cars would prove their worth. During the long hot summer of 1914 the Club *Journal* contained nothing to suggest that the Pax Britannica would ever come to an

BALFOUR ALOFT

Arthur Balfour, leader of the Tories, car enthusiast and early Club member, takes a short flight at the Hendon Car Demonstration in the spring of 1911. Clearly aviation was still seen as an extension of motoring.

MAGNIFICENT MEN

Several of the flying machines crash-landed during the Demonstration, but the pilots are splendidly self-confident. Fourth from the left is Claude Grahame-White, founder of Hendon aerodrome. Gustav Hamel, whose Blériot monoplane is pictured below, stands on the right.

MILITARY MIGHT

The First Lord of the Admiralty, Reginald McKenna (left), attends. But, despite bombing and shooting exhibitions, senior officers were 'not greatly impressed' by the aeroplane as a weapon of war.

end. Other matters attracted attention. There was an 'increasing dearth of that warm hearted road fraternisation between motorists' which had formerly prevailed. Symptoms of discourtesy were the incontinent use of raucous horns and the inconsiderate revving of engines, which sounded like Gatling guns; but folk who yearned for quiet found compensation in the spread of cars like the 'Noiseless Napier', which was advertised as having 'conquered the Alps ... *under the official observation of the Royal Automobile Club*'.

In July 1914 the *Journal* did report on 'a titanic struggle between two nations' – France and Germany. But this took place during the Grand Prix at Lyon between Peugeot and the victorious Mercédès team – a Sunbeam 'saved the face of the British industry by coming in fifth'. Even at this late stage the RAC was still recommending Germany as 'a touring ground' and 'a land of infinite variety'. True, its officials were self-important. But at bottom they were 'quite harmless' and villagers gave a warm welcome to foreign motorists who impinged on their secluded lives. Altogether the Germans 'are a gentle, unsophisticated people'.

When war broke out, on 4 August 1914, the RAC reacted with unusual speed. Other organisations took to heart the slogan 'Business as Usual'. Acknowledging that anyone who had prophesied a European war three weeks earlier would have been thought a 'mere alarmist', the RAC recognised that this conflict would be different from any previous one thanks to 'the very movement that our Club has fostered'. Of course, boot leather, horseflesh and steam trains were the vital elements in the struggle for mobility. But this was also to be a 'war of motor vehicles'. Lorries, buses, cars, motor-cycles, ambulances, tanks and aircraft, made significant contributions to the war effort. Eager to volunteer its own expertise, the RAC threw itself into the fray. As early as 7 August the Club appealed to members to join the British Motor Service Volunteer Corps, which it quickly formed. Within a fortnight 12,000 cars had been registered and their drivers were engaged in a wide variety of war work, from ferrying generals around to helping with the harvest where horses had been requisitioned. By the end of August, when the ordinary life of the Club had come to 'a standstill', 28,000 motorists were ready to serve the War Office.

Among the first to leave for France, at six hours' notice, was H. Stanley Westcott. Engaged on dispatch duties, he had many adventures, including being arrested by the French authorities as a spy – they were evidently not impressed by his plain khaki uniform whose only distinguishing mark was a brassard worn on his left arm bearing the RAC badge. For the benefit of the Club *Journal* Westcott sent back a graphic account of dodging shells and skidding into ditches in his new forty-horsepower Hispano-Suiza. Because of its radiant fittings, troops christened the car 'Silver Grill'. G. D. Pearce-Jones also took an active part in early operations. During the retreat from Mons he 'had to drive his car over banks and gullies in an attempt to pass an apparently endless line' of troops, guns and transport wagons, 'the drivers of which were often asleep'. Another Club member, G. V. Pringle, who saw the German dead 'piled up so high that they form[ed] a sort of barricade', wondered how his automobile stood up to ploughing through shell holes two feet deep.

Frederic Coleman, an American member, was always, as General Smith-Dorrien said, 'close to where shot and shell were flying pretty merrily', and he wrote an entire book about his experiences. Perhaps, though, he somewhat exaggerated the importance of the role played by himself and his heroic fellow-motorists. One of them, E. F. Baring-Gould, noted that nine out

MOTORISTS MUSTER

The Club Journal of 31 July 1914 praised Germany for legislating against 'nerve-racking motor warning devices' such as sirens, buzzers and whistles, but said not a word about impending war. It came as a general shock, though Britannia seemed invincible at sea. However, the RAC was quick to mobilise motorists for the land conflict.

of twenty-five RAC members' cars on active service in France were *hors de combat* at any time. But there is no doubting their drivers' quixotic devotion to duty. Attached to the General Headquarters staff, Baring-Gould sometimes drove his Cadillac for thirty hours at a stretch. Yet he enjoyed the experience and doubted whether he could ever again reconcile himself to 'stiff collars and daily baths'.

While the war of movement continued motor cars could be of strategic significance. The largest single contingent sent abroad took part in the doomed attempt of Winston Churchill, then First Lord of the Admiralty, to stop the enemy from capturing Antwerp in October 1914. It consisted of about fifty cars, accompanied by lorries and red-and-white double-decker buses still sporting their London destination plates. But the Germans stamped with 'iron footprints' (as Churchill put it) on the courageous defenders, including the men of the Royal Naval Division. Within days the conflict settled into a bloody stalemate in the trenches. Automobiles were still widely used, especially in other theatres of operations. Between 1914 and 1918 British forces alone employed 19,000 Model T Fords. They proved particularly effective in the desert, seeming to sail over the sand, and became the 'Jeeps' of World War I. British models were also put on their mettle. Lawrence of Arabia enthused about his armoured Rolls-Royces. In 1915 Petty Officer C. F. Haining, who had worked in the RAC's post office before the war, wrote home from South West Africa, where the temperature was 110 degrees in the shade: 'The Touring Department know something about roads, but nothing like these. Boulders everywhere, dead mules, graves of dead Germans everywhere.... Our 25/30 Wolseley used up ten gallons of water in 62 miles.' Lieutenant Pardo, formerly of the general manager's office in Pall Mall, faced similar problems in Palestine where his motor-bike 'got a touch of the sun'.

Even in France, though, automobiles came into their own. Daimler, for example, built staff cars as well as ambulances and lorries. Its fleet was so conspicuous that the Prince of Wales remarked: 'It seems to me that the Daimler people are running this war.' Their limousines for brass hats were equipped with map tables and seats that could be converted into bunks. The cars were mobile headquarters in which some staff officers practically lived for months. Those less privileged nicknamed them 'Kitchener's greenhouses'. As the roads in northern France deteriorated and became increasingly congested, some cars were involved in accidents. Commander Mansfield Cumming suffered one in which tragedy and comedy were strangely mixed. Acting as his chauffeur, Mansfield's son drove a Rolls-Royce into a tree near Meaux, killing himself and seriously injuring his father. According to a lurid legend fostered by the Secret Intelligence Service, which Cumming (alias 'C') ran, he extricated himself from the wreckage by hacking off his smashed leg with a penknife. Certainly Cumming lost a foot in the crash and thereafter acquired a wooden substitute. But he was always impatient with slow motion. So he bought a child's scooter and 'learned to propel himself at speed along the War Office corridors'. On the road Cumming 'continued to terrorise both pedestrians and police'.

Even when the potential of mechanised road vehicles became plain, the British were slow to employ them. In 1914 they had 185 lorries per division: two years later this figure was still only 235. In 1916 Verdun was saved by an incessant convoy of lorries which kept it supplied along a single road, the 'Sacred Way'. Yet despite studying the French method of sustaining 'an army engaged in a great battle almost entirely by motor transport', the British made little

WHEELS ON SAND

Cars proved their worth where a war of movement continued. A convoy of Fords (right) scuds across Mesopotamia. Mechanised conflict comes to Arabia in the shape of T. E. Lawrence's Rolls-Royce (below). Lawrence used his 'steel chariots in the desert' to ambush trains and said that 'Armoured car work seemed fighting de luxe'.

attempt to copy it. On the Somme they stockpiled ammunition instead of having it driven up as required, thus sacrificing the element of surprise. Sir Douglas Haig, a cavalry general, did not appreciate the importance of maintaining 'good roads' for motor traffic. He also failed to take proper advantage of tanks, the mechanical elephants with which Winston Churchill had hoped to attain victory. Churchill (now out of office) lamented: 'My poor "land battleships" have been let off prematurely and on a petty scale.'

Yet despite military tardiness, the war fostered new inventions and stimulated technological progress. Where components such as magnetos had previously been imported from abroad, they now had to be made in Britain. Most motor manufacturers devoted themselves to munitions work, expanding their factories, applying the new techniques of mass production and earning large sums which could be used to finance postwar car building. The industry would be protected by the 33⅓ per cent duty on luxuries such as foreign cars imposed by the Chancellor of the Exchequer, Reginald McKenna, in 1915, an emergency change in the system of free trade which lasted (more or less) until the 1970s.

The war also introduced large numbers of men (and, at home, women) to motor vehicles for the first time. Anyone with mechanical knowledge, such as the RAC's 100-strong force of Road Guides, most of whom 'answered the country's call' at once, was likely to be paid extra and employed in military transport services. But countless new soldiers who had no idea about motor matters found themselves drafted into armoured-car or motor-cycle detachments. On the other hand, some RAC stalwarts were consigned to the infantry. Major Hume, formerly the Club's Assistant Secretary, wrote home from the Dardanelles in September 1915: 'The landing on the ever memorable (to me) Saturday is a thing I would not have missed for worlds. I saw it from a transport close in, and had a fair share of shells and bombs around. Since then we have been ashore and very much in the thick of it.' Lieutenant L. C. Fox, who had been in charge of the Road Guides Department at Pall Mall, also served in Gallipoli. He too wrote blithely about the 'strenuous time' he was having in the 'Purgatorial Peninsula'. In particular, he dilated on the charm of spending a night two yards from a dead Turk, when the 'decomposed deceased' had been in a '"Stilton" state' for some time. Fox's unit lost two-thirds of its officers and half its men, but 'that's quite an ordinary programme for Gallipoli'. He himself 'sustained a puncture', a bullet in the foot. Hume was invalided home with rheumatic fever and died on board ship, near Gibraltar.

Other members of the RAC staff told of their doings on the Western Front. They wrote of whole platoons being wiped out, of the incredible devastation caused by the German artillery, of being waist-high in water for days on end, of 'hell upon earth'. Yet amid the protracted agony they were full of dogged cheerfulness. B. Brandon, once a swimming-pool attendant at Pall Mall and later killed in action, was typical. He compared trench warfare to 'a game of hide and seek' and said that he was 'not a bit downhearted' despite the heavy fighting.

It was simply slaughter. We were over our boots in mud, but our fellows went over the ground as though they were in a race. It made you feel proud you were an Englishman. While they were waiting to charge they were joking, and they started singing a song. Everybody was anxious to get over the parapet.

BRITAIN GOES TO WAR

London buses transport the 2nd Battalion Royal Warwickshire Regiment to the front on 6 November 1914. They defended Ypres, which was to become the symbol of British resistance.

FRANCE'S LIFELINE

Verdun, the symbol of French resistance, was supplied by 12,000 vehicles using a single road. One passed along the 'Sacred Way' every fourteen seconds and a whole division was kept permanently occupied doing repair work.

Evoking as they do the immense tragedy of the Great War, these accounts read today with almost unbearable poignancy. They reflect contemporary feelings in conventional terms. However, the simple patriotism of the front line was mild beside the rank jingoism which soon blossomed on the home front. Serving RAC staff often wondered about what was happening at Pall Mall in the absence of so many male staff. One fantasist thought that 'it must be glorious to be a member of the Club now. Why the Sultan's harem isn't in it.' Actually, in the first months of the war the Club became the scene of an outburst of rampant xenophobia.

It was sparked off by at least two unpleasant incidents that occurred in the Pall Mall clubhouse. At about six o'clock on the evening of 9 September 1914, a certain H. C. C. Gittings was engaged in an animated Smoking Room discussion about a letter he had written to the Chairman, signed by 143 fellow members. It advocated the removal from the Club of all 'alien enemies' (as they were then called). As Gittings was holding forth about naturalised Englishmen of German or Austrian parentage being spies and conspirators, a member whom he did not know expressed forthright disagreement. Gittings said that the stranger, who turned out to be Sir J. T. Walters, a British MP of German extraction, 'began speaking to me in an angry tone about my action against the Germans in the Club'. When Gittings refused to engage in argument, Walters exclaimed: 'Damned scoundrel!' Gittings then 'struck him in the face'. Friends of the two men intervened, abusing one another in 'violent language'. Finally Orde appeared and restored calm. In due course the Club Committee heard a full account of the fracas. It ruled that Gittings should be 'requested not to use the Club during the continuance of the war'. It also established a subcommittee to examine the position of foreign-born members of the Club.

This body deliberated too slowly for the likes of some commentators. *The Motor*, for example, criticised the Club's 'apparent indifference' to the presence of alien enemies and wondered if it was connected with hopes of re-establishing continental tourist facilities after the war. The magazine contrasted the RAC's sloth in this matter with the 'veritable tornado of enthused patriotism [which] has permeated the whole of the A.A. organisation'. The subcommittee's collective mind was further concentrated by a second altercation in Pall Mall, which took place on 26 October 1914. It involved Richard Meyer, a German-born stockbroker who had been a naturalised Briton since Queen Victoria's reign and had served with the Rand Rifles during the Boer War. In the card room Meyer asked a Mr Kelton whether he thought things were going well at the front. Another player, Mr Wyndham, remarked loudly: 'Fancy a bounder like that asking you such a question.' Meyer protested but Wyndham continued, 'What right have you to ask a British officer for information from the front; what right have you got to be here at all, I should like to know?' To avoid further trouble Meyer started to leave the room, only to be confronted by E. R. Chittenden, who mouthed the words: 'Spies, spies.' Other slanders were uttered after Meyer had gone. He complained to the Club Committee, declaring himself to be 'a thoroughly loyal British subject' who found it incredible to be so attacked in 'free liberal England'. Meyer added that he would shun the Club until after the war. The committee now took a new line. It accepted the feeble defence of Wyndham and Chittenden, though rebuking them mildly. It also 'appreciated' Meyer's undertaking not to enter the Club for the duration, while regretting 'the circumstances' which had led to its being given.

MOTORISED CAVALRY

Armoured vehicles, pioneered by F. R. Simms, were produced when it became plain that horses could not stand up to barbed wire and machine-guns. This one is an Austin.

GENERAL-PURPOSE VEHICLE

Major-General Thwaites (above) boards his Rolls-Royce Silver Ghost at Fouquevillers in March 1917 – note the RAC badge on the bonnet. Below, WAAC drivers pose beside their humbler Studebaker.

In May 1915 the Club resolved to ban all alien enemies, whether as members or guests, while hostilities continued. It acknowledged that many of them were loyal but felt that 'this is not a time when discrimination can be exercised'. In retrospect this seems a harsh decision, not improved when the RAC tried to make its officially appointed hotels apply a similar exclusion order to their own staff. But the Club was overwhelmed by the current climate of hysteria. Spy mania, atrocity stories and invasion scares were rife. Anything connected with the 'Germhuns' was likely to be boycotted, from Liebfraumilch to Beethoven, from dachshunds to Mercédès. One Club member thought it would be 'unpatriotic to be driven around London in his German Adler' and had it re-bodied as an ambulance. The persecution of people with Teutonic names was ubiquitous, reaching into the royal family itself. Institutions as well as individuals were rechristened: Mayfair's Coburg hotel became the Connaught and Bechstein Hall became Wigmore Hall. Already, in October 1914, all London's fifty golf clubs had excluded 'alien enemies' who were naturalised and expelled those who were not. Orde said that the RAC had made its decision in order to prevent further friction in the present 'state of public opinion'. Even if the Club had wanted to, it could hardly have resisted the contemporary mood of intolerance.

Furthermore, the RAC was itself under threat during the war years. Private motoring, though never forbidden, was severely restricted. Petrol rationing was even tougher than it would be during the Second World War. Gas-bag propulsion was unsatisfactory, though in 1917 the RAC arranged for a char-à-banc powered by coal gas to take members from Epsom station to Woodcote Park for golf. It was frowned on to employ able-bodied drivers who might be in khaki. Such chauffeurs were regarded as loafers and the RAC helped to find substitutes 'beyond the age acceptable by the War Department'. Powerful headlamps were prohibited because of what they might reveal to Zeppelins, a ruling which, as Montagu observed, 'makes the avoidance of accident purely a matter of luck'. Above all, joyriding was deemed 'selfish and unpatriotic'. Club members themselves wrote to the *Journal* suggesting that motorists should place their cars at the disposal of the nation in order to 'wipe out for ever the stigma which has been cast upon them for years of being a useless and selfish class of the community'. But the call was not widely heeded. Montagu went so far as to justify 'joy-riding'. He said that 'the magnificently upholstered and equipped car' could hardly be scrapped or modified with 'real economy' and that it might offer its owner a refreshing break from 'present anxieties'. The RAC was associated with self-indulgence at a time when the state was in danger.

Soon official posters were put up that said: 'DON'T USE A MOTOR-CAR FOR PLEASURE.' Newspapers printed descriptions of people who ignored this injunction: 'a two-seater with a second lieutenant and flapper with a double pigtail'; 'a large car with two men and three women luxuriously furred'. Attempts to embarrass those who employed their motors for frivolous purposes were not confined to the press. Lord Derby harried Lord Curzon, one of the Club's most distinguished members, for his 'scandalous abuse of a Government car'. Curzon not only drove it to parties and dances but allowed his wife to use it for shopping expeditions. The parade of extravagance by a few 'aggressively opulent' people, as *The Autocar* called them, brought both automobilism and the RAC into disrepute. As social tensions reached breaking point some 'joy-riders' had their car tyres slashed and their windows broken. The War Savings Committee stated: 'We cannot with any effect ask the poorer classes to save, as long as

HEAVY METAL

*Because early pneumatic tyres were so prone to
puncture manufacturers tried to produce substitutes.
More experiments took place later, especially in
Germany, where the rubber shortage was acute during
the war. The steel-sprung wheels on this Protos were
said to have worked well.*

they see well-to-do people enjoying an expensive luxury.' Owen John blamed magistrates, who had once fined motorists 'more heavily than wife-beaters', for sympathising with 'offenders of their own rank'.

With the slump in ordinary motoring the RAC saw its Associate membership vanishing away and its major occupation almost gone. As Arthur Stanley said in 1915, there was 'practically no money for the encouragement side, which was after all the greater part of their work'. To make matters worse, 'the Club as a social institution, pure and simple, cannot hope for a continuance of the support which it has hitherto received'. Members stationed abroad or marooned in the country had little incentive to renew their subscriptions. For the first (but not the last) time the RAC's pride and joy, its clubhouse, threatened to become an insupportable burden. It now cost £35,000 a year to run and, in the words of an appeal which Orde sent to those who resigned during the early months of the war, 'any serious loss of income from members' subscriptions would tend to cripple' the Club. Orde, whose only son was killed after winning the DFC, presided over the staff at Pall Mall in what one valet called a 'masterly (I might say fatherly) way'. But, all too aware that the 'RAC is a commercial undertaking', the efficient Secretary knew how to make hard decisions.

First No. 83 Pall Mall, which the Club had purchased on an eighty-year lease in 1912 to provide larger offices for the Touring Department, was handed over to the British Red Cross – of which Arthur Stanley himself had also become chairman. Then the Club *Journal*, which had been run by Lord Montagu since 1911, was incorporated into his magazine *The Car*. Montagu had once asserted that the *Journal* was 'not necessarily dull because it is official' and then acknowledged that its dullness 'cannot be helped'. Yet amid a mountain of dross the *Journal* contains rich veins of interest as well as nuggets of pure gold. Altogether it is an invaluable chronicle of the heroic age of motoring and the pioneering days of the Club. Its demise as an independent entity leaves an aching gap in the historical record and was a serious loss to the RAC, which never again essayed such a weighty publication.

Finally, in November 1915, the Club held an Extraordinary General Meeting to endorse a revolutionary scheme devised by Orde and the Committee. In a bid to attract up to one hundred thousand full members (an astounding figure to aim at) it agreed to abolish the 25-guinea entrance fee and halve the ten-guinea annual subscription. Evidently, too, the Club lowered its social qualifications for admission. Wartime officers known as 'temporary gentlemen' were understandably welcomed. But the Committee also discussed 'whether a candidate whose name was over a shop should be elected' and agreed that 'each case of the kind must be considered on its merits'. By broadening its base the Club showed that 'it was not, as some of its critics have been so fond of alleging, steeped in sloth and luxury'. Stanley hoped that members would now regard the clubhouse not as an end in itself but as an 'incident merely in the great work that still remained for the Royal Automobile Club, as a society for encouragement, to perform'.

The RAC was generally congratulated for having tackled a problem that faced almost every London club during the war. But some of its own members opposed the 'sweeping change'. In a letter to the press, which was indiscreet even by his standards, S. F. Edge damned as 'ill-judged' the Club's announcement, 'Half-price sale now on!' The scheme would lead to overcrowding, he wrote, and impecunious new recruits would not help the dining room to pay.

RESCUING THE WOUNDED

*In a war which produced so many casualties needing urgent
treatment, motorised ambulances played a vital part. Among
their makers were Sunbeam (above) and Ford (below). The
RAC did much work for the Red Cross and set up an
ambulance repair shop at Boulogne.*

'I hate snobbery of all types,' Edge declared, 'especially pocket-snobbery.' But 'if the five guineas is a consideration, is the man concerned the sort of man for whom the Club, especially with the present clubhouse, was intended?' Acknowledging that the RAC, for which he felt 'a sort of reverence', '*must* be a commercial undertaking', Edge recommended that it should appeal to 'the trade'. Car manufacturers, now 'making a lot of money out of the war' by producing munitions, owed the RAC a 'debt of honour' which they would surely repay. Shocked fellow members considered that by publicly canvassing the Club's private affairs Edge had acted in the 'very worst taste'. They themselves were not anxious to see the Club deluged by 'an immense influx of new blood'. But this was infinitely preferable to Edge's ludicrous suggestion that the RAC should become 'a creature of the trade'. There had been suspicions enough about this in the past and the RAC could not sacrifice its impartiality by putting itself under the kind of obligation that Edge proposed. Moreover, the new strategy might work. And it did. Within eighteen months membership had nearly tripled, to reach 19,000, and the RAC's balance sheet was in a satisfactory condition. As one old member sagely remarked, it was 'better for a club to be rich and cosmopolitan than insolvent and exclusive'.

Apparently the success in Pall Mall cut no ice in Whitehall. In January 1917 Sir Alfred Mond, the Commissioner of Works (who later founded ICI), determined to commandeer the clubhouse under the Defence of the Realm Act (DORA) and turn it into government offices. There was a brief power struggle behind the scenes. Assisted by Orde, Stanley invoked the aid of influential members ranging from Mansfield Cumming to the Duke of Connaught, who apparently spoke to the King about the matter. Diplomacy was complemented by publicity. According to *The Autocar*, the Club had traditionally scorned self-advertisement: 'the premier body in the motoring world' was 'probably by far the least addicted to blowing its own trumpet'. This was because the 'wonders' it performed, especially during negotiations with the Chancellor over motor taxation, often had to be kept secret. Now the RAC reversed its policy of modesty, plying the press with information about its war work. The War Office, the Admiralty and other government departments had used its premises for various purposes day and night throughout the conflict. It housed many officers (twenty to thirty in the Turkish bath alone) and served 800 meals a day. The Club had 'practically become a Service Canteen and it might to-day well be described as a "Union Jack Club" for officers'.

Some newspapers accused Stanley of having 'lodged a selfish protest against handing over R.A.C. premises'. Stanley himself said that he was only trying to show that the clubhouse was more useful to the war effort *as* a clubhouse. This view prevailed. But a compromise was reached whereby, in March 1917, the Pall Mall palace became the headquarters of the Royal Overseas Officers' Club. This meant that a new Committee would be in charge, headed by General Sir Francis Lloyd. It involved changes such as the provision of more bedrooms and the covering of the swimming pool in order to convert it into a dormitory. In future, too, civilian members of the RAC not doing war work (only about an eighth of the total number) would be excluded from their own clubhouse. One suggested that alternative accommodation could be found for them by requisitioning the 'German embassy'. The RAC's motoring interests might now be, as Owen John pointed out, 'defunct'. But the Club was not, as others asserted,

MILITARY MOCK TUDOR

*This corrugated-iron assembly hall was
part of an encampment built in the grounds
of Woodcote Park for soldiers of the Public
Schools and Universities Corps. Many men
had their last taste of fun here before going
up the line to death.*

extinct. In fact, to quote the magisterial words of *The Autocar*: 'The Royal Automobile Club has no more ceased to exist than has the British Empire.'

This was partly because the new regime seems to have winked at the entry of all or most old RAC members. In due course the favoured status which they allegedly enjoyed provoked a public outcry. Walter Long, then Colonial Secretary, tried to stifle it. In a public letter to Sir Arthur Stanley (as he had become in October 1917) Long said that by giving 'splendid and lavish hospitality' to overseas officers the RAC had 'absolutely fulfilled the contract you entered into with the War Office in January 1917'. There was 'no foundation whatever' in charges levelled against the Club. But the popular press was determined to treat the issue as a 'scandal'. The *Evening News* said that the clubhouse would have made an 'ideal' government office but that Sir Alfred Mond had 'bolted at the first shot fired by "Lord Orde"'. Orde had smuggled back RAC members not carrying out tasks of national importance 'as soon as public indignation died down'. According to the *Evening Dispatch*, the RAC clubhouse was now nothing more than a 'heavily camouflaged resort'. Once again the Club had to defend itself. Stanley recited a further litany of the Club's wartime achievements, later printed as a pamphlet.

It was not an especially impressive catalogue but it was a surprisingly extensive one. At the outbreak of war RAC Tour Guides had helped to rescue stranded motorists on the Continent. The estate of Woodcote Park had been handed over as a training ground for the University and Public Schools Brigade, who built a hutted camp there – the War Office found the place so useful that they hung on to it until 1923. The Engineering Department was exceedingly active: it examined and valued second-hand chassis and lorries acquired by the Red Cross and the War Office; it designed motorised field kitchens capable of feeding up to 900 troops a day, of which fourteen were made; it constructed six motor field workshops; and it established a permanent plant for ambulance repair in Boulogne which quickly assumed 'a ship-shape and business-like appearance'. The RAC supervised further signposting at home, encouraged a 'Safety First' campaign, fostered road improvements and successfully urged the adoption of a system of standardised hand signals for drivers. It supported the Society for Checking Abuses of Public Advertising in its endeavour to rid roadsides of 'aggressive' billboards.

It did much other war work, such as sending ambulances to Russia and dispatching food and clothing to interned British chauffeurs. Between March 1917 and December 1918 the clubhouse provided 119,296 officers with bath, bed and breakfast at five shillings a head. They were also entertained by performers ranging from Glee Club singers and lantern lecturers to conjurors and Maori dancers. The Rifle Range was put at the disposal of the National Guard. The Great Gallery was lent out for free concerts, entertainments, Red Cross functions, even meetings of Sir Ernest Flower's Dumb Friends' League. During the war the members' owner-driver Volunteer Corps provided an average of thirty-five cars a day for the purpose of recruitment, medical aid, remount work, general inspection, women's welfare and so on. They travelled a total of thirty-seven million miles. RAC Driving Certificates 'assumed a national importance' as they provided a useful qualification to that vital new part of the labour force, women 'who desire to do the work of men'. The Club's examiners tested forty women a week in London alone. They found that some failed through 'sheer nervousness', though one young lady who crashed into the back of a cart during her test exclaimed: 'Now, wasn't that bad luck?'

PEACE AND VICTORY

*King George V and Queen Mary leave St Paul's on
Armistice Day, 1918. The patron of the RAC rides in a
horse-drawn carriage, which was now seen primarily as
a ceremonial rather than a practical vehicle, lending
dignity to royal processions and pageants. George's son,
Edward VIII, disappointed the crowds in 1936 by
driving to the State Opening of Parliament in a closed
Daimler instead of an open carriage.*

Female drivers also became victims of the aggression of male taxi-drivers who seemed 'dead nuts' on them. Other motorists, though, treated them with exaggerated courtesy. Montagu worried that they might come to 'rely upon the gallantry of the sterner sex, and take it for granted that they will receive a little more consideration than is their right'.

Because it had so many strings to its bow the RAC made a better showing during the war than the single-minded AA, which was 'dormant' for most of the time. The Club was therefore well placed to take advantage of a peace in which the productive and automotive advances achieved in the crucible of conflict would lead to mass motoring. As Owen John wrote in 1917, when the RAC rose from 'its tabbed and khaki ashes' after the war it might 'pick up the threads of its tango period' but it stood a good chance of becoming the 'centre of motordom'. This was a position of outstanding importance because 'motorists will not be looked on as freaks and rarities any more ... motoring is going to be "it"'. Postwar manufacturers would beat their iron tanks into char-à-bancs and their armoured cars into automobiles. Soldiers who had come into contact with the internal combustion engine for the first time would become chauffeurs and motor mechanics. Lloyd George would build a world fit for motorists to live in – with the help (if *The Car* had its way) of MPs specially elected to give 'intelligent representation' to the vital automobile interest. It would be a world in which more and more people could afford their own transport, and the vehicles of democracy would crush the standard-bearers of revolution. To quote Owen John again: every time workers saw a decent car they would not sing the 'Red Flag'. For they knew that 'the future of the world is going to be wrapped up in engines and machinery, and that by their aid humanity is going to secure the remedy that will heal all the damages of war'. The RAC, however, was looking less to the future than to the past. Soon after joyriders had celebrated victory in November 1918 aboard everything from Rolls-Royces to traction engines, Orde announced that the Club was turning its mind to 'the re-instatement as far as possible of pre-war conditions'. For the RAC itself, this was a sinister omen.

CARRIAGE TRADE

*Most pre-war Austins were high-quality
vehicles like this fifteen-horsepower,
four-cylinder town carriage, which cost
£495 in 1909. The driver sits over
the engine to give passengers room to
spread themselves.*

CHAPTER SEVEN

MOTORING FOR THE MILLION

*The growth of middle-class motoring changed the face of
Britain during the 1920s and '30s. Happy to salute a few
Rolls-Royces and Bentleys, the RAC now had to help regulate
a host of Austin Sevens and Morris Minors.
It achieved mixed results.*

STEPPING UP IN
THE WORLD

*During the 1920s
advertisers came to
realise that they could
use the glamorous
connotations of smart
cars to boost the prestige
of other goods on
the market.*

THE YEARS BETWEEN THE WARS were 'the golden age of motoring': cars, in vastly increased numbers, were being driven ever faster and further on open roads. But the Royal Automobile Club lost momentum, rested on its laurels, harked back to Edwardian glories. Even during celebrations held in 1922 to mark the Club's first quarter of a century there were signs that it could not keep up with the pace of change. An anguished debate took place over the question of whether members should wear white kid gloves in the presence of their chief guest, the Prince of Wales. It was decided that they should; but the future Duke of Windsor arrived to greet them bare-handed and hundreds of pristine gloves were hastily stuffed into pockets. At this anniversary occasion, Sir Arthur Stanley himself appeared almost bemused by the growth of the motoring movement. He exclaimed:

> Surely no movement has gone so far in such a short time! When
> one looks back on the old days to that extraordinarily
> uncomfortable vehicle, the hansom cab, and the old 'growler,' with
> straw on the floor for the feet when it was cold, and the omnibus
> with passengers perched on the knifeboard on top, it almost seems
> to me as if we were going back hundreds of years instead of only
> twenty-five.

Needless to say, the RAC had no wish to turn the clock back where technical matters were concerned. But the Club was hard put to adapt to its new social circumstances. After the war full members gradually ceased to be an embattled élite and became part of a mass (though still a minority) movement. The slogan 'Motoring for the million' was coined in 1919. It was then an aspiration, for there were only 100,000 cars on the road. Ten years later the hope became reality, and by 1939 two million Britons owned cars.

The man who sparked off this revolution was a bristling square-cut, bowler-hatted engineer well known in Pall Mall – he invariably arrived at the Club with so little cash in his pocket that the porter had to pay his taxi fare. Sir Herbert Austin, as he had now become, was a pioneer who had moved from making sheep-shearing equipment to motor manufacturing. In 1895 he built one of the earliest British cars – some say the first. Ten years later he established his own company, based at Longbridge near Birmingham. 'Pa' Austin, a nickname which acknowledged him to be 'the father of the British motor industry', took part in many of the Club's events. What he lacked in competitive skill he made up for in bloody-minded determination. Tough, frugal and self-reliant, qualities strengthened by his time in the Australian outback, he could 'swear for twenty minutes without once repeating himself'. Some members of the Club held him in low esteem. 'He *was* a navvy, of course,' wrote one. He was also 'a bit of a bully'. However, Austin possessed commercial vision to match his engineering facility, itself so remarkable that he could make sophisticated designs using a pencil in each hand simultaneously.

Like his great rival, William Morris (later Lord Nuffield), Austin learnt the lessons taught by Henry Ford. He saw that there was a huge market for a cheap, reliable, mass-produced family car. The hunger felt by less affluent people for personal powered transport was illustrated by the popularity of cycle-cars immediately after the war. One seller of them attributed his success to the enormous 'number of customers who have ordered two cars – one for each boot'. Some of these cars suggested even flimsier footwear than roller-skates: the Grahame-White Buckboard 'resembled a bedroom slipper on pram wheels'. Austin used similar terms to denigrate the manufacturers of motor-bike combinations: they were 'only a step above perambulator makers'. So in 1922, when he himself faced bankruptcy because the postwar boom had turned into a slump, Austin produced a motor car that would, he prophesied, 'knock the motor-cycle and sidecar into a cocked hat and far surpass it in comfort and passenger-carrying capacity'. The Austin Seven was born. When William Rootes, who held the important Austin agency in Maidstone, first saw the design he protested: 'My dear Sir, the public will just not stand for this.' Austin replied: 'My dear Sir, I am educating the public.' With this strange little car its creator hoped to realise his audacious ambition 'to motorise the masses'.

At first, as Rootes had feared, the Austin Seven excited ridicule. People called it a 'Chummy', a 'bath on wheels', or 'The Bed Pan'. One motoring journalist incensed 'Pa' by referring to it as a 'baby' car. It was, insisted Austin, 'A SMALL CAR'. In advertising parlance it became 'The Mighty Miniature'. This was the concept which stuck. When the initial mockery subsided the public saw the Austin for what it was – a sturdy, scaled-down version of a large car. Its components looked expensive. The first production model had a water-cooled, four-cylinder, seven-horsepower engine; three forward gears and one reverse; internal-expanding, cable-operated, four-wheel brakes; dynamo lighting and electric starting. According to optimistic claims the car's top speed was 50mph and it could cover that distance on a gallon of petrol, a rate of fuel consumption twice as good as that of the 'bullnose' Morris Cowley. The Austin Seven's total running costs were a penny-farthing a mile. In 1923 the car sold for £225, a price which fell by the end of the decade to £125 for the open tourer, £135 for the saloon. This

'PA' AUSTIN

*Herbert Austin, patriarch
of British motor
manufacturing, was as
formidable as he looked.
His savage temper and
Spartan habits were
legendary; but he could be
bearishly benign.*

AUSTIN MOTORS

*Before 1914 Austin
designed a seven-
horsepower car (above),
though it was built and
mainly sold by Swift. But
his breakthrough came in
1922, when he began
selling the Austin Seven
(left and below).*

The AUSTIN SEVEN

DIMENSIONS
Full car length · · · 9ft. 2in. (2,796 mm.)
Full car width · · · 3ft. 10in. (1,169 mm.)
Wheel base · · · 6ft. 3in. (1,905 mm.)
Track · · · 3ft. 4in. (1,016 mm.)
Road clearance · · · 8½in. (220 mm.)
Weight of touring car · · 8¼ cwt. (430 kilos.)
Height to top of screen · · 4ft. 9in. (1,450 mm.)
Height to top of hood when raised · 5ft. 4in. (1,625 mm.)

ENGINE—4-cylinder, water-cooled, detachable head; bore 2.2in. (56 mm.), stroke, 3in. (76 mm.) Total capacity, 747.5 c.c.
R.A.C. rating, 7.8; b.h.p. 10.5 at 2,400 r.p.m. The crankshaft has roller bearings. Aluminium pistons.
FUEL SUPPLY—By gravity from 4-gallon tank (18 litres).
IGNITION—By magneto.
COOLING—Radiator and fan.
LUBRICATION—Engine lubrication is by means of a gear pump. Chassis lubrication is by grease gun.

TRANSMISSION—Single-plate clutch. The ratios of engine to road wheels are—1st speed, 16 to 1; 2nd speed, 9 to 1; top, 4.9 to 1; reverse, 21 to 1. Gear changes are effected by a lever mounted centrally on the top of the box. Final drive is by helical bevel gear. The rear axle is of the three-quarter floating type, with differential and torque tube.
BRAKES—The pedal-operated brake acts on the drums of the rear wheels, and the hand lever applies brakes to the front wheels. The adjustment of both sets is extremely accessible and quickly carried out.
STEERING—Steering is of the worm and worm wheel type, with provision for taking up wear. Over the steering wheel are the throttle and ignition control levers.
SUSPENSION—Semi-elliptic cross spring in front : those at the rear are quarter elliptic. Shock absorbers, front and rear
TYRES—Tyres are 26x3in. Dunlop Cord Reinforced Balloon, and the wheels are of special wire type
EQUIPMENT—Electric starting and lighting, carburetter air strangler, spare wheel and tyre, electric horn, speedometer, blank number plates.

Chassis :
Price £112
Complete at Works.

The AUSTIN SEVEN "Easily the best small car in the world."

A Small Touring Car, to seat two adults and two to three children or a third adult, up to a total weight of 30-32 stone. Hood, screen and side curtains afford complete weather protection for all occupants. It has every quality demanded of a larger car, is thoroughly reliable, and will give continuous hard service. Typifies the most economical method of conveyance known Wonderful efficiency Perfect performance. Simple control.

Full equipment including electric starting and lighting, air strangler, electric horn, speedometer, automatic windscreen wiper, license holder, shock absorbers, spare wheel and tyre, and blank number plates. Triplex glass £4 0 0 extra

Price £145
Complete at Works.

'CHUMMIES'

*The 'Baby' Austin grows up (right). Thirty
years after the model was born, the A30 became
the first unitary-construction Austin. Although
the butt of many jokes, the 'chummy' was so
solid, well-equipped and cheap to run that it
became, in effect, the British 'People's Car'.*

brought it within range of the professional middle class, aided by hire purchase. Austin's midget proved to be a commercial giant. By 1938 350,000 people had purchased an Austin Seven. This 'brilliant idiosyncrasy' had become 'a landmark in the evolution of road transport'.

Even more remarkable were the aims and achievements of William Morris – autocrat, hypochondriac, munificent philanthropist and entrepreneur of genius. Like Austin, Morris rejected the old notion that cars were essentially custom-built luxury items for wealthy sportsmen. He believed in volume production. Not until Morris workers went to their Oxford factory by car, he said, would 'we have touched more than the fringe of the home market'. To this end he paid a 'moderately high wage'. And he met the postwar slump by lowering his prices and dramatically raising his sales. Whereas in 1919 two cars out of every five on British roads were Fords, Morris (assisted by a swingeing tariff) was turning out over forty per cent of the total by 1925. He had produced, one contemporary remarked, 'a Ford with an Oxford education'. Actually Morris could not match Austin, or even Ford, as an engineer, though he was outstanding as a businessman. He concentrated so ferociously on costs and sales that he once absent-mindedly put his suit on over his pyjamas and then complained about the heat in the factory. But he adopted 'mongrel designs'. And he relied heavily on parts bought from outside suppliers, which were assembled at Cowley – often with difficulty. Some of his pressed-steel car bodies leaked so badly that a factory wit suggested that they should advertise Morris as an all-weather car – 'it would let all the weather through'.

Where Morris did score, though, was in selling his cars complete with the modern fittings that became available between the wars. During the decade after 1924 he equipped his new models with brakes on all four wheels. These were such a novelty that they had to be used with 'great consideration' and some drivers put red triangles at their tail-end or notices saying, 'Danger. Four-wheel Brakes.' Bumpers, shock absorbers and Triplex safety glass were included as standard. So were electric headlights, which could be made to dip: thus the last oil lamps and acetylene flares were scrapped and the business of night driving was transformed. Similarly chromium plate and cellulose paint revolutionised the process of making cars gleam: previously it had been necessary to caress the top coat of craftsman-applied varnish with a 'chammy' (chamois) leather to prevent scratching, and to polish brass and nickel fitments for an hour a day to keep them shining. Automatic windscreen wipers and better side-curtains guarded automobiles against rain and snow. But open cars were now becoming less popular than saloons, nicknamed 'tin gin palaces'. This marked an important change, for by 1929 'practically every motorist' used his car all the year round instead of 'laying it up when the short dark days arrive' – a fact reflected in the RAC's making its winter and its summer service the same.

Morris also adopted the syncromesh, four-speed, twin-top gearbox, which lessened the old-fashioned wrenching, double-declutching and gnashing of teeth. Finally, low-pressure 'balloon' tyres toughened with cord-fabric were fitted, giving better grip and longer life. Such innovations were taken up piecemeal by rivals like Singer, Clyno, Swift, Humber and Standard. They made driving a car cheaper, simpler and more attractive to those who had never before aspired to one but were now prospering – paradoxically the affluent society began during the period usually associated with the Depression. Like many a conservative capitalist before him, Morris regarded the bourgeoisie as 'the backbone of the country'. 'From the first,' he said, 'I set out to

MORRIS MOTORS

William Morris (above), an abstemious bicycle-maker who became a bounteous automobile tycoon, was the most successful British pioneer of mass production. Cowley, though generally less advanced than American plants and still lacking a moving assembly line in 1929 (top left), became in 1939 the first British factory to produce a million cars.

MORRIS FOR THE MASSES?

Morris hoped that 'any steady-going working man in regular employment' would be able to buy a Cowley product like this 1939 eight-horsepower saloon (right). But it remained a bourgeois luxury until long after the Second World War.

cater for the "man-in-the-street" – the potentially large class of enthusi-astic but not too well-off owner-drivers – and aimed at producing a reliable, economical, easy-to-drive and look-after vehicle.' His family cars of eleven to sixteen horsepower dominated the market during the 1920s. Morris, above all, brought motoring to the middle class.

They took to it with unbridled enthusiasm. The car afforded not only mobility on a scale hitherto undreamt of, but the intrinsic thrill of *auto-mobility*. It represented an escape from, even a rebellion against, stiff Victorian conventions which had threatened to strangulate the white-collared segment of soci-ety. Sunday church-going was the first casualty of this vehicle of freedom. Instead of attending a place of worship, middle-class motorists drove into the country, visited the seaside, picnicked at beauty spots, or went off to play tennis or golf. Golf held a peculiar fascination for automo-bilists. 'It grows upon a man like collecting china or butterflies, but it is a mile and a half better than any indoor hobby like that, because it fetches a man out of himself.' Such, at any rate, was the RAC's view as recorded in Montagu's magazine *The Car*, which in 1922 changed its name to *Car and Golf*. Churchmen damned the new craze. Rural folk were inclined to see every-thing from the spread of disease to the ruin of rural shops, from soil infertility to a diminution of the duck population as 'a judgement of the Lord upon this generation for Sabbath-break-ing in motor cars'.

Motorists and golfers preferred clothes which assisted freedom of movement. So the strict dress code of former days began to relax, assisted by the advent of light new materials like rayon. Commenting on the 'sartorial revolution' fostered by the car, Owen John rejoiced at the way in which cumbersome, antediluvian garments had been discarded in favour of 'our gladdest of rags'. 'Summer motoring to-day conceals nothing, and, some say, almost inclines to reveal too much. Which is, of course, absurd.' Mrs Grundy did not consider it in the least bit absurd. Like Marie Corelli, she censured fast ladies of 'the new Motor-School of Morals'. She condemned cars as part of the decadent postwar culture typified by cocktails and cigarettes, lipstick and jazz. It was an import from the United States, the nation which had invented sin in a flivver. J. Edgar Hoover, head of the FBI, denounced cars as 'camouflaged brothels'. John Steinbeck declared, 'Most babies of the period were conceived in Model T Fords and not a few were born in them. The theory of the Anglo-Saxon home became so warped that it never quite recovered.' Everything seemed to point towards Aldous Huxley's *Brave New World* (1932), a mechanised civilisation where the godhead was Ford, to be invoked in litanies of sexual liberation. Ironically, Henry Ford employed inspectors to invigilate the private lives of his workers. But English puritans would doubtless have agreed with the American preacher who described automobiles, cinemas and dancehalls as the 'triumvirate of hell'. Even members of the RAC were doubtful about some of the new fashions. How could the short-skirted, Eton-cropped flapper sit for a hundred miles 'on the storm-tossed seat of her "boy"'s motor-cycle apparently enjoying the experience to the full, and still apply the word "gentler" to her sex?'

Lord Cottenham, who became something of an arbiter of automobilism during the inter-war years, spoke for Club members who felt ambivalent about the spread of motoring to the

THE CAR OF SUPERB REFINEMENT

THE characteristics of Humber cars have always been individual, something different—something superior. Not only in dominating road performance but in appearance, utility of equipment provided and in super-finish of coachwork. Will you accept a copy of our descriptive Catalogue?

Three Models: 8/18 h.p., 12/25 h.p. and 15/40 h.p.

Eleven different types of bodywork.

Prices from £240 to £845

Dunlop tyres to all models.

CARS

HUMBER LTD., COVENTRY

LONDON:

City Showrooms · · · · · 32, Holborn Viaduct, E.C.1
West End Showrooms & Export Branch Office 94, New Bond St., W.1
Repair Works and Service Depot Canterbury Rd., Kilburn, N.W.6

DEALERS EVERYWHERE

middle class. He celebrated the triumph of the internal combustion engine and the way it brought 'fresh air, better holidays, and greater enjoyment to millions'. But he lamented the vulgarisation of what had been an exclusive pleasure. Bright Young Things in MG Midgets were all very well, but they would say 'sports' cars instead of 'sporting' cars – an ill-bred term similar to 'gent's natty sports suitings'. Those who sold Bentleys might still be public school men, but Morris and Austin salesmen often paraded themselves with an 'exaggerated waist, yellow cardigan, violet shirt, and patent leather shoes'. Lord Cottenham conducted a relentless campaign of elementary motoring education in the *Daily Express*. Evidently his *noblesse* obliged him to give a lead at a time when even the automobile aristocracy was being diluted.

> Where the Rolls Royce, the Daimler or the Sunbeam in days gone by might have been occupied by those to whom the well-being of their tenants and their servants was as important as the upbringing of their children, to-day those cars are occupied far too often by the war profiteer or the nouveau riche, to whom, after the manner of their kind, the maintenance of their 'dignity' and the satisfying of their appetites alike are gods.

Like those who glamorised the expensive car as a marque of gentility, such as the novelists Dornford Yates and Michael Arlen, Cottenham was indulging in snobbish nostalgia for a mythical Edwardian Elysium. On the other hand, the sheer number of new motorists did present serious problems.

Since the only qualification for getting behind a wheel was to have reached the age of seventeen, competent drivers were scarce. In the words of one journal, 'Thousands of new motorists have no idea of "road sense"; the consequence is that, unwittingly, they are a source of danger to themselves and others.' Voluntary Safety First campaigns were no substitute for compulsory driving tests, particularly when the former were undermined by eminent figures like Lord Baden-Powell. He denounced 'Safety First' as a mollycoddling American slogan and urged his followers to live dangerously. It was 'British', he said, to step off the kerb without looking and die asserting that 'the road belongs to foot-sloggers'.

Erratic behaviour was not confined to foot-sloggers. The writer Ursula Bloom bought a decrepit Lagonda in 1922 and drove it 'without ever using the gears, because I had no idea where they were'. Sir George Sitwell designed his own limousine, incorporating a second-hand lorry engine into a vast structure which enabled him to lie down by the side of the driver. Having twice landed his car in a neighbour's pond, Siegfried Sassoon was confronted by a sign saying, 'THIS POND IS PRIVATE.' When V. S. Pritchett's Christian Scientist father acquired his first car, in the early 1920s, he relied for guidance on the Divine Mind. Unfortunately, as Pritchett junior wrote, 'the Divine Mind was the most dangerous driver I have ever known. It hit banks, tore off the sides of hedges, chased pedestrians, scattered people about to get on buses.' Error also kept creeping in to J. B. Priestley's conduct of cars. He found driving 'too easy to demand concentration' but 'too difficult to be safe'. The climax of his driving career occurred when he crashed into a lamppost in Newport, Monmouthshire, and was menaced by an angry crowd. Thereafter he hired chauffeur-driven Daimlers.

BRITAIN'S CHANGING FACE

*Rural pubs, like Ye Olde Windsor Castle at Little Bookham, Surrey,
pictured above in 1922, started to cater for motorists. During the period
immediately after the First World War the building of metalled roads
lagged behind the growth in motorised traffic. As a result, it was not as easy
as it would be in a few years' time to reach country pubs and restaurants
eager to welcome the motorist. In provincial towns such as Farnham,
pictured below in 1924, motor vehicles began to fill the streets and to
obscure the lower part of buildings.*

That option was denied to most middle-class motorists, whose misdemeanours attracted the attention of the police. Having set up the Flying Squad to deal with serious motorised crime in 1921, they also resumed speed trapping. Because the limit was still set at an unrealistically low 20mph, they came into conflict with an ever-growing section of the community. An anonymous member of the RAC retaliated with this parodic 'Ode to a Policeman':

> A greasy pocket-book beneath the bough,
> A punctured tyre, a motor-trap, and thou,
> Beside me, taking down my evidence!
> Ah! Surely you have evidence enow!

CHAPTER OF ACCIDENTS

As more cars travelled faster, traffic accidents grew in frequency and seriousness. They reached a peak in 1934, when driving tests, a 30mph speed limit and other safety measures were introduced.

There was evidence in plenty about the tragic death toll on the roads: 120,000 people were killed between 1918 and 1939. But contemporaries still could not agree about the cause of this slaughter. The RAC's Safe Driving Committee (formed in 1925) made extensive recommendations, including 'wider roads, better surfaced, reduced gradients, ample warning signs and the abolition of dangerous blind corners'. But the Club also took refuge in euphemisms. In 1927 the RAC asked the Home Secretary to insist on the official use of the words 'traffic accidents' instead of 'motor accidents'. More mealy-mouthed still, the AA preferred to speak of 'road incidents'. Whatever the terms used, the authorities were influenced by the growing strength of middle-class motordom. Relatively fewer people were charged with traffic offences and magistrates became noticeably more lenient. Satirising the trend, A. P. Herbert said that soon, when the remains of a mangled pedestrian were found in the road, the automatic verdict of a coroner's court would be 'death by natural causes'. Plainly, though, the spread of automobilism was in itself a danger. The press printed many attacks on 'The Deadly Motor Car'. Prompted by a double misprint, *The Times* dubbed drivers 'motorious carbarians'.

The carbarians were at the gate. There was no ignoring them. The clatter of petrol engines was heard throughout the land. Morris Cowleys droned over smooth, dark highways, carrying commuters between cities and suburbs. Austin Sevens hummed like gnats along narrow country lanes, once known only to horses and carts. Motor-bikes, never more popular than in the 1920s, when they tripled in number to reach nearly a quarter of a million, roared up airy mountains and down rushy glens. Caravans, so much the rage that the RAC set up a separate department to deal with them in 1925, lurched to distant seashores. Char-à-bancs rumbled into remote villages, sometimes taking the inhabitants out of their own district for the first time and, as Laurie Lee said, 'rattling away to the ends of the earth'.

There was much to be said for all this. The motor-bus was a means of deliverance for those hitherto confined by a life sentence of rustication. It did more towards the disappearance of the village idiot, Aldous Huxley memorably and tendentiously remarked, than all the lectures on eugenics. Its arrival told the rural poor that 'motors wouldn't always be for the rich'. Indeed, as J. B. Priestley said, this 'voluptuous' vehicle 'annihilated the old distinction between rich and poor travellers' by offering luxury to all. Complementing the wireless, the motor bus brought national newspapers to the most isolated districts on the day of publication. All told, the

internal combustion engine had a profound impact on prevailing standards of fashion, speech and thought. It transported the city to the country and vice versa. It finally snapped the fetters of locality. It helped to transform Britain from a congeries of regions into a united kingdom.

However, even long-standing champions of mechanical propulsion were inclined to lament (paraphrasing Dr Johnson) not so much that old England was lost as that the motorised millions had found it. By sheer numbers they threatened to destroy the unique heritage of the past, like mass tourists following in the footsteps of Grand Tourists. Take the Cornish hamlet of Morwenstow, for example, so remote in space that its celebrated Victorian vicar, Robert Stephen Hawker, reckoned it was 250 years behind his own times. He also said that a parishioner who had journeyed to a distant market town was rendered 'an oracle among his fellows'. For Edwardian members of the RAC visiting the West Country, Morwenstow was 'a Mecca'. It was, as one wrote, 'a shrine of romance' to be reached by twentieth-century pilgrims 'in luxurious cars instead of painfully afoot'. They were few. But during the decade after the war char-à-bancs brought trippers in droves to admire Hawker's rocky coast and, Montagu complained, they were 'low-bred enough to disfigure the countryside'.

Lord Cottenham resented motor coaches not only because they competed with motor cars but because they represented the obstruction of the élite by the mass.

> One can weary very soon of the back view of the 'Southern Belle', the 'Sunshine Seeker', or the 'Silver Queen' behind which one is temporarily eclipsed. Often but for the noise and smell, I would have tarried to ask the driver how long he had owned the Hastings road.

As early as June 1919 the RAC (which had just initiated a coach service between Pall Mall and Woodcote Park) expressed concern over the 'inconvenience caused by motor chara-à-bancs'. Doubtless many members sympathised with the efforts of refined resorts like Frinton to ban them, along with motor-bikes, from their smarter purlieus.

BY THE MID-1920S old stalwarts of the Club such as Claude Johnson found Britain's roads 'too crowded for pleasure-motoring'. Jaded journalists like Owen John agreed: it was years since he had 'gone out for a "joy-ride"'. Others were less blasé. In the words of a '20s Bentley driver, 'romance still lingered in the world of motor-cars; the roads were not yet overcrowded, and a week-end run to the coast never terminated in an endless queue headed towards London'. Cars were rare enough in the countryside, even as late as the 1930s, for drivers to cut corners on the wrong side of the road. Yet there were also traffic jams, especially during Bank Holidays or at race meetings. Cities grew ever more congested, though England was in a far better state than America where, it was said, 'automobiles are gnawing like termites at the bases of our skyscrapers'. As early as 1919 the Metropolitan Police found car parking a serious problem. Directing vehicles at busy junctions became increasingly difficult: in 1925 the city of Lincoln employed five RAC Guides to assist police with traffic regulation. In 1927 Wolverhampton and Leeds introduced automatic traffic lights. Other provincial towns followed suit and London, worse affected but slower off the mark, soon imitated their example. Further means were

HORSELESS CARAVANS

Early car-drawn caravans, like this one dating from 1924, were modelled on those of gypsies. They were too cumbersome for easy towing, but they did enable motorists to sample the wandering life and to experience (and erode) rustic seclusion.

RECRUITING DRIVE

Motorised escape from the city took many forms. Here a hundred women are setting off in char-à bancs from London's East End in 1925 to be entertained by the Marchioness of Salisbury at Hatfield House. The outing was part of a Tory campaign to fight Communism in the capital.

also employed to ease the flow: one-way streets, roundabouts, traffic islands, white lines. They only made room for more small cars.

These even started to go abroad, intruding on Europe's most fashionable preserves. 'There are so many Rolls down here,' Northcliffe told Johnson in one of his last letters, 'that some wag suggests that the place should be called not Monte Carlo, but "Monte Rolls"'. But in 1926, with the help of the RAC, Sammy Davis, racing driver and *Autocar* motoring correspondent, took an Austin Seven to the south of France. The patent slings for lifting the car aboard the ferry were too large and had to be adjusted. The owners of Delages, Hispanos and Rolls laughed at the Austin, a 'minnow among the tritons'. But it kept up a 'quite surprising average speed' and demonstrated the 'vast possibilities' of the vehicle. Others like it followed. Their inexperienced drivers often asked RAC Guides such questions as, 'What is foreign petrol like?' Once across the Channel they sometimes caused accidents by 'forgetting or not being aware that in France they must drive on the right'. Most novices quickly mastered a convention which enabled them to share the lyrical experience of the rich – soaring down the long, straight roads of France to the Riviera. The new motorists helped to turn it from a winter into a summer resort.

They also made an indelible mark on the face of Britain. Spending on roads increased from £26.4 million in 1920 to £65.6 million in 1938. These sums were inadequate to the nation's needs and they were certainly nothing like enough to satisfy the RAC. But they did pay for general road improvements (such as the use of bitumen instead of tar) as well as major new highways and bypasses, especially during the 1930s. The consequence was ribbon development, building along the margins of roads. Verges, hedges and trees were obliterated under bunga-lows, 'semis' and detached dwellings, to say nothing of roadhouses, factories and Woolworths. Larger residences were increasingly advertised as 'car villas' – they included garages or space for them. Since automobiles were now domesticated, some garages were decked out in Mock Tudor or even thatch. Others were integrated into dwellings, occupying part of the ground floor. Where the street had been an extension of the home during the Edwardian period, the home was now becoming an extension of the street. Unlike America, Britain eschewed drive-in banks, cinemas and churches. However, the Act of 1935 which attempted to restrain 'ribbon development' was ineffective. Suburbia grew so fast during the 'devil's decade' that people feared London would come to resemble Los Angeles, but without its multi-lane carriageways.

The RAC denounced ribbon development not only as an 'evil' in itself but because it prevented the widening of main arteries like London's North Circular Road. Ironically, the con-straint on widening was increased by the spread of kerbside petrol pumps, which the motoring organisations vied with each other to encourage. The first one had been established in 1913 and by 1929 there were 28,000. They were testimony to the fact that automobiles no longer required mechanical attention every time they took in fuel. As a motoring journal said:

> Quietly and almost unnoticed, a revolution has been wrought in recent years. We now have, in fact, cars that will run for 20,000 or 30,000 miles without need of adjustment, and it is because of this that the idea of the Filling Station is so growing in popularity.

In 1923 (after some hesitation) the RAC formulated a scheme for appointing petrol pumping stations throughout the country, whose accuracy of measurement, fairness of pricing and

TRAFFIC JAMS, 1928

Road works cause congestion in the Strand (above). The
Boscombe promenade (below) is crowded with motorised
holiday-makers and rally competitors. Usually delays were
slight but the 1928 Derby attracted 40,000 automobiles,
many of which were stuck for hours. Traffic lights soon helped
to relieve police and RAC men from arduous point duties.

purity of spirit it would ensure. Soon afterwards the Club complained to *The Times* about wayside petroleum billboards and the 'disfiguring signs erected by the AA'.

Tension between the two motoring organisations was all the more acute between the wars because several attempts to amalgamate them were frustrated. During the war itself they had been severely criticised for wasting resources by duplicating one another's efforts. It was, wrote Massac Buist, 'nothing less than a scandal'. At a conference held in June 1918 to devise 'a working arrangement' between the RAC and the AA, their respective chairmen actually agreed with Buist. Stanley said that the war had demonstrated the 'disadvantages of overlapping'. Joynson-Hicks deplored the fact that they had previously behaved as 'opposed institutions'. It was 'ridiculous that the two bodies should have rival signs on the roads, and rival signs on hotels, and rival touring sections', not to mention rival handbooks. Joynson-Hicks acknowledged that the Club was the 'premier organisation' and proposed that it should continue with its social, technical and sporting functions while the AA concentrated on 'outside work'. The idea was that there should be division of labour 'without loss of dignity'.

In subsequent discussions, however, the RAC insisted on the 'fundamental point' that the new body should be called the 'Royal Automobile Club Association'. Furthermore, its Chairman and a majority of Committee members should come from Pall Mall. This, Joynson-Hicks objected, 'would mean the swallowing of the AA by the RAC'. He had a point. But the RAC felt that it must have full control as it 'could not risk another Motor Union dispute'. Motoring journalists urged that nothing should stand in the way of 'amalgamation'. Foch had proved that 'unity is strength', wrote one, whereas the motoring organisations had separately shown 'an utter failure to make their weight felt'. But although negotiations dragged on into 1919 nothing came of them except mistrust and a degree of bitterness. In that year Stenson Cooke told the annual general meeting of the AA, 'we are out to fight the RAC, in a perfectly friendly way'.

Nevertheless, there was some co-operation between the competitors during the tube and rail strikes of 1919. Together they organised parties of private motorists to take workers home, helped with milk and mail deliveries and showed (in the opinion of the press) that motor transport was not just 'an auxiliary to the railways' but was 'essential to the very existence of the State'. The new minister of transport, Sir Eric Geddes, was widely supposed to be a 'railway maniac', a suspicion which also drew the champions of the motorist together. But in general the AA under Stenson Cooke was politically too 'extreme and unrealistic' to be a congenial ally for the RAC. The Club formed an independent parliamentary committee which included Stanley, Montagu, Jeffreys, Moore-Brabazon and Manville. This group pursued a policy of studious moderation. Although it lobbied for a petrol tax in 1920, it accepted vehicle duties as being in the national interest. Cooke, by contrast, mounted an unscrupulous campaign for a levy on fuel, designed to make commercial vehicle users subsidise private motorists. The campaign backfired, exposing the narrow partisanship of the AA. But the strategy had a populist appeal to new car owners who felt embattled and persecuted.

Certainly the AA grew much faster than the RAC between the wars. This was chiefly because it concentrated on the provision of road patrols. By contrast, motorists complained for several years after 1918 about the 'entire lack of service from the RAC patrols'. They were seen 'very rarely indeed' as compared with the 'dozens' of busy AA Scouts. At first the RAC Guides

BUILT-UP BRITAIN

Ribbon development along main roads, such as the Sidcup bypass (right), increased between the wars and more semi-detached houses were built with garages or car spaces. But many people condemned the urban sprawl.

THE PARTING OF THE WAYS

In Morden (right) pioneering efforts were made to segregate pedestrians, bicyclists and motorised transport. New arteries, such as the Kingston bypass (below), were opened to keep traffic flowing. Dual carriageways separated vehicles travelling in opposite directions.

were employed for weekends only; then just during the summer months. In effect the Club, which was in two minds about mass motoring, did not focus its attention properly on the needs of its Associate members. A more immediate cause of its failure was Sir Julian Orde's long illness. He received a knighthood in 1919. But it was Sir William Joynson-Hicks (actually a fussy, prissy solicitor-cum-politician aptly nicknamed 'Jix') who was hailed as 'the Alpha and Omega of motor matters and the Generalissimo of all motoring progress'. Not until Orde resigned from the Secretaryship in 1923 (amid tributes to his 'great personality') were the RAC Guides organised into an efficient, full-time force. But even by 1925 this only numbered 500 officers and men, about a quarter of the AA's strength. Moreover, Cooke was quicker to equip his Scouts with motor-cycles and sidecars. He also put up more roadside telephone boxes – 637 by 1938, compared with 550 RAC boxes (some designed by Edwin Lutyens) ten years later.

Because the RAC had comparatively few patrols, it harped on their quality. AA Scouts were still the 'Yellow Peril' whereas its own Guides were made of such sterling stuff that if their blood was spilled it ran RAC blue. The Club publicised stories about Guides who stopped bolting donkeys and runaway carriages, extricated motorists from accidents and resuscitated them with first aid, returned tools to car owners who had scattered them over miles of road, performed automotive miracles with matchsticks and shoelaces. When the lady whom one Guide had rescued in difficult circumstances said that 'he must be one of the very best men the RAC had on the road,' he replied with a bow: 'Madam, on the contrary, I am the worst!' She promptly allowed herself to be signed up as an Associate member.

Such anecdotes may be taken with a pinch of salt. The Guides were haphazard in their methods. Earning a basic wage of only forty-five shillings a week (the same as AA Scouts), they could hardly be an élite force. However, there were genuine cases of heroism: in April 1936 Guide Hayward died of injuries sustained when he tried to save the life of a child at Elveden crossroads in Suffolk. The Guides worked incredibly long hours: from 9 a.m. until 8 p.m in summer (dusk in winter), getting a single weekday off each week and an annual seven-day holiday which had to be taken during the winter. Moreover, the RAC's 'Get-You-Home Scheme' remained more effective than any service which the AA had to offer. Claims on it increased from 1,350 in 1919 to 10,000 in 1928, nearly half of them due to failures in the power units of cars. More telling still, Stenson Cooke did his best to denigrate the scheme. He was successful to this extent: by 1938 the AA had 700,000 members; the RAC, despite a lower subscription which was cut still further during the Depression, had fewer than 250,000 Associates.

In spite of the rivalry, and indeed because of it, each organisation was under pressure to amalgamate; for both were burdened by the cost of duplicated services. In 1923 Charles Jarrott, still a member of the RAC though he had just taken over the chairmanship of the AA from Jix, made a serious effort to unite the two bodies. This found favour in Pall Mall. Some members did worry that the RAC's 'financial resources might be seriously embarrassed' by any loss in foreign customs triptyche deposits: these amounted to £49,000 in 1923, though soon afterwards the cash deposit system was abolished. But the Club reckoned to save £3,400 a year by a merger because it was giving such a heavy subsidy to the Associate Department, which already had an overdraft of £17,800. However, the usual difficulties arose and Stenson Cooke proved so obstructive that Jarrott resigned in disgust. Yet again, though, the two bodies were

FILL HER UP

Pumping petrol could still be a part-time job: Mrs Weaver (right), hostess of the 'King William' in Tunley, was equally adept at pulling pints. But petrol stations developed rapidly after 1918 and during the 1930s many installed automatic pumps.

able to collaborate over matters which they thought 'detrimental to motoring interests'. Indeed, under its new Secretary, Commander Francis Armstrong RNVR, OBE, the RAC endorsed policies advocated by the AA such as a tax on fuel and abolition of the speed limit. But, like Cooke, Armstrong resisted this and later pressure to amalgamate, arguing that rivalry was a 'spur to efficiency' and that monopoly could 'bring in its train great evils'.

Armstrong had wide experience of the motoring world. The son of the proprietor of the *Globe* and founder of the Sunday *People*, he had written much about cars in the press. Armstrong had first become a member of the RAC's Committee in 1904 and afterwards served the Club in many other capacities. But he seems to have acquired his basic instincts at Charterhouse, where he was captain of football, and in the RNVR, where he was a martinet. Tough but unimaginative, efficient but unenterprising, he ran the RAC for nearly two decades as 'a very tight ship indeed'. So punctually did his big Armstrong Siddeley, distinguished by its full member's badge on the roof above the windscreen, make the journey between Pall Mall and his house in Lymington each weekend that RAC Guides could set their watches by it – and woe betide the patrolman who gave it a sloppy salute. Armstrong, whose chiselled features matched the razor-sharp creases in his trousers, imposed strict discipline on the Guides. He reinforced a quasi-military culture with its rituals and its ranks – Guide, Inspector, Superintendent. This culture was already strong because of the preponderance of ex-servicemen recruited and trained by the RAC, and it lasted until the 1980s.

Guides who smoked on duty or were 'flighty' with girls were liable to instant dismissal. Failure to enrol one new member a week during the summer months was punishable by suspension. Spit and polish was the order of the day, especially when patrolmen were equipped with gleaming Norton motor-bike combinations during the 1930s. Typically, Armstrong used aerial photographs to ensure that Guides organised the car parking with martial precision at Ascot, Goodwood, Aldershot and other big events – a significant (though loss-making) part of their work between the wars. Any irregularity in the neat lines of vehicles, which were mustered in a herring-bone pattern by means of long rolls of brown marking tape, provoked a Secretarial reprimand. Stanley, who had been more than a figurehead under the 'tactful and autocratic rule' of Orde, became a mere 'honorary boss' during the stern dictatorship of Armstrong. Club staff treated him as 'a deity'. Young members found him 'rather frightening'. The Committee's laconic minutes increasingly noted that matters had been 'left to Commander Armstrong'.

The first serious matter he had to face was the General Strike. About this he agreed wholeheartedly with Stenson Cooke and Joynson-Hicks: it was part of a 'Bolshevik conspiracy'. Actually the General Strike, which began on 3 May 1926, was not an incipient revolution but an industrial dispute which got out of hand. However, since all transport workers withdrew their labour the strike could have created, as *The Autocar* said, a 'paralysis of activity utterly disastrous to every branch and section of the people'. Motor vehicles could prevent this paralysis and the government had laid its plans accordingly. The Ministry of Transport had called in Armstrong the previous October and asked him to arrange for a large force of volunteer drivers to assist in any emergency. Their duties would be to keep ministers, MPs and top officials mobile.

Armstrong launched a recruitment drive which elicited an 'excellent response'. More than 2,000 motorists and 600 motor-cyclists 'enrolled' for duty. Armstrong also registered, trained

MOTOR ORGANISATION

The 'Premier Automobile Association in the World' began to advance from pedal power in 1922, when a few patrolmen got two-stroke Ivy motor-bikes (above). During the 1930s more were equipped with Norton combinations (below). Though a disciplined force, Road Guides generally worked alone and learnt to use their initiative.

and deployed another '2,000 volunteer lorry drivers' – 'scabs' in trade union parlance. And he stocked up with coal to keep the Club boilers burning. On the eve of the strike the Secretary received a message from the Ministry of Transport asking the RAC to deliver requests to hundreds of voluntary workers that night to operate the power stations if the men there walked out. He agreed, despite the short notice, and passed the word around neighbouring clubs. He also proposed 'to send notice to the theatre queues urging owners to bring their cars' to Pall Mall as 'a matter of vital urgency'. The second expedient proved unnecessary. By midnight Clubland had provided 180 cars, many of them parking in Carlton House Terrace, and 'the necessary dispatches were delivered'.

On the first morning of the strike, according to Winston Churchill's emergency propaganda sheet *The British Gazette*, motor vehicles rode to the nation's rescue: 'squeezed into cars, standing in vans, riding pillion, pedalling on cycles, swarming Citywards by every road and route, London came … doggedly and cheerfully to work'. Despite the congestion, RAC drivers helped to keep the wheels of government turning. Their operations were co-ordinated from an office set up in the Strangers' Room in the clubhouse, which 'became in effect a Department of the Ministry of Transport'. At first one of its officials worked in harness with Armstrong but 'dual control' proved unsatisfactory and soon the Secretary was in sole command. He dispatched Club members to act as chauffeurs to senior figures in Westminster, Whitehall, Scotland Yard, the Port of London Authority, the London County Council, the Air Ministry, the railway companies and so on. When it rained these important passengers were provided with black waterproofs bearing the letters RAC, 'a somewhat unusual advertisement for the Club'. Drivers arriving back at Pall Mall late at night were given sustenance and 'shake-downs' in an atmosphere of 'heroic improvisation'.

Throughout the provinces the RAC made similar efforts, most dramatically after the wreck of the Scottish express, when its 'emergency service was able to provide a fleet of cars' to take 400 passengers to Newcastle. Armstrong detailed his Guides everywhere to assist the police with their duties. The co-operation continued after the strike: the RAC later had a company in the motor section of the London Police Reserve, which held 'mufti parade[s] with cars'. An immediate result of the accord was that main roads became racetracks. As a smiling Lord Howe, racing ace and RAC loyalist, told one of the many drivers who helped to distribute *The British Gazette*: 'There's no speed limit, and the police are out to help.' A few motorists sympathised with the strike, but even they were not always able to assist: it took the virgin driver W. H. Auden seven days to conduct a car from Old Marston to Oxford, a distance of two miles. But the vast majority of motorists, many of them women who 'acquitted themselves like men', supported the government. When it won, generous plaudits were bestowed on those whose work had been 'an epic of devoted service to the state'. The RAC received official thanks from the Minister of Transport, which added to its dignity and associated it even more intimately with the Establishment. Wags might call the Club 'the Chauffeur's Arms'. But, wrote Owen John despairingly, 'One might as well try to annoy the Dean of St. Paul's by stroking the dome of the Cathedral the wrong way as make fun of the RAC nowadays.'

Car owners wanted a more practical show of appreciation from the state. The Ministry of Transport acknowledged that 'the motoring community saved the situation and the country is

DRIVING THROUGH THE STRIKE

Motorists, like their organisations, backed the government during the 1926 General Strike. But they jammed roads into London by driving to work. Still, at a time when public transport was paralysed, private cars gave some mobility. They also demonstrated, as The Autocar *said, 'the paramount importance of road transport to the whole community'.*

SHOW OF STRENGTH

Volunteer bus drivers were sometimes attacked and they got police protection (right), but it was probably unnecessary to escort supply convoys (like the one above in Hyde Park) with armoured cars. Foreign observers were 'amazed by the general peacefulness' and the future Lord Brabazon praised the 'public-school spirit' of the strikers.

left in their debt for the wonderful work they performed'. But, motorists asked, would the government 'discharge this debt'? The answer was no. Winston Churchill, Chancellor of the Exchequer, determined to continue with his policy of raiding the Road Fund for purposes of general taxation. Motorists, he maintained, were a privileged class who had 'the great good fortune to rush about the country'. Doubtless his mind was filled with notions of wealthy Edwardian scorchers recalled from his days in the RAC – he had resigned in 1921 amid a wrangle over whether his subscription was due, eventually scrawling in red pencil on Orde's dunning letter the angry instruction to his secretary: 'All right, pay.' Anyway, motorists made to pay denounced Churchill's fiscal measure as the 'most audacious' larceny since the imposition of Ship Money. To the horror of some members of the RAC and most members of the AA, Sir Arthur Stanley supported Churchill, arguing that parliament could not for ever be bound by Lloyd George's pledge to devote to roads all revenue raised from motorists. However, many in Pall Mall endorsed Stanley's view that it was the duty of responsible organisations to help the Chancellor balance the nation's budget. Stanley told the Minister of Transport, 'The bombshell thrown by Winston has fluttered the motoring dovecots, but unfortunately the doves are all rather inclined to fly in opposite directions, and if we don't take care the doves will end by looking like asses.' To avoid this eventuality, the RAC pressed Churchill to reduce the basic horsepower tax after the General Strike. But the Chancellor did not give even meagre concessions until a general election loomed. That was in 1929 when, he hoped, motorists would forget that they were motorists and remember that they were Conservatives.

Whatever way they voted, power fell into the hands of a minority Labour government, which proved surprisingly – and unfortunately – willing to listen to the motoring organisations. Herbert Morrison, the Minister of Transport, not only consulted them but went so far as to attack 'reckless walkers'. In 1930 he passed a Road Traffic Act which abolished the obsolete speed limit of 20mph. Morrison justified this measure by saying that MPs could not 'enforce the law which they themselves had no intention of observing'. However, he failed to impose a new speed restriction though he did lay down heavier penalties for dangerous driving. Here he was following the conventional wisdom of the experts, the RAC, the AA, the police and even road safety organisations. The Club actually declared that speed was 'pure good', because it got drivers out of trouble. Morrison also avoided bringing in driving tests, an issue on which the RAC had dithered before concluding (with the AA) that they had 'no utility'. Morrison did, though, introduce compulsory third-party insurance, which the Club opposed on the ground that solvent motorists should not have to subsidise insolvent ones.

As the road accident rate rose after 1930 (reaching a peak of 7,343 deaths in 1934, a figure not exceeded for thirty years), Armstrong and Mervyn O'Gorman persuaded the National Safety Congress that the shocking statistics merely reflected 'increased activity in obtaining records'. The national government did not share that opinion and in 1934 it passed a new Road Traffic Act imposing a driving test and a speed limit of 30mph in built-up areas. The motoring organisations gained a concession, later revoked, that the limit should not apply between midnight and 5 a.m. The Act also introduced pedestrian crossings, then marked with white or yellow herring-bone lines and amber globes on posts known, after the Minister of Transport, as Belisha beacons. The crossings, modelled on those in France, were among the

SERVICE WITH A SALUTE

The RAC issued much in the way of publicity material, but the reality was not always as encouraging as the advertisements. Patrolmen found stranded motorists less by science than by serendipity. Their work often brought them into conflict with what one called 'spivs and undesirables'. Even their telephone boxes were violated; and one American tourist thought they were 'cute little toilets'. However, RAC men worked hard and did much to earn public trust – even affection. The Club rightly believed that 'the service of touring Guides on the road is the best form of propaganda'.

Club's more enlightened recommendations, as was standardised signposting, to which the government paid some heed. But in general its views were partial and blinkered. Accordingly the motoring pundits of Pall Mall were much criticised during the 1930s, though the criticisms were by no means always consistent. Law reformers like Lord Cecil of Chelwood accused the RAC (and the AA) of being prepared to sacrifice road safety in the interests of the trade. Car drivers expressed indignation that the Club had accepted with 'complacency ... successive restrictions imposed on motor users'. Caught in the crossfire, the RAC was further castigated by its own members. On the Committee E. C. Gordon England, the glider pilot who became a racing driver and a talented design engineer, mounted a general assault: the Club had 'done little' to promote 'constructive legislation'. Other members made similar protests outside the confines of the Club.

In 1935 *The Motor* printed a hostile letter whose signatories were the cream of the motoring aristocracy. They included racing drivers such as Charles Jarrott, John Cobb, Woolf Barnato, J. W. Benjafield, Raymond Mays and Archie Frazer-Nash as well as authentic peers like Lord Garvagh (formerly the Hon. Leopold Canning), the Earl of March (later the Duke of Richmond and Gordon) and Lord Cottenham. They stated that the RAC was so lethargic and unimaginative that it had failed to pursue 'any single constructive policy continuously' since the war. They further declared that no improvement was possible 'under the existing constitution of the Club'. This charge stung because of the recent cancellation of a meeting of the Club's only remotely democratic forum, the General Council. Associates and members of affiliated clubs were represented on this body, but Armstrong had brusquely informed them that 'there were no matters of importance to bring forward'. Stanley said weakly that the Club's 'efficient and hard-worked' committees were doing much and that its only fault was in not giving their achievements more publicity. The campaign on behalf of Associates 'who are deliberately kept voiceless' continued. One protester wrote, 'It seems incredible that members who provide an income of about a quarter of a million a year should be given no opportunity to express their views or even to hear how the money is spent.'

The fact was that the Club was becoming a gerontocracy. It is true that in the decade after the war many of its outstanding senior members had died: Sir Boverton Redwood in 1919, Lord Northcliffe and Sir Alfred Bird in 1922, Captain Sir Mansfield Cumming in 1923, Sir David Salomons in 1925, Claude Johnson and Roger Wallace in 1926, Frank Butler in 1928, Worby Beaumont and Lord Montagu in 1929. But many other pioneers survived to form an oligarchy of the old. As *The Motor* pointed out in March 1935, the RAC's Committee included one man of eighty-nine, two of seventy-nine, two of seventy-six, six more over seventy and a large majority who were well over sixty. Some of these were able, distinguished, even brilliant men: F. R. Simms, Sir Arthur Stanley, E. Shrapnell-Smith, Rees Jeffreys, Sir Herbert Austin, Mervyn O'Gorman, A. F. Mulliner, Frank Lanchester, Sir A. L. Guinness and K. L. Guinness. But at this stage in their lives they could not infuse the Club, as Lord Cottenham wanted, with 'a more youthful and energetic spirit'.

Indeed, they were apt to focus on parish pump. They were easily distracted by such questions as whether to readmit the swindler Clarence Hatry to membership after he had paid his debt to society or whether to expel a member who had threatened to horsewhip one of the

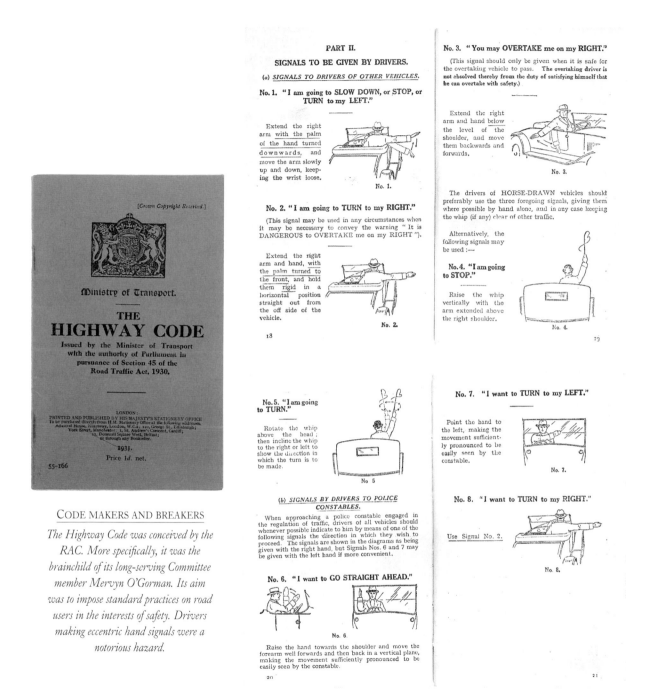

[Crown Copyright Reserved.]

Ministry of Transport.

THE
HIGHWAY CODE

Issued by the Minister of Transport
with the authority of Parliament in
pursuance of Section 45 of the
Road Traffic Act, 1930.

LONDON:
PRINTED AND PUBLISHED BY HIS MAJESTY'S STATIONERY OFFICE
To be purchased directly from H.M. Stationery Office at the following addresses:
Adastral House, Kingsway, London, W.C.2; 120, George St., Edinburgh;
York Street, Manchester; 1, St. Andrew's Crescent, Cardiff;
15, Donegall Square West, Belfast;
or through any Bookseller.

1931.

Price 1*d.* net.

55-166

CODE MAKERS AND BREAKERS

The Highway Code was conceived by the RAC. More specifically, it was the brainchild of its long-serving Committee member Mervyn O'Gorman. Its aim was to impose standard practices on road users in the interests of safety. Drivers making eccentric hand signals were a notorious hazard.

PART II.

SIGNALS TO BE GIVEN BY DRIVERS.

(a) *SIGNALS TO DRIVERS OF OTHER VEHICLES.*

No. 1. "I am going to SLOW DOWN, or STOP, or TURN to my LEFT."

Extend the right arm with the palm of the hand turned downwards, and move the arm slowly up and down, keeping the wrist loose.

No. 1.

No. 2. "I am going to TURN to my RIGHT."

(This signal may be used in any circumstances when it may be necessary to convey the warning "It is DANGEROUS to OVERTAKE me on my RIGHT").

Extend the right arm and hand, with the palm turned to the front, and hold them rigid in a horizontal position straight out from the off side of the vehicle.

No. 2.

18

No. 5. "I am going to TURN."

Rotate the whip above the head; then incline the whip to the right or left to show the direction in which the turn is to be made.

No. 5

(b) *SIGNALS BY DRIVERS TO POLICE CONSTABLES.*

When approaching a police constable engaged in the regulation of traffic, drivers of all vehicles should whenever possible indicate to him by means of one of the following signals the direction in which they wish to proceed. The signals are shown in the diagrams as being given with the right hand, but Signals Nos. 6 and 7 may be given with the left hand if more convenient.

No. 6. "I want to GO STRAIGHT AHEAD."

No. 6.

Raise the hand towards the shoulder and move the forearm well forwards and then back in a vertical plane, making the movement sufficiently pronounced to be easily seen by the constable.

20

No. 3. "You may OVERTAKE me on my RIGHT."

(This signal should only be given when it is safe for the overtaking vehicle to pass. The overtaking driver is not absolved thereby from the duty of satisfying himself that he can overtake with safety.)

Extend the right arm and hand below the level of the shoulder, and move them backwards and forwards.

No. 3.

The drivers of HORSE-DRAWN vehicles should preferably use the three foregoing signals, giving them where possible by hand alone, and in any case keeping the whip (if any) clear of other traffic.

Alternatively, the following signals may be used:—

No. 4. "I am going to STOP."

Raise the whip vertically with the arm extended above the right shoulder.

No. 4.

19

No. 7. "I want to TURN to my LEFT."

Point the hand to the left, making the movement sufficiently pronounced to be easily seen by the constable.

No. 7.

No. 8. "I want to TURN to my RIGHT."

Use Signal No. 2.

No. 8.

21

waiters for serving coffee too slowly. Hearing in 1939 that Pall Mall was 'seething with rumours' not about motor taxes or even about the imminence of war but about a 'wrangle over the card room', journalists asked: 'Is everything all right with our august leading motoring body?' It was scant comfort that the AA was in a worse state. Sir Stenson Cooke (as he became in 1933, to his immense glee) was increasingly eccentric, alcoholic and autocratic. He boasted that he *was* the Committee of the AA and installed loudspeakers at its headquarters so that he could give the staff ten-minute 'pep talks' once or twice a week. In these circumstances Armstrong was hardly well advised to insist that, despite the healthy competition between the two motoring organisations, there was essentially '*no difference between us whatever*'.

The RAC was not helped by Stanley's resignation as a result of ill-health in 1936. He was warmly thanked for the 'immeasurable services' he had rendered 'to automobilism'. But his successor was a lacklustre figure called Lieutenant-Colonel James Sealy-Clarke, who only got the chairmanship because Lord Lloyd refused it. Sealy-Clarke's sole qualification for the post was long service and general benevolence. He knew personally every member of the clubhouse staff, in many cases by their Christian names. But though he showed himself to be utterly indifferent to the bombs during the war he otherwise made little positive impression. Moreover he was ultimately responsible for an RAC version of the government's appeasement policy.

Admittedly, until the spring of 1939 most motorists (and most citizens) tended to hope and think that Neville Chamberlain's 'gamp was mightier than the sword'. Furthermore, they admired Hitler's autobahns. Having sent delegates on an official visit to study the German road network in 1937, the RAC itself recommended the construction of a British 'system of motorways'. It would provide work and reduce accidents, while making room for an anticipated doubling of motor traffic within the next fifteen years. This was a positive conclusion at a time when the AA opposed such a scheme on grounds of cost. However the RAC knew, not least from the reports of Mervyn O'Gorman at the Paris Touring Congress, that the 'tied' automobile clubs of Germany and Italy were mere instruments of totalitarianism. It had also received protests about the exclusion of Jews from organisations like the Tyrol Automobile Club, expressing its 'sympathy' but regretting that it could 'take no action'. So its bestowal of an honorary membership on Dr Fritz Todt, the German minister in charge of roads, was a craven gesture. Lord Howe's advice to the brilliant English racing driver Richard Seaman – that he should carry on as a member of the Mercedes team despite politics - proved to be tragic as well as misguided. In June 1939 Seaman was killed during the Belgian Grand Prix: Hitler sent a wreath to his funeral and the RAC wrote the Führer a letter of thanks. Worse still was the RAC *Handbook*'s geographical concession: it described Austria and later the Sudetenland as 'provinces of Greater Germany'.

Nevertheless, despite the Club's shortcomings, there were bright spots in its record. The Foreign Relations department maintained close contact with developments abroad. Its leading light was Mervyn O'Gorman. He wanted Britain to adopt what was good from Europe, including a 'grammar of road signalling' as recommended by the League of Nations. But, as usual wry and irrepressible, he resisted 'the unnecessary Frenchification of sporting terms

in English-speaking countries' and ignored the abuse of Gallic newspapers – 'let *sleeping liars lie*'. O'Gorman's comments on the undesirability of importing the French system of *priorité à droite* (which the AA favoured) were characteristically trenchant:

it is worth mentioning the absurdity which will develop whenever four law-abiding drivers reach four crossroads at about the same time. All must stop, and none can ever proceed except backwards, since each has a car on his right, to which he insists on giving precedence, thus recalling the oft-repeated situation when an unbalanced politeness prevents certain continental gentlemen from getting through a Committee Room door without argumentation. In the case of the four motorists, if all have a sound sense of humour they may *all* proceed and *all* collide.

O'Gorman spoke French with equal fluency and acerbity. He gave the RAC an influential voice at the Association Internationale des Automobiles Clubs Reconnus (AIACR) at a difficult time.

At home, when local clubs became moribund, the RAC often arranged to convert them into district offices of its national organisation. Ten such were established by 1928, many with reading rooms and other facilities for Associate members. In London the Legal and Engineering Departments were busier than ever. The Technical Committee continued to carry out a useful programme of tests and trials, while refusing to countenance those set up by rivals who challenged the Club's position as the 'governing body of the automobile movement'. At the request of the Ministry of Transport, it gave counsel on everything from headlights to hand signals. By awarding driving certificates from 1935, RAC examiners raised the standards of instruction in officially appointed schools. The Touring Department grew to six times its pre-war size by the mid-1920s and provided members with 'wonderful service', including more than twenty million miles of routes a year.

The RAC also did 'wonders' in examining and appointing reliable garages and hotels, such as those in the new 'Coventry Knight on the Road' chain, which were specially built for motorists. But Associate members still had many complaints. This was partly because trustworthy inspectors, often the targets of bribes and threats, were hard to find. Also, British standards were low. The RAC inspectors exposed many disobliging, dirty and dishonest establishments, some of them run by hoteliers who make Basil Fawlty seem like César Ritz. In the summer of 1933, for example, the proprietor of the Beach Hotel, Teignmouth, became 'mad drunk, caused a disgraceful and disgusting scene, and the police had to be called'. The local RAC manager confirmed that, although this was 'not a common occurrence, it is likely to happen at any time' and the hotel's appointment was cancelled.

The RAC kept an equally firm grip on motor sport. Its authoritarian tone was set only a few months after the war's end, when it declared that 'no entry of enemy-made motor vehicles shall be accepted … for competition' under RAC or associated club rules. The edict was later annulled, but it indicated the scope of the RAC's arbitration. In fact only two British manufacturers made a real mark on the sport during this vintage era of motor-racing, Bentley and Sunbeam, both dogged by cash problems. Each distinguished itself in the first Tourist Trophy Race which the RAC held after the war. It took place on the Isle of Man in 1922, over roads which the Club had treated with calcium chloride to lay dust. Instead the rain poured down,

TRAVEL DOSSIER

Since its foundation in 1903, the RAC's Touring Department had done much to simplify bureaucratic procedures for motorists going abroad. But it still had to undertake a vast amount of paperwork to enable W. E. C. Watkinson to tour the Continent in 1933.

the roads became shallow rivers and the chemical, splashing into drivers' eyes, caused agony. They scarcely paused. The Sunbeams screamed through the murk like black wraiths. The Bentleys stormed along like battleships. A Sunbeam, driven by Jean Chassagne, won. But Bentley, the only firm to field modified touring cars as opposed to frank racing cars, gained a team prize hastily improvised by Orde. H. O. D. Segrave's Sunbeam did the fastest lap of the day over a course which he considered the most interesting in Europe and second only to the Sicilian Targa Florio in severity. Despite his stinging eyes, he paid tribute to 'the splendid work which is done by the Royal Automobile Club'. In foresight, fairness, concern for safety and general expertise, it was 'a pattern to all other motor racing bodies'.

The Bentley enterprise was given a much-needed boost by its success in the TT race. It had been started three years earlier, at a time when, according to its founder W. O. Bentley, trying to construct a new car without substantial capital was like attempting to build a house on a desert island with a penknife. But W. O. – 'short, stocky, dark, inclining towards ocular fierceness, deliberate, monosyllabic and decidedly dour' – proved equal to the task. When his prototype burst into life, complaints from a nearby nursing home provoked the immortal comment: 'A happy sound to die to – the exhaust roar of the first 3 Litre Bentley engine!' This was certainly the view of the 'Bentley Boys', enthusiasts such as Woolf Barnato, Sir Henry 'Tim' Birkin, Jack Barclay, Glenn Kidston and George Duller, who raced the cars 'for glory'. At full throttle they felt an irresistible urge 'to break into some wild war song' and they were quite capable of throwing old spark plugs or even potatoes at slowcoaches who would not let them overtake. Barnato once raced (and comfortably beat) the Blue Train from the Riviera, earning himself a sharp rebuke from the RAC, which outlawed such private competitions.

Some of the most glamorous figures ever to haunt Pall Mall, the Bentley Boys lived at an equally cracking pace. Their cars were dreams of extravagance. Jack Barclay's Rolls-Royce Wraith (JB1) included a cocktail cabinet, a walnut backgammon board, a smoker's companion in the armrest full of Havana cigars, and American novelties such as a glass roof, a heater and a demister. The Bentley Boys' social doings filled the gossip columns. At one of Barnato's parties the waiters wore racing kit complete with crash helmets and the table décor was a miniature Brooklands. A note pinned to the menu advised guests: 'Before parking his or her chassis, each driver should ensure that his or her carburettor is flooded with at least two cocktails.' Needless to say, there were many Bentley Girls. In 1931 some of them took part in a women's car race at Brooklands organised by Barbara Cartland (who herself did not know how to reverse) and gave a display of dangerous driving which horrified spectators.

Barnato was notorious for being one of the richest and stingiest members of the Club. He was particularly mean with his 'gaspers' and one Bentley Boy claimed to bear scars on his knuckles from the flange of Barnato's gold cigarette case. Yet Barnato paid tens of thousands of pounds to keep the Bentley business afloat until 1930. The cars were not suited to the Tourist Trophy Race as run on the Newtownards circuit – the RAC moved it there in 1928 to help the economy of Northern Ireland. The race, which took place on a 13.6-mile, kite-shaped course full of challenging bends and gradients, favoured small cars because of the complex system of handicapping. As the Duke of Richmond and Gordon suggested, W. O. Bentley, whose vehicles grew steadily bigger, might have learnt lessons from the TT competition about 'the

THE BENTLEY BOYS

W. O. Bentley (below) did well in the 1922 TT, despite grazing 'all four hubcaps simultaneously' on the Isle of Man's dry-stone walls. Newtownards (centre) was even less suited to Tim Birkin's super-charged Bentley. But Le Mans (bottom) saw the triumph of 6½-litre Bentleys, the victors in 1930 being Barnato and Kidston.

THRILLS AND SPILLS

Eager to witness the excitement, spectators packed every vantage point around the TT circuit in Northern Ireland. They were seldom disappointed by drivers such as R. F. Oats (top left) and Malcolm Campbell (above), who is trying to put out a fire which has engulfed his Bugatti in the pits.

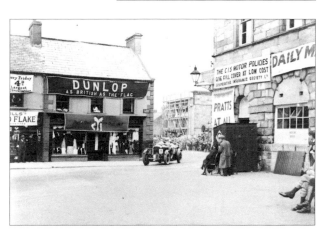

up-and-coming efficiency of smaller cars'. More pointedly, Ettore Bugatti was supposed to have said that Bentleys were 'the fastest motor lorries in the world'. Still, during the late 1920s, these magnificent machines completely dominated the gruelling Le Mans twenty-four-hour race. Mervyn O'Gorman called it a thrilling 'test of courage, skill, nerves, eye-sight, endurance, good engineering and scientific progress'. No car caught the imagination of the time more dramatically than the Bentley, the motor of Lord Peter Wimsey. No car more vividly embodies the spirit of the 'roaring twenties'. The marque was revered, even after its unhappy takeover by Rolls-Royce. When, at the outbreak of war, the new 4¼-litre 'Corniche' model was destroyed by a German bomb while coming back from a test run on the Continent, its key was salvaged and returned in 1945 by 'the faithful R.A.C. Port Representative at Dieppe'.

Sir Henry Segrave (as he became in 1929) was even more of a social idol and an ornament to the Club than were the Bentley Boys. A clean-cut Old Etonian, a tight-lipped war hero whose wounded left foot was held together with silver plates, a well-groomed amateur who eclipsed professionals, he seemed to embody the best of British characteristics. Yet, ironically, the Sunbeam cars on which he rode to fame were 'Fiats in British Racing Green'. To be sure, the beautifully engineered, streamlined and (from 1923) supercharged cars from Italy were 'models for nearly every notable Grand Prix car of the next forty years'. But the Sunbeam in which Segrave became the first British driver to win a Grand Prix, at Tours in 1923, was a virtual copy, apparently based on a full set of blueprints brought to England by a Fiat design engineer. Despite this victory and other good showings, the cost of racing impelled Sunbeam to seek publicity by breaking speed records. Thus in 1927 Segrave piloted the so-called 'thousand-horsepower' Sunbeam at just over 203mph at Daytona Beach in Florida. Thanks to bureaucratic perseverance by the RAC, the world record was officially accepted. Segrave was hailed as the 'fastest man on earth'. Three years later, after having broken the land speed record again in the stupendous *Golden Arrow*, he was killed on Lake Windermere while in pursuit of the water speed record. The Segrave Trophy, awarded in his memory to those with the 'Spirit of Adventure' to promote mechanical progress, has been won by other swift and celebrated members of the Club including Sir Malcolm Campbell, John Cobb and Stirling Moss.

The RAC could not by itself transform a British culture in which engineering was regarded as 'socially quite unacceptable ... little better than casual labouring'. Nor were all its motor sporting ventures between the wars a success. Brooklands' dullness as a venue for Grand Prix racing, as organised by the Club in 1926 and 1927, was exposed by the excitement of Monza, the new Italian circuit. MGs and Rileys kept the Union Jack flying, but the TT races at Ards did not so much foster British industry as enable foreign cars to shine, especially Alfa-Romeos and Mercedes-Benz. The titans of the track also proved to be foreign, notably Tazio Nuvolari and Rudolf Caracciola. Moreover, the 1936 race ended in tragedy, when six spectators were killed in a crash. W. O. Bentley thought it a miracle that such a disaster had not happened before in view of the 'hair-raising positions' taken up by onlookers. But after offering compensation and fighting a long legal battle, the RAC was vindicated in its conduct of the race. The TT competition was moved to Donington Park in Derbyshire, where it was held without accident. So, in general, were the myriad other events put on under the RAC's auspices, sprints, hill-climbs and local club contests, as well as the revived 'Old Crocks' Race' to Brighton.

THE LURE OF SPEED

Sir Henry Segrave, the preux chevalier *of motor sport, had an unquenchable zest for* celerity. *But even he was impressed by the Sunbeam below, actually driven by two 420-horsepower aero engines. Segrave thought he would not be bored during his 1927 attempt on the land speed record. The Segrave Trophy (right) commemorates his intrepid spirit.*

Most successful of all, when the government imposed a 'moral ban' on Monte Carlo Rallying because of the financial crisis, was the Club's domestic rally. Proposed by *The Autocar*, approved by Armstrong and masterminded by A. W. Phillips M.C., later general manager of the Associate section, this 'jolly all-British affair' began in 1932. It was essentially a test of reliability and it attracted 341 entrants, many of them Club members. All were dressed smartly in suits, though one or two ladies flouted convention by wearing trousers. Starting at different points, the competitors drove a thousand miles without serious mishap. The Countess of Drogheda, though, had placed her rally plate over her radiator grille with the result that the water inside boiled continually and she had to be rescued by an RAC Guide. The drivers finished at Torquay (other seaside resorts being chosen for later rallies) where tests were held on the promenade to determine the winners. The most unusual one was to see how *slowly* a car could travel. The overall victor Colonel A. H. Loughborough triumphed when his Lanchester, assisted by a 'fluid flywheel', maintained a snail's pace of 0.66mph.

The RAC examiners had to keep their wits about them: one back-seat passenger was found to be controlling the progress of his automobile with his feet, which protruded through a trapdoor in the floor. Other wiles were employed during the *concours d'élégance*. Some drivers got 'their girl-friends to sit on the bonnet and hoist their skirts above the knee'. The presiding judge was a dynamic but puritanical Scottish accountant called J. Duncan Ferguson, who would later become (in the opinion of some members) 'the evil genius of the RAC'. Against the names of those who had tried to make him stray from the path of virtue Ferguson wrote a note to deduct marks. It consisted of three letters, ASA, which stood for 'Anti-Sex Appeal'. This sedate 'gymkhana type of test' was remote from the fast and furious professional competition into which the RAC Rally later evolved. Yet before the war, by its very gentleness and gentility, the event contributed to the prestige of both the car and the Club.

Like the British motor industry itself, the RAC – with Commander Armstrong in the driving seat – survived and even thrived, despite the Depression. Of course, there were casualties among car firms and half of the fifty makes existing in 1930 had disappeared by 1935, including such famous names as Clyno, Invicta, Star, Swift and Trojan. There were also casualties among motoring organisations: in 1933 the Luxembourg Club went bankrupt after its secretary defaulted and committed suicide. Just after midnight on 1 August 1934, the RAC itself suffered a calamity: Woodcote Park caught fire, probably as the result of an electrical fault. The alarm was raised and everyone was safely evacuated, but a strong south-west wind fanned the blaze. 'It quickly became a raging storm which could be seen for miles around,' recalled Frank Bradley, one of the porters. The fire brigade drew water from the new swimming pool and the lake. Little could be salvaged, though the local police rescued the contents of the bar and disappeared into the rhododendrons. With a crash the upstairs floors fell into the cellars, 'leaving only gaunt walls eerily illuminated from within'. 'The ash covered what were then the squash courts from roof to ground, so completely that it could have been sprayed on by hand,' said Bradley, 'and the ruins smouldered for a week.'

Yet the setback proved temporary. When the Club wanted to raise £44,000 from debentures to help with the rebuilding, members offered to subscribe £250,000. Within two years Woodcote Park had risen like a 'phoenix' from the ashes. At its reopening dinner Stanley

MONTE OR BUST

Monte Carlo was the Queen of Rallies. With its international entry, far-flung starting-points and severe Alpine stages, it attracted drivers who were keen to test their skills and cars to the limit. But when the pound was devalued in 1931 and foreign jaunts became taboo, loyal Britons stayed at home.

1937

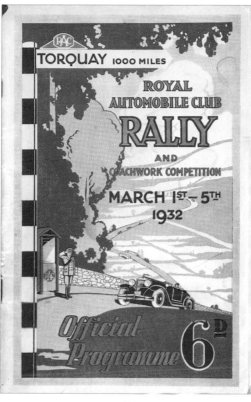

1932

1993

1989

RALLY ROUND BRITAIN

Appealing to patriotism, the RAC invited drivers to take part in its first Rally, in 1932, with the slogan: 'Enter the Rally and See Britain.' Down the years the event became ever more demanding. Today it is not so much a tour as a tour de force.

1956

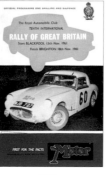

1961

1973

1982

reminded members that they had originally purchased Woodcote without having the money to pay for it, the Club's financial policy being at that time 'a blend of ignorance and impertinence'. However, the policy had worked. They were now secure in their wonderful 'new home' thanks to the 'nice fire'. Ironically, Woodcote Park regularly lost some £13,000 a year before the war, a deficit which the Club had to make good.

Like the cars produced by the Big Six motor companies, Morris, Austin, Ford, Rootes, Standard and Vauxhall, which developed more curved and raked lines during the 1930s, the RAC also made efforts to streamline itself. In 1937 it planned a pension scheme for the Road Guides, now numbering 800, some of whom were disaffected enough to have talked to their AA counterparts about joining a trade union. The clubhouse kitchens were modernised at a cost of £21,000, thus improving the monotonous but 'really good nursery food' served in the members' dining room and the already 'excellent cuisine' provided by the restaurant. The RAC's recommendations became more realistic. In 1938 it proposed that underground car parks, which could double as 'bomb-proof shelters', should be built beneath London squares. The Club campaigned for cycleways as well as motorways. It also wanted synchronised traffic lights, more roundabouts and a bridge over the Severn estuary.

Protected by tariffs and favoured by a degree of imperial preference during the 1930s, British manufacturers found a ready market at home and abroad for their low-cost, high-performance cars, despite their technological backwardness. The United Kingdom became the world's second largest producer and exporter of automobiles after the United States, which made fifteen times as many as Britain with only twice the workforce. The RAC was also wedded to old fashions, but it was sustained by wealth, tradition, *esprit de corps* and royal patronage. By the 1930s it had probably become the world's most respected automobile club. Its delegates were greeted with particular warmth at an AIACR conference held in America in the summer of 1939. Franklin D. Roosevelt's words of welcome were effusive. He praised 'the cultural and recreational values of automobile travel,' which answered an urge 'as old as mankind itself'. 'Travel contributes conspicuously to the stimulation of the spirit of understanding and good will among the peoples of the world,' he concluded, 'and it is my sincere hope that your work at this conference will further the promotion of the international friendship which we all so ardently desire.' The President's hope was to be swiftly disappointed.

FIRE ENGINE
*Like Ford's Tin Lizzie, the Morris Minor
was a maid of all work. Here a £125,
847cc two-seater speeds firemen to a blaze.*

CHAPTER EIGHT

AUSTERITY MOTORING

*As Britons fought to win the war against Hitler, civilian
motoring ground to a halt. And it only picked up slowly as they
struggled not to lose the subsequent peace. But from the blackout
to the dawn of affluence the RAC maintained its
'esprit de Club'.*

BEFORE AUGUST 1914 Britons had thought that a European war was
inevitable but impossible; before September 1939 they considered a further
conflict incredible but inescapable. Of course, right up to the last moment
'wishful thinking was rife'. Even so, when Hitler occupied Prague in
March 1939, motorists, like other citizens, concluded that he was bent on
war. Before then, broadly speaking, they had favoured appeasement. In
February, for example, the motoring press was filled with pictures of the
Führer opening the German Motor Show amid 'magnificent pageantry'
and taking a 'considerable interest in British cars'. Hitler recalled, incidentally, that his first personal vehicle, which he had used when organising
the Nazi party, was an Austin Seven – it was built under licence in Germany,
becoming the first BMW car. At the same time Lord Austin himself (as Sir
Herbert had become) was dismissing war scares as 'bogies'. But after the
invasion of Czech territory to which it had no conceivable claim, the Third
Reich became an object of odium and fear. Its clanking bureaucracy was
derided: one English motorist gave publicity to a notice displayed in a
German customs shed which prohibited the import of 'seditious, obscene
or pornographic material … except in quantities necessary to the journey'. The sinister implications of autobahns were now anxiously discussed: they 'revolutionised ideas on the speed of
military convoys'. It seemed clear that these great roads were leading to 'the first almost entirely mechanised conflict in history'.

Actually the horse still had its champions and it was to play a significant part in the
transport of both the British and the German armies. In the 1930s British cavalrymen had continued to resist 'those petrol things': tanks. One progressive Colonel, 'Chink' Dorman-Smith,

satirised this attitude by circulating a design for a new tank with a special attachment at the rear for releasing horse manure. This amiable fantasy was trumped by another cavalry officer who was so keen to maintain his regiment's 'equine standards of dash and glory' that he installed a saddle in place of a seat inside his tank even though it meant that his head permanently protruded from the turret. When war broke out the British army was not fully motorised and even where Artillery regiments had got self-propelled guns they retained 'elaborate procedures' for controlling non-existent horses, which slowed their rate of fire. It was only with North American help that the deficiencies in automotive equipment were remedied. At Anzio in 1944, for example, the Allies had 18,000 vehicles for 70,000 men. Churchill remarked dismissively, 'We seem to have a great superiority of chauffeurs.' But this was a war won by engines and, for all his much-vaunted tactic of Blitzkrieg, Hitler's armies were more of a 'military anachronism' than a 'mechanised juggernaut'. When he invaded Russia in 1941, he fielded 3,350 tanks and 650,000 horses – over four times as many as Napoleon had in 1812.

To return, though, to the summer of 1939 in Britain: here the chief threat seemed to be posed by Hitler's other mechanised force, the Luftwaffe. Most people believed that, in Baldwin's famous words, the bomber would always get through. It was expected to wreak havoc and bloodshed on an apocalyptic scale. Many feared that the first raid would result in a panic-stricken flight from cities, with refugees being systematically machine-gunned from the air as they got stuck in traffic jams. The authorities instituted elaborate air-raid precautions. Everyone became acquainted with shelters, searchlights, sandbags, gas masks, evacuation exercises, strips of sticky paper across windows, silver barrage balloons in the sky and the ominous blackout on the ground. Nevertheless, a curious air of unreality prevailed. As Ursula Bloom wrote in August, 'it did not seem feasible that there could be a war when everybody was going about their daily tasks in the ordinary way'.

Pall Mall was typical. Clubmen sauntered about and traffic flowed at its usual pace. Not all of it was generated by members of the RAC for, as those characteristic contemporary humorists Fougasse and McCullough pointed out, there was now

> in Great Britain one car to every 33 persons – that is to say, one to drive it, two to give advice from the back seat, one to oil and grease thoroughly and remove all tools, three to step in front of it and one to visit them and eat their grapes, one to devise means for speeding it up and four to devise means for slowing it down, one to draw pictures in the dust on the back, one to keep on taking it in part exchange, two to salute at crossroads, fifteen to lean their bicycles against it at traffic stops, and one to fail to understand what's come over everybody nowadays.

Yet order reigned around the temple of motordom, where, according to time-honoured custom, RAC Guides directed the parking of members' cars. Inside the clubhouse business (and pleasure) went on as usual. The head porter, a flamboyant Irishman called John Quinn, ran everything with brio and panache. Magnificently smart, he seemed to 'exude authority' and it sometimes seemed that 'he owned the place'. He reputedly knew all the members' names and, standing by the front door to greet those coming in for lunch, he resembled an archbishop welcoming a congregation at a cathedral before morning service. Under Quinn's eye the page

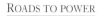

ROADS TO POWER

*Hitler opens the autobahn
between Frankfurt and
Darmstadt in 1935. He adored
these motorways, frankly
admitting that they were
instruments of dictatorship –
'All strategic roads were built by
tyrants.' But he also valued
them for reducing unemployment
and augmenting Germany's
economic strength.*

boys quailed, though they were not above furtively pinching one another as they sat, clad in RAC livery and pillbox hats, on a bench at the top of the hall stairs. The customs of the Club had hardly changed since Edwardian days. Committees deliberated upstairs while downstairs sportsmen exercised. In the little bar known as 'The Seaside' members drank the very best bitter. In the Great Gallery uniformed waiters served tea from silver teapots and dispensed cucumber sandwiches from silver trays to the strains of a string quartet playing 'Palm Court' music. Meanwhile small boys, perhaps brought in for a swim or a treat, gorged on chocolate éclairs and squirmed in creaky wickerwork chairs which left patterns on the backs of their bare legs. Their discomfort was often compounded by the Club barber, who, having given them the obligatory 'short back and sides', plastered down their hair with a 'concoction called something like "RAC Honey and Flowers", which had a strong smell and a "Grip-fix" like quality'.

Ladies too were inclined to be ill at ease in the clubhouse. They were bustled into 'that awful waiting room as soon as they put a foot inside the door'. Members' wives could order tea on their own but could not pay for it unless they had been issued with a voucher. Some doubtless observed the notice which read: 'Members are requested not to bring undesirable women into the Club unless they be wives or relatives of members.' But the misogynists were not alone in demanding what they took to be propriety. When a male guest suggested that he should fetch his host from his bedroom, the head porter replied crushingly: 'We do not allow gentlemen in other gentlemen's rooms in this Club, Sir.' In short, the Club exuded old-fashioned fustiness. This was precisely the quality that appealed to dyed-in-the-wool members, some of whom had themselves become living traditions. John Lewis, for example, puffing at his cigar and wearing his bowler hat, was a permanent fixture in front of the Smoking Room fire. Equally ubiquitous was a member called Wyatt, who spent his days telephoning his bookmaker and 'when his horse lost … would smack the face of the bust at the entrance to the main lounge'. At a time of impending cataclysm, the RAC seemed immutable.

It was therefore in some ways less well prepared for the expected war of 1939 than for the surprise conflict of 1914. True, many immediate matters had by now become almost routine. After war was declared on 3 September the RAC helped to rescue motorists stranded on the Continent. Also well practised was the slimming down of staff and the letting out of superfluous office space for war work. Most Road Guides had already enlisted in the Royal Air Force Volunteer Reserve and only about a hundred key men were kept. Enemy aliens were again expelled from the Club, while over five thousand serving officers at the War Office, the Admiralty and the Air Ministry became temporary honorary members. Experts in the Technical Department, soon known as 'the Brains Trust', calmly dispensed advice about conserving fuel: keep sparking plugs clean, get into top gear quickly, stay at 20–30mph and coast as much as possible. The Club's engineering depot at Lupus Street in Pimlico, later badly bombed, devoted itself to munitions work. The RAC soon extended its 'Get-You-Home' scheme to those who ran out of petrol. It arranged free lifts for servicemen stranded at railway stations after dark. It shared RAC road telephone boxes with the authorities, who paid an annual rental of £400. It supplied maps and routes to the military and civilian services. However, Club officials agonised about whether to give directions to men in mufti who might be spies. Nuns were also viewed with the gravest suspicion.

WAR FOOTING

In September 1939 barrage balloons are inflated, troops man anti-aircraft guns in Hyde Park and civilians carry gas masks. But much business could not go on as usual because of petrol rationing. Some footsore Britons found this the hardest of all wartime privations.

The full-scale blackout, which involved masking motor car headlamps and reducing traffic signals to shuttered slits, was as much of a shock to the RAC as it was to everyone else. Harold Nicolson described London without lights as 'a pall of black velvet'. Accidents of all sorts multiplied alarmingly. The road toll almost doubled. During the first three months of the war – admittedly, the Phoney War – more people were killed by motor vehicles than by enemy action. One cartoon showed Hitler inspecting an accident and saying to Goering, 'If they continue to annihilate themselves at this rate, we shan't have to bomb them after all.' Drivers paid garages one shilling and sixpence to paint their cars' bumpers and running boards white while they waited. The authorities also applied white paint liberally, to kerbs, bollards, lamp-posts, trees, Belisha beacons. The roads were full of daubers with brushes, lawn-markers and machines like ancient tricycles. Motorists were annoyed that it took a war to produce the clear road markings that had been needed in peacetime every foggy day. But the carnage continued. A correspondent of *The Autocar* made the hair-raising suggestion that after dark motorists should drive on the right so that they 'could more easily follow the white-painted kerbs'.

Eventually, on 1 February 1940, the government introduced a speed limit of 20mph in built-up areas during the blackout. The RAC opposed the move, saying that it was 'a sop to those who kicked up a row' and that it would induce pedestrians to take less care. The best that can be said about this reaction is that it was less obscurantist than the response of *The Motor*. Doubtless the magazine was provoked by press attacks on 'the Juggernaut of the road driven by a modern Moloch who lives by human sacrifice'. But, in what was still an astonishing outburst, it accused Chamberlain's 'Hitler regime' of 'applying Nazi methods to motorists' while using 'Gestapo' sleuths to protect foolhardy pedestrians who should themselves be regimented. There were, to be sure, cases of sentries shooting motorists who failed to stop when challenged. Sometimes they drove on because they were carrying contraband pigs or ladies of the night; but sometimes they were deaf or otherwise innocent. In any case they did not deserve to be the victims of trigger-happy soldiers and the RAC protested to the War Office accordingly. It also complained about 'irksome regulations' imposed by officious bureaucrats without consultation. The ban on car radios (supposedly because they could be turned into transmitters) was particularly fatuous. However, just as some factories continued to produce automobiles (30,000 of which were exported in the first seven months of the war), so pleasure motoring was still possible. Cars could not go far on a ration of four to ten gallons a month (depending on size). But drivers enjoyed 'motoring as we used to know it' – when horizons beckoned, pulses raced and hedgerows became a blur. For the roads were empty once again and Britain had reverted almost to its pre-automotive state. There were convoys of lorries, a few sleek Bentleys carrying officials and occasional miscellaneous motor vehicles. Otherwise pedestrians, milk carts, pony-traps and farmers with their livestock reoccupied the roads.

Even in London (where buses and trams were packed) the smell of petrol fumes vanished and the crisp, clear air of the first winter of war seemed a tonic. Sitting in his Great Portland Street office, the motoring journalist Dudley Noble had views south to Oxford Street and north to Regent's Park, and often in 1940 he could not see a single motor vehicle. Special events still attracted great clusters of cars. As late as June 1941, ten thousand automobiles gathered at Epsom on Derby Day, which was not 'criminal' (noted *The Autocar* nervously) though it might

GAS GUZZLER

*During the war determined motorists employed
ingenious but unsatisfactory methods to fuel their cars.
This 1935 Morris 16 is propelled by gas. But it could
only travel a dozen miles after the bag was filled, and
inflation took ten minutes.*

be 'injudicious'. Actually, for at least a year before that date the public had been waxing indignant about 'the continued use of motor cars for more or less selfish purposes'. The RAC was unmoved. While it refused to sanction competitions and said that trials had 'no military value', it did carry on issuing occasional permits, known as 'Moto-Auto-Bateau', to drivers going to France for touring or business purposes. And in the spring of 1940 the RAC requested an extra ration of petrol for Easter and published a leaflet entitled 'Why lay up your car?'

The Club's collective mind was concentrated by Hitler's conquest of France and his threat to invade England. Furthermore, a former habitué of Pall Mall, Winston Churchill, now moved into Downing Street. It was surely no coincidence that, as Sealy-Clarke observed four months later, 'the Club has the ear of the Government to a greater extent than ever before'. This was not just empty boasting. RAC representatives, having met the Home Secretary, were 'largely responsible for the comparatively innocuous requirements' concerning the immobilisation of cars. The Club advised the War Office about the diffusion of petrol stores, a problem pointed up by civilians who were prosecuted for hoarding fuel in open washtubs and leaking barrels. It assisted the government out of the muddle caused by a press campaign to 'camouflage your car' – service chiefs were worried that civilian vehicles might be confused with military ones, so colouring private automobiles khaki was prohibited. The RAC was also given privileged information about the boundaries of Defence Areas, in which movement was restricted. A Club minute gloated: 'It is certain that the AA has no such map.' Finally, the RAC was charged with removing, cataloguing and storing some 70,000 signposts which might have assisted the German panzers. As it turned out, this vast enterprise merely spread confusion on the home front. Motorists had to navigate with maps and compasses, even by the stars. Eventually the top brass themselves called for a partial restoration of direction boards. Cynics maintained that the signposting of London and other big cities was so haphazard that 'it might well have been retained for the purpose of baffling the enemy'.

The evacuation from Dunkirk at the end of May 1940 brought the war home to Britain in more senses than one. The RAC clubhouse provided a haven for many who had escaped, often with nothing but the clothes they were wearing. But though it was a busy scene, as the staff struggled to cater for the unexpected influx and to provide extra beds in the Turkish bath and the squash courts, not all was gloom in Pall Mall. Harry Stanley, nephew of the former Chairman, had rescued a jorum of rum from the ruins of Dunkirk. Clutching it like the Grail, he conveyed it across the Channel, back to London and as far as the clubhouse foyer. 'Do you like rum?' he asked Quinn. 'It's mother's milk to me,' the head porter replied. Quinn conjured up two white army mugs and was soon 'drunk as a fiddler's bitch'. As members arrived for luncheon he bawled at them, 'Get out you buggers!' He then retired to his cubby-hole and passed out, having added an entirely new dimension to the term 'Dunkirk spirit'.

No less colourful was Colonel Richard Meinertzhagen, the ornithologist and former secret agent who organised the RAC's unit of the Local Defence Volunteers in the summer of 1940. Introduced to the Führer before the war, the Colonel had returned the 'Heil Hitler' greeting with a 'Heil Meinertzhagen'. Now he applied his extravagant talents to securing Clubland and Westminster against the Nazi invaders with a 'Dad's Army' of retired senior officers, portly professional men and aged patricians equipped with dummy rifles. Impatient and

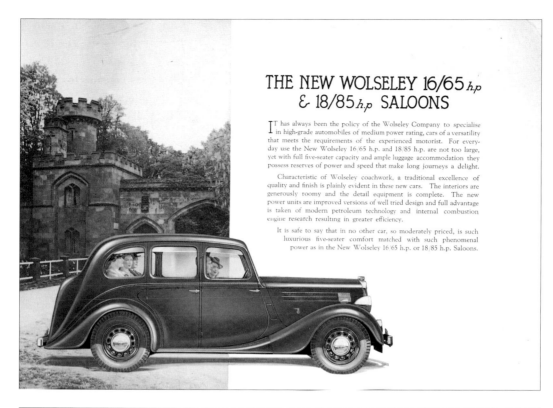

THE NEW WOLSELEY 16/65 *h.p* & 18/85 *h.p* SALOONS

IT has always been the policy of the Wolseley Company to specialise in high-grade automobiles of medium power rating, cars of a versatility that meets the requirements of the experienced motorist. For every-day use the New Wolseley 16/65 h.p. and 18/85 h.p. are not too large, yet with full five-seater capacity and ample luggage accommodation they possess reserves of power and speed that make long journeys a delight.

Characteristic of Wolseley coachwork, a traditional excellence of quality and finish is plainly evident in these new cars. The interiors are generously roomy and the detail equipment is complete. The new power units are improved versions of well tried design and full advantage is taken of modern petroleum technology and internal combustion engine research resulting in greater efficiency.

It is safe to say that in no other car, so moderately priced, is such luxurious five-seater comfort matched with such phenomenal power as in the New Wolseley 16/65 h.p. or 18/85 h.p. Saloons.

CAPACITY & COMFORT

WAR PRODUCTION

During the first half of 1940 the production, export and advertising of cars continued. At home Britons had 130 models to choose from and there were 3,500 registrations a month. But in July the government took over all stocks of new cars and banned their purchase except under special licence. In the interests of victory, motor manufacturing (like much else) succumbed to state control.

insubordinate, Meinertzhagen soon clashed with higher authority. He was hauled before Lord Cavan, head of the Home Guard, who announced, 'You're sacked, sir.' The Colonel replied, 'I am not going to be spoken to like that by an Irish field marshal.' Meinertzhagen stormed out and hailed a taxi. While taking him home it was hit by a bomb and he was seriously injured.

When the Blitz began, Gascoigne, the night porter in the RAC clubhouse, was involved in another memorable incident. During one air raid the front-door bell rang and a policeman asked to be let in with a baby. It proved to be an unexploded bomb, which he plonked down on the porter's desk. The hall staff protested and the policeman retorted, 'Pat baby.' When he did so himself, the operator of the cumbersome hydraulic lift in the hall took flight to the top floor and later handed in his notice. All this doubtless helped to turn Quinn's attention to the Luftwaffe. He used to go out into the street during the blackout, wave his fist at the bombers and shout at the top of his voice: 'Bloody 'uns!' On the night of 14 October 1940 they retaliated.

German aircraft dropped large numbers of high-explosive and incendiary bombs on the West End. The force of the blast was such that close to the RAC clubhouse two heavy metal coal-hole covers flush with the pavement were sucked up and whirled into the middle of the road. At least five fires were started in Pall Mall, which became, in Winston Churchill's words, a 'vivid flame picture'. The Carlton Club, a solemn Tory mausoleum whose atmosphere resembled 'that of a Duke's house – with the Duke dead upstairs', was devastated. Chunks of masonry weighing several tons fell into the street and the dazed staff were led in single file to the safety of the RAC clubhouse. There were 'waiters in their evening dress and the girls in their smart uniforms, all blacker than the hounds of hell'. Inspecting the Carlton the following day, Churchill expressed amazement that no one had been killed; a Labour colleague explained that 'the devil looks after his own'. Other clubs were also battered, including the Athenaeum, which gave one member 'a shocked sense that this time the Nazis had definitely gone too far'.

The RAC's headquarters got off lightly. The staff's fire-fighting section quickly put out small blazes and prevented a large one spreading from the Carlton Club. About twenty-five members sustained minor injuries, mostly from flying glass. Many bedrooms and bathrooms were damaged, and a few had to be temporarily closed. The gas was cut off, so members could obtain only a Continental breakfast the next morning. But, as one recalled, the day after he was served his usual repast of 'grilled kippers followed by egg and bacon'. Later raids left the clubhouse virtually unscathed. But on 20 February 1944 it did suffer 'severe damage' when a bomb pierced the terrace over the Great Gallery. Again fires were put out by the staff, whose work was praised by Sealy-Clarke. On this occasion the fire brigade took two hours to arrive.

The clubhouse, its doors protected by sandbags and its windows criss-crossed with strips of tape, remained open throughout the war. Moreover, it tried to maintain pre-war standards. This was a struggle because the Club was not immune to rationing or shortages. Early in 1940 members could still get a four-course meal for half a crown. Two years later the price had doubled, only three courses were permitted and the à la carte menu was abolished. The crisp bread rolls provided for breakfast shrank to minuscule proportions. Spirits were rationed and the price of a bottle of champagne rose first to five shillings and then to ten or more. Eventually members were reduced to drinking cheap Algerian wine, 'dreadful stuff, as harsh as inferior vinegar'. Yet the wartime RAC was acclaimed as an 'oasis' in a desert of austerity, 'not so much

HOME FRONT

The Luftwaffe failed to smash civilian morale, not least because it bombed the West as well as the East End of London. This strengthened the belief that every citizen was serving at the front in a people's war. During the Blitz the RAC made its own contribution to national unity by organising the 'Help Your Neighbour' car-sharing scheme.

a club as a caravanserai'. Always crowded, it served about 60,000 main meals a month, chiefly to members of the armed services. Fruit and vegetables were supplied from the four-acre market garden near Woodcote Park (itself a farm for the duration) which the Club rented for £100 a year. It also managed to keep on the menu such items as jugged hare and grilled herrings in mustard sauce.

The Club was understandably popular with officers from abroad. The Free French forces later gave the RAC an engraved silver cup as a token of thanks for its hospitality. Americans found it 'the nearest thing to one of their clubs England had'. They were made especially welcome: in July 1942 the bowling alley was reopened for their benefit, though the question of whether to allow mixed bathing was deferred until after the duration. As the war progressed the trickle of foreign uniforms became a flood. Some alien members made themselves almost too much at home. Tales were told of effervescent young men 'glissading down the highly polished steps of the palace of automobilism'. A tall Polish Colonel with a chestful of medals habitually approached any attractive female who seemed available, often as her escort was settling the bill. His refrain never varied: 'You like to make an old man happy – yes?' Apparently the answer was always no.

As the Blitz intensified Londoners found it increasingly hard to reach home. The buses, which provided only a skeleton service because many had been requisitioned as ambulances and petrol was in such short supply, generally ceased to run during raids. This left queues of tired, hungry people exposed to the bombs and the elements. Morale began to suffer. But the towering, beetle-browed Minister of Transport Sir John Reith, whom Churchill called 'that Wuthering Height', dismissed a memorandum from Downing Street on the subject as 'silly'. So in early October the Prime Minister replaced him with J. F. C. Moore-Brabazon, a pillar of the RAC and, in the opinion of the motoring press, the first person to occupy the post who really knew what he was doing. Churchill now took up 'the transport problem with vigour' and sent 'drastic proposals to Moore-Brabazon'. To supplement 'exiguous buses' he wanted motorists organised into 'a regular corps'. They should ply the London streets, especially during rush hours, and carry off 'this painful accumulation of hard-working folk'. Moore-Brabazon consulted both the RAC and the AA, who in turn mobilised motorists. So the 'Help Your Neighbour' scheme was born. In return for extra petrol coupons, drivers picked up several passengers at bus-stops and elsewhere and took them home. These amateur chauffeurs thinned queues, eased the capital's transport problem and reduced the death toll during the height of the Blitz. When the scheme was called off in the spring of 1941, because of acute fuel shortages, the Minister of Transport thanked the Club. The scheme had 'helped very materially in an hour when things were critical'. It had also, according to the motoring fraternity, disposed of 'the bogy that to use a private car in war is unpatriotic'.

THE RAC CONTINUED TO WORK HAND in glove with the authorities. It agreed to the Ministry of Food's proposal that Road Guides should act as dispatch riders in an emergency. It answered the Ministry of Transport's request for confidential advice about

GENERAL SALUTE

After the fall of France the British government found accommodation for Charles de Gaulle in Waterloo Place, off Trafalgar Square. The RAC clubhouse offered a more tactful welcome to the proud embodiment of Gallic resistance, and to his Free French officers – as shown by their silver token of thanks.

HOME FROM HOME

Among many Allied leaders welcomed to the RAC were Generals Eisenhower and Sikorski and Crown Prince Olaf of Norway, whose Ministry of Defence rented part of 83 Pall Mall from the Club. It could not satisfy all their tastes. Ike longed for hominy grits while hating English cabbage and Brussels sprouts – his chauffeuse overheard him say that 'this must be the fartingest war in history'.

whether banning the use of motor horns would reduce accidents – on the whole the Club thought not. It provided the Ministry of Information with the slogan 'Go Easy on your Tyres'. Responding to new directives about meeting an invasion, the RAC told its provincial officers to 'destroy all maps' but keep cash books and the records of Associate members. The Club produced up-to-date information on roads for the War Office and lists of hotel vacancies for the Welfare Department. It also provided registered driving instructors for the military. This was a particularly valuable service since, as Sammy Davis said, 'the British Army's driving was calamitous'. Horse-loving officers were not entirely to blame: Davis doubted if there was any truth in the old joke that only soldiers deemed unfit to be batmen were made drivers.

The fault lay chiefly in the extraordinary diversity of vehicles introduced at the beginning of the war, with their 'hotch-potch of mechanical variations'. These were a result of 'uncertainty and ignorance' in the War Office, which had 'transmitted confused signals to British manufacturers'. But they also demonstrated that British manufacturers themselves had still not grasped the principles of Henry Ford. One of the most erratic of the maverick machines was the Covenanter tank, which was never 'considered battleworthy because of mechanical shortcomings'. They defeated Davis himself, for all his skill at the wheel – or, in this case, at the twin tillers. He once drove a Covenanter 'over a verge, up a bank, through a hedge, ricocheted off tree trunks, ploughed through bushes, and came to rest … on the much prized tennis lawn of a retired lieutenant-colonel who was enraged at the manoeuvre'.

The RAC's labours did not stop it becoming the focus of hostile scrutiny. In May 1942 an MP raised yet again the question of its amalgamation with the AA: the two rivals were vested interests whose services should be combined, 'thus saving public money and preventing overlapping and waste of labour'. The Minister of Labour, Ernest Bevin, himself no mean amalgamator (of trade unions), expressed some sympathy for this plea. However, after a conference of the interested parties, he was evidently convinced that the proposed fusion would save little or no manpower. The RAC showed that its Road Section had shrunk from 1,367 employees at the outbreak of war to 270 at the end of 1941. These figures referred to headquarters (but not clubhouse) staff, those running the thirteen provincial offices, and Road Patrols, nearly all of whom were now too old or unfit for military service. The RAC gave copious information about its contribution to the war effort, and officials of the Ministries of Labour and Transport appeared 'impressed by the magnitude and importance of this work'. Nevertheless, the motoring organisations had been spurred towards greater co-operation. One remarkable sign of this was the RAC's decision, in October 1942, to give honorary membership of the Club to its old enemy Stenson Cooke. It is tempting to suggest that shock killed him, for within a few weeks he was dead. In fact, heavy drinking and general debilitation were to blame. Anyway, the disappearance of this awkward, egotistical but strangely compelling man, whose 'initiative and energy' the RAC saluted, made it easier for the two organisations to collaborate.

So did the departure of the redoubtable Commander Armstrong, whose resignation Colonel Sealy-Clarke had to request in July 1941. This was a painful task since Armstrong had long been rendered incapable of work by illness. No obvious successor could be found, so the Club appointed his assistant, Geoffrey Samuelson, Acting Secretary. He was, in the words of Harry Stanley, 'a dear, beloved character'. But he was also woolly-minded, never had bright ideas and

WAR MATERIAL

After the fall of Singapore the rubber shortage became acute. New restrictions were imposed and only those with E (for Essential) petrol coupons could obtain tyres. RAC patrolmen were privileged because they assisted officialdom – despite bureaucratic concerns that their uniforms might be mistaken for the field grey ones of the Wehrmacht. Eventually it was shown that the RAC used exactly the same material to clothe its men as did the RAF.

lacked drive. Persuading Samuelson to 'take an initiative was like push-ing a ton of lead uphill'. However, his scope for initiative was diminished when the scanty petrol ration was stopped altogether in July 1942 and, for three years, 'pleasure motoring' virtually ceased. Cars, though subject to increasing restrictions, were still used for medical and other essential purposes. Women's Voluntary Service drivers were asked, 'Do you mind a young child being sick in the back of your car?' But the RAC now advised on laying up private vehicles, and later conducted a census to measure the results. It offered Associate members postwar incentives to renew their present subscriptions and surprisingly, in 1943, eighty per cent did so.

COWLEY CRUSADE
Thanks to the 'shadow factory' scheme, car manufacturers rapidly turned to producing armaments. Crusader tanks were made at Cowley and suffered from some of the defects of Morris cars. In addition to being undergunned, they were underprotected and unreliable. By 1944 British forces depended on the mass-produced American Sherman.

The Club was reluctant to compromise with the times. Though arranging exhibition snooker matches at the Club by Joe Davis and oth-ers to raise money for the Red Cross, it deemed a professional billiards player ineligible for membership. Though facing a deficit, it refused to impose a guinea capitation fee on members, as suggested by Frederick Simms – a voice from the past but a frequent presence in the Turkish bath, which he valued as an air-raid shelter. However, the Club did accept various economies. It terminated a costly and 'disadvantageous' relationship with the Commercial Vehicle Users' Association, which it had founded in 1903. It also managed to avoid paying several thousand pounds in customs duty (on foreign vehicles imported before the war) through a complicated 'wheedle'. Financial juggling was matched by diplomatic sleight of hand. In October 1943 the RAC established the Standing Joint Committee with the AA and the Royal Scottish Automobile Club. The real aim was probably to avert further talk of 'amalgamation', but the professed purpose of the Standing Joint Committee was to 'act in unison on questions of common interest'. This body still survives, but it was a rickety infant. When Edward Fryer, the new Secretary of the AA, sent the RAC a letter about ways of avoiding duplication it took Sealy-Clarke a year to reply.

Such dilatoriness seemed to justify the Club's critics. St John Nixon, for example, said that all its 'old driving force' was exhausted. *The Motor* took the same line in a vendetta against both the RAC and the AA which lasted throughout the war. 'They are moribund, unrepresentative and dead to the world.' What motorists needed was 'propaganda by firebrands, not pink-fingered pen-men'. The journal's sharpest barbs were directed towards the Club's venerable Committee, 'septuagenarians ruled by an octogenarian chairman'. Sealy-Clarke had done 'splendid work in the past' but now he was presiding over a secretive and self-perpetuating body. The Club's annual report was marked 'Private' and its accounts were 'Strictly Private and Confidential'. The retiring members of the Committee were monotonously re-elected and since Associate members had no vote and fewer than five per cent of Club members returned their ballot papers, there was 'little chance of introducing new blood'.

Similar charges might have been made about the succession to the presidency of the RAC, though no one ventured onto that delicate ground. When the Duke of Connaught died in 1942, at the age of ninety-two, Sealy-Clarke consulted the King about a successor who might be 'help-ful to the Club in the difficult times ahead'. On George VI's advice it appointed as President

his brother, the Duke of Kent. Something of a royal Bentley Boy, the dashing Duke was an appropriate choice. But in August 1942 he was killed in an aircraft accident while on active service. The Club then approached two less suitable royalties, the Duke of Gloucester and the Earl of Athlone, but without success. Finally Lord Louis Mountbatten, the RAC's third choice, accepted the office. The Club President is a kind of constitutional monarch who can exert a positive influence. Mountbatten, though dynamic, regal and rich, seldom did so. According to one well-placed member, this 'completely egocentric' man treated the RAC as just another stage to strut on.

Wartime critics of the Club often had a good case but often, too, they had an axe to grind. St John Nixon obviously resented the RAC's cool response to his book *Romance Amongst Cars*. *The Motor* sought to attract readers through what one of them called its 'vindictive' campaign. It also failed to recognise what the RAC did achieve, against the odds, during the final years of the war. The Club at last approved a change in the horsepower 'tax-on-bore' formula. This was a revolutionary step which would allow British manufacturers, as one of them said, to design 'engines, of whatever size, so that they provide maximum efficiency'. The Club put forward a comprehensive road scheme, including motorways that would '*completely segregate*' motor vehicles from other traffic in the interests of safety and efficiency. Wilfrid Andrews urged that it be implemented 'immediately after the war as a work of the first importance'. Furthermore the Club so far took notice of its attackers as to embark on a consideration of internal reforms. These did not amount to much. But as more pioneers died in the course of the war – S. F. Edge, Lord Austin, J. S. Critchley, Mark Mayhew, Frederick Simms, Charles Jarrott – new members came to the fore. Ten fresh faces appeared on the Committee in the spring of 1945. Soon afterwards Colonel Sealy-Clarke announced his resignation, on grounds of advancing years. Wilfrid Andrews was elected as his successor. *The Motor* was pleased to see signs of a change from 'immobility of action and senility of direction'.

Andrews was then fifty-three years old and for the next three decades, until his death in 1975, he dominated the RAC. By origin he was a Kent fruit farmer but as early as 1908 he rode a motor-bike and he became an enthusiastic participant in the Brighton Run. He was a keen sportsman, a golfer and a supporter of Arsenal Football Club. He also painted, though the art at which he really excelled had to do with the management of committees. Andrews had climbed to a high position in Rotary International and he had founded the American British Commonwealth Association. On the Club Committee he towered 'head and shoulders' above his peers. A bluff, burly, florid man, usually wreathed in cigar smoke and sometimes surrounded by an aura of Napoleon brandy, he had a 'great presence'. Andrews seemed a 'born leader' and 'the natural chairman'. One of his greatest strengths was that he was an impressive speaker, never using notes and never at a loss for words appropriate to the occasion. Hearing him give an impromptu address, the MP George Strauss exclaimed enviously: 'Makes you spit – yet he's an amateur and we're professionals.'

Andrews's oratorical style might be described as Rotarian-Churchillian. It is exemplified in his tribute to Arthur Stanley, who died in 1947. It was, said Andrews, 'as though a thread, woven through the life of the Club, had snapped'. Stanley had brought to the chairmanship 'great wisdom, great dignity and, above all, an obvious sense of courage which enabled him to

CDR. FRANCIS
ARMSTRONG

*Secretary between 1923
and 1941, Armstrong
(right) ruled the Club
with a rod of iron.*

ROYAL PRESIDENTS

*The Duke of Connaught (top left), Queen Victoria's favourite son,
presided over the Club from 1911 to 1942. He was succeeded by
the Duke of Kent (above), a keen motorist who once drove from
London to Portsmouth at an average speed of 100mph. After he
was killed in an air crash later that year, Lord Mountbatten
(right) held the office until his assassination in 1979.*

rise superior to physical disability'. He had been 'an inspiration' and he left a void which would be impossible to fill. Asked by one young Club member, John Crampton, how he made such good speeches, Andrews replied: 'I just open my heart and let it all pour out.'

Sentimental, charming and genuinely kind, Andrews was particularly solicitous towards older members of the Club. In 1947, to make up for the loss of founder members, he instituted the 'Senior Hundred' list which consisted of those who had belonged to the Club longest. They were given annual dinners and other privileges. When an aged and somnolent colonel positioned his Bath chair with its back to the proceedings at a Committee meeting, Andrews stopped members turning him round: 'If the old boy prefers it that way, leave him as he is.' Andrews was especially indulgent towards the few remaining figures who embodied the heroic days of motoring. One was Frank Lanchester, whom Andrews extolled as 'the first vice-chairman of the Club from the industry'. Another valued antique was Montague Grahame-White. Immaculately dressed and 'four times larger than life', he still haunted the Club, where he liked to drink 'a bottle of bubbly' at eleven o'clock in the morning. Andrews corresponded with this Rabelaisian relic of 'glittering Monte Carlo society', describing his struggle to maintain traditional 'standards here at the Club'. Grahame-White did his bit to keep up standards in Pall Mall by persuading a pretty waitress to have a drink with him and saying, when she insisted that it should be orange juice, 'That won't put lead in your pencil. Oh, sorry, you haven't got a pencil.'

As Chairman, Andrews behaved as though he were the father of an extended family. In the words of *The Autocar*, 'He established himself as the head of the household, almost in the Victorian style, respected, admired and a little feared, and a stickler for correctness.' Those who still remember the RAC during the Andrews era often comment on its sense of solidarity, its 'esprit de Club', sometimes to the detriment of the bureaucratic modern organisation. Then it was a clan not a company. Certainly Andrews never forgot the value of warm personal relations. When the clubhouse servants wanted to join a trade union in 1955 he said that they were 'friends' and that it was 'their business'. Often he bemoaned the fact that it was no longer possible to get staff 'who were like the servants in one's own home'. A conservative to the marrow, he had an old-fashioned, squirearchical view of the bond which should subsist between master and man. He expected deference. Indeed, Andrews was a stern as well as a benign patriarch. He believed in strict discipline and rigid formality. Whenever the Chairman visited a provincial office of the RAC he was greeted by a guard of honour, the patrolmen in their best blue uniforms. Even during meetings of the Club Committee members had to stand when addressing the Chairman. Andrews stood on his dignity. He resented any challenge to his authority. A paternalist on principle, he was by instinct an autocrat. His dictatorial propensities grew more pronounced over the years and were to have dire consequences for the Club.

Almost at once power, which had been exercised by the RAC's three dominant secretaries – Johnson, Orde and Armstrong – for almost the first fifty years of its history, fell decisively into the hands of the Chairman. Andrews ensured that this would be the case by making the compliant Samuelson permanent (instead of just 'acting') Secretary. The Chairman's position was strengthened by the RAC's healthy financial state. During the war the clubhouse had never been less than full. And the Associate section had managed to hold onto a loyal core of 150,000

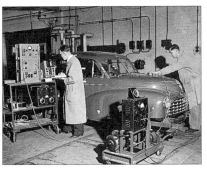

SLOW PROGRESS

Morris gears up for postwar production. But although new assembly lines are laid in 1945 (top right), the manufacturing methods are as old-fashioned (above) as the models. In 1948 the Morris Oxford undergoes electrical and freezing tests (right and below), but still looks like a pre-war vehicle.

members. Andrews, his confidence boosted by the Club's long waiting list, could therefore afford to impose a new policy. Whereas candidates for full membership had previously been elected 'unless there were reasons against', in future they 'should provide adequate reasons for their election'. The RAC would not be as strict as, say, the Beefsteak, which supposedly required its candidates 'to be a relation of God – and a damned close relation at that'. But it would give preference to sons of members, ex-servicemen, 'civil servants of administrative grade, principals of reputable firms, members of good London Clubs, public school and university men and regular commissioned officers of the Forces'. Foreign candidates should be 'vouched for by their respective embassies'. To prevent overcrowding, the Club was never to have more than 16,000 members and in 1945 their annual subscription was raised from four guineas to ten. In Pall Mall everything possible was to be done 'to maintain the standards of bygone days'. Associate members, meanwhile, were to receive 'post-war service at pre-war prices', a policy which led to road services being subsidised by the clubhouse.

ANDREWS'S ACHIEVEMENTS were limited because he was working against the contemporary grain, being a conservative reformer in an age of Labour austerity. The changing times were aptly symbolised on 26 July 1945 when the resigning Prime Minister, Winston Churchill, departed from Buckingham Palace by chauffeur-driven Rolls-Royce and his successor, Clement Attlee, arrived a few minutes later driving himself and his wife in a Standard 10. Less than three weeks afterwards, on 14 August, Japan's surrender ended the war and Lord Keynes warned the government that Britain was facing an 'economic Dunkirk'. With Lend-Lease about to be suspended, a huge foreign debt and massive war damage to make good, national bankruptcy was a real possibility. Only an American loan staved it off. But the government was obliged to institute a dual policy: Spartan self-denial at home and a relentless drive to sell abroad. It was a time of clothing coupons and bread units, shop queues and coal shortages, Woolton pies and snoek, dried eggs and watery beer, prefabs and spivs, the black market and red petrol (so coloured to prevent its illicit sale and use, though straining it through a gas mask removed the dye). But the car industry came into its own. When, in November 1945, Sir Stafford Cripps, President of the Board of Trade, told an SMMT dinner that he wanted fifty per cent of cars made in Britain to be exported, there were cries of 'No' and 'Tripe'. He riposted by suggesting that they thought Great Britain existed to support the motor industry, rather than vice versa. But within five years four-fifths of all cars produced in the United Kingdom were being sold abroad and Britain was the biggest automobile exporter in the world. MGs and Austins even found buyers in America. As Wilfrid Andrews said, British motor-makers 'have not only taken coal to Newcastle but have succeeded in selling it there'.

This was the bright side of a picture that was predominantly dark. Only in the artificial conditions created by the ending of the war could British car manufacturers make serious inroads into foreign markets. Their competitors in ravaged Europe were not yet geared up for production. And the global dollar shortage blocked the overseas sale of Chevrolets and Buicks, whose makers were anyway struggling to satisfy pent-up home demand. Moreover, the very success of British automobile producers abroad sowed the seeds of future failure. Their

SINEWS OF PEACE

After the war people queue for bread, now rationed for the first time, and other controlled goods. But the tightest controls were on the raw materials allocated to industry, which was switching to peace-time production – a conversion so abrupt that one cartoon showed a motor vehicle grafted onto a Spitfire.

overpriced pre-war models proved quite unsuited to rugged alien conditions. They were not backed up by adequate dealer networks to provide servicing and spare parts. British cars became a byword for unreliability. Furthermore Britain still turned out a bewildering multiplicity of models and components. After the war Morris manufactured 'ten different engines of three different valve configurations, nine distinct and different chassis and nine body types'. Yet Morris Minors were sent to Scandinavia without heaters as these were not standard fittings.

There is no doubt that leading figures in the industry were to blame, though it was admittedly racked by poor labour relations. Leonard Lord was literally liable to design Austins on the back of envelopes. Notoriously Lord Nuffield and Sir William Rootes rejected the chance to take over the manufacture of the Volkswagen on the grounds that it was 'too ugly and too noisy'. The former went on to build the 1948 Morris Minor, which he himself reviled as 'a poached egg' and which was cut in half shortly before going into production, the two sides being moved apart until it seemed to have the right dimensions. Rootes's prize performer was the Hillman Minx, which remained, until well into the 1950s, a 1938 model 'converted to unitary construction and superficially modified to look different'.

However, the government was also responsible for the parlous state of the motor industry. It sustained small, inefficient manufacturers with steel supplies because they were assisting with the export drive. For a moment the Labour administration, anyway committed to planning, seemed about to heed the RAC's advice on road improvement. But, when overtaken by budgetary problems, it reverted to the old 'patch and mend' policy. This encouraged the continued manufacture of high-revving, low-geared cars, fine for trundling along English byways but ill-adapted to speeding down alien highways. It was to promote the construction of more competitive cars that the government abandoned the RAC horsepower tax in favour, first, of an impost on engine capacity and then, in 1948, of a flat-rate licence duty. However, it ignored the RAC's further warning that the new policy would constitute a 'serious handicap' to smaller cars. Larger ones benefited, but towards the end of the 1940s Europeans wanted cheap models and they bought Volkswagens, Renaults and Fiats. These were also more economical on fuel than their British equivalents, the Morris Minor and the Austin A40 Dorset, partly because (from June 1945) petrol was rationed according to the mileage it afforded each car.

Almost everything that the Labour government did was anathema to Wilfrid Andrews. In this he was hardly alone. Many middle-class people felt outraged that the Socialists were the masters now – to quote the celebrated words of Sir Hartley Shawcross, himself later chairman of the RAC stewards, the final court of appeal in matters of motor sports. Motorists particularly resented Labour controls, nationalisation, austerity. In 1947 the popular high Tory novelist Angela Thirkell blamed most road accidents on wartime fatigue 'accentuated since the outbreak of peace by deliberate under-nourishment of the people of England to make them too listless to resist petty tyranny'. Although he may have nurtured such sentiments in his bosom, Andrews was at this stage studiously moderate. He insisted that 'Care must be taken, in stating the policy of the Club, not to have it overweighted by personal political opinion'. So the RAC followed its familiar, judicious policy of exerting influence behind the scenes. It invited several Labour MPs, such as F. J. Bellenger, to join the Committee. It tried to 'harmonise' the 'divergent views' of motorists and those who sought to regulate them. In particular it lobbied

SMALL WONDERS

*Cheap, new, sturdy, small cars like the Volkswagen 'Beetle',
the Citroën 2cv and the Morris Minor were destined for huge
success. But they were slow to appear after the war, opposed by
conservative manufacturers like Lord Nuffield. He denounced
the VW and shunned the Minor, only thanking its designer,
Alec Issigonis, after a million had been sold.*

against the publicity campaign to 'Keep Death off the Road.' The Club's claim that this was scaremongering gained substance when the Tory party adapted the poster, which featured a distraught woman in black, and captioned it 'I Voted Labour.'

The RAC's Committee was at odds over how far to oppose the 1947 Transport Bill, which placed railways and road hauliers in public ownership. O'Gorman thought that 'privately owned transport – as represented by the Club – was likely to suffer' by the creation of an inefficient state monopoly. Andrews himself considered that the nationalisation of small road operators amounted to an attack on 'the liberty of the subject', a view which many unhappy Labour MPs shared. But when a Committee member urged that the Club 'should come into the open' and denounce the Bill, discretion proved the better part of valour. Their sage conclusion was that the RAC must not 'embarrass itself with politics'. So the Club agreed to the mild and uncontroversial resolution, which the Standing Joint Committee would submit, that the government should deny any 'intention of restricting the freedom of movement of the private motorist on the road'.

The Club was more militant about the withdrawal, in August 1947, of the meagre petrol ration that remained. Actually some of the Committee at first wanted to treat the event as a 'fait accompli', but they were doubtless persuaded to engage in a 'nation-wide propaganda' campaign by the wrath of the RAC's full and Associate members. Many of them had cherished their laid-up cars during the war or bought second-hand machines at inflated prices after it. They clung to these vehicles, said a typical middle-class motorist, 'as a last link with comfort and luxury, having surrendered so many things, including annual holidays, library subscriptions and golf'. Thus the ban on petrol sales was widely seen as a vindictive form of 'class discrimination' and it came under fire on many fronts. *The Autocar* discharged a furious mixed metaphor: 'The heavy hand of totalitarianism has taken a step forward.' Demonstrators brandishing placards waylaid the Prime Minister as he travelled to attend a Labour rally. The Minister of Fuel and Power, Hugh Gaitskell, issued a newsreel film justifying the cessation of petrol supplies only to have it booed and hissed in a West End cinema when he himself was present – Gaitskell 'felt horribly embarrassed and really suffered agony'. Meanwhile the motoring organisations collected a million signatures to a petition calling for a restoration of the ration.

That autumn Labour did badly in the municipal elections. The party's local agents attributed its losses to middle-class disgruntlement and 'the way in which the AA and the RAC were able to sway motorists against voting Labour'. But the Club had been significantly more restrained than its jaundiced ally. As Captain Phillips told a group of delegates from motor sport clubs who met at Pall Mall in December, the RAC 'had not supported public protests organised against the petrol ban'. It did not consider this unfortunate policy 'an opportunity for a general political attack'. On the contrary, the Club 'desired to be constitutional' and 'enjoyed the support of members of the Labour Government today'. Annoyed that it was not creating enough of a splash, one delegate pleaded 'that the RAC should make its good works more public'. But in its own way the Club was being effective. It advised members how to get supplementary fuel rations, with which, as it acknowledged, the government was generous. To the astonishment of his own backbenchers Gaitskell even granted petrol allowances to 'masters of hounds for purposes connected with the hunt'. Doubtless this helped to endear him to

HIGH-OCTANE PROTEST

*The abolition of the basic petrol ration in 1947 united
motorists and motoring organisations, and proved the
power of the motoring lobby. When the million-
signature petition was delivered to parliament,* The
Times *thundered: 'The government now know that no
restriction has been more unpopular.'*

Andrews, who engaged in delicate negotiations for the restoration of the ration, which occurred in June 1948. The Chairman of the RAC told his colleagues that the attitude of the Minister of Fuel and Power was 'one of friendliness, reason and honesty'. Although the Club disagreed with Gaitskell, he said, it did not want to criticise him in public.

Meanwhile the RAC itself was having to cope with the rigours of austerity. Its road services were worst affected, especially as much basic equipment, including its stock of uniforms, had been destroyed by the bombing. Whether returning to their old jobs or newly recruited, many Guides (or Road Patrols as they were now called) had to dye their army battledress blue and their shoes black and sew on new badges. What the RAC did seem to have in abundance were scarlet sashes, to be worn on duty at all times on pain of dismissal. These were hated accoutrements because every time a patrolman bent over the first aid kit attached to the rear of the bandolier hit him on the back of the head. The red oilskins were also awkward, so stiff that after work they would stand up by themselves. And peaked caps, even with chinstraps, were no substitute for crash helmets (which were not issued until 1954). Many Patrols, moreover, had to supply their own bicycles (in return for a small allowance) and they were warned to restrict their mileage and watch out for 'saddle wear' since 'battledress trousers could not be replaced'. Some patrolmen went on pedalling into the 1950s because the ex-War Department Norton 16H motor-cycle combinations were slow to appear. No training was given in the use of these fiendish machines, which pulled to the left because of the sidecar box and froze their drivers because they were not at first fitted with windshields and hand muffs. As one former Patrol recalls, his motor-bike, which had a top speed of 40mph and no hydraulic suspension, 'was so old I thought it came out of the ark'. The tool kit was 'a bigger shock still. It consisted of a pair of pliers, a couple of open-ended spanners, a foot pump and a very old, bent screwdriver.'

Thus equipped, the Road Patrols kept busy on regular beats. They clocked in at RAC telephone boxes to call one of the sixteen regional offices. They gave news of local conditions, which enabled the RAC to provide a nationwide weather-reporting service. And they received information about breakdowns in their districts. Plenty occurred. Most cars were pre-war models, wheezing jalopies with bald tyres and geriatric bodies. They were, in John Steinbeck's phrase, 'rolling junk'. There seemed to be no restrictions on what second-hand car dealers could sell. One retired Patrol remembers 'a motorist asking me where the handbrake was on the car he'd just bought: there was none'. The 'ever-watchful' RAC issued warnings about dubious vendors. It also offered an inspection service to unskilled purchasers which exposed tricks of the trade such as filling rough gearboxes with heavy oil mixed with sawdust or ground cork. A garage owner in Chester found an ingenious way of ensuring that all his second-hand cars would be approved: he acquired an RAC uniform for one of his mechanics to wear. For authentic RAC Patrols, who numbered 600 by 1950, pay and conditions improved only slowly after the war. Most supplemented their wages by energetically enrolling new members and renewing the subscriptions of old ones. They earned a few shillings in commission on each transaction and raised membership to 400,000 by 1950 (as against the AA's million). Most patrolmen regarded an indelible pencil, for the signing of banker's orders, as their most vital piece of equipment.

Austerity cramped the RAC's style in other directions. On the menu in the members' dining room were items like bubble and squeak and tapioca pudding. The Club's proposed

SENIOR SERVICE

The RAC's road services were slow to get going after
1945 and the organisation remained so creaky that AA
wits sometimes called it 'Grandad'. But since most
Britons drove 'old men's cars' – either chugging
veterans or new models of antiquated design – RAC
Patrols and garages kept busy.

Victory Rally had to be called off because of the fuel shortage. Some compensation was provided in 1946 by the fiftieth-birthday Brighton Run. Huge crowds watched the progress of 137 'Old Crocks', 'a loving nickname', according to *The Autocar*, 'meaning as much as "Old Contemptibles"'. Only seventeen were unable to complete the journey, including Fotheringham-Parker's White Steamer, which went up in flames at the start, and Mrs Wood's Pieper, which had a faulty ignition and finally 'ran out of sparks'. St John Nixon had to help his de Dion tricycle on its way by vigorous pedalling. But this anniversary success was matched by the failure of the RAC's own Golden Jubilee celebrations. During the atrocious winter of early 1947, when the Club's restaurant and Turkish bath both closed down as they had never done during the war, events were planned more splendid than anything dreamt of in the philosophy of the SMMT, which was preparing its own 'Jubilee of the Motor Vehicle'. There would be banquets, balls, outside broadcasts, special-issue stamps, a dance at the Hammersmith Palais for 2,000 motor-cyclists, a dinner at Pall Mall with the waiters dressed as Road Patrols (Lord Howe's suggestion). But the following September almost everything had to be cancelled 'in view of national economic conditions', a balance of payments crisis which took Britain to the nadir of austerity.

That month the Club did salvage one event, as if in defiance of the times. It held a *concours d'élégance* in Regent's Park. Some women in the crowd were also in revolt against the contemporary drabness for they appeared in Dior's extravagant New Look. The cars, which ranged from a gleaming yellow 1897 Daimler to a sleek 1947 Armstrong Siddeley Typhoon, were equally voluptuous. The RAC also published a *Jubilee Book*. Hector Bolitho, the well-known man of letters, was originally approached to edit it, for a fee of 200 guineas. But in the event the motoring journalist Dudley Noble, friend of the Club's lively assistant secretary, Harry Stanley, undertook the task. Aided by members and staff of the Club, he endeavoured to produce a souvenir volume 'of an interesting and readable nature, as distinct from a mere record of facts'. That he did not quite succeed in this aim is suggested by O'Gorman's offer (apparently not accepted) to 'lighten the reading matter' with stories from *Punch*. The book is bland, trite, stuffy, scrappy and partial. Wilfrid Andrews himself damned it with faint praise as a 'worthy publication'. On the other hand, Noble's tribute contains much first-hand information. And the 20,000 copies, selling at £1 each, earned the Club 'excellent publicity'. Reviewing the book favourably, *The Autocar* repeated the comment it had made twenty-five years earlier: 'The history of the RAC is really the history of private motoring in this country.'

Postwar conditions also took their toll on motor sport. Petrol rationing ruled out the RAC rally until 1951. Brooklands was derelict and the War Office refused to release Donington Park, so no national racing circuit was available. Anyway, as Andrews indignantly remarked, there was 'no support for racing from the big four or five manufacturers'. Their attitude gave Lord Howe, chairman of the Club's Competitions Committee, 'a pain'. But at first all he could do to meet the demand for motoring contests was to raise the status of hill-climbs. Then, in 1948, Howe visited an airfield near Northampton called Silverstone. It was a bleak and desolate place which had been unofficially used by local racers. Howe inspected the runway and the perimeter road at a slow, dignified pace which was said to make him look like 'an ambulant cigar'. Having discerned its hidden promise, he persuaded the RAC to purchase a short lease from the Air

SILVERSTONE SPECTACULAR

The Autocar *congratulated the RAC in 1948 on its 'auspicious revival of full-scale motor-racing in England'. But Italy dominated the new course at Silverstone. Luigi Villoresi (above) wins the first Grand Prix in a Maserati. In 1950 Etancelin's Lago-Talbot battles with Kelly's Alta (below) but victory goes to the Alfa-Romeos. What is most striking about these pictures, however, is the total absence of crowd control. Animals as well as spectators strayed onto the course.*

Ministry and to put on the first Grand Prix in Britain since the war. The arrangements had to be completed within two months and one observer felt 'sheer bogglement at the magnitude of the task which by hook or crook the RAC has got to get through by 2 October'. On that day, standing at the starting grid, Howe brought down the Union Jack. Amid the howl of exhausts and the cheers of spectators, British motor racing was reborn.

The press was full of praise for the RAC's courage, energy and foresight. But in truth the Club was a reluctant entrepreneur. It was worried about making a loss but, as the governing body of British motor sport, embarrassed about making a profit. Andrews, who knew nothing about motor racing, intended merely to 'prime the pump'. The running of Silverstone could then be taken over by other organisations, perhaps the British Racing Drivers' Club (whose chairman was Lord Howe) sponsored by the *Daily Express*, both of which had already made a substantial contribution. Consequently the RAC was rather half-hearted about improving Silverstone. Conditions remained primitive for the 1949 British Grand Prix. The race control was lodged in a cowshed. The timekeepers were housed in an old bus. Lavatories were holes in the ground surrounded by canvas screens. The standard straw bales beside the track were the only form of protection. An additional hazard was posed by odd dumps of live ammunition and unexploded bombs. But nothing could discourage fans so long deprived of racing thrills.

Their excitement reached fever pitch in May 1950 when the first British Grand Prix d'Europe (a title bestowed by the Fédération Internationale de l'Automobile) was held at Silverstone in the presence of the King and Queen. Never before had a reigning monarch attended a motor race and the RAC spent over £20,000 to ensure that the event exceeded their expectations. The course was improved. Special grandstands and marquees were erected. A blue-and-gold royal box was built and embowered with yellow blooms, which Andrews insisted on having changed to blue ones on the morning of the meeting. Bunting, streamers and flags abounded; and the royal standard flew proudly in the warm spring sunshine. The day was also notable for the début in an English competition of Juan Manuel Fangio, 'the flying Argentinian'. He was denied the palm but nothing could prevent the victory of his team-mates in their all-conquering Alfa-Romeos. The new BRM, on which British hopes for future racing success were shakily pinned, did not take part in the Grand Prix. But the sleek, green torpedo did perform a couple of demonstration laps. They were inauspicious in that 'the peculiarly distinctive rising scream' of its exhaust caused some of the 120,000 spectators to stuff their ears with paper which had to be extracted by the rudimentary first-aid service. Nevertheless, the Grand Prix was hugely enjoyed, not least by the bowler-hatted, lounge-suited King George. He was cross at having to leave early to avoid traffic jams and at one point he urged Harry Stanley, who was acting as royal chauffeur in a large Humber, to 'keep up with the racing cars'.

About a fortnight later petrol rationing ceased and a new motoring era began. Despite the Korean crisis, people now sensed a chance of satisfying their craving for automobiles. That craving was apparent not only at Silverstone but at the postwar Motor Shows, the first of which, in 1948, had attracted 563,000 visitors. For the most part they were window-shopping, indulging in chromium daydreams. They gazed in hungry fascination at the glittering new models: Jaguar XK 120, Aston Martin DB1, Sunbeam Talbot 80, Morris Minor, Standard Vanguard. Their shapes were svelte, with door handles, headlamps, mudguards and running boards

GLEAMING VISIONS

One of the stars of Britain's first postwar Motor Show, in 1948, was this Hillman Minx, constructed in steel and perspex to reveal the working parts. But the gimmick was more novel than the engineering, which, like that of most of the cars on display, remained essentially pre-war. Still, the gloss was alluring and the export market was buoyant. These cars, it was said, would 'go down well in places like Port Said'.

merged into the bodywork. Beneath this integrated surface were other innovations, mainly from abroad, such as independent front suspension. But what these novelties suggested was not so much technical progress as a swift escape from a dark decade. As *The Autocar* said, 'the new cars radiate a heartening gleam. They may well prove to be the light at the end of the gloom-ridden road along which motoring has travelled over the past ten years.' Still more exhilarating were the exhibits in subsequent Motor Shows: the smooth Rover 75, the razor-edged Triumph Mayflower, the sophisticated young generation of Fords, Consul and Zephyr.

The Festival of Britain in 1951 also indicated improving prospects, its wire-suspended, floodlit, aluminium Skylon emphasising the shape of things to come like a giant exclamation mark. Under the nearby Dome of Discovery the Railton in which John Cobb had established a new land speed record of 394.2mph four years earlier occupied a prominent position. Equally eye-catching was the display put on in the Transport and Communications Pavilion, which demonstrated British automotive achievements over half a century. Its star attraction was the Rover Turbocar – JET 1. This was the world's first gas-turbine-driven automobile, an enticingly simple mechanism which could run on such unlikely fuels as peanut oil and tequila. Though ultimately disappointing, the revolutionary car won the RAC's Dewar Trophy. There was much that was modish about the Festival of Britain. It was also, in one sense, a triumph of hope over experience: the Skylon was said to resemble Britain in having no visible means of support. But the Festival, signposted by the RAC, seemed to point towards a brighter tomorrow. It promised an advance from austerity to affluence, which would occur with startling suddenness. There was no more potent symbol of affluence than the motor car.

TURBOCAR

Rover had been involved in developing Frank Whittle's jet engine during the war. Afterwards it built the first gas turbine-engined car, which reached 150mph but hit technical snags.

CHAPTER NINE

BLESSING AND BLIGHT

Mass motoring was a mixed blessing. Cars enriched the lives of millions with new freedom and mobility. But they also caused terrible problems of pollution and congestion. Hampered by old-fashioned leadership, the RAC responded slowly to the challenge of democracy in the driving seat.

BRIGHT FUTURE

Despite nostalgia for Victorian modes of transport typified by Emett's eccentric railway, the Festival of Britain ushered in two golden decades of economic growth and motoring progress.

DURING THE TWO DECADES after the Festival of Britain millions realised the dream of owning a motor car. The number of automobiles on British roads doubled in the 1950s and doubled again in the 1960s, reaching eleven million by 1970. What was still a luxury for the middle class when Winston Churchill won his second term as Prime Minister had become, by the time Edward Heath entered 10 Downing Street, a virtual necessity for the masses. Nothing could prevent the advance of motordom: not the Korean War, nor the Suez crisis, nor stop-go economic policies. Cars drove trains and trams off the rails; and buses could not compete with such shining models of comfort and convenience. Public transport could never fulfil private fantasies in the manner of E-Type Jaguars, Triumph Heralds and Minis. Like the Citroën DS, so memorably hymned by the philosopher Roland Barthes, they captured the imagination of an entire people. Cars today, said Barthes, 'are almost the exact equivalent of the great Gothic cathedrals ... the supreme creation of an era, conceived with passion by unknown artists'. They enabled the multitude, for the first time, to experience the joy of motoring, the ecstasy of speed, the ineffable glamour of personal powered mobility. Democracy became king of the road.

The trouble was that British roads were not ready for democracy. By 1959, the year in which the country's first major motorway opened, there were only 16,769 more miles of road than there had been in 1911. This represented an increase of 9.5 per cent, whereas during the same period the number of vehicles using the roads had risen by 3,400 per cent. By the end of the 1950s automobiles were carrying more passengers than public transport, lorries were hauling more freight than trains and almost half the population went on holiday by car (compared with a fifth in 1950). As a result British roads, though relatively clear by the standards of today, were by far the most congested in the world. Cities were threatened by 'traffic thrombosis'. There was 'a general clogging up of the whole civilised functioning of town centres'. During rush hours suburbs were threatened by stasis. Traffic jams snaked for miles along rural thoroughfares at peak summer periods. Restricted circulation harmed the economy and until at least 1960 British manufacturers continued to produce cars designed to run on roads that were little better than tarmacked cart tracks. There was a cost in blood, since most accidents took place on unreconstructed highways. Part of the purpose of the RAC's postwar campaign to 'Make the Roads Safe' had been to 'divert blame from motorists to out-of-date roads with their many hazards'. Yet investment in roads remained minimal. In an article entitled 'Roads: A Top Priority', written in 1955, Wilfrid Andrews indignantly declared that the government was spending £9 million on roads, or just two per cent of what it raised in motor taxes. The RAC hammered away at this theme throughout his long chairmanship. It was Andrews's most positive contribution to automobilism and it earned him the journalistic title 'Mr Motoring'.

Ever since the war the RAC had been 'respectfully' drawing the Ministry of Transport's attention to Britain's 'inefficient and out-of-date' highways. Not only did the Club plead for the construction of motorways to relieve 'the most heavily trafficked roads' on earth, it also harped on 'such urgent matters as street planning; a uniform system of street lighting; the general improvement of road surfaces; the provision of footpaths and cycle tracks; and the improvement in facilities for waiting cars'. Andrews continually stressed the RAC's 'importance in any scheme of highway reform'. The Ministry did not demur. Consultation took place over everything from flyovers to the standard height of hedges on the central reservations between dual carriageways. But since spending rose so sluggishly Andrews took other measures to galvanise the government. In July 1953, largely at his behest, the Standing Joint Committee published a booklet calling for 'A Revised Road Policy'. In January 1954 the *Manchester Guardian* devoted six pages to 'propaganda for more and better roads, which had arisen out of a publicity campaign organised by the chairman'. RAC members were encouraged to let the Club know about dangerous junctions, poor road surfaces and the like; and it passed these reports on to the authorities, who often acted on them. Motorists were also reminded that they should adopt 'Better Roadmanship'. The term, though not the practice, derived from Stephen Potter's comic 'carmanship' (itself a subsection of gamesmanship), whereby a passenger might rattle a driver by 'suggesting, with the minutest stiffening of the legs at corners', that he was going too fast.

Finally, keen to mount a 'full-blooded onslaught' on the government, which the RAC itself was inhibited from doing, Andrews founded the Roads Campaign Council in April 1955. It had the backing of all motoring interests, who were determined to promote serious investment in the nation's highways. In fervent pamphlets and passionate press releases the Council preached the gospel of roads. It produced films, held exhibitions and organised petitions. It took members of parliament to see German autobahns and then showed them the 'piecemeal and patchwork methods' by which British roads had been improved. It arranged for motorists fuming in Whitsun traffic hold-ups to be given leaflets saying: 'Get yourself out of this jam –

FANTASIES IN OVERDRIVE

The most imaginative cars of the age embodied the dreams of democracy. The Citroën DS ('Déesse' being the French for goddess) was more than a model of automotive sophistication. It was, in the words of Roland Barthes, a 'wholly magical object'. The E-type Jaguar was not just a 150mph sports car but, as almost everyone observed, a potent phallic symbol – a winning piece in the mating game.

Why is this car such a snip for £2,000?

press your MP for better roads.' So effective was the pressure group that as early as 1958 Andrews reduced the RAC's financial contribution to it, claiming that 'its objectives had now largely been achieved'. This judgement was premature. When the AA defected from the Roads Campaign Council to the British Road Federation in 1963, Andrews himself insisted that the Council should continue – as it still does, its longest-serving Chairman having been Jack Williams, a staunch and tireless member of the RAC's Committee. But the Council's impact had been such that all political parties paid lip service to it in their 1959 election manifestos. Annual spending on roads rose to £70 million by the end of the 1950s. The Council could also claim a concrete achievement in the shape of the first substantial motorway, the London–Birmingham M1.

This led Britain into the automotive age. It was safer than other roads. The motorway reduced congestion in bypassed towns and villages. It raised property prices and stimulated growth along the corridor it created. It fostered longer-distance commuting by car, permitting more people to enjoy country life. The M1 was the first branch of an asphalt network that would transform Britain. To quote Jack Williams: 'More than any man, it was Mr. Wilfrid Andrews who was responsible for getting the motorway programme off the ground.' The Chairman certainly posed a new challenge to RAC Patrols, who had to fit 'hundreds of yards' of new fan belts every year to cars which expired on its hard shoulders.

Yet, despite the Treasury's perennial reluctance to pay out, the RAC's Chairman had been pushing at an open door. Tory governments of the 1950s favoured the automobile as the most potent emblem of affluence. Reacting against socialist collectivism, Ministers of Transport such as Alan Lennox-Boyd and Ernest Marples aimed to set the individual driver free. They hailed the car as the vehicle of the future and accepted the view of *The Economist* that 'to restrict a country's motor-mindedness is to condemn it to technical backwardness'. However, they also recognised that the advance of the automobile inevitably meant further regulation. The right of one motorist to stop where he wished could violate the right of another to go as he pleased. Andrews failed to appreciate the limitations of laissez-faire. Thus, under his leadership, the RAC objected to the closure of roads in national parks as an 'encroachment on the liberty of the subject'. On the same grounds it hankered to increase the speed limit from 20 to 30mph in London's royal parks. Also, in the mid-1950s, it resisted the introduction of parking meters.

For a time, to be sure, the RAC considered it 'expedient to yield somewhat' on that question. This was because the Minister of Transport agreed to devote income from parking meters to provide more permanent spaces for cars. Also some of the Club's own members judged meters 'beneficial'. But many more resented this new imposition and criticised the Club for being 'placid' about it. So the RAC, like the AA, soon reverted to outright opposition. However, the Club's press campaign had an 'unfriendly reception'. The Ministry of Transport excluded the motoring organisations from its working party on parking meters and a Labour MP declared that the RAC's line was 'anti-social'. Andrews dismissed this charge as 'grossly unfair', but heretical doubts were being expressed on his own Committee. Harold Nockolds, the author of magisterial histories of Rolls-Royce and Lucas, thought that the Club was adopting a 'negative and defensive attitude'. Lord Howe declared that off-street parking, the RAC's

CONSUMER CONGESTION

*Cars struggle through Ashford, Kent, at 9.15 a.m.
on 6 August 1955. Such pictures supported the
view of the Roads Campaign Council, set up in
that year by the RAC, that motorways were
essential. They would not only ease the flow of
traffic but cut the annual toll of 5,000 road
deaths, which the Club Chairman compared to
a 'bloody war'.*

preferred solution, was problematic because of London's 'fantastic ground-values'. Andrew Polson, who was to succeed Wilfrid Andrews as Chairman, reckoned that the Club would have to revise its attitude if it could not put forward a plausible alternative to parking meters.

Andrews prevaricated, saying that at least they had an alternative to that other proposal which was upsetting motorists, the MOT testing of cars over ten years old. Instead of an onerous compulsory examination, the RAC wanted a 'system of "spot checks"'. This was hardly adequate to meet the case, as Andrews should have known from his regional inspection tours. For, ironically, some of the worst 'old bangers' in the kingdom belonged to the RAC. Its policy was to keep them on the road until they gave up the ghost, often with several hundred thousand miles on the clock. About his vehicle one Patrol exclaimed: 'Look at the holes in the wings. It plays God Save the Queen when I go over 40 miles an hour.' When John Robb became an inspector in the Glasgow area in 1952 he was given a decrepit Austin van with an insatiable appetite for oil. As he recalls, 'The side indicators only functioned when the driver thumped the door upright with his fist. Rusty headlamp reflectors produced lights like candles. There were no exterior rear view mirrors and unfortunately no heater either.' Crossing Rannoch Moor on dark winter nights, Robb had to stop regularly, lift the creaking bonnet, check the oil level and thaw himself out over the engine. Nevertheless Lord Howe supported the RAC's 'spot check' proposal. The new test gave too much scope for chicanery, he said, and since there were no spare parts for older vehicles 'the humbler classes of motorists would be legislated off the road'. Evidently he took no account of the argument that cars which needed spare parts were unfit to be driven. But at least Howe showed more grasp of motoring on a shoestring than some of his peers. Lord Jowitt suggested that testing would be unnecessary if others followed his way of keeping his own car in good order – he replaced it every year.

In the course of these disputes the RAC was increasingly attacked for being out of touch with ordinary motorists. Pall Mall, said the critics, represented nothing but itself. Andrews irately rebutted both accusations. The Club could speak for Associate members, he asserted, because its nationwide organisation provided 'a very clear idea of the feelings of its membership'. Andrews further claimed that information from 'various sources' in 'many quarters' enabled the Club to voice the sentiments of the entire motoring community. His case was unconvincing. The *Daily Telegraph* asked pertinently, 'Don't some of us think it quite reasonable that we should be charged a modest sum for cluttering up the Queen's highway for hours with great lumps of immobile metal?' The fact was that motorists were now so many and so various that the Club could no longer express their views as authoritatively as it had when they formed a smaller and more homogeneous constituency.

Furthermore, there was a gulf fixed between the Club's full members and its Associates. Samuelson would no more have dreamt of visiting the Associate headquarters next door than of contradicting Wilfrid Andrews. Many Associate members resented the Club's aloofness and saw themselves as the victims of social apartheid. Its consequences were not all bad. In 1956 the Associate Committee voted to 'review the desirability, or otherwise, of employing coloured people as patrols'. They were firmly told (by Andy Polson) that the RAC had previously decided, and now reaffirmed, that 'there should be no colour-bar to the employment of the Club's Road Staff'. Colour could be a bar to entry into the Pall Mall Club itself, however. In

MOTORWAY ONE

*Technically the Preston
bypass was Britain's first
motorway, but the London–
Birmingham M1 opened a
new era in road transport.
The motorway was, so to
speak, an extension of Henry
Ford's production line, a
traffic conveyor belt enabling
cars to travel more efficiently.
Many vehicles failed the
long-distance, high-speed test,
providing work for the RAC.
It issued a booklet entitled
'Know Your Motorway',
giving information and
advice such as 'Do not walk
on the carriageways.'*

1960 a prominent Indonesian was excluded in an insulting manner. His sponsor, Lieutenant-Colonel Bertram Ede, complained to Mountbatten, who replied that as President

> I never interfere in the internal affairs of the Club, which are handled entirely by the Chairman …. Speaking quite frankly and without implying any criticism, I think it would be fair to say that many of the members of the RAC have not got the enlightened attitude on world affairs and eastern folk which I hope you and I have …. I am sure that you agree that it is impossible to expect the Committee to accept as a member a person who they may have reason to believe will not be liked. I feel, therefore, we must accept their judgement, however much we may deplore it.

Whatever its degree and character, discrimination was generally practised with discretion.

That the RAC usually presented a united front and an attractive face to the world was due in large measure to good public relations. Senior figures like Harry Stanley, Tony Lee, Pat Gregory and Phil Drackett understood the media and exploited it to good effect. They were helped by the fact that the RAC was associated in the public mind with the glamour of motor sport. A racing driver such as John Cobb, for example, imbued the Club with an aura of excitement which was positively enhanced when he was killed attempting to break the world's water speed record in 1952. Cobb was promoted to the pantheon of the Club's heroes, Lord Howe hailing him as the 'finest sportsman and greatest gentleman he had ever met'.

Howe himself, whose brushes with death were legendary, was a persuasive defender of the Club's reputation. In 1955, recorded *The Autocar*, critics were left in no doubt that its Competitions Committee was 'fully capable of running anything from an egg-and-spoon race to the Mille Miglia'. Recognising that the Club's sporting image gave it a notable advantage over the AA, especially in attracting young members, Harry Stanley devised a motor sport membership badge. This displeased the volatile Captain Phillips, who did not want his members to be contaminated by anything racy. But in the spring of 1955 Wilfrid Andrews was persuaded to present the first badge to Stirling Moss, who accepted it on behalf of motor sport enthusiasts. Moss commented wryly that during the previous season's racing on European circuits nothing would have been more valuable to him than the RAC's Get-You-Home service. But that summer he became the first Briton to win the British Grand Prix.

The RAC was adept at exploiting trials, anniversaries, competitions, innovations. In 1955 it produced a fortnightly television programme entitled 'The World on Wheels', featuring matters like motor sport, new traffic laws and road safety. Using reports of traffic hold-ups telephoned in by Patrols, the RAC supplied news to the BBC and stole a march on the AA. In the competition for publicity between the two motoring organisations, though, the Club by no means always came out on top. In 1955, for instance, *The Autocar* published an embarrassing photograph of a car bearing the number plate RAC 1 and above it … an AA badge.

However, Harry Stanley and Pat Gregory, the RAC's public relations officer, pulled off a notable coup the following year, when the Soviet Union opened its borders to foreign motor traffic. They persuaded the Standard motor company to lend them a red-and-white Vanguard shooting-brake with a special TR3 engine and became the first Westerners to reach Moscow by car after the ban was lifted. Subsequently they published a booklet, 'To Russia and Back',

STIRLING WORK

Helmeted and goggled but otherwise ill-protected, Stirling Moss drives his Mercedes to victory in the 1955 British Grand Prix. Before a record crowd of 125,000, he completed 270 miles of the Aintree circuit at an average speed of 86.47mph.. He became the first Briton to win the Grand Prix Cup and to receive the RAC Motor Sport member's badge – which helped to invest the increasingly old-fashioned Club with youthful allure.

telling motorists what to expect behind the Iron Curtain. It advised them to take tools, spare parts, a tyre-pressure gauge, petrol and soap. The RAC duo also reported that the Automobile Club of the USSR had presented them with a 'Good Driver' badge. They omitted to mention that in the breakneck race against their AA rivals Stanley had not only frightened Gregory (who had never before driven on the Continent) but had terrified their KGB 'minder'.

The Club also took discreet advantage of its royal connection. Staff were instructed never to refer to the RAC, always to the Royal Automobile Club. Journalists were encouraged to play up the 'very special relationship' between the Club and its sovereign patrons. (Actually the Duke of Edinburgh sometimes supported AA events, which prompted a remonstrance from Mountbatten, who told him that the RAC was 'very shocked and deeply hurt'.) The Club celebrated its Diamond Jubilee with much ballyhoo. A splendid cavalcade of cars ancient and modern drove from London to Woodcote Park, among them Field Marshal Montgomery's khaki Humber Snipe. Lord Mountbatten presented a Diamond Jubilee trophy for outstanding achievements in motor transport, its first winner being the explorer Sir Vivian Fuchs.

The Club put on a travelling exhibition entitled 'The Age of the Motor Car' at which 250,000 people saw a unique panorama of vehicles from Cugnot's steam carriage to the latest jet machines. But the crowning moment of the celebrations occurred when Queen Elizabeth visited the Pall Mall clubhouse. She presented plaques to half a dozen surviving founder members, including Monty and Claude Grahame-White and H. J. Mulliner, and medals to patrolmen who had done long service or performed acts of gallantry. Summing up the general view, Gordon England said that the occasion had been 'full of dignity and sincerity' and 'made him proud to be British'. Behind the scenes, however, there had been a sharp contretemps. Harry Stanley had detailed certain members to meet the Queen in manageable batches. But just before her arrival Lord Mountbatten appeared in the vestibule. 'Where are the members?' he demanded furiously. 'I want the members to meet the Queen. Let them in!' 'Sir, I will do nothing of the sort,' replied Stanley. 'There are 16,000 members of the Club and it is impossible for them all to meet the Queen.' The Assistant Secretary, said to be the best-dressed man in England, had his way and his arrangements worked smoothly.

Soon afterwards Stanley resigned. Other senior figures went at about the same time. Captain Phillips retired in 1956. So did Geoffrey Samuelson. His able successor as Secretary, John Hanhart, lasted little more than a year, himself being followed by the more tractable Commander D. P. Little. All departed nursing a more or less virulent hatred for Wilfrid Andrews. He was, according to Harry Stanley, 'a total dictator'. He kept his top subordinates down and baulked them at every turn. He never acknowledged their contribution and boasted that 'There is no limit to what you can do if you take credit for other people's ideas.' He always liked to make headlines personally and to occupy the limelight by himself. Any little advantage gained by a member of his staff, from the award of an OBE to the enjoyment of a better room than his own in a hotel, became a personal slight. It was an implicit threat to his supremacy, a challenge to provoke a revenge. Like the deadly upas tree, Andrews ensured that nothing could grow in his shade. Moreover, his 'megalomaniac' tendencies grew with age.

There is no doubt that after the Diamond Jubilee Andrews himself should have retired. He was sixty-five and had done the Club some service. He had led it to recovery after the war and

DIAMOND JUBILEE

Queen Elizabeth enters the Pall Mall clubhouse on 18 March 1957, accompanied by the RAC's Chairman, Wilfrid Andrews. Its President, Lord Mountbatten, and the Duke of Edinburgh follow them. The Autocar *reported that this was a 'great day in the history of the RAC and in the lives of dozens who, seldom seen or heard, have served motorists well'.*

ROYAL HONOUR

The Queen honours venerable members of the Club and heroic patrolmen. On the right Patrol J. P. Drury, who rescued cattle from a fire, receives a gold medallion.

guided it safely out of the era of austerity. The clubhouse was a model of affluence. Indeed, by 1957 it was 'the most successful club in London', according to *The Autocar*, whose esteem was admittedly based on an odd criterion – the range of soups available in the members' dining room, which included shark's fin, bird's nest and kangaroo tail. Andrews had also presided over, and to some extent stimulated, 'the extraordinary growth of motor sport' after the war. Above all he had revived the fortunes of the Associate section. Membership had increased by leaps and bounds since 1945 and approached three quarters of a million by the time of the Diamond Jubilee. The Patrols were now motorised and radio communications were on the horizon. Many improvements had been made to the various services. Morale was high, team spirit was strong and the ethos of service was pervasive. Patrols worked, as one wrote, 'for the privilege of wearing the uniform and the respect'. 'It was,' says another, 'a vocation then.'

IN THE EYES OF THE PUBLIC the RAC's organisation certainly appeared glamorous and successful. Smart patrolmen saluted members. They helped stranded motorists, who sometimes offered to clamber under the car themselves rather than risk dirtying their rescuer's uniform. They assisted at accidents, often giving first aid in gruesome circumstances. They were chivalric figures who left cans of petrol in their telephone boxes and trusted members to pay for them. Their exploits often featured in the press. 'Tiger' Sinclair had to dig his telephone box out of the snow on Soutra Hill, south-east of Edinburgh, so often that local newspapers hailed him as the 'Soutra Sentinel'. Equally tough was Bill George, the RAC's 'loneliest patrol', whose Lake District beat included the Kirkstone Pass which was so steep that he often had to drive panic-stricken motorists across it in their own cars.

The RAC's weather-beaten patrolmen seemed to live lives of perpetual adventure. They delivered babies, helped the police catch criminals, herded sheep off moorland roads and cured leaking radiators with infusions of oatmeal or ground ginger. They breathed new life into the dead engines of Rolls-Royces and bubble cars, seagoing yachts and pantomime scooters. They were particularly adept at opening locked cars without doing damage. Richard Crossman described how a strange young RAC man with a piece of wire got into a friend's car in five minutes and exclaimed triumphantly, 'Well, I've never done a Mercedes before. That leaves only the Rover 3-litre and I'm longing to do that as well.' RAC Patrols also accomplished well-publicised tasks like sign-posting Holiday Routes: the first HR aimed to beat jams to the West Country and was appreciated by everyone except motorists who thought that the RAC was directing them to a Horse Race.

RAC patrolmen courted publicity because it helped in the all-important drive for members. Pressure to recruit and to renew subscriptions grew ever more intense. Patrol Herbert Kettlewell could never forget his superintendent's threat to dismiss him if he failed to sign up new members while doing point duty. The RAC stationed mobile enrolment caravans at strategic sites such as shopping centres, race courses and agricultural shows. It employed 'Patrolettes', young saleswomen in blue, air hostess-like uniforms with capes and high-heeled leather boots. Even in the early 1960s, apparently, the name 'Patrolette' sounded rather patronising and vain attempts were made to change it to 'Courier'. But Patrolettes did receive discreet hints about

PRESTIGE SERVICE

Being saluted by Patrols on gleaming Norton combinations made RAC members feel like captains of the road. Many motorists still joined the Club for the prestige as well as the service – which remained haphazard during the 1950s.

LION-HEARTED

RAC patrolmen had to be tough and resourceful since they received little help from their bosses and often faced difficult situations – some hairier than others.

employing their charms to solicit new members. One blonde, blue-eyed Patrolette managed to sign up twenty-five miners at Easington Colliery, County Durham, by dint of standing outside the pithead baths – which 'steamed up' rather more than usual on her appearance. The Club published a confidential 'Membership Promotion Bulletin' entitled *Signposts*. It was full of league tables setting out the achievements of the seventeen regional offices and exhortations to Patrols to exceed the magic number of 1,000 new enrolments a year. It did, however, enter this caveat: 'members of the public hanging from fourth-floor windows of a burning building by one hand should not be approached until they have been rescued'.

The regional offices also presented a brave front. They were semi-independent businesses, 'little RACs in their own right'. The area manager, pinstripe-suited and bowler-hatted, cut a dash in the local community. He was a figure at civic occasions, a pillar of the Conservative Club, 'Mr RAC himself'. At Bournemouth, typically, he was in charge of twenty office staff (mainly women), while his uniformed opposite number, the chief superintendent, commanded thirty-two Road Patrols. Despite the low pay, RAC provincial offices were often enjoyable places to work in. They operated on a human scale: employees were treated as 'people not statistics'. Outstanding managers like Tommy Burke-Bloor were father figures – firm, fair, humane. Sometimes they were even indulgent: in Stockport on very hot days L. J. Marshall bought his staff ice-cream. There were Christmas bonuses, dinner dances and outings subsidised by the Club. Rum incidents abounded: one member, on joining the RAC, insisted that he must receive a patrolman's uniform; another tried to pay his subscription in pigs' trotters.

Moreover these outposts of Pall Mall were repositories of encyclopaedic local knowledge. There was usually someone in the office who could locate a broken-down car from a telephoned description of its surroundings or devise an intricate route avoiding black spots but including beauty spots. Dennis Hall at Leeds was a walking road atlas: he could supply the best route for any journey in Britain, detailing road numbers, traffic lights, crossroads and so on, all from memory. But even he would have been hard put to meet some requests: for a route to keep clear of 'all towns and hills'; 'a route to avoid all traffic'; a route from Liverpool to Southend 'not using any roundabouts'; a route to Scotland beside the 'prettiest heather'.

Imposing though the RAC's façade was, however, serious cracks were developing in its fabric which would eventually endanger the whole structure. The Club was still rooted in the past, slow to modernise and reluctant to invest in plant or people. Budgets were usually written down on a single sheet of paper and then pigeonholed. Many of the regional offices were positively Dickensian. When Marjorie Pearce went to work for the RAC in Bristol in 1957, she was shocked to find a 'dreadful shabby office' with tatty linoleum on the floor, chairs that lacked seats, scratched tables instead of desks and 'grotty typewriters' such as 'Moses must have used to type out the Ten Commandments'. Often just as scruffy were the offices of managers, some of whom were little more than jumped-up clerks – literally so in the case of one man whose sole talent was to do a standing jump from floor to table, a feat he demonstrated to his bemused employees each morning. He and his kind frequently behaved like petty tyrants. John Howells ruled the Birmingham office with 'a rod of iron, sacked staff for any reason and terrified' nearly everyone. Others practised odious forms of harassment. Sometimes staff could hardly call their souls their own. It was, for example, 'frowned upon to become romantically involved

PATROLETTES

Patrolettes were anything but female Patrols. Their chief function was to recruit new members and sell the RAC's products. This they did with some success, despite the common belief, held by many in the RAC, that a woman's place was in the home.

BRIEF LIFE

The uniforms were modified for added glamour. But the role of the Patrolettes was never as well defined as their hemlines. During the late 1960s their careers, too, were cut short.

with fellow workers' and if a couple married one of them was expected to find another job. However, what made the turnover of office staff so high was the fact that wages were as poor as conditions – an experienced office worker might earn as little as £3 10s a week. Worse still, the service that the RAC provided at the regional level was creaky, confused and antique.

It had not changed much, indeed, since the 1920s – except that motor-bikes had replaced push-bikes. Patrols still rode about haphazardly 'looking for breakdowns' and seldom finding more than three a day. Their tool kits remained primitive, consisting of little more than spanners, screwdrivers, pliers and a puncture-repair outfit. Local RAC offices could only keep in touch by telephone, so Patrols had to be in their boxes at prearranged times. Occasionally this involved evicting squatters, such as strawberry sellers or call girls. Sometimes the system broke down and senior officers had to go in search of their men. A Devon inspector once surprised an errant Patrol at home digging potatoes while his Norton combination rested on its stand in a nearby stream, its rear wheel spinning in the current and clocking up an impressive mileage.

A regime which combined tight discipline with loose supervision was inviting misconduct. Moreover, positive incentives to good behaviour were lacking: during the Suez crisis, when petrol rationing diminished motoring, the RAC cut its Patrol force from 900 to 600 and made no redundancy payments. So there were cases of Patrols painting their houses with RAC blue paint, setting up in business on their own account, engaging in sexual adventures. Opportunities for dalliance certainly occurred, not least when female motorists broke down in lonely places. But perhaps one need not take too seriously letters sent to *Playboy*, purportedly from RAC patrolmen, describing acts in cars 'not mentioned in the Highway Code'.

Wilfrid Andrews extolled RAC telephone boxes as 'silent patrols' but by the late 1950s the Club's road service organisation was in desperate need of an improved communications system. The AA had introduced two-way radio into its London vans as early as 1949, extending it to motor-bikes in 1952. As a result its patrolmen were used with much greater efficiency than those of its rival. So in 1957 John Hanhart commissioned Captain Aubrey Thompson, a manager in the Associate section, to introduce an RAC radio-controlled rescue service. It would improve on the old 'Get-You-Home' service, used in the course of half a century by two and a half million people, which depended on garages.

The new service began with three second-hand diesel J2 Commer vans directed by radio to the scene of a breakdown. There RAC 'driver/mechanics', as they were called, would cope with anything but a major repair job. The Commers were soon supplemented by Mini vans, which gradually replaced patrolmen's Norton combinations, and Thompson began to establish a VHF radio network to deploy them. A control room was set up, first on the third floor of 83 Pall Mall and then in a specially designed chamber on the ground floor. The first transmission mast was at Jack Straw's Castle, a pub high on Hampstead Heath. Eventually sixty masts would be erected around the British Isles. The RAC's capacity to help its members, and to compete with the opposition, was transformed.

However, the mobile twelve-volt valve radios had a limited range and there were many 'blind areas', especially in hilly districts. The installations were sometimes faulty. On one famous occasion the Edinburgh radio landline became crossed with that of the horse-racing Tote, so that RAC Patrols with loudspeakers on their vehicles broadcast betting odds while book-

The old system

Relying on telephone boxes for communication and on garages for many repairs, the RAC could only deliver a patchy and inadequate service. Indeed, according to one canard, it petered out entirely north of Watford. Actually the Get-You-Home Service was the largest of its kind in the world and during the 1950s RAC Patrols dealt with tens of thousands of breakdowns every year. Nevertheless, the system was in urgent need of modernisation.

makers round the country received information about breakdowns. Investment in the radio rescue service was too little, too slow and too late – the Home Office only gave the RAC four frequencies (later increased to five) to the AA's twelve. Certainly the system soon proved itself. For example, in September 1964 RAC radio patrols kept the public in touch with events as King Olaf of Norway opened the Forth road bridge. Yet senior managers in the Associate section remained sceptical. Instead of this expensive, new-fangled apparatus they would have been much happier, remarked a cynical Patrol, with 'a tin can and a piece of string'.

In many respects the condition of British motordom at the end of the 1950s mirrored that of the RAC: the surface looked shiny and bright but underneath there were signs of rust and rot. Car production had more than doubled in the last seven years of the decade. Hire-purchase agreements on new cars had multiplied twenty-fold in ten years. Britain still had twenty-five per cent of the world car market. Austin merged with Morris to form the British Motor Corporation (BMC) in 1951, while Rootes acquired Singer in 1955. Profits were buoyant and expansion was in the air. Eye-catching new models rolled out of factories: Rovers, Triumphs, Rolls-Royces. The Jaguar, powered by a twin overhead camshaft six-cylinder engine, was especially compelling. The 1958 Mark IX saloon, for example, with power steering, disc brakes on all four wheels and optional automatic transmission, had everything that the American market could desire except tail fins. Still more exciting was the phallus-shaped 3.8-litre E-Type.

Not even this, however, could eclipse the true icon of the age, the Mini. Created by Alec Issigonis, an artist in engineering, this amazingly innovative little car had a transverse four-cylinder engine, front-wheel drive, tiny wheels and independent rubber suspension. The Mini, which did 70mph and 50 miles per gallon, seemed to justify the advertisers' claim that it was 'wizardry on wheels'. Compact but roomy, it clung to the road, manoeuvred easily through traffic and parked on a postage stamp. It became fashionable, classless and ubiquitous. It was driven by housewives and film stars, school teachers and racing drivers. The 'Orange Box', as it was christened at Longbridge, not only came to symbolise the 'swinging sixties', it initiated a revolution in car design that swept the world.

Yet the Mini can also be seen as an emblem of much that was wrong with the British motor industry. It was shoddily produced and plagued by teething troubles. Its clutch was defective, its sliding windows stuck, its wire door-pull snapped. Changing gears with its willowy stick was rather like water divining. Above all, the Mini often failed in the rain, which penetrated its body and extinguished its engine. This state of affairs was over-dramatised, declared Issigonis facetiously, by people who did not like sitting in a car with their feet awash, though he did admit the oddness of 'driving in galoshes'. In more serious vein, Issigonis justified the Mini's austere interior on the grounds that it was good for drivers: the hard seats kept them awake and they were not distracted by a radio. Such remarks prove the aptness of the nickname which the designer gave himself – 'Arragonis' – and perhaps explain why he was not universally esteemed at BMC. Yet BMC itself, which rarely recruited university graduates and managed its business by the seat of its pants, compounded the Mini's technical faults with disastrous commercial decisions. It produced so many versions of the car that sixty different varieties of speedometer had to be made. And, in a fatal effort to monopolise the cheap end of the market, BMC set the price too low. According to one estimate, each Mini the company sold lost it £30.

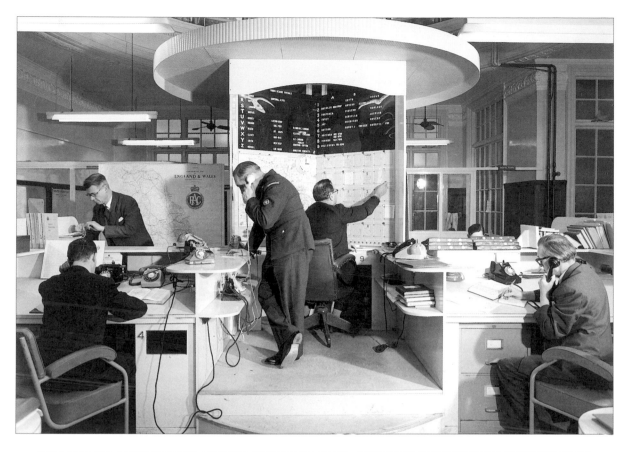

THE NEW SYSTEM.

During the late 1950s radio communications, linking the Associate section's headquarters with patrolmen in vans, began to revolutionise the service which the RAC could provide. The Pall Mall control room (top) was glass-domed and acoustically perfect. It was variously known as 'the goldfish bowl' and 'the snake pit'.

In contrast to the Ford Cortina, which from drawing-board to after-sales service was a triumph of planning, other British makes were dogged by serious problems. The Triumph Herald, which was put together like a jigsaw puzzle, leaked at every joint and fell to pieces in rugged conditions. The Hillman Imp's aluminium rear engine had a tendency to overheat, its pneumatic throttle functioned fitfully and its steering was suspect. The Austin 1800 had gear selection difficulties, an erratic indicator stalk switch and an improperly calibrated dipstick, which caused owners to overfill it with oil. Even Jaguar could not completely eradicate significant defects before production and the marque won a reputation for unreliability, especially in the United States.

At home the Consumer Association's magazine *Motoring Which?*, first published in 1962, subjected new models to ruthless scrutiny. Moreover, it obliged motoring journals, which had hitherto lived in symbiosis with the car makers who supplied their advertising revenue, to do likewise. It became increasingly clear that British motor manufacturing was inefficient because it was old-fashioned. Foreign technical advances were slow to arrive – disc brakes, radial-ply tyres, automatic gears, power steering, rear independent suspension, to say nothing of refinements like two-speed windscreen wipers and electric windows. This tardiness was not surprising in view of the antiquated plant on which British manufacturers relied. When Lord Rootes took over Singer in 1955 he recognised not only some of the men in the factory where he had served as an apprentice before the First World War but also some of the machinery.

In the event, the acquisition of Singer made the Rootes Group more ramshackle than ever. It was 'too small to make money ... too large to close down'. This was the situation of most British manufacturers and it led to a spate of takeovers and mergers during the 1960s. Rootes itself fell to Chrysler. The Leyland bus company became the implausible owner of Standard Triumph in 1961, adding Rover to its portfolio four years later. In 1965 Jaguar joined BMC to constitute British Motor Holdings. Finally, in 1968, the big two British car companies amalgamated. Under the managing directorship of Sir Donald Stokes, they formed the British Leyland Motor Corporation (BL). In theory this created a single world-class company which could achieve the same economies of scale as foreign giants like Volkswagen. In practice BL was not even well placed to take advantage of the boom year of 1972, when a record 1.9 million cars were produced in Britain. The fact was that BL had too many plants and too many models. Too little investment meant that its new cars (such as the Maxi and the Princess) were largely unsuccessful. After the Mini it certainly had no world-beater. Stokes rationalised neither the company nor its untidy dealer network. Its manpower remained high and its productivity low. In 1968 BL's 185,000-strong workforce made $1.9 billion from sales, whereas Chrysler in the United States, with about the same number of employees, achieved sales worth $5.65 billion.

The decline of the British car industry was by no means just a failure of management. Labour relations were atrocious and attempts to cure overmanning provoked crippling strikes. Of course, workers harnessed to assembly lines were inclined to rebel against what has been called 'the organisation of exhaustion'. One Ford worker complained that the company 'class you more as machines than men'. On the other hand, militant shop stewards even fell out with their own trade union bosses. Demarcation disputes, restrictive practices and unofficial stoppages were rife. Governments seemed powerless to improve the situation. Indeed, they made

More room in less space

EAST-WEST ENGINE

The Revolutionary
"QUALITY FIRST"
MORRIS Mini-Minor

A MINI SENSATION

Alec Issigonis's answer to the bubble-car, like Herbert Austin's riposte to the cycle-car, was a brilliant all-rounder. It did everything from carrying families (above) to winning rallies (below). But it combined astonishing versatility with worrying unreliability.

MADE IN MILLIONS

Now nearly forty years of age, the best-selling car in Britain is still being manufactured. Furthermore, today most of the world's automobiles have front-wheel drive and the space-saving transverse engine which Issigonis pioneered.

matters worse by treating the industry as a source of revenue and an economic regulator. The Treasury had a battery of fiscal weapons at its disposal: purchase tax, petrol duty, the road licence fee and credit restrictions. Usually they were deployed with scant regard for the industry itself. Between 1952 and 1972, for example, the rate of purchase tax changed twenty times.

More serious was the reduction of tariffs on imports, which, ministers hoped, would prepare Britain to join the European Common Market. By the end of the 1960s the duty had fallen from 33⅓ to seventeen per cent. At this stage fewer than ten per cent of automobiles sold in the United Kingdom had been made abroad. But Britain's share of the world car market had halved during the decade and there were ominous signs that foreign competitors were poised to attack. Japanese companies had virtually driven British motor-cycle manufacturers from the field and Japanese automobile production had multiplied more than tenfold, streaking past that of Britain. Arguably the British car industry was always a creature of protection. Certainly the collapse of tariff walls helped to destroy it.

MEANWHILE THE CAR ITSELF was ousting alternative forms of transport and causing increasingly serious problems. Bus services had remained adequate during the 1950s. But as more people bought cars a vicious circle set in: fares rose, passengers defected, profits fell and services were cut. The same process afflicted the railways. Many local lines became grossly uneconomic and in 1963 Dr Richard Beeching was appointed Chairman of British Railways with a brief to conduct brutal surgery. He axed 5,000 miles of track and closed a third of the country's 7,000 stations. At a time when only about half the families in the kingdom owned a car, the social cost of the contraction of public transport was immense. Rural areas again faced isolation, from which they had been rescued by the internal combustion engine. Those who could not afford a car were increasingly handicapped. Young people could not get access to further education. Old age pensioners were imprisoned in their villages. Housewives were stranded in the suburbs. At the same time, the quality of life in towns and cities was deteriorating sharply as a result of the automobile invasion. The car was a source of noise, fumes, vibration, congestion, visual pollution, injury and death. It was difficult, opined Professor Colin Buchanan in his book *Mixed Blessing* (1958), to think of anything wrought by the hand of man which had created havoc on such a scale – apart from war. Yet, he continued, the car was not only a vital element in the nation's social and economic affairs, it was to many people, including himself, 'little short of an object of worship'.

Buchanan was commissioned by Ernest Marples to study the impact of motor vehicles on urban life and his report, *Traffic in Towns* (1963), came to the same conclusion: the car was both a blessing and a blight. Everybody wanted an automobile but *en masse* they were destructive monsters. When regarded as part of '"the traffic problem" the motor car is clearly a menace that can spoil our civilisation. But translated into terms of the particular vehicle that stands outside the door, we regard it as one of our most treasured possessions or dearest ambitions, an immense convenience, an expander of the dimensions of life, a symbol of the modern age.' Buchanan's analysis of the problems posed by the glut of cars in cities was acute. And he skilfully exposed flaws in the solutions advanced by others. He revealed, for example, the environmental dam-

THE GOOD, THE BAD AND THE UGLY

The Cortina (left) was Ford's sharp reply to the Mini. Its engine was sturdily conventional but the car's lightweight body was a pioneering model of scientific design. The Triumph Herald's body (below left), which owed more to slick Italian styling, was assembled in sections that often did not fit. The Austin 1800 (below right) was far heavier and less reliable than the Cortina. And the stubby Hillman Imp (bottom) was a British reversion to rear-engine drive when the world was looking forwards.

The Triumph Herald 12/50 has an opening for a smart dad

How can you create the big impression
without seeming to show off?
Drive an Austin 1800.
The big impression is built in.

AUSTIN

WAIT
TILL
YOU
GET
INSIDE

HILLMAN ROOTES

age caused by Marples' well-publicised endeavours to make the most of existing streets. Traffic flow was certainly improved by urban 'clearways', linked traffic signals, parking prohibitions, pedestrian controls, 'No Right Turn' signs and more one-way streets (including, in 1962, Pall Mall). But these mechanisms inhibited stopping and thus access to nearby buildings, as well as enabling cars to be driven faster than their surroundings warranted. Similarly, although Buchanan wanted the 'canalisation' of traffic along main arteries, he showed that the kind of road network being built in sprawling Los Angeles was inappropriate for cramped London. A single motorway interchange took forty acres, rather more than the area bounded by Pall Mall, St James's Street, Piccadilly and Lower Regent Street. Buchanan declared that there were 'absolute limits to the amount of traffic that can be accepted in towns, depending on their size and density'. Restrictions were inevitable, probably in the form of a tough parking policy and some kind of road pricing. But in the last resort, Buchanan believed, Britain should meet the challenge of the car through comprehensive urban redevelopment, with 'multi-level schemes' to segregate pedestrians from motor vehicles.

This ambitious, if impractical, proposal must have appealed to Wilfrid Andrews. At any rate, the RAC welcomed the Buchanan Report's 'constructive approach' and made its author an honorary member of the Club. However, the Chairman continued to denounce parking meters as a 'disgraceful political swindle' long after the AA had decided that 'a price mechanism was inescapable'. He saw road pricing as a 'congestion tax'. And he fought for urban motorways with the zeal of a fanatic. London was an 'orphan city', he said, as it lacked clear proposals for urban motorways. The claim that such roads were crushing metropolitan America was 'as sound as a sinking pontoon'. Far from being 'an evil thing', they brought economic lifeblood into the cities, never 'meant to be museums to past glories'. 'I am staggered,' he fulminated, 'by the colossal impertinence of those who complain of the aesthetic atrocities of urban motorways.'

As this indictment suggests, Andrews had become an angry old man. He was increasingly out of sympathy with the times and his tone grew ever more shrill. He derided many road safety campaigners as 'cranks' and 'bigots'. He deplored 'hysterical outcries' about motor accidents. He damned official efforts to co-ordinate highway and town planning as a farrago of 'muddle and chaos'. (Ironically, in 1960 the RAC moved 700 of its Associate section staff from 83 Pall Mall to a modern, open-plan office block in Croydon in order to comply with government advice on decentralisation.) Above all, Andrews identified with the motorist, who was more embattled, he believed, than at any time since the days of Edwardian 'motorphobia'. The motorist was the 'whipping boy' of the world:

> Taxed to the hilt, bedevilled by parking meters and the like, harried by a special force
> of men in blue, recruited to aid the police in curbing his dreadful sins, the poor chap
> will at last be told, 'You are not to be allowed to drive your motor-car into the city centre.'

Evidently Andrews was suffering from a kind of persecution mania. Yet he did have some excuse for such outbursts, for the automobile attracted ever more antagonism as it moved towards the hub of the nation's life. That progress was inexorable. As the Labour frontbencher Patrick Gordon Walker said in the debate over the 1960 Road Traffic Bill, the ownership of a car was 'beginning to replace the ownership of a house as the expression of a man's sense of inde-

MONEY STICKS

The RAC protested that parking meters were 'just another way of hitting motorists in the pocket'. Ugly and voracious, they kept business out of cities and made 'no contribution whatsoever to solving traffic problems'. But motorists themselves were divided over the issue and many concluded that street parking charges were an inescapable part of the fight against urban congestion. The Beatles, also upbeat, sang, 'Lovely Rita, meter maid …'.

pendence and self-respect'. This was an international phenomenon, extending even into the Communist world. On a visit to London the Soviet premier Alexei Kosygin told Barbara Castle, Minister of Transport from 1965 to 1968, that the main aim of his own transport policy was to 'supply one car to every family'. Surprised, she complimented him on this good capitalist objective and added: 'Here, I am appalled by the difficulties which will be created when we have reached that point. In this crowded little island ....' Despite Mrs Castle's efforts to encourage public transport, British roads became ever more thronged and concern about the environment expressed itself in hostile scrutiny of the motor car.

HOLLYWOOD
BOULEVARD

The freeways of Los Angeles, says Jan Morris, are 'the city's grandest and most exciting artefacts'. But London had little room for urban motorways and even less appetite for 'spaghetti junctions'.

This was aggravated by the American champion of the consumer Ralph Nader, whose book *Unsafe at Any Speed* (1965) accused car manufacturers of wilfully putting their customers' lives at risk. Skimping on safety, they marketed danger. The automobile had killed three times as many Americans as all the country's wars put together and half the cars then on the road would be involved in an injury-producing accident. Nader's book was given added weight, and huge publicity, when General Motors was forced to apologise for having employed private detectives to spy on him. In the opinion of many people on both sides of the Atlantic the car itself became a vehicle of villainy. It was described as a 'bad machine'. One writer said that 'the invention of the private automobile is one of the great disasters to have befallen the human race'.

Nader made out a powerful case against the car-makers, who as a result were obliged to pay less heed to glamour and focus more on safety. Governments were prompted to pass laws about seat belts, exhaust emissions and so on. Nader's criticisms of the American Automobile Association (AAA) also had an impact. In the matter of car design, he asserted, the AAA's position had been 'one of curtsying whenever the automobile industry nodded'. Now it pursued a tougher line, complaining about hazards like protruding knobs and angular dashboards while calling for collapsible steering wheels and interior padding. Actually Nader's indictment of the AAA and, indeed, of the industry, was overstated. As one of his biographers has shown, it was absurd to claim that the 'entire traffic safety establishment', including the AAA, was 'a gigantic cabal' in thrall to the likes of General Motors. But Nader was right to stress the need for legislation to improve safety measures and to expose the inadequacy of well-meaning exhortations to take care. Some of his strictures on the AAA applied equally to the RAC.

Wilfrid Andrews still clung to the idea that road safety was primarily a matter of personal responsibility, not political regulation. Thus the RAC opposed the compulsory introduction of seat belts (though as early as 1961 Andrews had supported a plan to fit them to all Club vehicles). The car was a symbol of liberty and its occupants should not be told to 'belt up' by the 'nanny state'. For similar reasons the RAC resisted random breath tests to detect drunk drivers. It declared that the breathalyser was 'unreliable'. It favoured the sale of alcohol with food (but not otherwise) at motorway service stations. The Club also started to defend members charged with driving under the influence of alcohol. It objected to the raising of the age limit for motor-cyclists to seventeen.

Finally the RAC pushed for higher speed limits where possible and attacked the experimental 70mph restriction on motorways introduced in 1965. This was imposed after a series

of ghastly accidents and the Club said that it was 'a move of panic-stricken desperation' made by a minister (Barbara Castle) with a 'closed mind'. In fact Andrews was swayed in different directions on the speed issue. One Club Committee member maintained that excessive speed cost lives while another opined that doing 70mph on the motorway was 'extremely dull in a fast car'. Many Associates blamed the Chairman for being too acquiescent over the matter. *Autosport* described Andrews's support for 'realistic speed limits' as 'diabolical' and remarked rudely that he had 'left his mouth running while his brain was in neutral'.

Andrews often abused modern governments for mentally inhabiting the era when road loco-motives were preceded by men with red flags. But he himself never advanced much beyond the golden age when middle-class motorists could do pretty well as they liked. He did not appreciate that conditions which the few had enjoyed could never be available to the many. Consequently he was wrong about almost every major transport issue during the 1960s. Moreover, spurred on by militants, with whom he had a visceral sympathy, he largely abandoned the RAC's traditional policy of political moderation.

Thus a reformed AA was enabled to occupy the middle ground and the RAC lost influence as a result. Politicians like Anthony Wedgwood-Benn (as he then was) did not distinguish between the two organisations, describing the motoring lobby as 'the most hideous lobby of all'. But the press recognised that the RAC was now the more aggressive body and mainstream newspapers criticised it accordingly. In a leading article headed 'Save Your Breath', *The Times* said that the RAC had been 'unwise' to protest against the Home Secretary's instruction to chief constables on how to conduct breath tests. The *Guardian* also rebuked the RAC for 'Huffing and Puffing on Breath Tests'.

Andrews found Barbara Castle, a left-wing, non-driving female who used parking meter money to subsidise bus services, particularly uncongenial. What is more, he allowed his antipathy to show. Overt sniping replaced fruitful behind-the-scenes negotiations. After lambasting the 'backroom boys' at the Ministry of Transport for persevering with their 'money-grabbing' road-pricing scheme, Andrews pronounced:

> The RAC has been accused in some quarters of being reactionary, anti-this and anti-that. It's a jolly good job for the community at large that someone is, otherwise a great many restrictive and unnecessary practices would slip in without anyone being aware of it until it was too late.

After such vituperation the Ministry of Transport could hardly be expected to prefer, say, the RAC's driving instructor's qualification to its own. As a result the Club's Institute of Registered Motor Schools and Instructors (founded as an 'Association' when the driving test was introduced) had to be closed in 1970. By then Andrews was portraying the cohorts of the RAC as 'almost the only defenders of the motorist surviving'. In reality he had done much to marginalise and fossilise the organisation of which he was Chairman for so long.

―――――――――――

ANDREWS ALSO PRESIDED over the decline of the Pall Mall clubhouse. Ironically, this occurred partly because he was so determined to maintain traditional standards. Believing that

A NEW KIND OF CRASH

*'Motorway madness' was the alliterative cliché used to describe driving
which caused such fearful multiple pile-ups. It gave the impression that
motorways were swarming with homicidal maniacs. In fact they were the
safest roads in Britain, carrying twenty per cent of all traffic yet
accounting for eight per cent of the 5,000 fatal accidents a year.*

if tipping the staff were permitted 'the spirit of clubdom will be gone', he tried to enforce the rule against it, which members often broke in an effort to get better service. He insisted on high social qualifications for membership to the Club and saw numbers fall accordingly. Old-fashioned sartorial smartness was also a fetish with him. Ladies wearing trouser suits were not admitted until 1970 and then only after a prolonged wrangle on the Committee and an appeal from one of its members, Martin de Bertodano, for the Club to 'move a little more with the times'. During an argument about what should be worn at an RAC dinner for the Lord Mayor in 1969, another Committee member, Sir Norman Hulbert, said

SELLING THE SERVICE
Brochures dating from 1958 to 1972 reveal something of the RAC's relentless recruiting drive. It was quite successful, since the rescue service had made progress. Andrews complained that 'spoilt' members were overusing it.

that it was now 'possible to attend the most pompous occasions in a black tie'. But Andrews used his casting vote to insist on white tie and tails. Some 'old traditions' must disappear, maintained F. J. Bellenger, such as the provision of a special waiter to serve tea and coffee in the library after lunch, which was costing the Club £600 a year. Andrews ruled that the service should continue. Similarly the antimacassars were laundered daily. Important stocks of claret were acquired. The Chairman did, though, make some concessions. The Club orchestra was disbanded in 1962. Two years later the bowling alley was closed, much to Andrews's regret – its temperature of 63 degrees was ideal for storing cigars. But, however large the clubhouse deficit, the Chairman would not countenance the suggestion that it should install 'One-Armed Bandits'.

Attempting to run the Club on lavish pre-war lines, Andrews was reluctant to pay more than meagre pre-war wages. Thus many waitresses (among them Christine Keeler) had to find additional work in order to earn a living. Some employees took in kind what they were denied in cash. One defalcation, which was hushed up, cost the Club £70,000 and so worried Andrews that he wrote to Mountbatten: 'I feel that I have no need to assure you that I have not personally misappropriated or pinched any of the Club's money.' Andrews was also loath to spend the Club's money on the clubhouse. This was not because he was naturally frugal, quite the reverse. He bought brand-new limousines and at once had them 're-sprayed in RAC blue'. As one of his staff discovered on a trip to Monte Carlo, the Chairman's idea of austerity was to bypass a restaurant, park his Jaguar and settle down to a picnic, served by his chauffeur Dillon, consisting of caviar and smoked salmon sandwiches washed down with Moët et Chandon champagne. Andrews even took his car abroad when its sole function was to convey him between the Hôtel de Crillon in Paris and the headquarters of the FIA, a distance of seventy-five yards. However, Andrews was in thrall to J. Duncan Ferguson, a partner in the accounting firm of Andrew Barr. 'Fergie', as he was called, 'looked as though he hadn't two brass farthings to rub together'. He wore a grubby suit and had a trick of rolling a cigarette from side to side of his mouth. But, squat and rough as Andrews was tall and suave, he established a mysterious hold over the Chairman and became the second most powerful man in the Club. According to one senior RAC figure, 'Fergie played Rasputin to Andrews's Tsar'. But most Club employees invoked a more modern Russian comparison: Fergie was 'head of the KGB'.

Certainly he kept an 'iron grip' on finance and when any outlay was suggested 'his starting-point was always to say no'. He saved but he did not plan for the future: sufficient unto the day

was the expenditure thereof. Fergie's puritanical attitude appealed to some part of Andrews's epicurean soul. He had long been worried about the '"rising spiral" of costs' in which the Club was caught up, though he was slow to raise prices and subscriptions. The astute Fergie, who managed to become the RAC's auditor as well as its accountant while at the same time involving himself professionally in the affairs of Committee members, also encouraged Andrews's addiction to financial secrecy. This was forthrightly displayed during one of the many attempts to negotiate an amalgamation with the AA, much favoured by the Duke of Edinburgh, which foundered when its Chairman asked to see the RAC's accounts. 'Not bloody likely,' thundered Andrews, who swept up his papers and 'stormed out of the meeting'. That response was predictable, particularly in view of his hatred of the rival organisation, which he thought full of 'artful Charlies'. But Andrews also prevented his own Committee from properly scrutinising the accounts. He allowed copies to circulate for ten minutes once a year and then demanded their return. At one meeting he announced angrily that 'a gross impropriety' had occurred: somebody had not handed back his copy. Dennis Flather confessed and said that he could only approve the accounts if he could study them. Andrews forced him to surrender the document. Fergie would have applauded the Chairman's robustness. Together the two men formed not so much an alliance as a conspiracy. If one of them died, it was whispered in the Club, the other would have to 'hire a medium' so that they could remain in constant contact.

Fergie's shoestring financial management ensured that repairs and refurbishments to the clubhouse were skimped or postponed. By 1964 the red carpet in the vestibule had worn out but Fergie decreed that the Club could not afford a new one and it was replaced by a thirty-eight-year-old blue-green article which was barely an improvement. Buying a computer for the Club required 'a great deal of thought', said Andrews, and set up a subcommittee to study the proposal. The archaic boilers were patched up because installing modern oil-fired ones would cost a 'large sum'. The bedrooms remained unimproved though they could now be described as West End slums: their heating was supplied by flickering, sixpenny-meter gas fires and their hot water was delivered in galvanised iron jugs. Nor would Fergie sanction the 'very heavy expenditure' needed to redecorate the Great Gallery: instead its flaws would be hidden by 'floral decorations'.

Also on grounds of cost, the Committee refused a request from the Lord Mayor of Westminster to clean the exterior of the clubhouse in 1967, though members agreed that the Ritz's recent face-lift had been 'very successful'. As standards deteriorated fewer members used the Club. Often the restaurant was half empty. The quality of the food also declined and staff went so far as to advise disgruntled members to take their custom elsewhere. The Committee considered closing part of the clubhouse on Sundays but this, they decided, would worsen the 'vicious circle'. Anyway, as the 'Home of Motoring in Great Britain' and 'forum for vital discussions', the Club should remain open. It did, but visibly bedimmed: the light bulbs bought on Fergie's orders were of such low wattage that members could hardly see to read.

Andrews never fully appreciated the problems. In his view it was 'folly to allow ourselves to be driven into the belief that we have a Club which members no longer wish to visit'. But his view was blinkered by the fact that the Club was his castle and in it he lived like a king. Andrews always boasted that 'The clubhouse has not taken a penny from the Associate section

LONG-STANDING CHAIRMAN

*Wilfrid Andrews, Chairman of the RAC from 1945 to 1972,
is pictured in Carlton Gardens beside his Humber Pullman
limousine. It sports an AA badge as well as those of the RAC,
indicating his honorary membership of the rival body (which
he privately detested). Andrews himself aroused fierce passions
within the RAC, among both detractors and supporters.*

and I am not taking a penny from the Club.' But he cost the RAC £30,000 a year in expenses and behaved as though the Associate section were his personal fiefdom. For example, he used it to recruit his domestic staff and arrange his Continental holidays, which he took with a lady who was not his wife. And its managers treated him more as a deity than as royalty. He was seldom visible to them. As one said, 'You weren't supposed to see him any more than you were supposed to see the Lord.' In the clubhouse he manifestly reigned. He held court. He dispensed patronage. He sat at his privileged table in the restaurant as though 'on a throne'. Here he nodded to supplicants and indulged in his fondness for Lobster Thermidor. Attentive waiters flocked round him, anticipating his every wish, while at nearby tables neglected members fumed. They literally had to take the proceedings with a pinch of salt because Andrews had 'the only salt-cellar with a spoon'. At breakfast the Chairman somehow also managed to 'monopolise the marmalade'.

Woodcote Park was in an even worse state than Pall Mall. There had long been complaints about bad organisation, poor service, unhygienic kitchens and general dilapidation. Little was done to improve matters. When a member told the Epsom public health inspector that there was an infestation of ants at the country club, the Committee in London was more indignant about the 'extremely bad taste' of the informer than the presence of the pests. Woodcote was an admirable venue for RAC staff outings, though women resented their brusque exclusion from the members' bar – members perhaps compensated for this slight at annual staff parties by not only serving the food but doing the washing-up afterwards (a custom later abandoned). But these occasional visits could not make the place pay. Nor was it prudent to sell members single-acre building plots overlooking the golf course for as little as £3,000. Woodcote Park might have profited if it had applied for a club (as opposed to a justice's) licence in 1963 under the new act, which would have extended drinking hours. It would also have permitted only thirty members to call an Extraordinary General Meeting, whereas 200 members were required under the justice's licence. So Andrews forbade the change: 'one might get caught and have to listen to the complaints of the few', he said, which would be an 'intolerable situation'. F. J. Bellenger found it 'extraordinary that the Club were prepared to carry on with losses in revenue merely because it was desirable to prevent members calling an Extraordinary General Meeting'. But Andrews prevailed and Woodcote Park remained a monument to mismanagement.

Despite this the Club did attract some new members during Andrews's last years; but they were exceptional, even eccentric. The poet John Betjeman was perhaps the most distinguished. He joined in 1967, having resigned from the Athenaeum because its new décor made it resemble a Trust House. Betjeman much admired the RAC's Pall Mall building and felt comfortable among its faded splendours; it was, he wrote, 'one of the only places where you can find INK and a DIPPING PEN'. Betjeman liked to entertain his friends there, among them Lord Snowdon and Peter Sellers. The actor was an awkward guest: when barred for not wearing a tie, he gained admittance by putting one on *under* his shirt.

Betjeman enjoyed a swim before taking tea and anchovy toast. Once, another friend recalled, the poet involuntarily exposed himself by pulling his baggy black hired bathing costume high around his waist. But Betjeman did not notice because 'he was concentrating on two old club-men, who were doing vigorous exercises at opposite ends of the pool, swinging their arms

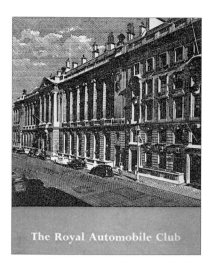

The Royal Automobile Club

CENTRAL HALL

THE PUBLIC FACE

The RAC presented a brave face to the world during the chairmanship of Wilfrid Andrews. He was concerned to preserve pre-war standards and to maintain the dignity of the 'home of automobilism'. But too little was spent on the clubhouses, which deteriorated sadly. By 1970 Andrews was shocked to hear a member suggest that 'the Club is on its way out'.

THE BUILDING AT PALL MALL

Ground Floor
(from Entrances)

To Right
Smoking Room Annexe (Chess Room), Lavatories, Message and Notice Boards, Cloakroom, Members' Smoking Room and Terrace, Lower Smoking Room and Bar, Billiard Room.

Centre
Bookstall, Cigar Stall and Post Office, Great Gallery and Terrace.

To Left
Ladies' Drawing Room, Restaurant, Theatre Ticket Office.

First Floor
Members' Dining Room, American Bar, Library, Motoring Library and Television Room, Lavatories, Committee Rooms, Lost Property Office.

Second Floor
Card Room, Cashiers and Badge Department, Secretary's Offices, Competition Department Offices.

Lower Ground Floor
Cloak Room and Main Lavatories, Hairdressing and Chiropody Saloons, Galleries to Squash Rackets Courts, Television Room, Telephone Booths.

Basement Floor
Snack Bar, Turkish Bath, Swimming Bath, Squash Rackets Courts and Changing Rooms, Dressing Rooms, Miniature Rifle Range.

Bedrooms
are situated on the 2nd, 3rd and 4th Floors.

THE GREAT GALLERY

R.A.C. COUNTRY CLUB
WOODCOTE PARK, EPSOM

Telephone: ASHTEAD, SURREY, 666

The R.A.C. Country Club is an integral part of the Royal Automobile Club, and no subscription beyond that for Full or Country Club Membership of the R.A.C. is required from Members in respect of the use of the Club House and grounds.

The Country Club was acquired by the R.A.C., as an added facility for its Members and their guests, in 1912.

The grounds consist of 330 acres of parkland adjoining Lord Rosebery's estate, 'The Durdans', and stretching to Epsom Downs and the Race Course.

23

No other London Club provides, in addition to all the facilities at Pall Mall, a Country Club, with an 18-hole and a 9-hole Golf Course, a Swimming Pool, Croquet and Tennis Lawns.

The building is a steel-framed structure with fire-resisting staircases and floors, to prevent any likelihood of the recurrence of the disastrous fire which destroyed the original Club House in August, 1934.

No expense has been spared which modern experience could devise, such as the provision of filtered draughtless air-conditioning of the public rooms, automatic panel and radiator heating, mechanical ventilation of kitchens and still rooms, to obviate the odour of cooking, and the softening of all water for drinking, cooking and baths.

DINING ROOM

IN THE GROUNDS

On the basement level are Golf Dressing and Locker Rooms, complete with showers, foot baths and drying rooms, and a comfortable bar for Members and male guests only.

On the ground floor are situated the Entrance Hall, an Inner and Outer Lounge, Cocktail Bar, Dining Room and Cloak Rooms.

The Dining Room, capable of seating 200 persons, has a dance floor laid and folding doors to enable the room to be thrown open to the air in fine weather.

On the first floor are the Library, Billiards and Card Rooms. A television set is installed in the Library.

There are thirty bedrooms, and each has a radiator, electric fire, hot and cold water, fitted wardrobe and telephone. All double rooms have separate bathrooms and lobbies to ensure privacy and quiet.

25

in a bizarre, geriatric manner, making John laugh a lot as he bobbed about in the water'. Betjeman also had a quirky interest in automobilism. Just as particular types of company car indicate an executive's position in the business pecking order today, so Betjeman artfully invoked Hillmans, Rovers, Austins and Lagondas to convey social nuances in verse. Betjeman himself was an impatient motorist who hated being delayed, even by lollipop men, or 'kiddie crossers' as he called them. They were, he maintained, 'thwarted power maniacs who had failed to get into the police force and enjoyed holding up traffic for the sake of it'.

The poet joined the Club a couple of years after its Motor Sport Division transferred from Pall Mall to 31 Belgrave Square, a move approved by Andrews, who frowned on the comings and goings of women in crash helmets. While the Chairman was concerned to keep up the RAC's tone, his financial guru and 'trusted confidant' was preoccupied with keeping down its costs. Fergie favoured Motor Sport's new premises since, despite the smart address, they were labyrinthine, derelict and cheap. In fact, the twin considerations of prestige and expense determined the RAC's policy on motor sport throughout the 1950s and '60s. Andrews worried that television pictures of cars spinning off the track at Brand's Hatch would give motor racing a bad name. Similarly the Club's image would be tarnished by crashes during Tourist Trophy races. In 1955 the worst accident in racing history occurred at Le Mans when Pierre Levegh's Mercedes somersaulted into the crowd at 150mph and killed eighty-three spectators. This proved that speed had outstripped safety and, bowing to public opinion, the RAC decided not to return to the hazardous course at Dundrod. Fergie feared the financial risks of motor sport.

Thus the Club generally avoided direct involvement except in the TT itself, the International Rally and the Brighton Run. Some Committee members such as Lord Brabazon and the Duke of Richmond and Gordon, wanted it to promote major competitions. But most preferred the RAC to licence other bodies to run the hundreds of events which occurred each year. The Club would merely keep a 'watchful eye on the interests of the sporting community', act as final arbiter and restrict its liabilities to a minimum. 'Fergie was the villain of the piece,' says Dean Delamont, then head of the Motor Sport Division. Not only was the little Scotsman tight-fisted over investment in the sport, he was close with the truth. Under his influence Andrews refused to tell the local clubs and organisations just how the RAC spent their licence fees. If this were divulged, he said, 'there will be endless irritation caused by nagging questions'.

Sometimes the RAC had to make awkward choices between kudos and cash, especially over the commercial sponsorship of motor sport. Andrews had an instinctive aversion to it. With a snobbish idealism born of the past, he regarded the Club as a service rather than a business. The AA might 'move into the realm of "trading"' (though not without damaging its 'brand image'), but the RAC, as befitted a royal institution, should hold aloof. It was as a service to members, not as a profit-making enterprise, that the RAC justified setting up its travel agency in 1958. Andrews thought it vulgar to put events like Autocross 'up for sale'. But he did feel obliged to encourage the renaissance of British motor racing. This was marked first by the success of drivers such as Mike Hawthorn, Stirling Moss, Jim Clark and Graham Hill, all duly saluted by the Club. The development of the Cooper-Climax and Cosworth engines followed soon afterwards, triumphs of British technology and vital elements in shaping the modern racing car. In 1965 Andrews was elected president of the FIA, 'no mean honour' in view of the fact that

DISASTER AT LE MANS

In June 1955 Pierre Levegh's car catapulted into a portion of the 250,000-strong crowd at Le Mans. It killed eighty-three spectators, injured scores more, some of them terribly, and left the grandstand looking like a battlefield. The race was continued so that rescue vehicles would not be blocked by the dispersing crowd, but many thought that the scale of the tragedy had not been appreciated. Across the Channel, the RAC tried to restore the reputation of motor sport.

he did not speak French. Three years later advertising on Grand Prix cars was permitted. Andrews reluctantly concluded that racing success depended on money that could only be contributed by commerce. In 1971, without consulting the Club Committee, he even allowed what had been the RAC British Grand Prix to be called the Woolmark British Grand Prix.

He also allowed himself to be persuaded that the RAC Rally needed sponsorship. Thanks largely to Jack Kemsley, an experienced rally driver recruited to make the Club's event one which would attract foreign competitors, the RAC Rally established a global reputation during the 1960s. Kemsley won it by the simple method of injecting the element of speed. Since racing on the public roads was impossible, he arranged for certain stages of the rally to take place on private land, much of it belonging to the Forestry Commission. Excited onlookers alongside its dirt roads witnessed driving as a form of dramatic art. The brilliant Scandinavian contestants, in particular, employed dynamic new techniques to corner more swiftly than ever before, locking their back wheels into a skid by left-foot braking while simultaneously accelerating. Kemsley transformed what had been a genteel trial into a gruelling contest. It was not the world's longest, fastest or toughest rally; but, as *Autosport* said, it was the most popular.

Even the 'amazingly hard-working' Kemsley, though, could not eliminate the mistakes which marred RAC rallies during the late 1960s. If the event were not to fall below international standards he needed a better organisation and more resources, which could only come from sponsorship. At that time, Kemsley observed, the Club 'wouldn't even allow advertising to appear in the Road Books. Mustn't sully the RAC's name and all that!' But he kept nagging until Andrews asked to see a car adorned with publicity material. As Kemsley recalled, a Ford arrived which was 'smothered in advertising. When Wilfrid Andrews looked down at this car sitting in Pall Mall, I thought he was going to fall out of the window!' But after the Chairman had recovered from the shock, Kemsley won his point.

Despite the bright spots it was clear, as Andrews's reign drew to a close, that the RAC was in a parlous condition, especially in relation to the AA. The Club was running a poor second to this increasingly computerised, commercialised and streamlined body. Except in political matters, such as the 'Cut Motor Taxes' campaign, the RAC tended to follow its rival's lead. After AA Scouts stopped saluting their members in 1962, RAC Patrols did likewise. When the AA raised its annual subscription from two to three guineas in 1967 the RAC followed suit in 1968. This was the first increase since 1921 and it was made necessary by the Selective Employment Tax and by the growing expense of the 'Get-You-Home' service. The RAC rescued about 375,000 motorists in 1968 but doing so cost it £800,000 and Andrews reckoned that the Club was being 'taken for a ride' by frequent users of the service. However, he recognised that it was the Associate section's chief selling-point. It certainly took pride of place in the Club's advertising, though even this drew on the AA's new techniques such as promotional films and shop window displays. The Club also kept a close eye on the AA's other ventures but it could seldom compete. The AA gave away its *Handbook* to members whereas the RAC had to charge (for what was a bigger and, it claimed, a better article). At Pall Mall one Committee member became so exercised by the inferiority of the RAC's insurance schemes that he vociferated: 'we are in danger of barking up the wrong tree and missing the boat in relation to the AA'.

1938

THE GREAT PRICE OF GRANDS PRIX

International motor races could only be organised properly with the help of commercial sponsorship. Newspapers gave good early support. But in 1971 sponsors were allowed to include their own names (while omitting that of the RAC) in the title of Grands Prix. Today beer ads have replaced cigarette puffs. And Silverstone is the only circuit able to hold Grands Prix. This may change after 2001. What is certain is that sponsorship has revolutionised motor racing, turning it into the highly professional sport it has now become.

1996

1948

1971

1992

1955

1986

1964

1968

1977

1980

This was an apt summary of the RAC's position by the time Andrews
retired. The Club's Associate membership stood at 1.5 million, compared
to the AA's 4 million. Its patrol force, which numbered 1,200 men, was less
than half the size of its rival's. RAC staff, who had enjoyed one of the best
pension schemes in the country during the 1940s, now endured 'one of the
worst'. Everywhere petty economies were imposed while necessary investment was stifled, and the Chairman announced that nothing would induce
him to emulate the high-spending policies of the AA. The voice was the
voice of Andrews but the hands were the hands of Fergie. The little
Scotsman was probably behind the move to exclude Sir Gerald Nabarro, a
flamboyant Tory MP who acted as self-appointed champion of the motorist,
from the benefits of the Club's legal services because he used them too heavily. Certainly Fergie bore a major responsibility for the grave situation facing the Club as his
patron prepared to depart at the beginning of the 1970s. Privately the Committee was deeply
worried. Publicly Andrews proclaimed that 'at no time in its long and proud history has our
organisation been healthier'.

Cynics might say that, as the inadequacy of Andrews's stewardship became more obvious,
he only remained in office because the Club was not subject to democratic control. There is
some truth in this. As early as 1949 Andrews had secured a change in the rule of the RAC's
holding company, Automobile Proprietary, which stated that directors had to resign on reaching the age of seventy. Six years later he waived the rule which disallowed a small proportion
of Committee members from standing for re-election. Thus Andrews kept it packed with his
cronies. Like the Chairman himself, many lived a long time, though death took its inevitable
toll: E. S. Shrapnell-Smith died in 1952, Sir Algernon Guinness in 1954, Mervyn O'Gorman
in 1958, Lord Brabazon in 1964 and Lord Howe in 1965. But Andrews ensured that amenable
and venerable figures filled the gaps. Several were keen to succeed him. But although Andrews
talked of 'being senile' and of retiring soon, he clung to power and kept them all dangling.

The most formidable pretender was Lord Chesham, who became Executive Vice-Chairman
in 1966. He was a former Minister of Transport and a master of the trenchant phrase: he said
that not having a national car parking policy was like 'bicycling backwards into the future on a
penny-farthing'. But Andrews consistently thwarted Chesham, who resigned in disgust after a
five-year struggle. One of Chesham's allies, Sir Norman Hulbert, insisted that a proper
tribute should be paid to him. For once the Committee minutes, almost always tantalisingly
bland, strike a note of acerbity. Andrews 'questioned whether Sir Norman had raised this
subject to cause trouble'. Hulbert challenged him to substantiate the allegation or withdraw it.
The Chairman refused to withdraw, saying that he 'had information in black and white which
caused him to make the remark'. The Committee supported Andrews by fourteen votes to four.

Yet the RAC's governing body was no mere flock of sycophants. It included younger men
of courage and integrity. There was Squadron Leader John Crampton, the son of a founder
member, who had won both the DFC and the AFC. There was Captain Martin de Bertodano,
who had run the shore staff of 'the Shetland bus', the flotilla of ships which sailed back and forth
across the North Sea helping the Norwegian resistance against the Nazis, and who had been

THE RISING DATSUN

At first Japanese competition seemed rather a joke: the cars looked as lacklustre as the advertising. But the eastern imports proved their worth, and the consequences for the British automobile industry were shattering.

2000 de luxe saloon

2000 De Luxe Saloon.
Luxury four door Saloon all steel body.
Fully reclining individual front seats form a bed. Tinted safety glass all round, overriders, whitewall tyres, carpets, childproof safety locks, reversing lights, heater, demister, screen washers, clock, cigarette lighter etc.

Specification

Engine	Six cylinder 1973 c.c. OHV 109 BHP at 5,200 rpm 8.2:1 compression ratio
Transmission	4 speed all synchromesh with floor gear change
	Ratios 1st : 3.549
	2nd : 2.197
	3rd : 1.420
	4th : 1.000
	Rev : 3.164
Performance	Maximum 93 mph
Suspension	Independent coil springs at front with torsion bar, semi-elliptic rear springs, telescopic shock absorbers, with torsion bar. Borg-Warner automatic transmission available at extra cost.

Recommended retail price £1,378

Nissan-Datsun (U.K. Concessionaires) Ltd.
Harbour Way · Shoreham-by-Sea · Sussex · BN4 5HX
Telephone: Shoreham-by-Sea 4410 / 4419 / 4624   Telex: 87445

2000 de luxe estate car

2000 Estate
Four door, six seater all steel body. Bench front seat.
1973 c.c. six cylinder OHV engine producing 109 BHP at 5,200 rpm.
A load capacity of over 1100 lbs. with three passengers plus electrically operated remote control rear tail-gate window, operated either from the driver's seat or from the rear seat, child proof safety locks, heater, demister, screen washers, etc.

Specification

Engine	Six cylinder, 1973 c.c. OHV 109 BHP at 5,200 rpm.
Transmission	4 speed, all synchromesh, with steering column gear change.
	Ratios 1st : 3.549
	2nd : 2.197
	3rd : 1.420
	4th : 1.0
	Rev : 3.164
Performance	Maximum 90 mph
Suspension	Independent coil springs at front with torsion bar. Longitudinal semi-elliptic rear springs and shock absorbers. Borg-Warner Automatic transmission available at extra cost.

Recommended retail price £1,398

YOUR DATSUN DEALER IS:

the Datsun range 68/69

DATSUN

1000 de luxe saloon

1000 De Luxe Saloon.
Four door, all steel body with separate reclining front seats.
Standard equipment includes: tinted safety glass all round, padded instrument panel, whitewall tyres, overriders, twin windtone horns, cigarette lighter, windscreen washers, two speed wipers, carpeting throughout, heater and demister, reversing lights and childproof safety locks.
A sturdy, comfortable and high performance 'big' car.

Specification
4 cylinder 988 c.c. OHV engine with Hitachi double choke down draft carburettor 62 BHP at 6000 rpm 8.5:1 compression ratio. Transmission Floor mounted gear lever, four all-synchro gears.

Ratios	1st : 3.76
	2nd : 2.17
	3rd : 1.40
	4th : 1.0
	Rev : 3.64
Overall length	12' 6.4"
Performance	84 mph
Suspension	Independent wishbones on front, with transverse leaf springs and telescopic shock absorbers with longitudinal semi-elliptic rear springs and telescopic shock absorbers.

Minimum turning circle 26.2ft

Recommended retail price £749

1600 de luxe saloon and estate car

and 1300 de luxe saloon

1600 De Luxe Saloon
Four door, Saloon all steel body with tinted safety glass all round, full-flow ventilation, fully reclining separate front seats, whitewall tyres fitted as standard. Front disc brakes, heater, demister, screen washers, reversing lights, child-proof safety locks etc.

Specification

Engine	4 cylinder 1,595 c.c. OHC 96 BHP at 5,600 rpm. 8.5:1 compression ratio.
Transmission	Floor mounted gear lever, four all synchromesh gears.
	Ratios: 1st : 3.38 2nd : 2.01 3rd : 1.31 4th : 1.00 Rev : 3.36
Overall length	13' 6"
Performance	Maximum 100 mph
Suspension	Front independent strut type with tension rod and stabilizer, rear independent semi-trailing arm with coil springs and telescopic shock absorbers.

Minimum turning circle 31.4ft
Borg-Warner automatic transmission available at extra cost.

Recommended retail price £947

1600 De Luxe Estate Car
Specification (as Saloon)
1600 de luxe Estate Car four door. Over 5½ cubic feet load space with rear seat folded.   Recommended retail price £1065

1300 De Luxe Saloon
Specification
1300 de luxe saloon. Separate front seats whitewall tyres, heater, demister, carpets, 4-speed floor change synchromesh on all 4 gears. OHC engine. 1296 c.c. 8.5:1 compression ratio. 77 B.H.P. at 6,000 rpm. Body and Suspension (as 1600) max. speed 90 mph.   Recommended retail price £869

1000 de luxe estate car

1000 Estate
Two door, Estate Car all steel body. Standard equipment includes: padded instrument panel, white wall tyres, overriders, twin windtone horns, cigarette lighter, windscreen washers, two speed wipers, carpeting throughout, heater, demister, reversing lights. Load capacity 2 persons plus 882lbs with counter-balanced upwards-swinging tailgate. Effortless cruising at 81 mph.

Specification
4 cylinder 988 c.c. OHV engine with Hitachi double choke down draft carburettor 62 BHP at 6000 rpm 8.5:1 compression ratio.
Transmission Floor mounted gear lever, four all-synchro gears.

Ratios	1st : 3.76
	2nd : 2.17
	3rd : 1.40
	4th : 1.00
	Rev : 3.64
Suspension	Independent wishbones on front, with longitudinal transverse rear springs and telescopic shock absorbers with semi-elliptic leaf springs and telescopic shock absorbers.

Recommended retail price £764

'very good at his job'. The loyalty of such people was quite genuine. They recognised the Chairman's autocratic nature but endorsed the many plaudits he received: it was, said one Club member, 'difficult to conceive of a man more dedicated and with greater fire in his belly – with drive, initiative and Churchillian determination'. They admired his oratory, still vigorous though increasingly repetitive, and his past achievements. At a time when the car was coming under renewed assault no one had championed it more boldly. Andrews was the high priest of motordom. He would have agreed with Barthes, or with Le Corbusier, who compared the best motor cars of the day to the buildings of Periclean Athens. This explains the fury he felt when a BBC *Panorama* programme claimed in 1970 that foreign cars were better than British.

So, for all his faults, Andrews was sorely missed when laid low by cancer in 1971. Praising his 'humour, kindness, anger, his wonderful abilities, his great character, his marvellous voice', John Crampton said that the Chairman was 'a man for all seasons' for whom his colleagues felt nothing but 'love and affection'. The sentiments were valedictory but the dying Andrews was unwilling to leave. Indeed, he took advantage of the benign atmosphere to stage an extraordinary last-ditch coup. Instead of actually resigning, Andrews sent the Committee an ingeniously word-ed letter saying that it must choose 'someone to carry on the responsibilities associated with the chairmanship'. In May 1972 it selected the 'exceedingly loyal' Andy Polson, who thereupon announced that his predecessor would now become 'Chairman d'Honneur'. This was a title and a position known in France but not in England. It enabled Andrews to retain control of the RAC even though he had one foot in the grave.

ASTON MARTIN 007

*In 1965, even without James Bond's
optional extras, the Aston Martin DB5
was probably the world's most exciting
car. It seemed licensed to thrill.*

CHAPTER TEN

CRISIS IN THE CLUB

*As Britain's car industry strove to contend with fierce
international competition during the 1970s, the RAC
engaged in its own struggle for survival – the result of long
neglect. After episodes both dramatic and traumatic, the
Club achieved a remarkable recovery.*

A NEW IMAGE

*Modernity, solidity and
uniformity – these were
the aims of the revised
(though still regal)
corporate logo, marking
the seventy-fifth
birthday of the RAC.*

AS THE EIGHTY-YEAR-OLD WILFRID ANDREWS settled into his luxurious retirement suite at Woodcote Park, the RAC was lurching towards the greatest crisis in its history. Yet outwardly all seemed serene. The succession had gone without a hitch. Hovering outside the Pall Mall committee room while his colleagues made their choice, Andy Polson had felt like a criminal 'awaiting execution'; but once appointed Chairman he had the sense of joining a 'family of friends'. Polson was a large, robust Scot who seemed to exude self-confidence. An energetic golfer who had been something of a playboy in his youth and still enjoyed a drink, he had become a Club member in 1935 when working with the Mercedes racing team. During the war Polson had served in a bomb disposal unit (once being called to deal with an unexploded 'Flower-pot' incendiary in the clubhouse) and in special forces. Beneath his ample waistcoat, it was said, 'beat a generous heart'.

However, Polson was always blunt and he sometimes 'treated his staff in the most brutal manner'. Doubtless he had the courage to tackle the fundamental problems afflicting the Club; but he lacked the will. On succeeding to the chairmanship he announced that he would not be a 'new broom' because nothing of the sort was needed. And he remained hypnotised by 'the power of Andrews's personality'. It was an extraordinary state of affairs. Andrews had long been an anachronism, 'the day before yesterday's man'. As Chairman d'Honneur he held no constitutional position in the Club. Above all, he was virtually moribund. Yet Polson travelled down to report to him at Woodcote Park several times a week. Although now free to go his own way, the new Chairman remained alert to the sound of his master's voice.

As a result he was slow to respond to the swiftly changing circumstances of the early 1970s. Polson himself said that it took him two years to comprehend the ramifications of the RAC, during which time economic freeze followed economic squeeze as Edward Heath's government vainly tried to contain inflation. This rose from six per cent in 1973 to sixteen per cent the following year, an increase that was partly caused by the tripling of oil prices after the Middle East war. In the scramble for higher pay the miners went on strike, a three-day working week was imposed and the Conservatives were defeated in the general election of 1974. During the same period purchase tax and Selective Employment Tax were brought to an end while Value Added Tax (VAT) was introduced. Moreover, Britain's entry into the European Economic Community led to a rapidly worsening balance of trade, especially in motor vehicles. In 1974, for the first time since 1913, car imports exceeded exports, mean machines such as the Volkswagen 'Beetle' selling far better than 'gas-guzzlers' like the Vauxhall Victor. To save energy the Ministry of Transport imposed a speed limit of 50mph, which also saved lives. But instead of welcoming such measures the RAC, its strings doubtless pulled by Andrews, treated those who favoured the conservation of resources as part of the 'anti-motoring lobby', to be fought tooth and nail. Actually the crisis showed that petrol had become the new *élan vital*, which the nation could on no account afford to waste. Without fuel to animate the automobile, civilisation as most Britons knew it would grind to a halt.

Keeping it moving, though, took an increasingly heavy environmental toll, something Polson also failed to recognise. In the spirit of Andrews, he dismissed as 'poppycock' the charge that motor cars were polluting the atmosphere. Urban motorways, he claimed, protected the environment better than pedestrian precincts. These were a mere capitulation to anti-automobile pressure groups. About the power of that lobby, at least, Polson was correct. Since the Westway had cut its giant swathe through London in 1970, there had been growing agitation for 'Homes before Roads'. Passionate protests had put an end to inner ring motorways in London and similar schemes elsewhere. Popular opinion was, in fact, swinging towards the past, aiming to turn the clock back. As recently as 1958 more journeys had been made by public transport than by private car; within a decade three times as many journeys were made by car as by public transport. By the early 1970s it was becoming clear to all but heedless partisans of the automobile like Polson that some integrated system, employing both mass transit and the motor car, was vital if urban communities were not to be irreparably damaged.

Such, indeed, was the destructive potential of the internal combustion engine that some considered civilisation itself to be on the road to ruin. A rash of books appeared whose titles expressed the current phobias and fears: Kenneth Schneider's *Autokind vs. Mankind* (1971); Ronald Buel's *Dead End* (1972); Emma Rothschild's *Paradise Lost* (1973). There were even forecasts of an automobile apocalypse. The protagonist of J. G. Ballard's novel *Crash* (1973) had a vision of 'the whole world dying in a simultaneous automobile disaster, millions of vehicles hurled together in a terminal congress of spurting loins and engine coolant'.

Britons were particularly inclined to conjure with notions of global doom at this time, perhaps because their own situation was so gloomy. The country's relative economic decline had been going on for at least a century, but by the 1970s it was vertiginous. There seemed to be no clear remedy for what was fashionably called the 'British disease'. Its symptoms were nowhere more painfully obvious than in the British car industry. This was now on its last legs thanks to low productivity, inept management, outdated designs, inferior quality control and

PETROL FAMINE

The government printed 16 million petrol ration books after the Yom Kippur war
in 1973, but to eke out dwindling supplies garages either closed down or imposed
their own rationing systems. Long queues formed outside those that remained open,
causing traffic chaos. The RAC campaigned for lower taxes on fuel.

chaotic labour relations. British Leyland dealt with twenty unions in seventy factories and sometimes negotiated several pay claims and faced several strikes in a single day. In the three years after 1971, itself the worst year for industrial relations since the General Strike, the company lost twenty-seven million man-hours.

At the top, Lord Stokes (as Sir Donald had become) approved a series of cars which ranged from disappointments to disasters. His personal favourite was the sporty Triumph Stag, suitably named in that its timing was apt to jump, causing valves to collide with pistons and wrecking the engine. Equally unpredictable was the Allegro: not only did its steering wheel consist of four shallow arcs instead of a circle, but its windscreen was liable to pop out when the car was raised on a jack. As for the unreliable and uninspiring Marina, it would not even sell in the United States when 'dumped' at bargain prices. By 1975 BL confronted a loss of over £20 million. It was nationalised by a government anxious to protect jobs and to preserve the last British-owned car giant. But, as Harold Lever warned his colleagues in Wilson's cabinet, they were rushing into a 'grandiose folly'; 'it was like a "bad Pharaoh's dream" in which we weren't even promised seven fat years after the seven lean ones'.

The RAC, in its different departments, was also having a thin time. The Motor Sport Division, based in Belgrave Square under the directorship of Dean Delamont, was suffering because fuel shortages restricted the number of rallies, races and other events on which its income depended. In fact it issued 34,000 licences in 1973; but even with permit fees, profits from the sale of programmes and so on, it made only £11,000. Pay was frozen, morale slumped and, as experienced staff left, service deteriorated. The Club's Competitions Committee was so worried by the situation that it expressed 'disgust' at the delay in solving the salary problems – a word to which Polson objected in vain. What particularly concerned Delamont and his supporters was the simple fact that the RAC had 'no God-given right to govern motor sport'. It ruled with the consent of the hundreds of affiliated clubs which organised their own competitions, local and national. In return for their affiliation fees, these clubs got a set of rules, an independent judiciary and a permit that allowed them to insure against accidents. So if the RAC had proved inadequate to the task, the affiliated clubs might have withdrawn and given their allegiance to a more efficient body – as had occurred in France, for example.

Aware of the danger, Polson agreed to set up a working party headed by Sir Clive Bossom, a former MP and a member of the Club Committee, with a view to reorganising the 'much-maligned' Motor Sport Division. However, Polson's handling of the business suggested that this was nothing so much as a delaying tactic inspired from Woodcote Park. In a stinging rebuke written in August 1974, one member of the working party, Peter Cooper, expressed 'utter amazement' at Polson's dilatoriness and demanded instant reform. The RAC was

> daily becoming more vulnerable to a takeover by an outside source, possibly with commercial interests, which would, in my opinion, be the death of the sport as we know it. Please ... let us revitalise and streamline motor sport now, not after the specialised staff at present in control come to the end of their tether.

Polson replied huffily that he was not dragging his feet. But he was pushed into agreeing that the old Competitions Committee should be superseded by a new, more professional RAC

MEDIOCRE MODELS

British Leyland's careful publicity photographs helped to give the Morris Marina (right) sales of 1.2 million, while the Austin Maxi (below) sold almost half a million in its dozen years of life. But nothing could disguise the derivative nature of these cars, which owed much to the Morris Minor and the Mini respectively. Moreover both vehicles had obvious faults (notably in the gear-box) and patently poor styling. The Maxi, which looked as if it were designed to travel sideways, was nicknamed the 'Land Crab'.

Motor Sports Council under the chairmanship of Sir Clive Bossom. This gave Dean Delamont more independence, especially in financial matters. It also opened a rift between Pall Mall and Belgrave Square which would, in due course, threaten to split the RAC asunder.

The RAC's motoring services were also in a parlous state. The Associate section had ceased to grow, for as fast as new members joined, old ones left. The number of road Patrols was actually falling, rates of pay being too low to attract fresh recruits. The organisation was as creaky as its equipment, despite the sterling efforts of loyal and experienced regional directors like Tony Andrews, 'Mac' Mackay, Jack Proud, Ken Sheridan and John Styles. When Eric Charles took command in 1969, having started as a clerk in the Leeds office over three decades before, he found that RAC vehicles were, on average, eleven years old. Certain improvements did occur. A Staff Association for RAC Employees (SAFRACE) was formed in 1970, though not before area managers had threatened to dismiss Patrols such as Terry Philips and T. H. Lowe, who had 'canvassed covertly' for it. The Club's seventy-fifth anniversary in 1972 was marked by newly designed badges and uniforms. The latter were both fashionable and practical: unlike the old uniforms, they had no exposed silver gilt buttons to catch under car bonnets. Even the unpopular beret was useful for cleaning windscreens. In addition to these cosmetic exercises, the RAC launched its Rapid Rescue service for motorways in 1973: specially designed 'Pick-U-Up' vehicles quickly removed broken-down cars, which were particularly vulnerable on interchanges with no hard shoulders.

Accordingly *The Autocar* dismissed the suggestion that the RAC was its rival's 'poor relation'. It had fewer members and their cars broke down only half as frequently as those of their counterparts in the AA, with the result that the pressure on the RAC's patrolmen was less intense. Moreover, the AA was in some respects *too* innovative. It bombarded its five million members with offers for goods and services ranging from villa holidays to *Drive* magazine, so much so that some damned it as a 'large "Mail Order House"' and left the organisation to enrol in the RAC. However, although the Club avoided that trap, it generally responded to the opposition's initiatives rather than taking the lead itself. This was particularly obvious in 1974 when the AA, prompted less by the RAC than by the emergence of new rivals such as the National Breakdown Recovery Club, founded its Relay service. It provided for the transport of a member's car and its passengers to any destination in mainland Britain if a major breakdown occurred. Despite initial problems and inbuilt restrictions, Relay proved both successful and profitable. The RAC was bound to react.

In 1975, therefore, the Club launched its Recovery service. This improved on Relay by delivering the immobilised car and its passengers to their specified destination in case of accident as well as breakdown. True, there was an initial element of bluff. Eric Charles bought a few Range Rovers and dressed them up in the RAC's smart and safe new livery (white predominating over blue and red) in order to give the impression that the Club deployed a fleet of such Recovery vehicles. In fact, garages did most of the work. Nevertheless, Recovery was a great leap forward for the Club. It 'created lots of excitement' and provided 'a service that had been missing'. It was also the biggest change that Patrols had seen since the coming of radio. Their motto remained 'Go not Tow'. But now they were relieved of some of the pressure to repair cars by the roadside as well as much of the business of getting them to a garage and

500,000+

RECOVERY

RAC Services Director, Eric Charles enrols television star Basil Brush as the half-millionth member of the Recovery Service

The RAC's Recovery Service dealt with twice as many cases and covered twice as many miles last year than it did the previous year.

Launched nearly three years ago, vehicles used by the service have driven nearly seven and a half million miles, and more than half of these were covered last year.

Mr. Eric Charles, the RAC Services Director, commented: "Our Recovery Service last year doubled its membership, doubled the number of cases handled, and also the number of miles covered.

"These figures prove beyond doubt that many motorists want the reassurance of ready help in the event of a major breakdown, and RAC members are getting that assistance through the Recovery Service."

Recently the 500,000th member of the Recovery Service was signed up at the RAC's headquarters in London—which means that nearly one in three of the RAC's total Associate members are now covered by the service which is complementary to the normal Rescue Service.

The fees charged by a garage to attend a breakdown and the cost of repairs, can make it a nightmare for a driver who finds himself stranded in the middle of the night in some remote part of the country and his car will not budge.

Explained Mr. Charles: "Those members who

they can do if the car is beyond immediate repair, except call for further assistance.

Even so, it can be a very expensive operation for a motorist to transport his family and car to his home or on to his holiday destination. He may be able to get it repaired locally, but this is not always possible.

This is where the RAC Recovery Service comes in. Under it a member, his car and up to three passengers will be taken on to their destination or returned home should they prefer.

The service covers vehicles involved in an accident, provided the car has not been so badly damaged to render recovery by normal means impossible.

In addition the member is covered no matter what car he or she is driving, and, like the normal RAC membership, the member's wife or husband when driving is also fully covered free of charge.

The Recovery Service, which is complementary to the existing RAC Rescue Service, comes into operation automatically for a member whose car cannot be repaired in a reasonable time either by RAC road staff or a local garage.

While the service does not provide for rescue of a car broken down within the immediate vicinity of a member's home, it does not specify distance. This is left to the discretion of the local controller because from experience of handling vehicle breakdowns, the RAC knows that in some remote parts of the country a driver can be stranded when only a short distance from home.

Please note: Recovery Service is not available in Northern Ireland

...ere's a reply-paid enquiry ...r you to send off for an application form.

RECOVERY

RAC RECOVERY

the service that gets you there-breakdown or accident

RECOVERING THE LEAD

The Recovery Service was masterminded by Eric Charles, head of Motoring Services from 1969 to 1985. An innovator in his day – in 1947 he coined the term 'black ice' – Charles finally concluded that computer-aided rescue was 'gilding the lily'. But in 1978, when Recovery had proved popular and profitable, he could afford to bang the RAC's drum – even to wag its Brush.

perhaps finding a nearby hotel where their owners could stay overnight – occasionally Patrols put up members in their own homes. The service was versatile, though it had its limitations. As Bossom said, the RAC 'assisted two elderly ladies who were accompanied by two ducks but we jibbed at the farmer who wanted us to take his prize bull aboard one of our Recovery vehicles'. Still, despite the extra £4 cost, a third of the RAC's 1.5 million members quickly subscribed to Recovery. What is more, the service made £1 million in its first year of operation. Polson was horrified. He told Eric Charles, 'It's obscene to make all that money.'

Plainly the culture of the RAC, with its stress on service, was remote from that of the AA, with its high-pressure salesmanship and slick marketing techniques, its television advertisements and Green Shield stamps. Like its competitor, the RAC offered a variety of products to the public. But in the words of a visitor to the head office of the Associate section, next door to the Pall Mall clubhouse,

> gentlemanly propriety seeps through the wall. At the counters where they sell books
> and maps and insurance, or offer advice on touring, the atmosphere is relaxed,
> deferential, slow moving but helpful. The pressure to buy would not be regarded as
> excessive in a church bazaar.

Upstairs in a 'rabbit warren of dark oak and dingy corridors, shared incongruously with Walt Disney productions', the office staff worked at an equally sedate pace. Among them was a bevy of old-fashioned eccentrics: one sported plus-fours; another would fret over the damage wet weather did to the permanent wave in his hair. High priests of the ledgers, they treated their professional knowledge as arcana to be kept from newcomers; and in consequence 'the chaos was amazing'. Their boss, Nelson Mills Baldwin, a gargantuan ex-sailor, inhabited a comfortable office decorated in the Edwardian style. He was a popular figure with a taste for high living and a desk which seemed to be empty unless furnished with a glass of whisky and ginger ale. But despite his forceful manner and his grand title – Director-General – Mills Baldwin had little drive and less authority. He once complained, 'I can't order toilet paper without going to see Polson.' By 1975, however, the Chairman was a shadow of his former self. His face sagged and to those not in the know he seemed to be permanently drunk. In fact, though he was too proud to admit it, Polson had suffered a debilitating stroke.

Thus the RAC was centrally governed but poorly controlled. Individual departments went their own way, with mixed results. The travel service, for example, contrived to be both small and cumbersome, not least because it dabbled in irrelevant matters like obtaining theatre tickets. Standards of service in the insurance department were poor and there were so many policies that it was difficult for the layman to distinguish between them. From 1970 computers were introduced into area offices on a piecemeal and haphazard basis – as late as 1983 there was not a single one in the Stockport office. More enterprising was the Foreign Routes Department directed from Croydon by Colin McElduff, a breezy former soldier and globetrotter whose life had been a series of colourful adventures. His nineteen staff supplied members with 50,000 foreign routes a year, in the process occasionally discovering roads – stretches along the Italian coast, for example – which had simply been omitted by the map-makers. Some itineraries were outlandish indeed: a route for Spanish motor-cyclists who wanted to drive to the top of Mount

THE NEW STYLE

RAC patrolmen had been involved in terrible accidents before 1973 because they were not visible enough. Conspicuous clothing and brightly hued vehicles saved lives. New uniforms also made Patrols look smarter – though the beret was a bugbear. And motorists had more confidence in uniformed rescuers, though some thought that RAC men were police spies.

Kilimanjaro; a path across the Sahara desert for an Anglican priest pushing a wheelbarrow for charity. The spirit of this department was summed up in the title of a book which the RAC published in 1981: *Turn Left – the Riffs have Risen*. One journalist suggested that the motto of international motorists should be 'Lead on McElduff'.

The RAC's peripheral maladies, however, were as nothing compared with the chronic condition at its heart. So solidly built was the clubhouse that it seemed not only to defy time but almost to sanction neglect. It appeared indestructible to the likes of Lord Camden, who had long presided over the house committee, which was responsible for its supervision. Actually this was a toothless body with no financial power, and its aged Chairman was ineffective. Camden, once Sir Henry Segrave's team manager, jocularly confessed that his 'family had got its title for killing Irishmen for Queen Elizabeth I', but he himself was putty in the hands of Wilfrid Andrews. So by 1975 the clubhouse was in an unprecedentedly dirty and dilapidated condition. The lifts worked intermittently, if at all. The steam boilers were at their last gasp. The floors were covered with black marks made by trodden-in chewing-gum. The carpets were so ragged that members tripped up on the threads. The kitchens were antediluvian. Against the odds, standards remained high in the restaurant, thanks to the 'suave and urbane' head chef, A. G. Trompetto. But the members' dining room was a mess. For years it had served ambitious and extravagant food. 'Finest jellied eels in London, old boy,' confided the editor of a national newspaper. But the meals had always been absurdly cheap: members boasted that they 'could have lunch at the Club and get change for a pound'. A sudden attempt to raise prices and curtail the menu led to such a fall in custom that the old ways were reinstated. But the damage was done.

In the words of one member, the clubhouse was like an impoverished country vicarage where 'respectability concealed decay'. A visitor compared it to 'a beached Cunard liner'. The whole place, according to another witness, was suffering from a 'hardening of the arteries'. Harry Stanley, now on the Committee, was 'horrified' by its decrepitude. Still more alarming was the steep fall in full membership: in 1975 it dipped towards 8,000, half the total which Andrews had considered desirable. Totting up the figures, Mills Baldwin painted a 'very disturbing picture' of the Club's financial position. The Committee worried endlessly over causes and cures. Some blamed the breathalyser, others parking meters, others VAT, others unclubbable times. Among the economies suggested was the introduction of paper towels, though Polson felt that only linen was in keeping with 'the dignity of the RAC' – the Committee overruled him and saved the Club £3,000 a year.

There were many proposals to gain added revenue from the Great Gallery, which Andrews had considered 'one of the finest banqueting halls in London'. But the Club restaurant had yet to move there and, according to de Bertodano, this splendid salon was the 'biggest "white elephant"' in Clubland. Sir Clive Bossom actually suggested converting it into a real tennis court. Polson objected to sacrificing the Great Gallery, or perhaps the swimming pool, for this project; but Bossom insisted that the RAC must 'look for new ways of attracting business'. That such an astonishing scheme should have been mooted was a measure of the Committee's desperation. As John Crampton said, 'This was the worst period' in the history of the Club. It seemed to be infected with a virulent strain of the British disease, to which no one could find a remedy. Some reckoned that it would have been better if Andrews, ill though he was, had

FOREIGN PARTS

The RAC's Croydon office provided routes to the ends of the earth as well as a variety of other touring services for motorists who wanted to take their vehicles abroad. The Club's travel organisation, based at Pall Mall, ventured into the long-haul holiday market during the 1970s. But the competition was fierce.

stayed on and Polson had never become Chairman at all. As it happened, both men departed together. Wilfrid Andrews died in February 1975. The following month Polson announced his resignation on grounds of advancing years.

MOUNTBATTEN PLAYED A PART in choosing his successor – at the behest, he said, of his 'niece', Queen Elizabeth II. His candidate was Sir Clive Bossom, who was proposed for the office of Chairman in June 1975 and accepted with 'alacrity and humility'. Bossom had known the Club from boyhood. His parents lived at 5 Carlton Gardens and he remembers playing rowdy games of Red Indians with his brother in the shrubbery during the late 1920s and being pelted with peanuts and olive stones by members wanting to enjoy a quiet drink on the terrace. Bossom has high connections. His father was the first life peer, while he himself served as a junior member of Mountbatten's staff in the Far East. His wife was descended from Lord North, King George III's Prime Minister, and he himself became Margaret Thatcher's first parliamentary private secretary. Bossom was a sportsman, a traveller and a director of several companies including Vosper Thorneycroft. Jovial and relaxed, he was a raconteur and a bon viveur in the spirit of Wilfrid Andrews. Though cautious and conservative, Bossom might well have succeeded under normal circumstances. But he had to pay the bill for Andrews's over-weening self-indulgence. He also had to 'take the rap for the awful catalogue of neglect' resulting from Fergie's Calvinistic penny-pinching. So Bossom became 'the most unfortunate man in the history of the RAC'.

However, the new Chairman was one of nature's optimists. He extolled the Club where possible, endeavouring to place it at the head of a united phalanx of motorists. He scored a propaganda coup when the AA not only imitated the RAC's practice of using rigid tow bars but recommended motorists to have a professional survey done of any used car they proposed to buy, a service provided by the Club. At Westminster Bossom had taken an interest in transport matters and he continued to campaign on the motorist's behalf with ebullience. When the Greater London Council threatened to levy a tax on vehicles entering the city centre he was not above canvassing on the street, stopping cars and handing out leaflets. This provoked charges from the Labour leader of the GLC that the RAC (like the AA) was being 'used by a small group of politically motivated men who are dedicated to opposing all reasonable controls on the worst excesses of the car and the juggernaut'. Bossom objected to fuel-saving speed limits, which were consistently flouted, and to legislation which compelled the use of headlights in built-up areas after dark. He declared that 'the motorist is still harried, still restricted and still a sitting duck for the guns of the tax-gatherers'. Bossom also mounted an outspoken attack on environmentalists protesting against motorways: they should 'come out of their caves, when they will find that the dinosaur is now extinct and the wheel has been invented'. These were routine sallies. But, as Bossom said, the RAC did have some new achievements to its credit even during this 'painful and traumatic period'.

Some stemmed from a report commissioned from Coopers & Lybrand, whose management consultants investigated the RAC's various activities. In the opinion of Brian McGivern, the youngest and one of the ablest members of Bossom's Committee, the report was little more than

ANDREW POLSON

A sturdy Scot, always known as Andy, Polson was Chairman from 1972 to 1975. But he never moved out of the long shadow cast by his formidable predecessor, Wilfrid Andrews.

SIR CLIVE BOSSOM

Genial old Etonian, regular soldier in the Buffs and Tory MP, Bossom was Chairman of the Club from 1975 to 1978. He faced the worst crisis in the history of the RAC.

SIR CARL AARVOLD

An eminent sportsman and judge, Aarvold was Chairman of the RAC between 1978 and 1981. With tact and cheerfulness he helped to resolve the crisis that beset the Club.

NELSON MILLS BALDWIN

Formed by Cambridge (double blue) and the navy, the cordial Mills Baldwin served as Director-General from 1971 to 1978. He looked more formidable than he was.

DEAN DELAMONT

Able and outspoken boss of the RAC Motor Sport Division, Delamont threatened a unilateral declaration of independence during the Club's crisis. But he himself was ousted.

BRIAN MCGIVERN

A forthright and popular sportsman, McGivern played a major role in saving the Club during the 1970s and in improving the clubhouses over subsequent years.

'an exercise in common sense'. Even so, certain of its recommendations (those, for example, seeking to make the Committee more accountable) were rejected. But most were accepted and formed the basis of a major reorganisation. Financial procedures were strengthened. The RAC radio network was enhanced. New vehicles were bought. Local offices (some of them, like Birmingham, 'a disgrace') were improved. The Associate section spent £2 million on its upgrading, much of that sum earned by the successful Recovery service. The RAC also intended to set up 'an effective marketing infrastructure designed to promote the varying RAC "products"' such as insurance and legal services. Perhaps inspired by the litany of commercial jargon, the Committee hoped that these measures would create a more aggressive 'corporate image'. It would be summed up in the phrase: 'RAC, the go-ahead organisation that cares for YOU.'

The Chairman had little to do with this aspect of the Club's endeavours. He thought Eric Charles was a 'first-class' manager of the Associate goose that laid the golden eggs and contented himself with exclaiming occasionally: 'Tell me what exciting things you're doing.' Bossom was personally more interested in motor sport. He attended many Grands Prix. He tried to reduce the noise made by rally cars. He struggled to persuade the BBC to accept 'full frontal' advertising on racing cars. He regularly went to meetings of the FIA and was 'impressed by how much the RAC was respected internationally'. However, the FIA President, Jean-Marie Balestre, was distinctly disrespectful and he rekindled old antipathies. Other nations seemed to be of little account, says Bossom, but 'we fought like tigers against the French'.

Bossom also fought to restore the clubhouse, but it was a losing battle. He himself felt that the Committee, still packed with venerable figures like Lord Black, Lord Camden and the Duke of Richmond and Gordon, was little help. His personal assistants were no better, being 'loyal but decrepit'. Dillon, the stately chauffeur whom he had inherited from Andrews, looked like a coachman and would only drive during the day because he could not see at night. Club members were unresponsive and, when Bossom wanted to increase subscriptions, uncooperative: in exasperation he told those who expected to continue to enjoy generous facilities for the small fixed sum of £25 a year that they were 'living in cloud cuckooland'. But Bossom himself failed to grapple with the problems. 'I came in fairly green,' he admits, 'and I should have been much tougher.' The Chairman, who worked (unpaid) for the Club every morning, took only palliative measures such as disguising the inadequacies of the committee rooms with swathes of dyed hessian. Yet despite the appointment of an experienced hotelier, David Unwin, as Secretary, the clubhouse was running out of control. It was overstaffed yet inefficient. Nothing was properly costed or priced. As the Committee's minutes noted incredulously, there was 'not a single facility within the Club which shows a profit'. A deficit of £50,000 was forecast for 1977, which was set to double the following year. Furthermore, massive expenditure on renovations was now inescapable. The boilers threatened to explode. The sewage system was in a dangerous state. The lifts, when they functioned, were death-traps. The electric wiring gave off sparks which started small blazes in a building that flagrantly breached the fire regulations. Then, one summer day in 1976, a health inspector was shown into Bossom's office. He announced that he was going to close down the Club's kitchens: they were not only infested with rodents but, marching across their floors, was the largest army of cockroaches he had ever seen.

MOBILE BILLBOARDS

As rallying costs rose during the 1970s, commercial sponsorship became vital. Ford got support from Cossack, a men's hair spray. Roger Clark, soon above driving an Escort RS 1800 to victory in the 1976 RAC Rally, declared in television commercials that thanks to Cossack his hair stayed in place even during rallies. The claim was all the more incongruous since his driving was seldom less than hair-raising.

GLOBAL EXPOSURE

General Motors also attracted sponsorship and enjoyed some rallying success with versions of the Vauxhall Chevette (above). But Ford's dominance was amply demonstrated by the victory of Hannu Mikkola's Escort in the London to Mexico Rally of 1970 (left). The Rally gained added publicity by linking up with the football World Cup, being played in Mexico.

Bossom exercised all his formidable 'charm' on this dour bureaucrat, who somewhat relented. Only the lower kitchen was shut, on the excuse that it was being redecorated. The Committee then agreed to spend £150,000 on a complete overhaul of the catering department, which included moving the restaurant into the Great Gallery – where it remains, to the great advantage of the Club. Some of the money would come from the sale of 87,000 bottles of port and claret laid down in the Club's cellars. More would be raised by increasing the Club's membership. The Committee puzzled about how this was to be done when the clubhouse lacked 'amenities commensurate with the 20th century'. One suggestion, made by Major Eric Strologo, was to open it to Associate members, though he admitted that there could then be 'no selection procedure'. Instead Bossom introduced corporate and then family membership, giving companies and women a stake in the clubhouse for the first time. However, the membership continued to dwindle, causing a drop of £30,000 in anticipated revenue by July 1977. Committee members looked into the abyss. They would need to borrow £100,000 in November and by the end of the year, their financial advisers warned, the 'Club will be insolvent'. 'Maybe our forebears could have been more prudent with better housekeeping when times were good,' said Bossom mildly, but this was the moment to create 'a new RAC'.

Various plans were put forward to raise the estimated £1.5 million necessary to modernise the clubhouse and to save the Club. Woodcote Park could be sold: it was a 'luxury we cannot afford'. But the country club, too, was run-down, patched-up and loss-making. Its kitchens actually rivalled those of the London clubhouse: two Committee members who had toured them with a public health inspector were 'absolutely amazed at what they had seen'. So Woodcote might only fetch a modest sum, which would quickly be swallowed up by Pall Mall. Perhaps instead the RAC should move to smaller premises. The Junior Carlton Club had fallen on evil days, being, as one RAC stalwart loftily observed, 'mis-designed and mis-used'. Its modern building, which had annual overheads of £200,000 as compared to the RAC's £775,000, might make a suitable refuge, though it lacked both swimming pool and Turkish bath.

More attractive was the prospect of selling the leasehold of the RAC's premises to European Ferries. This company proposed to convert the upper four floors into luxury apartments while letting the Club continue to occupy the lower four. But the building was not only listed as being of historical importance, it was protected by a covenant which prohibited any change of use. Accordingly the Crown Estates Commissioners would have to approve the transfer, which might be a long process. The RAC was running out of time. So, on 25 August 1977, a desperate Sir Clive Bossom sent members what amounted to an ultimatum. Unless they paid an annual subscription surcharge of £45 per head over the next four years, the Club would have to close its doors for good on 31 December.

Some senior figures were 'sympathetic and understanding', and about a quarter of the members were prepared to pay the extra levy. Doubtless they were encouraged by Lord Mountbatten, who gave Bossom his full support: 'I admire the firm way you have gripped the situation and I must say I think the letter you have written is splendid. I agree with it all.' But most members disagreed with it all. Furthermore, they were horrified by the state of affairs which the letter disclosed. They criticised mismanagement at the top, feared that a severe blow had been dealt to the RAC's 'corporate image', and raged that they had received so little warning about

RALLY RESULT

*Ford capitalised on its international rallying
success in 1970 by setting up an Advanced
Vehicle Operations production line to build the
Escort Mexico. This enterprise led to the famous
RS Ford range of sporting saloons. Sport
promoted commerce as well as vice versa.*

the Club's imminent 'financial collapse'. Some denounced Bossom's demand as blackmail, others as highway robbery: 'It was a real case of "Stand and Deliver".' Many thought that the Chairman's 'shock tactics' would not work and that he should resign. From this maelstrom of emotion came urgent calls for an informal meeting of members. Although anxious to get the 'minimum of press coverage', the Committee concurred and set a date for 26 September 1977. It proved to be one of the most dramatic days in the RAC's history.

It was also an exceptionally hot day, as over a thousand members converged on the large upper committee chamber, soon to be christened the Mountbatten Room. They overflowed into the corridors and down the stairs. The dynamic young editor of *The Economist*, Andrew Knight, who had joined the Club to keep fit, arrived late and spent half an hour fighting his way through the crush. Aghast that the clubhouse was so badly run, Knight had done some homework and reckoned that the RAC 'was sitting on a gold-mine'. Dominating London's grandest street, the Club was 'potentially the finest executive health and meeting forum in Europe'. Bossom was less well prepared, despite being warned that if he did not formulate a clear plan of action the proceedings 'would turn into a lynching party'.

Having dealt with Sheerness dockers, Bossom had a cavalier confidence that he could handle members of the RAC. But when, flanked by his Committee and with his back to the northern wall of the clubhouse, he got up to explain the position, he quickly lost control of the meeting. It erupted like a volcano as 'the members rose in their wrath'. They barracked, stamped, shouted, exchanged irate words with each other and jabbed accusing fingers at the hapless Chairman. 'There had been nothing like it since Rolls-Royce was wound up,' a witness later recalled. In this highly charged atmosphere little coherent argument was possible. Knight made an effort, and was afterwards told by Lord Gowrie that he had missed his métier as a politician. Then the microphone passed into the hands of a shrewd, resolute sixty-six-year-old solicitor named Sidney Lesser, 'who saved the meeting from total bedlam'. Possessed of a weighty manner and a gravelly voice, he made by far the most impressive speech of the day. Its burden was that a small 'ad hoc committee' should be set up in an effort to rescue the Club.

The proposal was accepted and six members were chosen to serve on the committee: Lesser himself as Chairman, Tom Beattie-Edwards, Andrew Knight, Jeffrey Rose, Richard Slowe and Bernard Jones, who soon dropped out of things, apparently because he was worried about his position on the Stock Exchange. None of the six had previously known the others, though they were soon accused of having plotted to take over the Club. The ad hoc committee set to work and within a month produced a preliminary report. It said that provisions to maintain the building had for many years been 'hopelessly inadequate'. The 'appalling trading losses' of the clubhouses had been going on for 'far too long'. Pall Mall had governed Woodcote Park badly and 'almost at arm's length'. When serious dangers became apparent Bossom's Committee had failed to take 'effective steps'.

What Bossom and, before him, Polson had done, the ad hoc committee discovered, was to obtain legal advice about which of the three entities in the RAC – the Pall Mall Club, the Associate section and the Motor Sport Division – owned what. The opinions of counsel, which could have determined the allotment of any remaining assets if the clubhouse did become insolvent, had been predictably equivocal and expensive. One QC had said that the position of

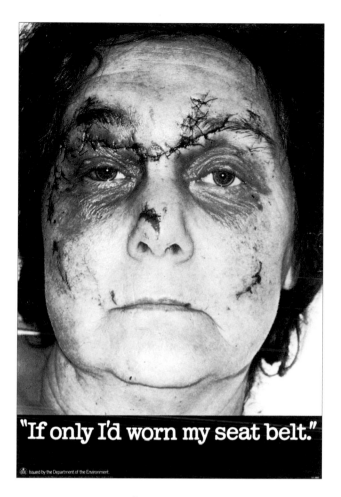

"If only I'd worn my seat belt."

Issued by the Department of the Environment.

SHOCK TACTICS

Horrifying pictures like the one above were used in 1972 'Clunk Click'
television commercials to induce people to use their car seat belts. The RAC
supported the policy of persuasion. But when 'belting up' was enforced in
1983 car deaths and serious accidents fell by 20 per cent.

the Associate section 'tends to elude precise legal definition'. Another authority had ventured that it was a 'shadowy area'. The ad hoc committee decided that the Associate section was owned and managed by the RAC's holding company, Automobile Proprietary, but governed by its own rules and possessed of funds which could not be used for extraneous purposes. Whether the Motor Sport Division also enjoyed complete financial independence was unclear – which alarmed Dean Delamont. Eventually, the ad hoc committee reported, the 'web of confused interwoven functions and costs' in which the RAC was enmeshed would have to be unravelled.

More immediately Club members, as members also of Automobile Proprietary, controlled substantial resources in one way or another. So the sudden decision to close the Club had been 'misconceived'. Now a new 'working committee', consisting of six members of Bossom's Old Guard and six members of Lesser's New Guard, should be formed with full powers to resolve the crisis. This recommendation was accepted at an Extraordinary General Meeting held on 21 November 1977. But, as the *Sunday Times* said, it was not easy to make the transition from Bossom's Committee, 'gilded by Debrett's, to a hybrid working committee dominated by activist businessmen'. At their first meeting, Lesser claimed, the Old Guard's representatives 'looked at me as if I'd just crawled out of a piece of cheese'.

Hostility between the supporters of Bossom and Lesser took every form, ranging from 'Machiavellian intrigue' to 'guerrilla warfare'. Bossom acknowledges that he 'tried to ride roughshod' over his opponents and that he 'must have been bloody rude' to Lesser. But the diminutive solicitor gave as good as he got. Ambitious, abrasive and ferociously outspoken, he was quite capable of ordering the Chairman to 'Get out of my office!' Lesser was contemptuous of Bossom. Bossom could not stand Lesser, whom he described as a 'pushy East End lawyer'. Lesser and several other members of the New Guard were Jewish and such expressions so concerned Andrew Knight that he telephoned Lord Mountbatten to protest. In fact, since the days of Sir David Salomons and King Edward VII, whose Jewish friends eagerly joined the Club of which he was patron, Jews had been prominent and accepted in its life. So when Lesser complained of being the victim of anti-Semitism he won some sympathy in Pall Mall.

Despite these corrosive antagonisms, the 'working committee' made astonishing progress. This was chiefly because it streamlined management by means of a ruthless division of labour. It delegated supreme authority in specific areas to various of its members. Brian McGivern and Andrew Knight, aware of the risk of trading while insolvent, concentrated on making the clubhouse pay. To achieve a fuller use of its facilities they started by coating all the public rooms with cheap but cheerful – even garish – paint. The Great Gallery, for example, was given green walls and aubergine pillars. Some members were outraged, but others came to see what all the fuss was about, and stayed to have lunch. Soon the improved restaurant became the financial 'engine room' of the clubhouse. Staff morale rose and so did standards of service. Other parts of the building benefited including the Turkish Bath. The bedrooms were smartened up and occupancy rates rose by twenty per cent despite increased prices. Subscriptions were standardised and the dozens of special concessionary rates were abolished. A recruiting drive produced a thousand new corporate members from 'top-name companies'. In March 1978 McGivern and Knight, respectively a printer and a journalist, launched a glossy new RAC journal entitled *Pell-Mell & Woodcote*. Resembling 'an upmarket parish magazine', it claimed

ANDREW KNIGHT

Educated at Ampleforth and Balliol, Knight was editor of The Economist *when the Club faced bankruptcy. He invested all his skill and energy in its rescue.*

JEFFREY ROSE

Devoted to the RAC, Rose was prominent among its rescuers. As Chairman he presided over its renaissance – one of the great corporate success stories of the age.

SIDNEY LESSER

A shrewd, strong-willed solicitor, Lesser took the lead in saving the RAC. But many members were alienated by his overbearing manner and he never became the Club's Chairman.

to express the *glasnost* which complemented the RAC's *perestroika*. It was, indeed, surprisingly frank. But it also contained so much propaganda about the revitalisation of the Club that some members likened it to *Pravda* – a charge which, to give the journal its due, it reported.

Another aim of the magazine, as its title suggests, was to eradicate the old 'them-and-us' feeling which existed between Pall Mall and Woodcote Park. This was compounded by rancorous suspicions about the *bona fides* of the New Guard and fears that the country club would be sold. Tom Beattie-Edwards was well suited to assuage these emotions. He was a golfer, a traveller in Outer Mongolia (which was about as cold, he said, as the first tee at Woodcote), a hail-fellow-well-met Liverpudlian who had made a fortune out of orange drinks and now lived in a house

THE HOUSE MAG

Founded to help revive the Club, Pell-Mell & Woodcote *harked back to history. Pall Maille, commonly called Pell Mell, was a game, played by Charles II among others, in which a ball was struck through a ring at either end of an alley. One of those alleys became the main street of Clubland.*

near Epsom called Wit's End. However, the disaffection at Woodcote was exacerbated by the 'working committee's' decision to stop separate membership of the country club at the end of 1978, which involved increasing annual subscriptions there from £55 to the Pall Mall level of £105. This prompted moves to declare unilateral independence, though it was not clear how that could be achieved. Woodcote's 'totally uncooperative' elected committee refused to submit accounts to Pall Mall and was said to be 'almost in a state of mindless revolt'. However, Beattie-Edwards cracked the whip and Lesser insisted that 'the financially non-viable country club could no longer expect to be subsidised from other resources'. Fifty members resigned. Others were converted when infusions of cash produced obvious improvements at Woodcote Park. But the crisis left a simmering legacy of mistrust and discontent.

Meanwhile Jeffrey Rose, himself partner in a firm of surveyors and property consultants, sought to capitalise on the fixed assets of the RAC. He never favoured the sale of the top floors of the clubhouse but he went through the motions of negotiating with European Ferries until the deal proved unnecessary. By the spring of 1978 the clubhouse was trading its way out of trouble: it was expected to make a surplus of £175,000 instead of a loss of £110,000. Nevertheless the 'working committee' needed well over £1 million to attend to what it alliteratively called 'daunting dilapidations … dangerously deferred'. To raise this sum Rose proposed to sell two properties: 83/85 Pall Mall, whose staff could join those at the Associate section's headquarters in Croydon; and 31 Belgrave Square, which would be bought by its present occupants, the Motor Sport Division. But the disposal of these buildings was problematic because no allocation of resources had yet taken place. To achieve that the RAC would have to cut through a 'formidable legal and accountancy tangle'. In fact, the Club needed a complete reorganisation. It required a new structure by which the various components were sharply separated, their assets were fairly apportioned and the chain of command was clearly defined. Lesser, ably assisted by Rose and Richard Slowe, and advised by accountants Peat, Marwick & Mitchell, worked out a plan along these lines to put before the combined Extraordinary and Annual General Meetings on 31 May 1978.

On this occasion Lord Mountbatten appeared resplendent in the uniform of Colonel Commandant of the Royal Marines. He had had no time to change after taking the salute as the Marines' Massed Bands beat the retreat at Horseguards Parade, and he assured the five

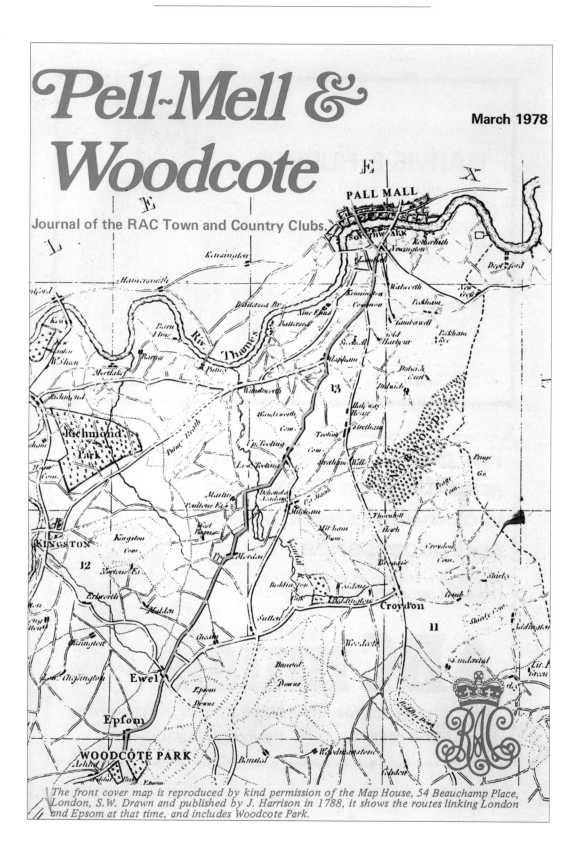

hundred assembled members that he was not, 'in this curious costume … modelling the new patrolmen's uniform'. Then he uttered a paean of praise to the Club. The Associate section was making substantial profits. The Motor Sport Division had won the Formula One Constructors' Association (FOCA) trophy for its work at Silverstone in 1977. The *Daily Express* had said that the RAC had the 'finest Clubhouse in the world, and for once I agree with the *Daily Express*'. However the 'problems' at Pall Mall had jeopardised the rest of the RAC's endeavours. So, declared the Club President, Sir Clive Bossom's 'time is up'. It was a cruel valediction, made worse by a roguish tribute. Mountbatten told the hackneyed story of Churchill's reaction to hearing the surname of Sir Clive's father: 'Bossom, that's ridiculous; that's neither one thing nor the other.' But, said Mountbatten, Sir Clive was 'one thing … a damn good chairman'.

Lesser, for all his denials, desperately wanted to succeed him. However, brusque to the point of brutality, he had made too many enemies in too short a time. Even the normally amiable Lord Nugent was vitriolic about Lesser. Nugent, a former Minister of Transport, was expected to take the chairmanship himself. He was urged to do so by Mountbatten, whose former ADC George Ritchie (himself Arthur Stanley's nephew by marriage) acted as his universally acceptable 'liaison officer' in the Club. But, when Nugent refused, the mantle fell on Sir Carl Aarvold, formerly Recorder of London and a steward of appeal in motor sport. Lesser had to content himself with the title of Executive Chairman. But he must have gained some comfort from the fact that the new Committee, which included Beattie-Edwards, Knight, McGivern and Rose, gained overwhelming support. Only five members voted against them. Lesser had a full mandate to press on with his 'corporate restructuring scheme'. He described it optimistically as 'a compendium family arrangement in which everybody gains'. But he might have reflected that no family feuds are more bitter than those which occur over the division of the inheritance.

THE MOTOR SPORTS COUNCIL, which had been formed to streamline that side of the Club's activities, was semi-detached and wholly suspicious. Dean Delamont had long been convinced that his surplus of £228,000, accumulated over five years and kept in the parent company's 'money-box', would be used to resuscitate Pall Mall. If that happened, he feared that 'the immediate reaction from the motor sporting community would be to break away from the RAC'. So at the end of 1977 Bossom, still Chairman of the Club, agreed to form a separate, independent company, the RAC Motor Sports Association, to take over the financial and business affairs of the sport. Bossom believed that the ad hoc committee was only interested in the clubhouse and would accept this *fait accompli*. It would surely prefer to relinquish control of motor sport rather than risk a 'head-on clash' with the new association, perhaps losing 'royal patronage as well because of messy publicity'. This was a miscalculation. Taking advantage of the many legal and administrative complications, the New Guard gave no ground in negotiations that lasted until the end of May 1978. Blaming their 'intransigence' and bent on asserting independence, Bossom and Delamont changed the name of their organisation to the British Motor Sports Association, eliminating all mention of the RAC. Then Lesser, newly elected Executive Chairman at Pall Mall, began the final round of his power struggle with Bossom, who remained the nominal head of motor sport in Belgrave Square.

NUMBER ONE

*The pre-eminence of British motor racing was
dramatically displayed in 1977. The RAC won the
FOCA award for organising the best Grand Prix
and Silverstone was dominated by Lotus (above)
and McLaren (below). These British cars sported
rival cigarette advertisements. But the McLaren of
world champion James Hunt also bore the magic
No. 1 – and he won the race.*

Encouraged by Aarvold, who was a master of the tactful phrase and the emollient gesture, Lesser began gently. He would be 'happy to re-open discussions in a new spirit, the object being to wipe the slate clean and reach an early decision that suits all parties'. Bossom replied in the same vein. But very soon positions hardened and ranks closed. One member of the Association's Committee, Dennis Cardell, sent a manifesto to regional clubs urging that motor sport must become 'master of its own destiny' and concluding, 'Let us man the barricades together.'

What provoked this rallying cry was a failure to agree on whether Belgrave Square or Pall Mall should have ultimate control of motor sport. Furious about the impasse and determined to 'restore our management to its former structure', Lesser revealed the iron fist. In a fierce, hand-delivered letter, he 'required and instructed' Delamont and his staff to 'cease and terminate any appointment with or in relation to a recently created rival company known as British Motor Sports Association'. Instead they must devote their time 'exclusively and loyally to the interests and affairs of our R.A.C. Motor Sport Division'. As employees, they had to comply on pain of dismissal. But Bossom, in concert with the major local clubs and circuit owners, talked of taking 'drastic action' and 'going it alone'. Exercising his talent for diplomacy, Aarvold pulled him back from the brink. Then, at the end of August 1978, Rose, McGivern and Knight met three representatives of motor sport, Basil Tye, Michael Southcombe and Jack Sears, to seek a compromise. They hammered out a series of resolutions which were acceptable to their principals. Aarvold congratulated the New Guard negotiators. But although they had reached the heart of the matter, this was by no means the end of the affair.

There was much haggling and wriggling over details. Relations were soured by leaks to the press, evidently emanating from Belgrave Square. It would function (according to one report) 'entirely independently' from Pall Mall, whose effete denizens had little understanding of 'the increasingly commercialised and complex mysteries of motor sport', which had become a 'growth industry'. Another source of friction was Aarvold's insistence that there was no place for Delamont in the new dispensation, despite the 'vast amount of fine work' he had done for the sport. On legal advice Bossom did a last-minute 'volte face' which incensed Rose and threatened to wreck the accord. But eventually, in the spring of 1979, it was signed.

The main provisions were that the RAC British Motor Sports Council (its agreed name) would be the parliament of the sport. The civil service, to be directed by Basil Tye, would be the RAC Motor Sports Association. This would be controlled by a board of directors, half of them nominated by the RAC's holding company, Automobile Proprietary, and half by the Motor Sports Council. Since the latter was a committee of the RAC this gave effective power to the Club, where it remains to this day. Finally the funds of the Motor Sports Association would be 'ring-fenced' and it agreed to purchase 31 Belgrave Square from the Club for £310,000. So at last the government of motor sport had been re-established along traditional lines and the RAC raised a substantial sum which was designated for clubhouse use. Ironically, it was never called down as all improvements were financed from successful trading.

Certainly a wind of change was sweeping through what had seemed to be for so long the mausoleum of motordom. It was perhaps too early to claim, as Knight did, that the RAC had mounted 'one of the most successful rescue operations in the history of clubland'. But the place buzzed with activity. Corporate members and women swelled the numbers using the clubhouse.

ROAD RACERS

Britain's sports cars benefited from the success of her Grand Prix racers. But they also suffered from familiar British ills, as these 1960s models illustrate. The Triumph Spitfire (above) sold well but its life was artificially prolonged. The MGB GT (below) was also popular but suffered a premature death. And the Lotus Elan (right), though a brilliant road-holder, was fragile and unreliable.

McGivern, who had served with RAF Fighter Command before going into business and joining the Club (to play squash, one of several racquet games at which he excels), led his colleagues in a long struggle to ensure that standards of dress were in line with the smarter appearance of the building. Subscription revenue increased from £481,000 in 1977 to £722,000 in 1978. The facilities were better patronised: in one week in April 1979, for example, 256 people used the gymnasium (recently converted from the rifle range); 1,400 meals were served in the Great Gallery and nearly as many in the Buttery and the Long Bar; the seventy-four bedrooms had an occupancy rate of over 90 per cent. New specialist staff, such as Nick Cranfield, marketed the banqueting rooms. The entrepreneurial spirit trickled down from the top: tipping was permitted, with none of the dire consequences forecast by Wilfrid Andrews.

Pell-Mell & Woodcote lauded the swimming pool where Johnny Weissmuller (the Hollywood Tarzan) had once practised. It also promoted the squash courts, where players ranged from Cardinal Hume, who modestly described his efforts as 'geriatric', to James Hunt, the motor racing driver, who bicycled to Pall Mall wearing shorts and a T-shirt, changed into a suit on the pavement outside the clubhouse, reversed the process on going home and never complained about the dress regulations. Knight also secured publicity for the Club's amenities from other members in the inky trade such as Harold Evans, Donald Trelford and Nigel Dempster. New equipment increased efficiency. As David Unwin said, 'We are trying to go from the quill pen to the computer rather quickly.' By the end of 1980 the best part of a million pounds had been spent on new boilers, rewiring, catering improvements and a modern telephone system. Massive further refurbishments were planned. The New Guard had halted the clubhouse's 'lurch to oblivion'.

The reformation was slower to affect Woodcote Park. Here, as one letter of complaint noted in 1978, the swimming pool was out of order, the tennis courts were bumpy, service in the almost deserted dining room was 'sloppy' and the cheese-cake was 'edged with mould'. Matters soon improved, thanks in part to Beattie-Edwards. More important, £250,000 was lavished on the country club, achieving not just a restoration but a resurrection. From now on the potential of Woodcote Park would increasingly be realised and, as Lesser hoped, it would never again be treated as 'the Cinderella of the RAC'.

By 1979 Lesser was widely hailed as the saviour of the Royal Automobile Club. In reality its salvation had been a joint accomplishment. The 'working committee' had justified its name: the likes of Rose, McGivern and Knight had laboured incessantly and without recompense, giving up time which they could ill afford. However, Lesser was chiefly responsible for devising the new structure of the RAC, together with the legal and financial disciplines that would keep it in place. He masterminded the division of its operations into half a dozen separate companies: RAC Motoring Services Ltd (formerly the Associate section); RAC Insurance Ltd; RAC Travel & Brokerage Ltd; the RAC British Motor Sports Association Ltd; RAC Pall Mall Clubhouse Ltd; and RAC Woodcote Park Ltd. Having solicited advice from accountants and the opinion of counsel, he resolved the 'ludicrous uncertainties' about what asset belonged to which enterprise. Thus, for example, he allotted the RAC's twenty-four local offices to Motoring Services while the clubhouse retained 83/85 Pall Mall. But while conducting these manoeuvres, Lesser behaved like an incipient dictator.

FENCING SQUASHED

The RAC clubhouse at Pall Mall has been described as 'the spiritual home of amateur squash'. Here the British amateur championships were held and members waxed so keen on the game that the fencing salle (above) was eventually converted to the purposes of squash. Woodcote Park boasts two international-sized doubles courts – thanks partly to the enthusiasm of Sir Michael Edwardes.

PROFESSIONAL STANDARD

Oke Johnson helped to raise the level of squash to such heights that the RAC has often won the Bath Cup, first awarded to the best London gentlemen's club in the 1922–3 season. The Drysdale Cup, given in 1926 to commemorate the RAC's outstanding player Dr Theodore Drysdale, is the most coveted trophy in junior squash.

THE BATH CUP

THE DRYSDALE CUP

He bullied, hectored and ranted. He claimed credit for every success and blamed any failure on others. He exercised a rare talent for intrigue and displayed an extraordinary capacity for alienating even his closest allies.

So there was no opposition in the summer of 1979 when the RAC board abolished Lesser's office of Executive Chairman. Lesser's reaction to being ousted, he told Mountbatten, 'was very much like Nescafé – pretty black and instant'. But really it was stronger and more bitter than that. He accused board members of 'stupendous folly': they had acted in a 'selfish', 'inept', 'unconstitutional' and 'grossly offensive' manner. Aarvold tried to mollify Lesser, paying tribute to his virtues and achievements but saying that his 'arrogance' and 'dictatorial' behaviour made the decision essential for the good of the Club. Mountbatten also soothed Lesser, who was appointed a vice-president of the RAC and given other perquisites. In particular he was invited to undertake the task of re-establishing good relations with the FIA. This sugared the pill of rejection and had the advantage of taking him away from Pall Mall.

There Jeffrey Rose was appointed Deputy Chairman and Michael Limb was given the title General Secretary, succeeding Nelson Mills Baldwin who died soon afterwards. The new team worked well. Limb was efficient and experienced. He had felt 'trapped' in the remorseless spiral of decline during Andrews's latter years, and now he rejoiced at the fresh opportunities offered by the RAC's revival. Rose had a vision of what the revival could become. Quiet, modest and charming, he was also cool, confident and calculating. Having been chiefly occupied with sorting out the RAC properties and keeping its motor sport activities on track, he now took a pre-eminent part in directing the fortunes of the Club.

The septuagenarian Sir Carl Aarvold was a 'typical non-executive chairman'. He was a popular figurehead rather than a charismatic leader. Tall and florid, Aarvold had been a distinguished sportsman and judge. Excelling at cricket and water polo, he had also played rugby in four successive Cambridge sides, a unique feat, and had won a place in the 1930 British Lions team. Invariably judicious, he was never pompous; he had a self-deprecating manner, always attributing his success to luck rather than judgement – 'I seem to have had such ruddy flukes.' His conversation was a feast of good humour punctuated by bursts of infectious laughter. Understandably this 'super chap', as Limb called him, was quite unprepared for the last twist in the tale of the RAC's protracted crisis.

The trouble arose in 1980 when four members of the Club Committee became disenchanted with the governance of Aarvold and Rose. The dissenters – Tom Beattie-Edwards, W. E. Norton, Douglas Richards and Richard Slowe – all seem to have had separate agendas. Beattie-Edwards, for instance, wanted to have a free hand at Woodcote Park and to rid the Automobile Proprietary board of employee directors, describing them (with some justification) as 'the payroll vote'. Moreover there was no love lost between the quartet on the one hand and the Chairman and his deputy on the other. An argument had taken place between Aarvold and Slowe, for example, over a car which the latter had wanted to purchase in order to carry out his duties as a director of the RAC's travel company.

However, the dissidents did coalesce around a single major personality and a single vital issue. They believed that the Club would be better run by Sidney Lesser. They also made the belated claim that the way in which the RAC's assets were being split between its separate new

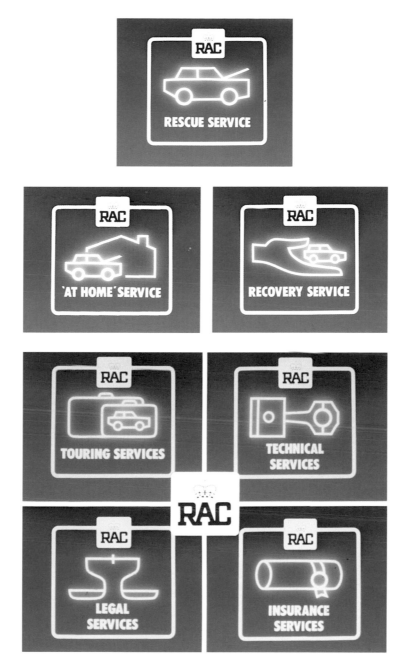

DIFFERENT DEPARTMENTS

According to the Sunday Telegraph *of 3 April 1977,
the RAC suffered from the historical accident that its
'motoring organisation is an appendage to the social
club of the same name'. But, as these symbols show, if
the motoring body failed to distinguish itself and its
various services from the gentlemen's club it was not
for want of trying.*

companies was unfair to the clubhouse. All RAC enterprises were in a sense the progeny of Pall Mall, yet the clubhouse was only receiving a fifth of the RAC's total worth (itself estimated at £15 million). 'In the Club, with its marble swimming pool and slightly dog-eared opulence, some members feel apoplectic at this proposal,' reported the *Observer*. But at the annual general meeting of 28 May 1980 Aarvold was taken completely by surprise when these sulphurous emotions bubbled to the surface. Slowe, a highly articulate lawyer with a flamboyant personality, conducted a noisy opposition which raised the temperature to boiling point. 'I'm not put off by boos or shouting,' Aarvold told hecklers, but he was certainly flustered. When warned that he might face a vote of no confidence, the Chairman replied with disarming candour: 'It's a matter of great surprise that anyone has confidence in me at all.'

Not since Bossom was howled down had there been such a 'commotion in London's Clubland'. But after three hectic hours only the resolution to approve the accounts was rejected. The meeting itself was adjourned for further study of the reorganisation. The next two months were filled with furious in-fighting. Writs, injunctions, court orders and lawyers' letters whirled to and fro like shrapnel. The affairs of the Club were virtually paralysed. The RAC's entire 'restructuring programme', of which Slowe had been an architect, was threatened with destruction. Supporters of the Chairman were appalled by opposition which they regarded as mischievous and irresponsible. However, the dissident group did have a point. The division of the RAC's assets was essentially pragmatic and could well have been challenged in a court of law. Ironically this was because the clubhouse might have been taking too large, rather than too small, a share. The RAC's finance director, Frank Shaw, warned Aarvold that the original acquisition of 83/85 Pall Mall had possibly been 'financed by the Associate section'.

Slowe and his allies also scored a technical victory by claiming that Aarvold was ineligible to be Chairman. He had been elected to the post as an honorary (instead of a full) member of the Club, thus perhaps inadvertently breaking the rules as they then stood. The RAC's own solicitor, Alan Levinson, concluded that the Chairman's position was clearly unsatisfactory. Then the dissidents tried to debar four directors loyal to Aarvold, including McGivern, from the board of Automobile Proprietary on the grounds that they had not been re-elected at the abortive meeting of 28 March. They retaliated with a High Court injunction which prevented the board from carrying out any but routine business until the situation was resolved.

The granting of the injunction imposed a temporary stalemate on the conflict. Slowe and Norton were frustrated in their attempt to replace Aarvold with Beattie-Edwards, who declared that he was 'amazed and hurt' by McGivern's accusation of plotting. However, Aarvold and Rose could themselves do little except encourage members of the Club to vote for them in due course. Their campaign was interrupted by another fracas which erupted at the beginning of July. Douglas Richards, one of the four dissidents and a former president of the SMMT, had lost the confidence of the main board during the year in which he had been chairman of the RAC's travel subsidiary and his contract was not renewed. Angrily declaring that this was 'an unholy business', he thereupon tendered his resignation from the main board. Richards denounced the 'unsuitable and unbusinesslike attitudes of those running the RAC', saying that its three thousand employees, 'all damned good blokes ... should not be mucked about like this'. He then wrote to all full members of the Club urging them

SHABBY GRANDEUR

Despite attempts to hide the signs of wear and tear in the clubhouse, they are all too apparent in these photographs taken during the mid-1970s. It was a long, hard struggle to escape from the vicious circle of increasing dilapidation, falling membership and shrinking revenue. But some preferred the club to be unfashionable – the spies Burgess and Maclean had lunched there inconspicuously just before escaping to Russia. And others liked the faded sense of peace, including one member who wanted to die in his favourite armchair – and did just that.

to vote for Lesser, 'the man who put the RAC back on its feet'. When the annual general meeting was eventually resumed, on 24 July 1980, the members disregarded his advice.

The day was again searingly hot and the temperature in the crowded Mountbatten Room was further raised by arc lights set up so that members in overflow rooms could watch the proceedings on closed-circuit television. This was the RAC's first electronic AGM, with portable microphones, computer terminals at the entrance and stewards clutching walkie-talkies. The dissidents had agreed that Rose should take the chair – Beattie-Edwards telexed the news to him, 'hoping this helps to clear a hopeless muddle'. Calmly but firmly, Rose began by condemning those who had 'brought discredit' on the RAC by seeking to disqualify Aarvold. Disclosing the excellent financial results – Motoring Services and the clubhouse had surpluses of £2.8 million and £400,000 respectively – he deplored the fact that the RAC's message to the world was nevertheless 'sour and discordant'. Cups of cold water were passed round the room and the board paraded its candidates 'like mannequins'. In the end its recommendations were 'resoundingly carried'. Delighted, Rose told the press: 'There has never been any concerted body of criticism. As in any organisation we have a few individual dissidents and from time to time, but only rarely, they have come together.' Now they had been routed.

The next day the High Court injunction was lifted and the RAC could 'operate without legal hindrance'. Aarvold was at once elected to full membership, co-opted onto the board and formally made Chairman. The attack on him, said McGivern, had 'demeaned the entire RAC'. All the dissidents resigned from their official posts apart from Lesser, who continued as vice-president, attending appropriate functions and treated with due courtesy, until his death in 1993. Slowe and later Beattie-Edwards also resigned from the Club. Jeffrey Rose's star, however, was in the ascendant. He was congratulated for having 'handled the AGM superbly'. He got credit for trying to heal the Club's wounds and avoiding further legal action. He was given the task of overseeing Motoring Services. Then, early in 1981, Rose succeeded Aarvold as Chairman. His elevation brought the Club's long, louring crisis to an end and opened the brightest chapter in its history since Edwardian times.

BOND BUG

Described as 'the Mustang of its class',
this vehicle was certainly a step up
from the Robin Reliant. But the
attempt to combine economy with style
had all the flair of, say, flared trousers.

THE TRIUMPH OF TECHNOLOGY

While the car boomed and British volume car-making busted, the RAC experienced a renaissance. Revolutionised by new management and modern technology, it sped into the outside lane of the 'information superhighway'. Motorists observed and members multiplied.

UPBEAT JOURNAL

The RAC's staff newspaper, glossily produced by the specialist firm Chandler Gooding, was launched in 1988. It aimed to keep employees in tune with quick-tempo change.

DURING THE 1980S THE AUTOMOBILE was favoured as never before but the British car industry collapsed like a punctured tyre. Margaret Thatcher openly boasted of 'never travelling by train' but she abominated British Leyland because it made demands on the public purse and should anyway have been a private enterprise. When Sir Michael Edwardes, the stocky South African boss of BL, called at 10 Downing Street in May 1980 to solicit further state subsidies, he felt as if he were on a 'suicide mission ....' She was in an enquiring mood, somewhat reminiscent of the Spanish Inquisition. "Now what's all this about? You're not going to ask for more money?" was her opening salvo.' He not only asked for, but got, almost a billion pounds. The Prime Minister acted against her most visceral instincts because she was 'absolutely horrified' by the impact that BL's liquidation would have on unemployment and the balance of payments. Also she had hopes of 'investing in success' since Edwardes, who had been Chief Executive since 1977, was transforming BL. Moreover he showed 'grit' in the face of 'trade union bloody-mindedness'. Edwardes had first spelled out his determination to resist the tiny minority of extremists at a meeting of the Guild of Motoring Writers at the RAC clubhouse in 1978. The audience was surprised because, at a time when labour relations were tending towards anarchy, militants were more vocal than managers. The motoring writers were also sceptical, since the boardroom appeared to be cowed by the shop floor. But between 1977 and 1982 the tough little tycoon, who kept fit by playing squash at Pall Mall, reduced strikes from 5.9 to 1.6 per cent of the hours worked. So at the very time when the RAC was caught up in its own mortal crisis Edwardes was struggling, with apparent success, to save the life of British Leyland.

When Edwardes took command at British Leyland he had been confronted with a plethora of problems more complex and deep-seated than any facing the Club. The company had too many old and uneconomic factories. It produced too great a variety of models, most of them overlapping, outdated and unreliable. Even new cars constructed in new plants were disappointments: the Rover SD1 came off its purpose-built assembly line at Solihull riddled with faults – a leaking boot, wheel arches prone to rust, inefficient electrical works and serious engine defects. British Leyland's accountants failed to provide a breakdown of costs on each model produced, so Edwardes did not discover for some time that every MG he sold in the United States lost the company £900. BL possessed no test track and its engineers 'had to resort to testing new vehicles at night on public roads'. Finally, morale in the workplace was 'very, very bad' and industrial relations were still worse. According to Edwardes's calculations, over a period of thirty months a single shop steward at Longbridge, Derek Robinson ('Red Robbo'), was responsible for '523 disputes, with the loss of 62,000 cars and 113,000 engines, worth £200 million'. Obviously drastic action was needed to reform BL. No one was more resolved to take it than Edwardes, whose style of 'macho management' aroused powerful feelings on both sides. Critics abused him as a 'poison dwarf' who aspired to be dictator of an industrial 'Bantustan'. Admirers hailed him as 'Mighty Mini', a pocket Hercules with the strength and guts to clean out British Leyland's Augean stables.

Like the New Guard at the RAC, Edwardes began by staring bankruptcy in the face. Unlike them, however, he could draw on the national exchequer in the last resort. In 1977 the motor industry was still Britain's largest exporter of manufactured goods and a Labour government, even more than a Tory one, felt bound to sustain it. Thus Harold Wilson had bailed out Chrysler (UK) in 1975. To bring jobs to Belfast his successor, James Callaghan, even financed the DeLorean sports car, a disaster on wheels of which its eponymous creator remarked prophetically: 'If Northern Ireland can build the *Titanic*, they can build this car.' Inevitably, therefore, the government came to the rescue of BL in 1977, though the cost was high in terms of public concern as well as cash. Indeed, the Prime Minister remarked: 'If we could get rid of the motor industry perhaps our image wouldn't be so bad.' The handout also had an adverse effect on BL itself, reinforcing the complacent conviction that the company need not stand on its own feet. But Edwardes now had the resources to undertake 'the most extensive restructuring of a major company that has ever been done in a very short period of time'.

It was in some ways a larger version of the reorganisation at the RAC. BL was divided into several sectors, each having a degree of independence and each being required to make a profit. There was a purge at the top: within six months 200 managers were redeployed and ninety were sacked. Others were promoted, among them a brilliant young man named Neil Johnson, who later came to the fore at the RAC. Plant was rationalised: nineteen out of fifty-five factories were closed, including those at Solihull, Canley and Speke. The product range was slimmed down and celebrated marques like Morris went the way of Hillman and Humber. The MG and TR7 sports cars also disappeared. BL's total workforce shrank from 193,000 to 108,000. Productivity per worker rose by 30 per cent and on assembly lines using robots it approached European and Japanese levels. Wage settlements were kept in low single figures despite ferocious pressure from organised (and disorganised) labour – pickets at Longbridge brandished placards saying

BL BLUES

*When Michael Edwardes (above) went to British
Leyland in 1977 he took charge of the 'largest public
sector lame duck of all time'. Most factories were old-
fashioned and stoppages were frequent. Edwardes
condemned the Speke plant (below) for 'gross
disruption and structured laziness', confronting
strikers in a painful effort to reform BL.*

'BL = BREAD LINE'. The Metro, launched in 1980 proved to be BL's first successful volume car since the Mini. An alliance with Honda produced the reputable Triumph Acclaim. Jaguars had traditionally been so faulty that Americans said they needed two to make sure that one stayed on the road. Under the chairmanship of John Egan the issue of quality was comprehensively tackled. As many as 150 problems were identified, most of them stemming from inferior components – failing switches, sticking radio aerials, misshapen tyres. By 1982 matters had so improved that Jaguar was both profitable and esteemed. Much remained to be done. But when the chief engineer of Daimler-Benz saw the XJ12 for the first time he exclaimed: 'Amazing, thank God you can make it.'

In spite of all these advances BL was steadily losing ground. Its share of the home market fell from 24.2 per cent in 1977 to 17.8 per cent in 1982. Over the same period its car exports declined from 293,316 to 118,615. By 1982, when Edwardes departed, BL had cost the nation some £1.5 billion. Hopes of a return on this investment were largely dashed by glum new models such as the Maestro (1983) – described as 'a "rattling good car", with the stress on rattling' – and the Montego (1984). In any case, the government regarded a successful car not as a worthwhile investment but as an opportunity for privatisation. So the Jaguar division of BL was sold in 1984 and others, such as the bus and truck divisions, followed. The process did not run smoothly. Just as MG drivers had held mass demonstrations in an attempt to preserve that marque, so patriotic admirers of Land Rover resisted its acquisition by General Motors. In an outburst of what Margaret Thatcher called 'pseudo-patriotic hysteria', John Bull opposed the incursions of Uncle Sam. But her government was determined to find an acceptable buyer for the remnants of a company (no longer called BL but the Rover Group) which was 'totally bankrupt and had been for years'.

It therefore gave exceptionally favourable terms to British Aerospace (BAe), which (to almost everyone's surprise) purchased Land Rover and Austin Rover in 1988. Indeed, the government was later blamed for selling Rover far too cheaply and paying BAe secret 'sweeteners' into the bargain. The Cabinet minister in the firing line, Nicholas Ridley, found the criticisms difficult to answer, especially as Rover had achieved higher levels of productivity by 1989 than Nissan in its new Tyne and Wear plant. Whatever the political rights and wrongs, the fact is that the last British car giant had collapsed and been dismembered. By the end of the 1980s, in one way or the other, foreign manufacturers dominated the domestic scene: Peugeot-Talbot (once Chrysler-Rootes); Ford (which took over Jaguar in 1989); General Motors (Vauxhall); Nissan and Toyota. BMW joined them in 1994 when it bought Rover from BAe. Britain still made (and makes) a significant contribution to the increasingly integrated global automobile business. Moreover, Britain remains the centre of international motor sport and British-built racing cars such as Williams, McLaren and Benetton are world-beaters. But despite the enormous amount of money and effort which had been devoted to it, the British-owned volume car industry was 'essentially non-existent'.

The decline and fall of a national enterprise with which it had been intimately associated from the start was an awful warning to the RAC. It too had weathered the storm of the 1970s but there was no guarantee that it would survive in the harshly competitive climate of the next decade. Indeed, in some respects the RAC symbolised what Margaret Thatcher wanted to

INVASION OF THE ROBOTS

*BL's Longbridge plant was
transformed by automation
during the 1980s. Robots,
mechanical workers that did not
tire or strike, raised rates of
production until they almost
reached those of Japan. Often,
though, the robots had been
made in Japan.*

sweep out of modern Britain. It was an old-fashioned vested interest which had almost succumbed to bad management, a body more wedded to ideals of service than to the disciplines of the market-place, a bastion of privilege and tradition. Yet the 1980s also presented the Club with fresh opportunities. The motorist, as the standard-bearer of private enterprise and freedom of choice, personification of the 'feelgood factor', was uniquely favoured by Mrs Thatcher's government. Her heaven, it was said, consisted of two cars in every garage, a filling station on every corner, and cities amounting to little more than streets and parking areas. Certainly she cut subsidies to public transport, deregulating and privatising where she could. Bus and train services declined while the number of cars multiplied from fifteen to twenty million. Expenditure on highways also increased, though the RAC complained that this represented only 30 per cent of the £10 billion raised annually from the British motorist – whereas Continental countries spent 55 per cent of their motor-tax revenue on roads. Such 'griping', a critic of the Club remarked, had become a ritual. The new challenge confronting the RAC, under the leadership of Jeffrey Rose, was to modernise its organisation to cope with the motoring boom.

During the clubhouse crisis Eric Charles had continued to run road services successfully. Associate membership climbed above the two-million mark and two-thirds of the new recruits availed themselves of the Recovery service. Surpluses were also comfortably into the millions despite soaring costs – fuel prices underwent a particularly dramatic rise as a result of the Iranian revolution. In 1979 RAC Patrols handled 750,000 breakdowns, a figure that reached a million by 1983. New lift-and-tow vehicles known as 'Jambusters' improved the rescuers' performance. So did individual initiatives like that taken by Patrol Mark Gatty in 1978. After a notably hazardous recovery over snowbound roads in the Lake District he got permission to use 'deep-grip tyres at all times', a practice which the RAC eventually made standard. Gatty was exceptionally good at his job: he later won the Club's accolade, Patrolman of the Year. Yet it is fair to say that most of the RAC's thousand-strong road force aspired to emulate the likes of Gatty, encouraged as they were by higher pay scales, a better pension scheme and improved relations between management and the staff association SAFRACE. Of course, a few were bunglers or impostors – sometimes both. One Portsmouth patrolman worked for a year before it was discovered that he had 'never taken a driving test' and that his mechanical knowledge was limited to lawnmowers. But in general the RAC's men in uniform lived up to their reputation of being benign 'gods of mechanics'.

Patrols took every opportunity to develop their skills, learning novel techniques for patching up vehicles so that they could reach a garage or get home under their own power. Among the more familiar 'tricks of the trade' were replacing a disintegrated rotor arm with 'a carefully shaped cork, equipped with a drawing pin and a paper clip', sealing a water hose with a spare spark plug, and creating a makeshift fan belt out of 'the legendary pair of ladies' tights'. Many cars were driven to the limit and beyond on the proliferating motorways. The result, as Bristol patrolman Dave Hurdle observed, was a huge crop of 'blown head gaskets, wrecked big ends and broken camshaft belts'. During summer holidays the hard shoulders were cluttered with ancient family saloons, often grossly overloaded and sometimes carrying inflatable dinghies on the roof which took off 'almost better than hang-gliders'. Winter also took its toll as cars ground to a halt suffering from ignition faults, flat batteries, worn-out tyres and radiator

FRESH START

A revived BL bore attractive new fruit. The Metro (right), produced at robot-ridden Longbridge, was smart and popular. The Triumph Acclaim (below left), resulting from BL's association with Honda, did not disgrace its name. The Jaguar XJ12 (below right) benefited from John Egan's drive for efficiency and sold well in America. Though by no means faultless, these cars were a marked improvement on the past.

problems. The root of the trouble was that, despite stringent MOT tests, Britons tended to ignore servicing requirements. Thus their cars were 'the least roadworthy in Europe'. The RAC assisted forty per cent of its members each year whereas the figure for motoring organisations on the Continent was more like ten per cent. The Club's Patrols responded to this challenge with enthusiasm. Moreover, their expertise extended well beyond breathing new life into old crocks. One went to the aid of the owner of a Jensen Interceptor on the M3, who complained: 'The car starts to misfire at about 110mph.'

The variety of tasks which Patrols were called upon to undertake was one of the chief attractions of their job. Vehicles of all sorts required assistance, some of them quite exotic: RAC men managed to jump-start or reactivate a train, a helicopter, an eight-ton Scorpion tank and a 350-ton minesweeper. Bicyclists were rescued, including an old lady who became confused about new road layouts while pedalling to her library and strayed into the outside lane of the M25. One RAC member was made mobile when a Patrol provided a bolt for his artificial leg. Vehicles containing animals often ran into trouble. Patrol Mark Tipton was called to mend the tail-gate of a red Ford Cortina estate, only to find that it had been broken by the thrashing tail of a nine-foot female alligator en route to a zoo. While opening a locked car outside a Manchester circus, Patrol Ian Williams discovered that it contained two Bengal tigers. Others had adventures with poisonous snakes, leopards, billy goats and brown bears, to say nothing of squirrels, birds, mice and hamsters.

Patrols encountered, too, all sorts of conditions of men and women, often in difficult or dangerous circumstances. They became involved in domestic dramas. They rescued nudist bathers and naked lovers who had locked their clothes in their cars. They acted as surrogate police and ambulance men, often arriving first at the scene of mind-numbing accidents. Patrol Charles Lewis was driving on a dual carriageway at night when

> two lads in an XR3i Sports Escort whizzed past me. Within an instant there was a huge ball of flame. The heat was so intense I could feel it through my windscreen. When I stopped behind the car the two lads were frozen with fright. The front of the car was written off and on fire – it was filling with acrid smoke. I shouted at them to get out and used my extinguisher on the flames. In the distance I could see what looked like a bin bag in the carriageway. It turned out to be the driver of a broken-down three-wheeler. Unfortunately the chap had been messing about at the back of the three-wheeler when the XR3i had hit it, causing the petrol tank to explode in his face and severing his legs at the knees. I did what I could but he later died in hospital.

Despite such horrors, Lewis reckons that being a Service Patrol was 'the best job in the world'. Many of his colleagues would agree. Certainly the work was hard and tiring, but it was also rewarding. It provided much freedom, constant interest and occasional excitement. It also afforded Patrols the profound satisfaction of serving the community.

On the other hand, they were prevented from doing their best. This was partly because the prevailing culture of the RAC stifled initiative. The organisation was a rigid hierarchy in which orders from the top were obeyed at the bottom. When Air Commodore Alec Leggett was recruited to develop computerisation at Motoring Services in the early 1980s, he found that 'the

THE BIGGEST PARKING LOT IN THE WORLD

Completed in 1986, the M25 ring road around London immediately became congested and derided. It attracted far more vehicles than planned, especially local traffic, which took advantage of the many entries and exits. Soon the surface began to crack under the strain. (Cars too felt the strain, which kept the RAC busy.) But, like other motorways, the M25 was a victim of its own success.

RAC was far more militaristic than the RAF'. As it happened, discipline in the AA was stricter still. But certainly no RAC employee, whether uniformed or not, was left in any doubt about where he came in the pecking order. It was possible to tell a person's position not just by the canteen he ate in (there were three grades) but by his office furniture: leather-inlaid desks, bookcases, cabinets and wooden panelling were all jealously guarded signs of rank. Even a business card differentiated a junior manager, who had to write his name on it, from a senior manager, whose name was printed. These were the officers: Patrols were Other Ranks. They stood to attention when their superiors entered the room. They saluted smartly and were reprimanded for any deficiencies in their dress, such as failure to wear a beret. They paraded for inspection beside ranks of gleaming vehicles. Uniformed staff were addressed by their surnames and excluded from some area offices – they had to speak though a guichet. Patrols were even 'discouraged from meeting each other without prior permission'. Prohibition was the order of the day: for example, RAC men were forbidden to change water pumps because one of their number had accidentally sheared an engine bolt while doing this job. Such edicts had a demoralising effect on a workforce distinguished by its 'genuine care and dedication'.

Patrols were hampered still more by inadequate equipment. The tools issued to them were basic. The RAC supplied spare parts but these were only the 'bare essentials'. Patrols themselves bought additional components, which they sold to members who needed them. This private enterprise benefited everyone. But the staff were 'filling in for management's failure', and the resulting service was erratic and unsatisfactory. The same could be said of the rescue service as a whole. A member requiring assistance had to find a telephone, feed it with coins and dial the correct emergency number (one of thirty-four on his membership card) to reach the nearest of the RAC's seventeen regional 'command and control centres'. These functioned twenty-four hours a day but a dearth of lines effectively rationed their output. If the motorist could get through he gave his membership number and type. This had to be verified before help was sent since, as one senior RAC man announced firmly, 'We are not clairvoyant.' Then the member would try to explain the location of his car, which often led to a miasma of misunderstanding. Sometimes motorists relied on maps so antique that they seemed more likely to reveal the whereabouts of dragons and hippogriffs than motorways and Milton Keynes.

The message-taker wrote everything down on a slip of paper, which took about three minutes, and put it on a conveyor belt leading to the operations room. Here a dispatcher made radio contact with an appropriate Patrol, whose position was indicated by means of a pin on a large map. Because of limited frequencies and 'blind areas', as well as the huge volume of voice traffic, communication was often problematic. So was finding the stranded vehicle. Indeed, every stage of the complex process possessed the potential for confusion and delay. The system was made to function reasonably well by a loyal office staff who were often inundated with calls. They worked twelve-hour shifts. They lived on their wits in lieu of training. They learnt to cope with every kind of problem, from identifying unpronounceable Welsh hamlets to soothing the anxious, the angry and the afflicted. One young female message-taker was telephoned by a furious motorist who demanded to be put through to a man so that he could 'have a good swear'. 'Go ahead,' she replied wearily, 'I'm past caring' – which broke the ice and turned his exasperation to amusement. Eric Charles, who put his many years of valuable experience to good

JAMBUSTERS

This was what the RAC called both its 'lift-and-tow' trucks, introduced in 1980, and its motor-cycles, reintroduced in 1986. The name was rather optimistic since the trucks were liable to get stuck in traffic jams and the 581cc Nortons, though they reached stranded members in sixteen minutes on average, could only carry a limited amount of spares and equipment. But the aim was good – to clear busy routes of broken-down vehicles.

effect, was 'the ace organiser of the paper-driven regime'. But the regime had by now reached the end of its tether. The RAC could hardly make further progress while its database consisted of handwritten dockets and, as Alec Leggett said with pardonable hyperbole, its 'most important piece of technology was the rubber-band'.

Furthermore, the comfortable 'duopoly' which the RAC had for so long enjoyed with the AA was now under threat. Over the years the two motoring bodies had learnt to live in relative harmony. The AA was the acknowledged market leader, though it relied on the same kind of system as its rival and had recently made some serious mistakes. The RAC, by dint of its heritage, possessed the greater prestige. Neither seriously poached on the other's preserves. But by the 1980s a number of fledgeling rescue organisations had sprung up and the most vigorous of them, the National Breakdown Recovery Club (NBRC), was offering particularly fierce competition. True, the NBRC and its ilk used garages rather than patrolmen and so dealt with only half their breakdowns at the roadside, whereas the RAC repaired two-thirds – a great advantage. But the small fry, with fewer overheads and no frills attached, were generally cheaper. They were also quicker to reach members in need, three-quarters of whom professed to be 'very satisfied' with their service, while the figure for the RAC and the AA was only two-thirds. These developments were of special concern to the RAC, which was the more vulnerable of the veterans. But the AA was also worried and there were persistent rumours that the two oldest motoring organisations would be 'prompted to merge'.

NOTHING WAS FURTHER FROM THE MIND of Jeffrey Rose. He felt a preternatural loyalty to the Club and on becoming Chairman had set himself the goal of enhancing both its reputation and its influence. Accordingly, he felt it essential to maintain 'the integrity of the RAC as a single institution while recognising the differing interests of individual sections'. This explains why he had fought so hard to ensure that motor sport remained under the RAC's wing. Rose also believed that the Club had a duty to support the general interests of motoring and the motorist in the spirit of its Victorian founders. It should not therefore be 'driven too much by the profit motive, which can easily cause worthwhile initiatives and services to be dropped'. For example, Rose would not accept proposals to do away with the RAC's costly function of erecting road signs to special events – indeed, under his auspices sturdy plastic signs with adhesive computer-produced graphics replaced the old hand-stencilled boards. However, Rose had been appalled by the lack of financial controls which the ad hoc committee discovered. He had helped to select a new Finance Director, Frank Shaw, an excellent accountant of the old school. After this appointment fresh mechanisms were put in place to set budgets and measure performance; and on these much of the future success of the RAC's enterprises relied. In other words, Rose recognised that although the RAC was a mutual trading company, responsible only to its members, it must adopt the best business practice of a public limited company with obligations to shareholders. It had to generate a substantial income, not in order to pay dividends but to improve efficiency. Rose grafted a culture of commerce onto a tradition of service.

To a great extent the achievement reflected its author, since Rose was a businessman for whom business was not an end in itself. Born in 1931, he had been head boy of his grammar

THE COMPETITION

*By the mid-1980s the fast-growing
National Breakdown Recovery Club
posed a real threat to the two major
motoring bodies. The NBRC was quick,
flexible and cheap. But unlike the AA, a
sometimes ponderous giant, it relied on a
network of garages instead of uniformed
patrolmen. It also did less repair work
by the roadside and offered fewer
subsidiary services.*

school in Essex before going on to do national service and being commissioned in the Royal Artillery. Here he found that, though incapable of decarbonising the family car as his father could, he was able to explain complex technical matters in simple terms – useful to a gunnery officer much engaged in running training programmes. He also developed an appreciation of wine, which later made him an asset to an RAC Wine Committee notable for its expertise. Rose got into trouble for travelling to a London wine-tasting on behalf of the Regimental Mess in the only vehicle available, a three-ton truck: it was seen parked in St James's Square by the GOC London District, who caused enquiries to be made. After National Service he began to read law at the London School of Economics. But in 1954 his father died and Rose left to go into business. He made use of experience gained in a vacation job and started a successful television maintenance and rental firm. Early on he sold part of this enterprise, celebrating the acquisition of his first capital with Krug and oysters at Wilton's. Near him, also having lunch alone, was Randolph Churchill, who suggested that they should join forces and toss for who would pay. They enjoyed a gargantuan meal, and Rose eventually found himself on a train with all his cash intact, so he presumably won the toss. But, like others who shared a table with Randolph Churchill, he has only hazy recollections of the event.

Rose then moved into the world of property development and investment. He acted on his own behalf and for important clients such as GEC and Grand Metropolitan. After arranging a particularly lucrative deal for Young & Co's Brewery, he was invited by the Chairman, John Young, to join the board and served as a non-executive director for sixteen years. As a master of intricate entrepreneurship, some of it carried out abroad, Rose prospered. He married and became the father of three children. He also found time to cultivate a taste for the finer things of life, music, drama, art and books – his abiding passion is for P. G. Wodehouse. He loves walking and swimming – preferring the sea even to the RAC's sumptuous pool – and watches a variety of sports. Motoring is also a perennial enthusiasm. Rose doted on his first car – a Sunbeam Alpine, one of several which had been modified for the works team led by Sheila van Damm to drive in the Monte Carlo Rally – in spite of 'that awful steering column gear change, which was a bit like putting a knitting needle into a rice pudding and waggling it'.

Other models followed, including a Jaguar XK 140 drop-head and a Bristol 405, his favourite. Today he likes to drive the Club's 1937 4.3-litre short-chassis Alvis in the Classic Car Run, which was started in 1986 on the initiative of Michael Southcombe, Chairman of the RAC British Motor Sports Council. Now the largest event of its kind in the world, it is particularly attractive because of the scenic routes chosen and the places of interest visited, such as the Grand Prix circuit at Silverstone, which are normally inaccessible to the public. Rose also looks forward to driving the RAC's gleaming 1901 Mors on the Brighton Run. The appeal of this Veteran Car outing is universal. Rose recalls arriving in Brighton at the same time as Cecil Parkinson, then Secretary of State for Transport, who remarked on what an unusual experience it was for a politician to 'drive for hours in an open car and be cheered every yard of the way'.

Rose joined the RAC to play squash and took no part in its proceedings until 1977. Then, in order to help save the Club, he was among those who agreed to pay the surcharge requested by Bossom. For the same reason he spoke at the crisis meeting and consented to serve on the ad hoc committee. Rose found the challenge facing them 'utterly compelling'. But although

SIGNS OF THE TIMES

Hand painting has given way to computer-generated graphics and the old free service now aims to cover its costs. But RAC signs continue to advertise the Club and to direct traffic to special events. Actually local authorities are resisting the proliferation of 'street furniture' and the RAC is finding new markets. But it still puts up 35,000 road signs a year to help motorists find their way.

a champion of reform, he was the antithesis of Lesser. Rose remained personally on good terms with many of the old Committee such as John Crampton, Jack Williams, Earl Howe, Lord Camden and the Duke of Richmond and Gordon. Discreet, polite, tactful and considerate, he often persuaded them to support his proposals for change. In fact, Rose denies that there was any straightforward cleavage between the Old Guard and the New. Certainly his own diplomatic skills, which complemented those of Aarvold, helped to bind the Club together after 1979 – one of his paramount aims. But Rose, a compact figure of medium height with a mane of greying hair, was made of sterner stuff than his strapping predecessor. The new Chairman of the RAC had, and has, a steely tenacity and a flinty self-possession that most find formidable and some find intimidating. Furthermore Rose possesses a mastery of detail not always agreeable to those who feel that he should have delegated more and intervened less.

From the first he took tough decisions: in 1981 Rose shut down the RAC's unprofitable travel operation. He was unafraid of spending more money and developing new operations. So in 1982 the 'At Home' service was begun to enable members to receive help at their doorsteps. The following year the Recovery service was extended to cover a fifty-mile radius around Calais, thus meeting the needs of the two million British cars which passed through that port each year. Staff were encouraged with an improved pension scheme, whose architect was Frank Shaw. Rose also galvanised them by setting new and testing targets, notably for the recruitment of Associate members. More publicity was generated: in 1983 the RAC challenged the AA's *Drive* magazine with its own quarterly *Road & Car*. It was distributed to buyers of the *Sunday Times* and the *News of the World* as well as to RAC members, an audience of eighteen million. But because of the difficulty of appealing to such a diverse readership it was dropped soon after *Drive* ceased publication in 1985. More usefully, the RAC initiated a 'radio signs' experiment, indicating to motorists the frequencies on which local stations broadcast traffic news.

Rose was also prepared to embark on ambitious ventures, not all of which succeeded. The most frustrating of these began in 1984 when the RAC purchased Beddall Bradford, the firm of insurance brokers which had been acting on its behalf (paying a commission on each RAC policy) in a distinctly unenterprising fashion for nearly thirty years. In the course of a prolonged negotiation the price rose to £9.5 million – too high for some members of the RAC board, one of whom said that they were buying 'a pig in a poke'. But Rose believed that the acquisition was essential. The Club would be able to provide competitive insurance for members and earn 'substantial extra income' to subsidise motoring services. The RAC could exploit and enhance the power of its name, which enjoyed a '98 per cent unprompted recognition'. Beddall Bradford would also supply details of those already insured and obviate the difficulties of making a 'cold start' in a hotly contested business. All told, the RAC would be augmenting its synergy, to employ the vogue term for getting different parts of an organisation to contribute to the good of the whole. But in practice it was almost impossible to identify RAC members, and thus sell them products, through Beddall Bradford's database. Its systems were antiquated and the problems proved intractable. The insurance operation kept raising hopes only to dash them. A future Chief Executive, Arthur Large, called it 'my Spanish ulcer'.

It was, however, incidental to the main challenge facing Rose: how to revolutionise the 'paper-driven regime' in the core business of Motoring Services. He searched far and wide for

SPREADING THE WORD

In 1983 Road and Car *was the largest and, the RAC claimed, the 'most powerful' motoring journal in the world. But this specialist quarterly, even though it was produced in association with News International, found it hard to hold a general audience. Still, as the first issue shows, it did convey solid information about new models, DIY car maintenance, road safety and so on.*

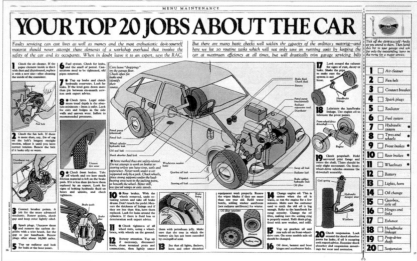

a solution, invoking the aid of Norman Austin, who had risen through the ranks of the RAC to become Director of Operations at Croydon. Canny and open-minded, Austin studied the systems employed by motoring organisations at home and abroad. But it was Rose who found the answer. In November 1982 he and Michael Limb attended a conference of the Alliance Internationale de Tourisme (AIT) in Sydney, Australia. Here they visited the National Roads and Motorists' Association (NRMA). It was then the very model of a modern motoring organisation, with a 'phenomenally successful' insurance company as well as a superb computerised rescue service. By substituting the latest press-button technology for pen, paper and speech, it had streamlined the entire process of bringing aid to motorists. The system was confined to Sydney but Rose perceived its nationwide potential.

On his return to London he gave a talk to the RAC board, setting out his 'vision of the future'. He envisaged that the stranded RAC member would dial a single toll-free number and that his call would be answered without delay. The message-taker would tap all the relevant details into a computer, which would confirm his entitlement to service and provide other information. This would include the location of the member's car, pinpointed by means of an electronic gazetteer or nationwide directory indicating not only street names but local landmarks such as supermarkets, cinemas and pubs. The computer would also identify the appropriate Patrol to go to the rescue and the dispatcher would flash instructions to a printer in his vehicle. Rose's oration must have sounded like science fiction. But he intended to make it fact.

Much preparatory labour was undertaken. Some of it caused friction with staff, especially those belonging to the Transport & General Workers' Union (TGWU), who were well aware that computers could cause job losses. In the words of one of the RAC's five excellent regional directors, Tony Andrews, 'industrial relations were in a chaotic state – management and union were at loggerheads at almost every avenue of progress'. Rose and Austin gave anxious consideration to the costs, consequences and problems of establishing a single national freephone service. For it to work properly the RAC would have to make its own regions conform to those of British Telecom. This in turn pointed to the desirability of moving and consolidating control centres. Rose, for whom the huge property implications held no terrors, urged his more hesitant colleagues to grasp the nettle. But his most important preliminary task, as Eric Charles approached retirement, was to find the right person to implement the new technology and to transform Motoring Services.

In 1984 Rose, who had by then become the RAC's first paid, full-time Chairman, discovered someone with the right qualifications to succeed Charles. This was Arthur Large, small of stature but with great abilities. Large understood science and technology, having read chemical engineering at Birmingham University and worked for IBM in San Francisco during the 1960s. He was also an accountant with wide business experience in Canada, Italy and France. In 1975 he had been recruited by BL, where he was first shocked by its 'anarchic' procedures and later awed by Sir Michael Edwardes's 'revolution'. Large recalls that he always sat on the edge of his chair in the presence of Edwardes, who had an alarming capacity 'to speed-read a document yet point out a spelling mistake on line twenty-three'. Edwardes had promoted Large to be Company Secretary at BL and now recommended him to Jeffrey Rose, who took a prodigious amount of time and trouble to get this vital appointment right. Large, Edwardes

NORMAN AUSTIN

Having joined the RAC in 1947 as a £5-a-week accounts clerk, Austin had become its chief administrator by 1980. In this capacity he helped to prepare 'the most important technological change in the Club's history' – the Computer-Aided Rescue Service (CARS).

MICHAEL LIMB

General Secretary of the Club from 1978 to 1994, Limb was the first employee to become a director. A calm, ubiquitous presence, he was responsible for much, including the introduction of computers.

ARTHUR LARGE

A human dynamo and an inspiring leader, Large was the chief executive of Motoring Services between 1985 and 1991. He not only transformed the technology of the RAC, but also revolutionised its culture.

FRANK RICHARDSON

Hired as a hard-headed professional in 1987, Richardson became managing director of Rescue Services, until 1996. He produced a surge of innovations, not least the REFLEX service.

told him, possessed 'energy', 'shrewdness' and 'commercial acumen'. He had first-rate qualities of 'leadership'. Above all, he was a doer and 'not a mandarin'. All this was true (though it was not the whole truth). Large proved an inspired choice to take command at RAC Motoring Services. Even today its staff speak of him in devout tones: 'He was our saviour.'

At the beginning of 1985 Large underwent an agreeable induction, which included visits to motoring organisations in Europe and north America. But when he took up the reins at RAC Motoring Services in March, he realised that until a comprehensive computer system was introduced progress in other directions would be blocked. Thus although telephone communication was soon improved with the installing of an automatic call distribution system, computer-assisted dispatch was essential if the sophisticated Linkline service were to be introduced. It was essential, too, if new deals were to be struck to provide motor manufacturers with superior RAC services. However, while research and development were taking place there was much that Large could do in the interim. The most important change he accomplished was a cultural one. Rose, though personally reserved and anything but a populist, had already gone some way towards modifying the autocratic character of the RAC. Unlike Andrews, whose cronies did his bidding, Rose surrounded himself with colleagues whose acquiescence had to be won by discussion and argument. Now, with the Chairman's encouragement, the Chief Executive set about eradicating the military ethos of Motoring Services and substituting for it an 'informal and friendly style more suited to a modern company'.

First, though, Large revealed that he could fight hard if necessary. He refused to be intimidated when the TGWU 'blacked' personal computers in 1985. He also stuck to his guns when the union objected to the 200 redundancies, mainly among sales staff, which Large imposed swiftly and without negotiation during the same year. Taking a leaf out of Edwardes's book, Large insisted that his changes were vital to 'the survival of our company'. The argument impressed Bob King, the national officer of the TGWU. He thought it was about time that the RAC, which had relied on its 'club image' for so long, got rid of its 'paternalistic attitudes towards staff'. Subsequently, through an elaborate process of consultation, 'understanding and trust' were built up between union and management. Concord also 'filtered down' to the workforce as a whole. The RAC contributed to the process, in King's view, by 'freeing up information, discussing forward plans, and moving from a hierarchical organisation to an open one'. Large reaped the benefit later, when he brought in full computerisation. Despite some rumblings, not a single day was lost through industrial action.

Arthur Large's own personality played a significant part in accomplishing this harmony. Ever since his days at a tough grammar school in south Wales, Large had been a good mixer. He describes himself as a 'chameleon character', just as much at home in the staff canteen as in the Great Gallery at Pall Mall. He exuded warmth, had a photographic memory for faces and never stood on ceremony. So white-gloved salutes became a thing of the past and people were called by their first names – though old-fashioned bosses uttered them through gritted teeth. Superintendents went out and in came Service Team Managers (STMs). Telephonists were instructed to say 'RAC' instead of the more high-falutin' 'Royal Automobile Club'. Open-plan offices became standard. Large's office, with its unclosed door and its glass partitions, was an emblem of transparency. He himself was candid to the point of indiscretion,

SOCIAL MOBILITY

*Cars move people upward as well as onward and
different models convey subtle gradations of status.
During the early 1980s so-called yuppies favoured
the Ford XR3i (above), the i being a sign of vertical
thrust. The BMW M3 (right) conferred enough
prestige to give a new owner a fresh identity. The
Porsche 924 (below) impressed more by the name
than by the VW/Audi engine, but it was good for
cutting a dash without spending a fortune.*

which earned him an early rebuke from Rose. But staff found his frankness refreshing. They were invigorated by his dynamism. They warmed to this 'passionate Welshman' with his 'tremendous intensity of purpose'. Although he seldom had to be reminded that the RAC was 'a people business', Large was fascinated by new technology and could not resist playing with it. 'Let's kick the tyres,' he would say. When heavy demand caused delays, he did not think it beneath his dignity to stand in as a telephone message-taker. On one such occasion he received a call from an irate member who demanded to speak to the Chief Executive. Large said that he was the Chief Executive but the member refused to believe him and harsh words ensued.

FAST CARS

The RAC's Computer-Aided Rescue Service originally used a network of seventeen regional command centres (supplemented by the Octagon commercial vehicle recovery service). But in 1992 command and control operations were consolidated at five Supercentres.

If Large led by example he also created mechanisms to get the best out of his 4,000-strong workforce. These were adapted from the 'lean production' methods which made Japanese car factories so efficient. Large noted that every Japanese operative had a red handle by which he must stop the assembly line if faced with a problem he was unable to solve, whereas in Western plants only the director could stop the line. Yet Western lines halted at least once a day, achieving only ninety per cent of capacity to the detriment of both product quality and industrial relations, whereas Japanese lines kept going without a pause for weeks on end, achieving 100 per cent results. This was because the Japanese applied two principles: *ichibon*, whereby 'each individual is accountable for his own work and proud of it'; and *kaizen*, whereby 'all problems are thoroughly analysed and resolved as part of a process of continuous improvement'.

The first step towards implementing these principles in a service industry, Large believed, was to set out a clear, quantifiable objective. He conducted research and held discussions. Then he announced that RAC patrolmen should try to reach eight out of ten members within an hour of their calling for help, a performance well above the RAC (and AA) levels at that time. To achieve it he recruited another 120 Service Patrols, paying for them by making administrative and other savings – extravagant status symbols like directors' dining rooms were ruthlessly axed. Additional revenue, Large hoped, would come from the enhancement and expansion of the insurance business. Shipton Insurance Services was acquired largely for its branches, to give the RAC's own operation a presence in the high street. It also brought the RAC a small stake in the mechanical breakdown market, supplemented significantly in 1986 by the purchase of London Wall. More pertinently, Large ensured that every individual accepted the RAC's 'commitment to customer satisfaction'. He also monitored shortcomings, not referring them to a customer complaints department but, where possible, eliminating them at source. Thus, before the end of 1985, he hit his target. Employees were responding to management's determination to give members what they wanted and had a right to expect. As Large said, 'It was like taking the cork out of a champagne bottle.'

He could not complete his programme of 'people empowerment', however, without electronic assistance. So in February 1986 Large joined an RAC delegation led by Rose, and including Limb and Austin, and flew to Sydney. There they subjected the NRMA's system to final, minute scrutiny. Like Rose before him, Large was intensely 'excited' by what he saw and felt that it provided a virtual 'blueprint for what we had to do'. His colleagues concurred

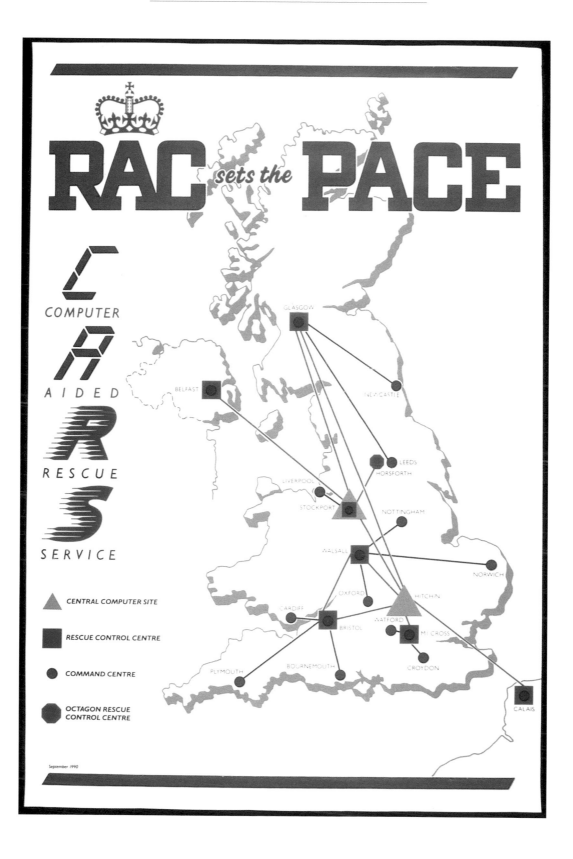

and Rose reached an agreement to licence it: no money would change hands but the Australians were to be given the benefit of any improvements made in Britain. Actually the NRMA bosses, convinced that their metropolitan system could not be adapted to nationwide use, thought the RAC men 'were living in cloud cuckooland'. But they did agree to Rose's request that their Systems Director, Howard Graham, should come to England for a year. Here he would work on the essential modifications with Elliott Roper, an Australian software wizard, and teams of RAC experts, to be led by Maurice Buck, former Chief Constable of Northamptonshire. Graham, who was quiet, diplomatic and formidably clever, would master-mind the technology of an operation more sophisticated than anything of its kind. The Computer-Aided Rescue Service, CARS, was 'staggeringly brilliant and childishly simple'. The most important technical advance in the RAC's history, it would revolutionise the service offered to members and motorists.

The pace of change now quickened. The board agreed to embark on the biggest single investment the RAC had ever made. Motoring Services had a nest-egg of some £60 million, built up from members' subscriptions skilfully husbanded over the years. Rose proposed to spend about two-thirds of it on modernising the organisation via computers and RAC control centres in London, Bristol, Walsall, Stockport and Glasgow. It was decided that the new build-ings should be ultra-modern and prominently located close to motorways, though suitable sites were hard to find. The first 'Supercentre' faced the junction of the London–Birmingham motorway and the North Circular Road. 'M1 Cross', as it was called, opened in 1987 and became the metropolitan headquarters of RAC Motoring Services. But it did not take over all the functions which had been carried out at Croydon, where the RAC's lease was about to expire. Some of these moved out of London. Thus, for example, Legal and Member Services went to Bristol, eventually being housed in the Bradley Stoke Supercentre at the intersection of the M4 and M5 motorways. The Rescue Services Division was transferred to Walsall, where the glossy, glassy Bescot Supercentre was constructed beside the M6.

Bescot was also to be the focus, incidentally, of an astonishing renaissance in the RAC's automotive expertise which resulted from an investigation commissioned by Large in 1986. It was undertaken by Brigadier Charles Maple, formerly head of the army's Vehicle Testing Establishment. He reported that the Club's technical service had deteriorated 'to an unac-ceptable degree. It had become a poor relation', understaffed, underfunded and undervalued. Maple recommended the recruitment of a chief engineer and other well-qualified staff, the acquisition of new equipment, and the provision of a library and an electronic database. All this came to pass and in due course members reaped the benefit. Patrols went on training courses at Bescot. They were supplied with manuals, to be regularly updated, containing 63,000 details on 1,100 motor vehicles. And they were given sophisticated devices such as the AVO M2005 Multimeter, which identified electrical defects in cars. John Wood, the outstanding new chief engineer, deserved much of the credit for this. His achievement was to give the RAC pre-eminence in the crucial field of diagnosing and curing faults in motor vehicles.

As the complex development work on CARS proceeded, Large exerted a relentless pressure towards change in other directions. Barbara Williamson, who in 1953 had started at the RAC's Leeds office sitting 'in front of an ancient Underwood typewriter with the letter "s" missing,

CAPITAL CONTROL

Overlooking the start of the London–Birmingham motorway, M1 Cross handles 30 per cent of all the RAC's rescue work. When CARS was introduced in 1988, staff felt that they had been 'thrown in at the deep end'. But today M1 Cross is a treasure-house of technical wizardry and human expertise which will see the RAC into the next millennium.

which had to be handwritten in afterwards', was now faced by Filofax time systems, Prestel print-outs and project targets. Many staff, senior as well as junior, could not take the strain and there was a considerable turnover. But Large drove the enterprise forward, though, as he later acknowledged, not without going up 'many blind alleys, [and taking] many false turns'. He reorganised the RAC's port offices, cutting some jobs and hiring student labour for the summer months when eighty-three per cent of the business was done. He bought Octagon Recovery, one of the RAC's smaller rivals, which had expertise in commercial vehicle rescue. He increased wages and commissions on sales. Advertising expenditure also rose and Large got the RAC to take part in newsworthy operations like the Ministry of Transport's development of 'Autoguide', an automatic route guidance system for motor vehicles. In 1987 the RAC's membership leapt from 2.75 to nearly 3.5 million. Large bought more vehicles and took on more Service Patrols, who numbered 1,200 by 1988. They carried out more work since more members could now get through to the control rooms. Then Large equipped each one with a Lucas spare parts kit. Roadside repair rates at once rose by 2 per cent and customer satisfaction increased in proportion, all as the result of a relatively modest investment of £390,000. Some worried, though, about the overall cost of doing more business. Large claimed plausibly that this was a penalty of success: the RAC was needed.

Even when Motoring Services dipped into the red in 1987-8 Jeffrey Rose loyally supported Large. The Chairman was confident that their strategy was sound despite the objections of certain board members. They were alarmed about maintaining levels of expenditure 'embarked upon against a bull market which was not likely to be there as the plan unfolded'. Rose did, it is true, restrain Large from plunging more deeply into the difficult insurance market. Large was also prevented from offering complimentary membership of the Pall Mall Club as 'a powerful tool' to achieve his commercial ends. Further control was exerted by merging the boards of Automobile Proprietary (shortly to become RAC Ltd) and Motoring Services early in 1988. However, everyone took comfort from the fact that CARS was performing well in its initial trials. Indeed, its prospects looked so promising that in 1987 Volvo became the third manufacturer (after Fiat and Jaguar) to sign a MOTORMAN contract. This was a deal, tailored to suit each car-maker's needs, whereby new vehicles were sold with RAC membership included to give added value. Thus Jaguar, which billed its arrangement with the RAC as the 'Finest Partnership in Motoring', provided buyers with a year's membership of the Club as part of the vehicle warranty agreement. The Volvo contract covered the life of the car so long as its servicing schedule was maintained. This sensible agreement brought the Club an additional 60,000 members each year. Over the next few years the MOTORMAN scheme was to prove a powerful engine of growth for the RAC.

AFTER RIGOROUS TRAINING and meticulous preparation, staff at Stockport took the first CARS call on 8 December 1987. The early results were encouraging, but it would be almost three years before the system was complete and fully operational. Until 1989, for example, Patrols were still subject to information bottlenecks since they could only be reached by two-way radio. This was because the experiment of fitting RAC vehicles with printers had

DASHBOARD MAGIC

Mobile Data Transmission units (MDTs) made two-way radio seem like semaphore. Fitted in 1989, these computers completed the CARS system, providing instant information about breakdowns. Patrols regretted the loss of voice contact but welcomed the gain in efficiency.

CHIPS WITH EVERYTHING

By 1993 Patrols could train on computerised machines which simulate car faults (above). A year later electronic technical manuals – CD-ROMs (right) – were introduced.

proved unsatisfactory. So it was decided that Patrols should have Mobile Data Transmission units (MDTs), which would flash up computerised information on liquid crystal display screens. However, this 'fast-track solution' threw up 'hideous problems' of its own. Initially the MDTs garbled messages, caused intense frustration and cost extra money, because back-up cellular telephones had to be bought. Eventually the bugs were eliminated and Patrols hailed the MDT as 'pure magic'. But as CARS started to function, centre by centre, other faults occurred. M1 Cross suffered worst.

This was, and remains, by far the busiest Supercentre as far as rescues are concerned and the birth of CARS here was premature. During the first months of 1988, for various reasons, the system almost collapsed. Bad weather created a heavy demand for RAC services. Overloaded computers went blank. The electronic gazetteer was so detailed that it had taken thirty-six 'person-years' to compile but identical place-names in different parts of the country caused confusion: one Patrol went on a rescue mission to the Kensington district of Liverpool when help was needed in Kensington, London. Even so, the system proved its resilience. When breakdown calls from the M25 were handled by the Glasgow Centre, to reduce the load on M1 Cross, there were no adverse effects on service, though a number of members expressed surprise at the high proportion of Scottish ladies apparently working in north London. However, many staff left because of the strains of trying to implement the new technology, occasionally compounded by verbal abuse from furious motorists. There were even cases of nervous breakdowns among RAC employees. This was not altogether surprising for, as management recognised, 'the transition from manual practice to computerised communications was a cultural shock of the greatest magnitude. The effect could be likened to casting aside the faithful Morris Minor and stepping into a fine-tuned Formula 1 Grand Prix car.'

Large did his utmost to commit staff to the change. He circulated a video setting out its advantages. Believing that 'a lot of management is theatre', he presented a dramatic 'roadshow', complete with lasers and dry ice, entitled 'The Future ... Now'. The propaganda continued in *Newslane*, a glossy staff magazine started in 1988. The following year, when MDT killed voice communication and left many Patrols feeling isolated and deprived of personal contact, 'Call Sign' was initiated. This was a bright and breezy monthly magazine programme on audio tape cassette which Patrols could play in their vehicles. Featuring RAC news reports, interviews with staff, 'tricks of the trade', technical bulletins and competitions, it has proved a highly effective and hugely popular means of communication. At the same time Large came up with a catchy acronym to maintain the human dimension in the midst of technological revolution and to ensure that everyone kept up with the change of PACE – which stood for 'Personally Accountable, Caring and Enterprising'. This message was reinforced by a long-term training programme, devised by psychologists whom Large commissioned, entitled 'People in Mind'. Its aim was to realise his 'mission', embodied in a much-publicised statement, that the RAC should 'provide the best services to Europe's motorists'. The jargon of management was tired but Large invested it with genuine energy. Moreover, an ambitious advertising campaign, supervised by Large's 'terrific' new lieutenant Frank Richardson, helped to motivate RAC staff as well as to attract more RAC members. Puffing CARS and featuring the 'New Knights of the Road' driving computer-directed RAC Sherpa vans, it urged motorists to 'Save Pounds, Lose

SHINING ARMOUR

*These advertisements attempted to combine and
project two discordant images – old-fashioned
chivalry and up-to-the-minute sophistication. The
campaign was largely successful and it raised the
RAC's 'public profile' to new heights.*

Wait'. Richardson thus assisted in transforming the RAC's 'old-fashioned and elitist' image; increasingly it now seemed 'modern, high-tech, professional, responsive'.

This impression was strengthened when the Bescot Supercentre opened in 1989. Members of the Club Committee had expressed concern about this spectacular building because, being designed (by the Building Design Partnership) specifically for the RAC, it might be worth less than the cost price if for any reason it was put on the open market. Rose was able to reassure them by pointing out that the rental cost of a premium poster site on London's Cromwell Road was £250,000 a year. Traffic volumes passing the Supercentre along the M6 are huge: in fact, this is the busiest section of motorway in Europe, so the value of the building as a 'poster' for the RAC represented a substantial capital sum. Certainly the futuristic steel and glass edifice, sometimes nicknamed the 'Tardis' after Dr Who's time-capsule which was bigger inside than out, attracted attention. Drivers stuck in traffic jams had plenty of time to gaze at the RAC's newest 'shop window'. Many gave it 'rave reviews'. So did the jury of the Royal Institute of British Architecture when bestowing a regional award for innovative design. The shiny Supercentre made a compelling statement about a 'high-profile and high-tech' RAC which was ever watchful on behalf of motorists. It was said to resemble 'an eyeball overlooking the motorway'.

All the Club's vigilance would have gone for nothing if CARS had crashed. But the mature system (which still continues to evolve) more than realised Rose's early hopes. Over eighty per cent of members' calls, made to the single freephone number 0800 828282, were answered within ten seconds. They were instantly routed through a telephone network designed to find available capacity at any one of the five Supercentres. So a motorist who broke down in Kent might get through to Bristol, where the microvax computer could identify him by his vehicle registration number or even his postcode. Priorities could also be established, with preference being given, for example, to a doctor on call or a lone female stuck in an intimidating multi-storey car park. The motorist's location would be fixed by the electronic gazetteer, constantly being brought up to date and able to distinguish between, say, each of Britain's sixty-six Newtowns and every one of Heathrow's twenty-seven car parks. The gazetteer provided a fairly good substitute for local knowledge. But Large, who believed that 'small is beautiful', set great store by having an RAC presence throughout the land and retained the seventeen regional offices. So it was from them that dispatchers sent out the appropriate rescue Patrols. Using their MDTs, they in turn reported progress stage by stage. Patrols, whose shift patterns were rescheduled to meet demands forecast by CARS, reached over eighty per cent of break-downs within an hour. Their average 'travelling time' came down to twenty minutes, as did their 'fixing time'. This was an astounding advance on the old business of riding around haphazardly and undertaking three jobs a day. The RAC gained an enormous advantage over competitors and its customer satisfaction ratings rose to new heights. Some ninety-two per cent of members who used the RAC's breakdown service renewed their annual subscription.

The provision of such data was a largely unforeseen but colossally important by-product of CARS. Since every action was logged by computers, the RAC could monitor and improve staff performance at every level. Its information was commercially valuable in other respects. Between 1987 and 1990 the RAC captured three-quarters of the lucrative fleet rescue market

BESCOT SUPERCENTRE

The RIBA jury said that 'as memorable landmark, as a positive contribution to an otherwise bleak urban environment, as an example of architecture as dynamic image making, the new RAC building in Walsall is an heroic achievement'. It is also designed to service CARS.

not just because of the service it gave but because it could provide fleet operators such as Lex Leasing with key facts about 'the economic operation of their company vehicles'. Similarly, manufacturers who gave RAC membership to purchasers of their vehicles got not only an excellent dedicated service but incomparable intelligence about any problems affecting their new models. A concerted sales drive stressing these advantages produced a surge of MOTORMAN clients in the late 1980s, among them Renault, Lotus, Ford, Toyota and Vauxhall.

By 1991 sixty per cent of all new cars carried RAC membership and their makers learnt about faults so quickly (in one case by daily e-mail) that they were able to make modifications early in the production run. One manufacturer was given early warning of defects in the handbrakes and alarm systems of a new model, which were swiftly corrected. Another was alerted to a weakness in a new fuel pump relay, also soon put right. The RAC benefited because the rate of breakdowns on new cars was so low and its membership growth was so rapid. Car dealers, who saw a reduction in the revenue they had earned from the failure of vehicles under guarantee, were less happy about MOTORMAN. But the Club 'walked that tightrope with some success', claiming that its scheme promoted 'customer loyalty' to a particular model and thus to its dealer. However, MOTORMAN involved the Club in an inescapable conflict of interest. Instead of giving manufacturers the information provided by CARS the RAC might have made it available, in the manner of *Which?* reports, to motorists themselves. Large was uneasy about the situation. But the RAC concluded that it could best serve the interests of automobilism in general by helping to improve motor vehicles at source.

According to one of Large's senior managers, David Johnston, working for the RAC in the late 1980s was 'a bit like riding a rollercoaster'. One initiative succeeded another with breathtaking speed. An RAC credit card was issued, in conjunction with Mastercard. Motoring Services broadened their scope on the Continent and the CARS system was installed in the Calais office. RAC family membership was introduced, with the automobile rather than the individual being covered. Fresh vehicle inspection schemes were begun for cars, fleets and caravans. New rescue services were started to help motorcyclists and disabled drivers. The latter, known as RESPONSE, was the first of its kind and provided specially trained Personal Incident Managers (PIMs) to look after the needs of the country's million handicapped holders of orange badges. This was, in fact, a development of the so-called REFLEX service, which the RAC initiated in 1989. It provided personalised care to those who joined the scheme from the moment of accident or breakdown until they reached their final destination, giving them everything from alternative travel arrangements to message-relaying facilities. Looking after people as much as vehicles, REFLEX offered motorists the most comprehensive rescue package in the land.

However, the dips in the RAC's switchback could be alarming, especially when the new technology did not live up to expectations. In 1988 Large commissioned IBM to create a revolutionary computer system to handle all the new business he was generating. It was christened RESPOND, which stood for Responsive On-Line Database. The system was billed to cost about £10 million and designed to record particulars of the millions of new members joining the RAC. Then, in theory, RESPOND would link up that information with data collected in all the other divisions of the RAC. It would thus constitute a uniquely powerful tool for mar-

Repmobiles

As a MOTORMAN client, Ford learnt much from the RAC about the performance of its successful fleet car the Sierra. Launched in 1982 at a competitive price, this was a traditional rear-wheel drive vehicle with an 'aerodynamic' body (often called a 'jelly mould'). It was popular with salesmen, who sometimes gauged their standing by which of the six engine sizes they got.

keting and management. For example, through a few strokes of the keyboard RAC Insurance Brokers would have access to motoring members' details and could thus ensure that every sales pitch was on target. The system offered enormous improvements in service and productivity. But RESPOND, which should have complemented CARS, was not a success. It was written in 'fourth generation language', an advanced form of communication which 'added massively to the complexity and caused long time and cost over-runs'. So when Large launched new motoring or insurance services, which invariably attracted a host of potential customers thanks to the pulling power of the RAC's name, his office staff were overwhelmed. Worst affected were those at Bristol towards the end of 1989. The existing computers could not cope, switchboards jammed, mail went unanswered, members complained, employees resigned. Before painstaking, piecemeal solutions were found to these administrative problems, the RAC experienced 'a traumatic period'.

The troubles with RESPOND were not calculated to increase Jeffrey Rose's confidence in Arthur Large. The setback was compounded by continuing disappointments in the RAC's insurance business, of which Large took personal control for a time. The Chairman and the Chief Executive had further differences over strategy and finance. Large wanted the RAC to hasten into Europe whereas Rose was more cautious. There was a disagreement about how corporate overheads should be apportioned. But the crucial issue over which they differed related to the degree of independence which Large should enjoy. In theory the Chief Executive accepted the authority of Rose, who spoke for the RAC's main board. But Large resented interference and was inclined to behave as though Motoring Services was a separate fiefdom. Rose, who attached supreme importance to keeping together the disparate elements of the RAC, sometimes found him 'utterly intransigent'.

Although both liberal-minded conservatives, keen on cars new and old, the two men lacked a personal rapport. As Large recalls, 'We were very much chalk and cheese.' Large himself was effervescent and outspoken, a creature of impulse and emotion. Rose was calm and deliberate, a cerebral character who played his cards close to his chest. For that reason, perhaps, Rose was able to devise a short-term means of resolving their policy disagreements, which Large describes as 'brilliant'. At the end of 1988, when they had reached an impasse, the Chairman suggested that they should go on a twenty-mile walk together across the South Downs. It proved a success: Rose was interesting and amusing; Large felt relaxed and revitalised. Afterwards he wrote Rose a warm letter of thanks, paying tribute to his achievement in rebuilding the RAC, saying how highly esteemed the Chairman was by his colleagues and pledging that Motoring Services would continue to function within the Club's constitutional framework. Other 'walkabouts', as staff came to call them, removed subsequent difficulties. But in January 1991 Large stubbornly insisted on pushing ahead with plans to set up a subsidiary company, which could attract equity funds, to improve the operation of the RAC's rescue services. Since the board had not approved this proposal Rose forbade it and when Large demurred they came to a final parting of the ways. No one was sorrier about this than Rose himself, who says of his erstwhile

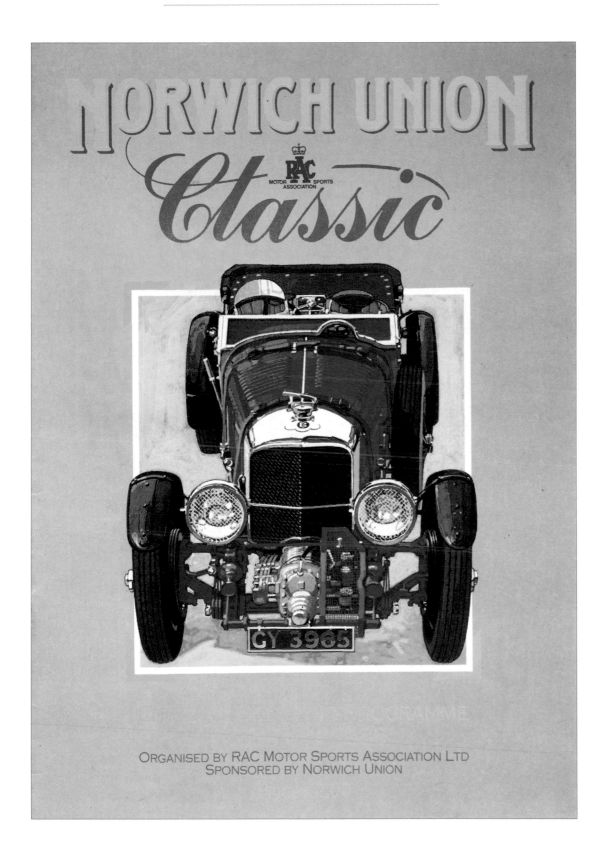

colleague: 'I have the greatest regard for his ability and integrity and regret that he could not come to see himself as a team player in the RAC.'

When Large's departure was announced the RAC 'reeled'. Shock waves travelled throughout the organisation. Many employees mourned the loss of their 'Messiah'. In the surge of emotion Large's charisma obscured his cussedness and his victories concealed his defeats. By humanising the culture of the RAC he had earned the gratitude of the entire workforce. Moreover his commercial achievements had been extraordinary, especially when measured against the yardstick of the Club's leading competitor. In five years the RAC had doubled both membership and sales revenue. It had trebled profits to £7.2 million on a turnover of £155 million, compared to the AA's profit of £4.1 million on a turnover of £231 million. MOTOR-MAN deals had given the RAC 'a massive marketing advantage' over the opposition. The RAC had streamlined both manning and management: it had 4,400 employees to attend to the needs of 5.2 million members, whereas the AA had 13,500 staff and a membership of 7.5 million. In 1991 RAC Patrols reached eighty-two per cent of breakdowns within the hour, as compared to its rival's sixty-six per cent. Its customer satisfaction rating had also overtaken that of the AA – seventy-eight as opposed to seventy-four per cent. *Which?* gave the RAC (along with Britannia and National Breakdown) its 'Best Buy' accolade but did not recommend the AA. After a detailed comparative study, *Management Week* concluded in May 1991: 'the RAC has got the AA on the run'.

Most of this advantage stemmed from the triumph of CARS. The system was a daring monument to the 'enterprise culture', created during a decade when the car was king but the British automobile industry was going to the wall. CARS was also a superlative vehicle of change which took the RAC out of its paper-strewn cul-de-sac and onto the 'information superhighway'. During this arduous and sometimes hazardous journey the Chief Executive was in the driving seat. But the Chairman had planned the itinerary. The RAC followed the route to progress which Rose had charted on his trip to Australia in 1982, when he had divined the possibility of giving his own members hitherto undreamt-of levels of service. Large thus fulfilled Rose's vision of how the RAC could be transformed by technology. Their association, for all its vicissitudes, could hardly have been more productive.

SPACE TRAVEL

The Renault Espace was the first
in a range of fast, comfortable
'people-movers' which set a
fashion for the 1980s.

CHAPTER TWELVE

MOTORING INTO THE FUTURE

*The unstoppable growth of car ownership excites fears that
civilisation is facing 'Autogeddon'. The true-blue RAC now
promotes 'green' motoring. But this is only one of many
initiatives which the century-old Club has taken to streamline
itself for a motoring millennium.*

THE CHUNNEL

*Having long advocated a
fixed link across the
Channel (though it had
usually favoured a road
– bridge or tunnel), the
RAC helped to organise a
spectacular Inaugural
Rally in 1994.*

THE AUTOMOBILE HAS NEVER had an easy ride but its road grew rougher in the run-up to the third millennium. During the recession-ridden 1990s confidence in the car, which Margaret Thatcher had done so much to sustain, began to sag again. Hopes that new roads might keep pace with the volume of traffic, which grew by eighty per cent on motorways and fifty per cent elsewhere during the 1980s, were soon dashed. When the M25 opened in 1986 it was 'immediately dubbed the biggest roundabout in the world' and plans were made to add extra lanes. The announcement of a £6 billion inter-urban 'Roads for Prosperity' programme in 1989 was the last great boost to motordom before the official consensus in favour of the car began to collapse. In 1990 the government published a White Paper entitled *This Common Inheritance*, which considered the impact of motorised transport on the environment. Dwelling especially on the hazards of air pollution and ecological degradation, it recognised the need to reduce the use of cars and increase the role of public transport. This acknowledgement coincided with growing anxiety about the dangers which the internal combustion engine posed to health and safety. Cars and lorries notoriously caused accidents and choked cities. But it was now a commonplace to accuse them of being cosmic vehicles of doom, of destroying the resources of nature and contributing to global warming. When Malcolm Rifkind became Secretary of State for Transport towards the end of 1990 he quickly began to consider transferring freight from road to rail. In his first parliamentary speech as minister he referred to the environment as the 'new dimension in transport'.

The RAC had anticipated him. Early in 1990 Jeffrey Rose appointed David Worskett, formerly a civil servant in the Departments of the Environment and of Transport (where he had been Head of Road Safety), to succeed Tony Lee as the RAC's Director of Public Affairs. Worskett shared Rose's view that the Club must be much more sensitive to the citizen's interests, especially where they clashed with those of the motorist. Of course, the two categories of people were becoming almost identical, a fact that Worskett would cheekily exploit by launching a 'Motorist's Charter', which designated the road user as a customer entitled to satisfaction, at the same time as the government's 'Citizen's Charter'. But it was clear that the RAC had lobbied for too long on behalf of its own narrow constituency, straying from the tradition of responsible automobilism which dated back to the Club's Edwardian days. As late as 1983, for example, the RAC had said that road humps were not a safety measure so much as a 'potential danger'. A year later it had resisted European Community proposals on exhaust emissions 'which might unreasonably prejudice motorists' interests'. Subsequently it had opposed the law making rear seat belts in cars compulsory. The time was ripe for the Club to take a less adversarial and a more enlightened line, especially where motoring measures had an impact on the general quality of life. Almost Worskett's first action was to submit proposals whereby the Chancellor could encourage 'cleaner' motoring through relevant tax concessions. He then commissioned a public opinion survey which revealed that drivers themselves favoured environmentally friendly motoring. So he began to campaign for unleaded petrol, carbon monoxide testing, catalytic converters, Park-and-Ride schemes and car sharing.

The RAC set out further such proposals for tackling urban traffic congestion in a pamphlet entitled 'Cars in Cities'. It acknowledged that little more could be done in the way of road construction except for bypasses and the enhancement of major arteries. But since vehicle speeds had fallen to about 12mph in central London and the number of cars in Britain was projected to reach twenty-five million by the year 2000, it urged optimum management of the existing road network. This would encourage smoother flows, which would in turn reduce exhaust emissions – research carried out by Saab suggested that one stationary vehicle may generate up to five times as much pollution as it would if travelling at 50mph. The RAC therefore proposed (among other things) more efficient public transport linked to decent parking facilities on city outskirts, better signs and junctions, properly co-ordinated street maintenance, computerised traffic lights assisted by closed-circuit television cameras, 20mph speed limits in residential areas backed up by traffic-calming schemes. The recommendations, which aimed to make cities more 'pleasant and safer places in which to live, work and pursue leisure activities', were wide-ranging and progressive. But they still bore the unmistakable stamp of the motoring lobby.

Even as they were being formulated, therefore, Rose and Worskett sought a more independent and authoritative approach to the complex issue of reconciling cars with conservation. In October 1990 Rose convened a meeting with some half a dozen leading figures in the motor and oil industries. His aim was to get their support for establishing 'a sound programme of high-quality objective research into key aspects of transport and the environment'. The response was discouraging since each of the moguls seemed to have his own agenda. Rose thus determined to bring together a group of distinguished scientists, with expertise in transport, engineering, land use and the environment. On the advice of Sir Henry (later Lord) Chilver, Principal of Cranfield College of Technology, he invited a 'generalist' to be Chairman. This was Professor Sir David Williams, an eminent academic lawyer and the Vice-Chancellor

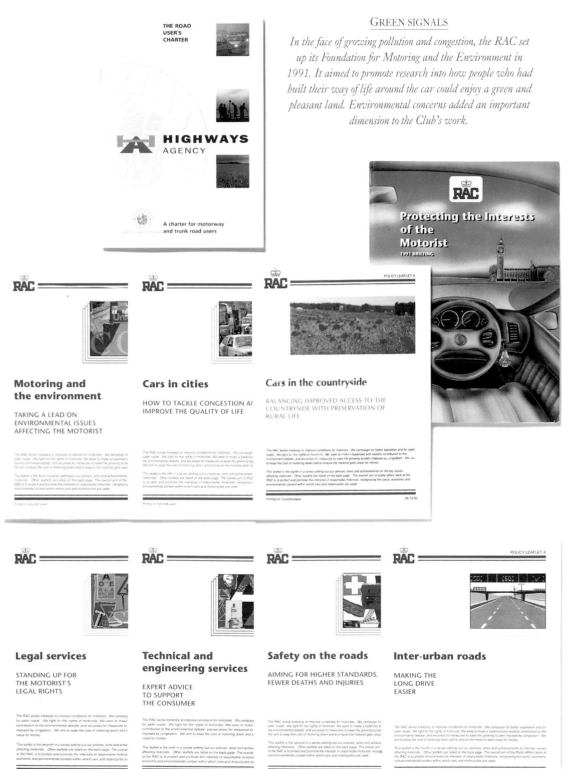

THE ROAD
USER'S
CHARTER

HIGHWAYS AGENCY

A charter for motorway
and trunk road users

GREEN SIGNALS

In the face of growing pollution and congestion, the RAC set up its Foundation for Motoring and the Environment in 1991. It aimed to promote research into how people who had built their way of life around the car could enjoy a green and pleasant land. Environmental concerns added an important dimension to the Club's work.

Protecting the Interests of the Motorist
1991 BRIEFING

POLICY LEAFLET 8

Motoring and the environment

TAKING A LEAD ON
ENVIRONMENTAL ISSUES
AFFECTING THE MOTORIST

Cars in cities

HOW TO TACKLE CONGESTION A
IMPROVE THE QUALITY OF LIFE

Cars in the countryside

BALANCING IMPROVED ACCESS TO THE
COUNTRYSIDE WITH PRESERVATION OF
RURAL LIFE

Legal services

STANDING UP FOR
THE MOTORIST'S
LEGAL RIGHTS

Technical and engineering services

EXPERT ADVICE
TO SUPPORT
THE CONSUMER

Safety on the roads

AIMING FOR HIGHER STANDARDS,
FEWER DEATHS AND INJURIES

POLICY LEAFLET 4

Inter-urban roads

MAKING THE
LONG DRIVE
EASIER

of Cambridge University. He agreed to participate and in the spring of 1991 an independent charitable body was established called the RAC Foundation for Motoring and the Environment. Its brief was to initiate research into means of reconciling 'the need and desire for personal powered mobility with the protection of the environment'. The true-blue RAC was becoming green.

The first report of the Foundation, published in 1992, set the tone for the RAC's future policy-making. It acknowledged the damage done by the motor car, which produced pollutants contributing to 'the greenhouse effect, to acid rain, to health problems, and to a range of other difficulties associated with "quality of life" including noise, community severance, and visual intrusion'. At the same time it recognised the fact that the automobile brought incomparable social and economic benefits to the community. Moreover, car ownership had become 'a prime aspiration to many people because of the personal freedom it confers'. The report went on to consider ways of solving the problems caused by the car without imposing unacceptable constraints on its use. Cleaner, quieter and safer vehicles were already being manufactured, thanks to what has been called 'the renaissance in automotive technology'. Further research along these lines was desirable. But, according to the report, claims made for the electric car were overstated since its means of generating power merely shifted 'the pollution from one source to another'. Congestion, particularly in view of the 'sheer numbers' of cars involved, was a more intractable difficulty. It could not just be resolved by a single strategy such as road construction and improvement, better traffic management, improved public transport or even road pricing. More fundamental changes were needed by which, for example, people could get access to shops without driving – during the decade after 1985 half the retail floor space opened in Britain was in 'out-of-town shopping centres'. Thus the report was a serious challenge to standard views about the functioning of a modern society and a developed economy. New ways should be found, it concluded, to reduce 'dependence upon the car'.

This verdict, as David Worskett intended, gave rise to several important research projects. In January 1993 the RAC issued a report on 'Cars in the Countryside' which warned that curbs would be imposed on access to sensitive areas unless urgent action was taken to manage traffic in ways that protected rural life. Three in every four Britons visited the countryside each year, four out of five of them going by car, which in most cases was the only feasible means of transport. But although these visits added 'enormously to the quality of life of many individuals ... cars threaten to destroy the environment in which they seek rural escape'. The difficulties were amply demonstrated by an investigation into the impact of car usage on the North York Moors National Park. Commissioned by the RAC's Foundation in 1994, the study was carried out by a research group from Oxford Brookes University. Surprisingly, they encountered less opposition from motorists, who recognised the need for constraint, than from local people who feared that restrictions would discourage the lucrative tourist traffic – thirteen million visitors a year, all in search of 'peace and solitude'. The research group continues to wrestle with a rural problem that seems to require 'urban' solutions, such as entry fees, better public transport, parking charges and Park-and-Ride schemes.

The RAC came to similarly radical conclusions in its review of the government's proposal to charge for motorway use in 1993. Although eighty-six per cent of motorists opposed this, the

CORNERING THE SUPERMARKET

Out-of-town shopping centres invade the countryside and hurt the high street. But the habit of weekly bulk buying at supermarkets is now established, the car being the last link in the food distribution chain. The RAC wants better planning.

Club concluded that, in the current economic circumstances, a toll was probably inevitable. It should be collected by electronic debiting technology because the cumbersome business of paying at booths would discourage travel on Britain's safest roads. Only by raising revenue in this way, the RAC maintained, could the country afford an effective system of

> roads and railways which bring environmental relief to local communities, and which are themselves built to the highest environmental standards. Tunnels and trees, reduction of noise and the eyesore aspects all cost more and more.

However, the RAC warned that motorists would only come to accept charges if the money was entirely 'dedicated to the motorway system'. Government ministers and Whitehall mandarins took RAC advice increasingly seriously because it was more objective and better informed. Particularly influential was David Worskett's effort to focus attention on 'gross polluters'. These were buses, lorries and the ten per cent of motorists who, as revealed by special roadside monitoring equipment which the RAC imported from America, caused more than half the harmful emissions from the nation's cars. The RAC advocated the use of 'green cameras' which could be as effective in enforcing environmental traffic laws as speed cameras were in reducing accidents. Rather touchingly, during a 'Green Week' organised by the RAC in the summer of 1994, fifty of its staff demonstrated their devotion to the environmental cause by taking part in the annual charity bicycle ride from London to Brighton.

Pedal power was all very well, but the RAC remained committed to the cause of the environmentally friendly motor car. This, however, was increasingly deemed a contradiction in terms. In October 1994 the Royal Commission on Environmental Pollution launched a sustained attack on excessive car use as being harmful to national health and efficiency. Many of its proposals – for example, to reduce exhaust emissions and car dependence while improving public transport and traffic management – echoed those of the RAC. Furthermore, according to one member of the Royal Commission, when submitting evidence the RAC's representatives 'behaved like angels'. But they frowned on the Commission's most radical recommendations. It wanted to discourage motoring by doubling fuel prices over the next ten years, charging for urban road use and restricting work on trunk roads, which were said merely to generate traffic. The RAC countered these proposals with arguments expressed by Jeffrey Rose himself in an article for the *Daily Telegraph*. The economy, he said, which was ever more reliant on 'just-in-time' delivery techniques, required a modern highway system. Roads carried ninety per cent of the nation's passengers and freight though they received only fifty-six per cent of the transport budget, an overwhelming tribute to their efficiency. They were also a vital factor in sustaining the '"just-in-time" lifestyles which were built around personal, flexible mobility: the car'. It enabled women to combine a career with motherhood, for example, to earn a second income and to take their children to school. Pricing such activities out of the market would limit freedom and cause significant social problems. The Royal Commission's report, Rose declared, was 'characterised by breathtaking naivety'.

The Chairman of the RAC ventured onto still more contentious ground when he claimed that further bypasses and motorway lanes made a positive contribution to the environment. Certainly they saved lives and improved conditions in towns and villages relieved of traffic. But,

CLEARING THE AIR

Much effort is put into monitoring the level of exhaust fumes in cities, not least by the RAC, which campaigns against 'gross polluters'. Environmentalists and others show their concern, especially about the effect of vehicle emissions on the health of children. The problem remains serious but cleaner engines are on the way.

as the *Observer* noted, the government's £18 billion road programme was 'hugely controversial and unpopular'. Some new road schemes, especially when they involved the despoliation of areas of outstanding natural beauty, the nicking of Dartmoor or the slicing through of Twyford Down, aroused enormous and legitimate anxiety. The Royal Commission had given wide currency to the view that, as one newspaper headline put it, the 'reign of the car must end'. More and more people seemed intent on overthrowing the 'tin tyrant'. Their endeavours ranged from peaceful demonstrations to violent protests. Opponents of roads lobbied parliament and marched in the streets. They lay down in front of bulldozers and conducted treetop sit-ins. They agitated for 'car-free zones' and blocked traffic with 'human zebra crossings'. Fiercer still was the rhetoric of pressure groups such as 'Reclaim the Streets' and 'The Land is Ours'. For them motoring was not just politically incorrect, like smoking; it was morally wrong, like drug-dealing. Their talk was not only of 'gridlock', 'juggernaut jungles' and the 'automotive nightmare', but of 'auto-terrorism' and 'Carmageddon'. In *Autogeddon*, playwright Heathcote Williams's extended anathema against the automobile, streets became 'open sewers of the car cult' and 'alfresco gas-chamber[s]'. The language of hysteria inflamed those who rebelled against planning procedures, public enquiries, the processes of democracy. It fed 'green fascism'.

ROAD OUTRAGE

Protesters demonstrate against the Newbury bypass in 1996. Many ordinary citizens were infuriated by the desecration of the countryside and the resistance was marked by violence. But most people in Newbury wanted an end to traffic congestion.

The intransigence of extremists did not rule out the possibility of a moderate consensus. Jeffrey Rose, in particular, thought it

> wrong to define the debate as essentially between conflicting factions. The reality is that nearly all of us drive cars, and the car provides transport for about 40 per cent of the journeys of those who do not possess one. Yet at the same time we are all mothers, fathers, brothers and sisters desperately concerned about the environment.

But there could be no meeting of minds while prejudice was sustained by ignorance. So in 1995 the RAC published its report on *Car Dependence*. Produced by the wholly independent Oxford University Transport Study Unit, this was the most substantial and sophisticated research project which the RAC's Foundation had thus far commissioned. It reveals that the automobile plays a more vital part in the life of the nation than had hitherto been appreciated. Twenty per cent of journeys 'have to be done by car', while for another sixty per cent the car, because of its speed and convenience, is the only rational choice. Good alternative means of transport are available for the remaining journeys, especially the eight per cent which are of less than a mile. However, as the report makes clear, reliance on the car is not a steady state: it grows through custom and practice. It is encouraged by all sorts of social and psychological pressures, reinforced with car commercials (which account for about a fifth of all British spending on advertising). By conferring freedom and flexibility on their owners, cars are seen as the appurtenances of a 'superior lifestyle'. Motorists think not in terms of car dependence but in terms of personal independence.

Thus in a country where 'the average driver spends one and a half hours a day in the car' (nearly ten per cent of his waking life), reliance on the car is set to increase. Yet there is scope

for reducing its use by about a fifth. Significant benefits might flow from marginal adjustments. The report concluded that concerns about

> global environmental change and local environmental damage, health effects of noxious emissions, obesity due to lack of exercise, problems in the development of independence among children, perceived and actual danger on the streets, waste of economic resources in congestion, problems of the commercial viability of town centres, difficulties in arranging for the efficient distribution of goods, and frustrated expectations of personal mobility – all tend to point to the unsustainability of current trends, and have revived interest in the important roles to be played by the long under-valued modes of walking, cycling and public transport, and by the recently unfashionable idea of strategic land-use planning.

COMMERCIAL
CORRECTNESS

Advertisements reflected the growing concern about fuel conservation and road safety. In 1984 the Vauxhall Nova, though little more than a souped-up shopping car, was presented as a racer. In 1993 the Toyota Supra's top speed – more than twice the legal limit – is not even mentioned.

These ideas were much ventilated during the 'great transport debate' initiated by Brian Mawhinney when he was Transport Secretary. They also appeared in the Green Paper, 'Transport: The Way Ahead', which his successor issued in 1996. But this was widely inter-preted as the expedient of a government anxious to invest less on roads before an election in order to 'pocket the savings'. As *The Economist* concluded, 'all political action to reduce car use seems as gridlocked as downtown New York'. The Green Paper largely ignored the realities about growing automobile dependence set out in the RAC Foundation's report. Yet the report had been widely praised, not least by the Environment Secretary John Gummer, who was, along with the Transport Secretary, present at its launch. The Green Paper failed to recognise what Jeffrey Rose had called 'the central role of the car as the key transport provider of the future'. It adopted the strategy about which the Foundation had issued a dire warning when it was first established: to do nothing and allow rising levels of congestion to regulate traffic was 'the most inefficient transport policy of all'. The RAC's own transport policy may have been open to crit-icism but at least the Club could not be accused of inactivity.

BECAUSE OF EXCEPTIONALLY DIFFICULT trading conditions, RAC Motoring Services also had to be exceedingly busy during the early 1990s. The economic downturn, sharp cost-cutting by competitors, the Gulf War crisis, the blow to staff morale caused by the departure of Arthur Large, to say nothing of the IRA car bomb that rocked M1 Cross in 1991 (itself a small matter compared with what the RAC's Belfast office had endured) – all presented the organisation with serious problems. For almost two years Jeffrey Rose himself took the helm, with Frank Richardson managing a rearranged and simplified core business. They steadied the ship, which made progress despite the adverse circumstances. Each year Patrols set new records for the number of jobs done, which reached 2.76 million in 1992. Improved training for dis-patchers (who were entrusted with so much of the RAC's spending power) ensured that every breakdown got the right resources. The results were reflected in higher customer satisfaction ratings. The RAC's rescue service even won a seal of approval from the British Standards

SMALL, YET HANDLES WELL OVER A TON.

You should hear the things they're saying about us in the motoring magazines.

"Difficult not to use superlatives when discussing the handling," said Autosport.

"Even when it's flicking left right left through a series of S bends, the SR remains remarkably flat, balanced, poised, unruffled," reported Motor.

These same journalists are also fond of nicknaming the Nova SR the "Super Nova."

Quite right, too.

At £5,404 the SR is top of the Nova range: a powerfully built 5 speed 1300 that can unleash 70bhp.

It can get you from 0-60mph in just 10.6 seconds. And up to a top speed of 103 mph a few seconds later.

But just as there's true grit under the bonnet, there's also true grip under the SR's flared arches.

Anti-roll bars, front and rear. Uprated springs and dampers. And low profile tyres.

The inside is just as well-equipped. You'll find there are rally-style seats, head restraints, tinted glass, a 4 speaker radio/stereo cassette and a full array of sports instrumentation.

Actually, in these few column inches, it's hard to describe all of the features packed into the SR's 12 feet.

So instead, we'll leave it to Autosport to sum up:

"For those who must have 100 mph plus performance, the SR is the fun car par excellence."

Exactly.

THE 103 MPH VAUXHALL NOVA SR.

Better. By Design.

AERODYNAMITE.

In designing the new Toyota Supra, we took on the heavyweights in the world of the supercar.

The Italians would describe that sweeping bodywork as super leggera. Because aluminium and newly formulated plastics lightened the car by 220 pounds.

For the Germans, the engine has Wagnerian overtones. It's got 24 valves, six cylinders and twin turbos that work in sequence. Linked to a 6-speed manual or 4-speed automatic gearbox, it delivers a stirring 326 bhp

from just three litres. To put this in perspective, the new Supra can reach 60mph from zero in 4.9 seconds. In other words, it's the car in front of the Ferrari 348 and the Porsche 911 Turbo.

Slip into the leather seats. Seal yourself into thermostatically air-conditioned cabin. And reassure yourself that this is also the car in front on safety features.

They go far beyond the driver and passenger air bags and side-impact bars. Take the Supra's electronic traction control

system. It never feeds the wheels more power than they can handle. There's the new 4-channel ABS system, too, with spirally ventilated discs. It lets you brake from 60mph to standstill in 120 feet. In a straight line, even in the wet.

And that rear wing heightens your control. With the speed-activated front spoiler, it harnesses air to push the Supra squarely against the tarmac.

At every stage of its development, the new Supra was track tested by racing drivers across the world. That's why

every inch of this car makes you feel at one with it.

At £37,500, it comes with Toyota's comprehensive warranty, three years or 60,000 miles, and 3 years' RAC membership.

Only a few Supras are available this year from selected Toyota dealers. For your nearest, turn the page or call 0800 777555 free. Obviously, these cars will go very quickly.

THE NEW *Supra*

THE CAR IN FRONT IS A 🅣 TOYOTA

Authority, the first motoring body to do so. MOTORMAN continued to grow and new deals, incorporating insurance as well as recovery, were struck with manufacturers such as Mazda and Nissan. By 1992 the RAC covered two-thirds of new vehicles in Britain, a million a year. MOTORMAN even secured its first motor-bicycle clients, Enfield and Yamaha.

Other initiatives abounded. Abroad the RAC began to erode the AA's monopoly in Eire and continued with the European drive begun by Arthur Large. In 1991, for the first time in its history, the Club sold roadside assistance to French drivers. The following year its Croydon-based unit ROADATA set up a hotline to give motorists information about blockages and delays during the French lorry drivers' strike, answering a total of 23,000 calls. In January 1993 the RAC moved its Continental headquarters from Calais to the centrally located city of Lyons. At home, in 1991, the RAC practised what it preached about pollution, outlawing smoking in its offices – less than a decade after refusing a non-smoking hotel entry in its Guide on the ground it had no graphic symbol to denote such a place. The Club also made fresh efforts to secure the safety of lone female drivers, of whom there were more than ever on the roads. The press applauded and journalistic tests showed that the RAC generally 'lives up to its priority promise for women'. But when the *Sunday Times* demonstrated that the New Knights of the Road were sometimes slow to rescue damsels in distress the Club was accused of 'trying to scare women into taking their service'. A week later, though, the newspaper printed a letter from a female motorcyclist who had often broken down on lonely stretches of the A1: 'the RAC's response was fantastic …. Every time I felt reassured that I was top priority.'

At the end of 1992 David Livermore, an outstanding fifty-two-year-old senior executive from IBM, was appointed to take Jeffrey Rose's place as Managing Director of Motoring Services, which then seemed set to beat the economic trend. As Rose told the Club Committee early the following year: CARS had been 'handsomely vindicated'; budgets were 'consistently being met' and 'cash flow was strong'. Between 1991 and 1993 profit after tax rose from £5.9 to £12.1 million. Furthermore, a dramatic new move was in train which transformed the public face of the RAC. During 1992 command and control operations were concentrated at the Supercentres – in London, Bristol, Walsall, Stockport and Glasgow – which also housed specialist operations such as legal services or technical training. This meant that eleven regional command centres and twelve member reception centres closed, with the loss of 200 jobs. Shutting down these offices (some of which, like the one in Norwich, had only just opened) avoided duplication and saved enormously in overheads. Because the CARS location system was so good, and improved still further with the introduction of screen maps and graphic displays, dispatchers had less need of local knowledge when they were trying to pinpoint breakdowns.

Nevertheless, many regretted the loss of 'the personal touch' and the 'friendly club image'. Local offices had given Patrols a focus and kept the RAC directly in touch with the community. Now it seemed to be a wholesaler rather than a retailer of services. Or as one Patrol put it, 'Members have gained a supermarket and lost the corner shop.' Members, indeed, had become customers. And, according to some staff, they themselves had become items in a balance sheet. But other employees were pleased with the change of emphasis from Club to company, especially when the company looked after its pensioners so well and had such 'tremendous

RAC
FRANCE

LES DIX COMMANDEMENTS DU DÉPANNEUR RAC

1 - Tu seras toujours précis sur l'heure d'arrivée du dépannage.

2 - Tu seras courtois envers les membres du RAC et toujours tu les réconforteras.

3 - Tu seras toujours compétent et tu essaieras de faire une réparation sur place.

4 - Tu seras toujours efficace et tu remorqueras avec des véhicules spécialement adaptés.

5 - Tu assisteras toujours de ton mieux en toutes circonstances et de sous-traiter, il ne te sera pas permis.

6 - Tu informeras toujours nos chargés d'assistance de tous les problèmes.

7 - Tu auras toujours du matériel et des locaux propres.

8 - Tu te rappelleras que les pièces détachées sont à la charge du client et non du RAC.

9 - Tu enverras rapidement la facture détaillée au RAC.

10 - Tu seras toujours professionnel et la qualité sera ta devise.

FAITES ATTENTION!

The RAC pronounces its Ten Commandments in French. They were directed at operators of the rescue service it established for French motorists in 1991. This was a preliminary to a panEuropean enterprise called FASTRAC, which proved … très problématique.

integrity'. What had once been a family had turned into a business, employees said, and 'thank goodness for that'. They agreed with Large, who thought that the emphasis on customers was useful because it reminded everyone that 'the customer is king'. Moreover, most RAC staff felt proud of the stupendous increase in efficiency which the Supercentres made possible. One senior manager expressed 'great elation and satisfaction that we were now competing with all opposition and winning hands down'. From being a regiment, with little outposts scattered throughout the kingdom, the RAC was manifestly consolidating itself into a national service. It was an enterprise that was not just 'high-tech' but 'high-profile'.

The most prominent sign of this was the Supercentre at Bradley Stoke. As the recession persisted, wits nicknamed the depressed area outside Bristol 'Sadly Broke'. But the RAC's £16 million flagship, whose twin masts towered 215 feet over the M4/M5 interchange, invested the neighbourhood with new character and confidence. One observer wrote, it exudes 'more authority and reassurance than Mission Control, Houston'. Designed by Nicholas Grimshaw & Partners, the building is a dark-glazed three-decker snugly berthed in its own super-bowl, which is crossed by a footbridge. Cam-shaped – triangular with curved corners – it might be a gigantic space station about to whirl into orbit from its landscaped silo. But the building is also a monument to green values. Outside there is a kidney-shaped car park planted in the manner of an orchard, and a fragrant sunken garden including a sun-and-moon design symbolising the twenty-four-hour working pattern of the RAC. Inside, the open-plan floors seem to float around the central atrium. This is full of foliage and leads into the restaurant and fitness centre. Glare and noise are excluded by 718 panes of sloping, tinted, toughened, double-glazed panels, each one weighing a quarter of a tonne. The air is conditioned by an energy-efficient displacement ventilation system and the atmosphere is, in more senses than one, transparent. The technology is sustained by a mass of electronic entrails, including 290,000 linear metres of cable – enough to cover the distance from Bristol to Liverpool.

The 500 staff work in specialist units like legal and membership services as well as manning the RAC's south-western command and control centre, which handles up to 4,000 calls a day. A visitors' room like a huge crow's nest poised halfway up the masts presents those who have a head for heights with a panorama of the motorways, which are often at a standstill. More important, from the RAC's point of view, is the powerful image which the award-winning Supercentre conveys to the motorist. In the excited words of *Marketing* magazine, the RAC's Bradley Stoke development and its four sisters were the 'ultimate superposters'. 'The blend of design, function and branding is a marketeer's dream.'

The Supercentres would merely have been an impressive façade had not David Livermore appreciated better than most that technology never stands still. He was determined to ensure that Service Patrols would reflect the sophistication of their headquarters by meeting the challenge posed by ever more advanced automobiles. In theory, these should have been less liable to go wrong. In fact, 'the number of faults is proportional to the number of components', which increases every year. Old defects are eradicated but new ones occur. In 1993, for example, Patrols attended 110,000 cars whose drivers had locked themselves out – a few had even managed to lock themselves *in* – and they had an excellent success rate even though security devices have become so complicated. Car alarms and immobilisers also prove to be the

BRADLEY STOKE SUPERCENTRE

This avant-garde building is the RAC's nerve centre in the South West. A beacon to motorists in the dark, it is an emblem of space-age sophistication in daylight. With its rotating lines and floating surfaces, the Supercentre seems to be in perpetual motion – as is the RAC.

cause of problems, and more recently radio signals from traffic sensors, walkie-talkies and other similar sources have tended to neutralise remote-control key-fobs.

Patrols were better able to cope in 1994, when they received CD-ROMs in place of unwieldy printed manuals. The Panasonic device was 'a portable electronic encyclopaedia' which could store 160,000 'pages' of information and display it on a screen with words and diagrams. The CD-ROMs are kept up to date by engineers at the Bescot National Technical Centre, which supplies Patrols with a disc each month containing fresh data, all carefully code-protected to frustrate thieves. To improve the roadside repair rate still further, the RAC had developed computerised machines, each the size of a large trunk, which simulate a car's electronic systems. They replicate faults which Patrols diagnose and cure under the guidance of instructors. Oddly enough, however, motorists whose cars break down do not regard fixing them as the priority. More important is that help should arrive swiftly and that Patrols should be friendly, sympathetic and obliging. David Livermore was keen on scientific solutions, as evidenced by his pushing ahead with CARS II – so called because it further improved the RAC's communications via, for example, a computerised system for generating locations from telephone numbers. But he did not ignore the human factor. His motto, endlessly reiterated in uplifting speeches and mission statements, was 'Customer Driven Quality'.

This dual approach achieved some good results. In 1994 the RAC beat off stiff competition to supply a recovery service for Eurotunnel. Under the terms of the £2 million, three-year contract, its fifteen-strong team became responsible for removing any vehicle which broke down around the Folkestone Channel Tunnel terminal. To keep traffic flowing onto Le Shuttle speed is essential: so at any time of the day or night Patrols have to be able to clear an immobilised vehicle from the crucial Red Zone within eleven minutes. Consistently voted the best fleet breakdown service, the RAC negotiated deals with big operators such as Hertz and Swan National, who had been with the AA and National Breakdown respectively. It forged stronger links with MOTORMAN clients like Ford and Toyota, and signed up new recruits such as Proton and Hyundai. It arranged special low-cost RAC membership for the one million members of the Transport and General Workers' Union (to which 1,800 RAC staff belonged). It clinched a multi-million-pound contract with the Norwich Union insurance company to provide a unique helpline linking its policy-holders to the Club's services.

Never had the RAC been more visible. It brought the disturbing phenomenon of 'road rage' to the attention of the public. It waged war on 'bull bars', dangerous designer bumpers on pickups and jeeps. It campaigned for side-impact bars, however, and better head restraints to guard against whiplash. It agitated against private companies which carried out indiscriminate wheel-clamping and spot checks on cars. Its revamped sign service broke new records, though it had to contend with souvenir hunters to whom the signs were irresistible, to say nothing of entrepreneurs who tried to trick the RAC into directing people to acid house parties by calling them names like 'Elixir Exhibition', 'Fantasia' and 'Heaven and Earth'. Finally, the RAC, whose advertising has never been really first-rate, launched a new series of press and television commercials. Previously these had stressed the trauma of breakdown: now they concentrated on the relief of rescue and the satisfaction of reaching one's destination. Under the RAC logo the slogan read, 'It Says You've Arrived.'

INSIDE THE ARGOSY

The floors of the Supercentre resemble decks, and staircases zigzag through the green atrium – like companionways on a ship. The whole interior is light and open, conveying a sense of community in the workplace.

Accentuating the positive was well and good; but the advertising campaign was much criticised and negative aspects of the RAC could not be ignored during the final stages of David Livermore's stewardship. In 1994 Vauxhall declined to renew its MOTORMAN contract although 'totally satisfied with levels of service' it had received. The car manufacturer's decision seems to have been determined by the fact that the AA undercut the RAC to the tune of £1 million, a figure which gave the impression that the new business was acquired as a 'loss leader'. Nevertheless, it was a blow. Like Arthur Large, Livermore believed that Europe presented the RAC with 'a fantastic opportunity', but it has yet to be realised. In 1995 Livermore set up FASTRAC, a company offering breakdown assistance and other services across the Continent for corporate customers like car-makers and fleet operators. It was assisted by local partners and sustained by EUROCARS, a version of CARS with added refinements such as automatic translation facilities. However, the difficulties of breaking into the European motoring services market, estimated to be worth £3 billion a year, are considerable and the business remains fragile. Equally disappointing was the start of BATTERY ASSIST, a mobile service established to supply, fit and dispose of batteries. This enterprise catered for the motorist's most pressing need – battery problems account for nearly a fifth of all calls for assistance made to the RAC. It therefore seemed to have the potential of making millions. But it proved difficult to implement and the RAC's Service Patrols were unhappy with the scheme.

Staff morale had plummeted generally: an independent survey revealed that only fifteen per cent of the employees at M1 Cross 'were satisfied with the RAC'. One reason for this was low job security. This was also a feature of life in the RAC's beleaguered Insurance Services, which in 1994 fell victim to murderous competition from companies selling direct to customers by telephone. Livermore, who believed that the RAC had for years been guilty of 'fiddling and dabbling' in the insurance business, followed suit. He closed local offices, fired 250 staff, introduced computerised telephone sales techniques, made special offers. This strategy, jointly agreed, was in some respects effective and gave grounds for optimism. But Jeffrey Rose and his colleagues had heard 'optimistic forecasts' before and they continued to see a fall in profits (though the RAC's £5 million gain looked good beside the £27 million loss chalked up by the AA in 1994). On 3 October 1995 Rose told Livermore of the 'profound disquiet' he felt about 'the low level of achievement in the principal objectives of the company'. The following day, by mutual consent and with sadness on both sides, David Livermore stepped down from his position as Group Managing Director.

A successor was waiting in the wings. He was Neil Johnson, who had been appointed General Secretary to the Club on the retirement of Michael Limb, in January 1994. For the post of 'principal civil servant' to the RAC, Rose had sought a candidate of the 'very highest calibre'. The forty-four-year-old Johnson came with 'excellent credentials', though his *curriculum vitae* was hardly orthodox. At his excellent Cardiff grammar school he had had 'a chequered career in every respect'. But he did well at sport and engineering and finished as head boy. Johnson went on to Sandhurst. However, after the defence cuts of the late 1960s he saw no future for himself as a professional soldier. So he left to become a sailor, like his great-grandfather. Starting 'before the mast', he spent three years ploughing the seven seas aboard Strickline cargo ships. It was, he recalls, 'a wonderful experience'. But after taking his second mate's

KINGS OFF THE ROAD

The Range Rover (left) was born as long ago as 1970. With its four-wheel drive this sovereign vehicle could master rugged terrain, but it soon became fashionable with people who seldom roved beyond tarmac. Other manufacturers followed the trend, producing models such as the Ford Maverick (below), actually built by Nissan. Despite some forecasts, the reign of the luxury jeep seems set to continue.

MACHO MACHINES

Used in Australia to stop kangaroos damaging cars, 'bull bars' became a popular 'fashion accessory' in Britain during the late 1980s. Unlike conventional bumpers they do not crumple on impact, thus causing serious injuries and deaths. The RAC began to campaign against them in 1994, its spokesman remarking sagely: 'You don't see many kangaroos down the King's Road.'

ticket and becoming a 'navigating officer', Johnson decided not to go on following his 'own version of the hippie trail'. Nor did he want to join his father's commercial vehicle engineering business though he had caught the 'automotive bug' early, having learnt to drive a huge breakdown truck at the age of ten. Instead Johnson became a graduate trainee with the Lex Service Group. He rose rapidly, occupied positions of heavy responsibility on the commercial vehicle side and learnt the latest managerial techniques. Considered too young, at twenty-four, for general management, he set up a small engineering and motor business in Aberystwyth before being 'head-hunted' by British Leyland in 1974. His first task was to oversee customer services across Europe. When Michael Edwardes took over the following year Johnson, like 500 other top managers, was obliged to undergo psychological assessment. He found the process of 'being shrunk vaguely absurd but reasonably amusing'.

Johnson's psyche passed muster and he did a succession of tasks at the heart of a reinvigorated BL. He supervised strategic marketing and planning. He took part in securing the Honda alliance. He helped to save the Mini and to launch the Metro. For nearly two years he ran the service division, streamlining warranty processes and introducing computerisation. He became Managing Director of European Operations, attending to sales and marketing. Early on, incidentally, he encountered the *ancien régime* at the RAC. Johnson wanted BL to become the first manufacturer to offer a roadside assistance scheme as part of its sales package – the germ of MOTORMAN. But Eric Charles, to whom he made his initial approach, showed no enthusiasm for the arrangement; so Johnson went to the AA, which created 'Supercover'. In 1982 Johnson accepted John Egan's offer to become Sales and Marketing Director at Jaguar, a job which was said to be 'the next best thing to suicide'. But he revitalised the dealer network and made a crucial contribution to the recovery of the famous marque, assisted by what he now calls 'a naive reluctance to believe that it was impossible'.

Then, in 1986, Johnson accepted an even more daring challenge, this time from the War Office. Long a Territorial, he agreed to take command of the 4th battalion of the Royal Green Jackets. For three years Johnson served as a Lieutenant Colonel in England, Germany and Northern Ireland. In exercises, his superiors reckoned, he reached the same decisions as regular officers – but sometimes by a different route and in half the time. After this 'marvellous mid-life break', as Johnson called it, he returned to the world of commerce. As Director of European Operations for the Rover Group inside BAe with a seat on the main board, he achieved good results, boosting the sales of Rover cars and Land Rovers on the Continent and launching the successful new Land Rover Discovery. Finally he spent two exciting years learning a lot about Westminster and Whitehall, not all of it pleasant, as Director General of the Engineering Employers' Federation. Johnson's qualifications were matched by his qualities, which made him particularly attractive to the RAC.

Tough, astute and competitive, Johnson is also charming, open and amusing. His aquiline features frequently soften into a broad grin. Quietly cultured, he enjoys opera, studies military history, reads novels and poetry. He loves sport, especially if it involves cars. He is fond of country walking and skiing in company with his three daughters. He mixes easily with all sorts and conditions of people. No one expected David Livermore to depart so precipitately; but it was understandable that, from the first, Johnson was groomed for stardom.

DAVID WORSKETT

Appointed Head of Public Affairs in 1990, Worskett became the champion of 'green' motoring policies.

DAVID LIVERMORE

Managing Director of Motoring Services between 1992 and 1995, Livermore promoted new technology.

SIR JOHN ROGERS

Air Chief Marshal Rogers has been a strong Executive Chairman of the RAC Motor Sports Association since 1989.

JOHN QUENBY

An experienced business manager, Quenby became Chief Executive of RACMSA in 1989, achieving excellent financial and public relations results.

NEIL JOHNSON

After Sandhurst and an unconventional but outstanding career in the motor industry, Johnson was appointed Chief Executive of the entire organisation in 1995. He faces the challenge of leading the RAC into the next millennium.

Rose himself recognised the need to make a phased withdrawal, thus avoiding the trap into which Andrews had fallen, of remaining in office for too long. He thought now was the moment to begin that process, which would culminate in his full retirement after the Club's hundredth birthday. The RAC should have a '"hands on" and high profile leader' and the Chairman would concentrate on 'non-routine strategy' as well as arrangements to celebrate the 1997 centenary. Johnson, as Chief Executive Officer, agreed to work out an overall 'plan of campaign'. This he did during the next few weeks. It involved an interesting return to the principles and practices of Johnson's predecessor and namesake, Claude. Like the Club's first Secretary, Neil Johnson believed that it had to be run as a unit, with each of the disparate elements contributing to the whole and clear lines of command running down from the top. Previously there had been too many grey areas, breeding-grounds for inefficiency and intrigue. Now the Chief Executive (who remained General Secretary), answerable to the board of the RAC Ltd, would 'see across the entire organisation'. So in January 1996 Rose became non-executive Chairman. Having played a principal part in saving the RAC during the 1970s and having led it to become the most technologically advanced motoring organisation in the world during the 1980s, he prepared to bow out gracefully during the 1990s. Before that, however, Rose had approved a structure and a strategy which was calculated to ensure the RAC's progress into the next millennium.

When the Chairman's name is mentioned loyal Club members are liable to intone: 'Cometh the hour, cometh the man.' Yet to a considerable extent his emergence had been a matter of luck: the Club might equally have saddled itself with another Wilfrid Andrews. Because of the strength and independence of the RAC's board, that sort of mishap is unlikely to occur again. Yet there is certainly scope for further constitutional reform at the RAC. Although its General Council gives some representation to ordinary members, and ever since 1924 has elected the Associate Committee which looks after their interests, this is hardly a democratic body. Indeed, as the *Sunday Telegraph* has argued, the 'Parliament of Motoring' is more a 'self-perpetuating oligarchy' – like the AA. Both bodies, declared Arthur Large after leaving the RAC, 'are without accountability to their beneficiaries – the motorists who are mutual members'. As S. F. Edge had perceived soon after the Club's foundation, the very fact that it is a hybrid makes the fullest possible integration of individual motoring members all the more necessary.

Even more anomalous, in the modern world, is the fact that women are denied representation on the RAC board. They are ineligible because, however high they may rise in the ranks of Motoring Services, they cannot be full members of the Pall Mall Club. This is an absurd anachronism, particularly as the RAC rightly prides itself on being an 'equal opportunities employer'. It takes a strong line, for example, against sexual discrimination and harassment in the workplace. Pressure is mounting to shatter the so-called 'glass ceiling' which blocks the progress of women, who are, incidentally, thirteen times less likely to commit serious motoring offences than men – a fact which the RAC acknowledged by teaming up with Norwich Union in 1991 to provide cheaper breakdown and insurance cover for the 'safer sex'. As this droll expression suggests, however, there is much atavistic prejudice to be overcome. Opinions are still sometimes heard in Pall Mall which seem to leap straight from the pages of the Club's Edwardian *Journal*. One member asserted that if there were 'several young women together and

JAGUAR AT LE MANS

The driving force behind Jaguar's racing triumphs in the 1980s was Neil Johnson. Then Marketing Director, he appreciated the commercial value of victories over BMW and other top European manufacturers. Johnson got Tom Walkinshaw (above left) to run the racing team, which owed much of its success to this swashbuckling Scot.

personable looking males came in, they would start to preen themselves' and each would tend to converse in a louder voice, this, in his opinion, 'disturbing the atmosphere of serenity in the place'. There is nothing to stop other gentlemen's clubs from institutionalising misogyny. But the RAC, with its responsibilities to automobilism, a constituency in which women amount to forty per cent, must surely soon accept the view of members who wish it to become 'a gentleperson's club'.

NEIL JOHNSON INTENDS to grapple with this divisive issue in due course. Meanwhile he has made a promising start in the highly volatile and competitive commercial arena. Like Arthur Large, he began by taking employees into his confidence, meeting as many of them as he could, explaining his policy at a series of roadshows and in a video. First he cited a recent opinion survey which had found that staff did not understand how management was trying to develop the business and doubted if those at the top had a clear vision either. This was understandable. There had been too many fuzzy initiatives. Profits had dropped to £3 million in 1995, on a turnover of a quarter of a billion. Group purchasing power had not been fully exploited. Twenty senior managers had been obliged to drive 20,000 miles a year to attend formal meetings, which 'has to be mad ... even [for] a motoring organisation'. All told, what was a relatively straightforward enterprise had become too complicated. So Johnson cut out two layers of management and increased the number of people reporting directly to him. He focused attention on providing outstanding service to the customer, without whom there would be no business. He hoped that they would all have some fun reviving it but warned that some changes would be painful. He also pledged that the RAC would provide Patrols with skills and systems to engage in the crucial 'battle for our success ... [which] will be fought and won by the roadside'.

That battle is being transformed by technology. Soon, as Johnson pointed out, twenty per cent of 'the value of a new car will be in its electronics', compared with only two to three per cent in the mid-1980s. Among the impending advances are in-car faxes and CD-ROMs to give drivers access to almost unlimited amounts of information, navigation systems which flash up maps on the windscreen and utter voice directions, 'intelligent' cruise controls which automatically adjust speed to traffic flow, 'anti-collision radar, thermal imaging systems to improve visibility, and sensors detecting drivers falling asleep at the wheel'. All this poses challenges to Patrols because cars will contain more components that can fail. But it also offers opportunities to the RAC because 'smart' equipment already exists which can identify faults under the bonnet. Before long transmitters will be added to send data about defects to Supercentres via a satellite, which would also fix the location of the vehicle.

The RAC, as one newspaper breathlessly reported, is even 'working on a top-secret SOS Patrol that arrives *before* your car has gone wrong. The crystal ball service uses an on-board computer to diagnose early symptoms of engine failure hours before the car grinds to a halt.' Furthermore, the RAC is seeking to develop 'virtual reality helmets'. Worn by Patrols, this futuristic headgear would have a mouthpiece, earphones and a camera to transmit pictures of malfunctioning machinery from the scene of a breakdown back to base, where it can be analysed by specialist engineers. In sum, the motoring changes of the next ten years are going to be more

THAT'LL BE THE DAEWOO

Gone are the days when British designers produced identifiably British cars. The design of automobiles, like their manufacture, has become global. As this extraordinary Daewoo Mya (left) suggests, the designers of new cars know no national boundaries. They are restricted only by the limits of their imagination.

THE SHAPE OF THE NEW

Peugeot produced the Asphalte (right) to 'put the fun back into driving' – there are no doors and to get in and out you remove the steering wheel. Ford's bubble-like compact (below) is less streamlined, but it could be the shape of city cars to come.

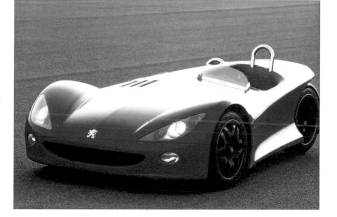

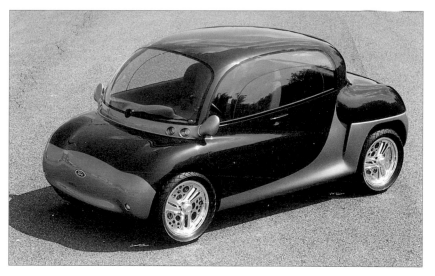

dramatic than those of the last fifty. But such is the proliferation of 'intelligent transport systems' that great human intelligence will be needed to discern their true potential. Johnson is determined to choose 'the technologies that will come out on top'.

He will have more time and resources to devote to this task as a result of the sale of RAC Insurance Services (RACIS) to Guardian Royal Exchange (GRE) for some £68 million in the spring of 1996. The previous autumn it had become clear to Rose and the RAC board that drastic action was finally needed to solve their most intractable and long-standing problem. The difficulties with RESPOND were far from being overcome and despite heroic efforts from the workforce in 1995 they were still being outstripped by the competition. The RAC board supported discussions started with several major insurance companies, including GRE. Rose made initial contact with GRE's Chief Executive and let it be known that he had a high figure in mind – something he was always confident of achieving, though others had doubts. Months of complex negotiation followed. Neil Johnson took a major role in bringing off the deal with GRE, assisted by Finance Director Alastair Miller and the Club solicitor Ian Mavor. This was, on the face of it, an extraordinary coup. An insurance business which has consistently performed in a fashion that Rose himself regarded as dismal and disappointing, hardly breaking even over the years, was sold for more than seven times what it cost to buy in 1984. Admittedly, had the initial sum been wisely invested it should have achieved a growth of some £25 million in twelve years and the business would have avoided substantial capital and general costs.

Nonetheless, the deal was a great achievement, prompting City analysts to say that the price paid was 'a little on the high side'. However, Guardian Royal Exchange was acquiring a stake in the RAC's name, which obviously has immense value, as well as taking over its 325,000 policies. RACIS will continue to trade under its own name (and with its own staff), but as part of GRE it will have access to new resources and expertise in underwriting, processing and systems technology. Furthermore, joint venture agreements were reached whereby GRE will sell insurance services to the RAC's six million members and the RAC will market its roadside assistance services to GRE customers. This should prove highly advantageous to the RAC. In addition it retains its own London Wall/RAC Mechanical Insurance business, a profitable, fairly self-contained operation run by a specialist staff and expertly managed, since 1990, by Dick Rogers.

The other elements in the RAC were also in good fettle. After its troubles in the 1970s, the RAC Motor Sports Association (MSA) had encountered further difficulties during the mid-1980s as increasing sponsorship and the resulting commercial pressures made the sport more professional. Its governing body could not be anything less. But in May 1988 the MSA moved out of its old rookery in Belgrave Square to a new open-plan office near Heathrow. This was hard to reach for commuters on the wrong side of London and there was a loss of experienced staff. In July Peter Hammond, newly appointed Chief Executive of the MSA, was killed in a motor-cycle accident on his way to Silverstone before the Grand Prix. Finding a replacement was problematic and it soon became apparent that neither day-to-day management nor long-term strategy could be properly handled from Pall Mall. Safety, especially, was at issue: minimising the ever-present risk of disaster is the heaviest responsibility which the governing body of motor sport undertakes. Rose says, 'I did not feel we were adequately discharging that responsibility.' Quite by chance he soon found the man to do so.

REINVENTING THE WHEEL

Unveiled in 1996, the Mercedes-Benz F200 prototype (above) has a guidance system instead of a steering wheel. The controls would look more at home in an aircraft cockpit. But the concept seems a great leap backward – to the tiller.

SEEING THE FUTURE

Jaguar's new vision-enhancement display (left) shows science giving practical help to motorists. The car is fitted with an infra-red camera which transmits holographic images to the windscreen so that the driver can see better at night and in bad weather.

ELECTRONIC MAPS

Computerised car navigation systems already exist. Soon they will be commonplace – the motor industry's contribution to its customers' marital harmony.

Air Chief Marshal Sir John Rogers had recently retired after a distinguished career in the RAF. Starting as an apprentice electronics engineer, he had risen to become Controller Aircraft at the Ministry of Defence, in charge of procuring air systems for all three services. When not engaged in these high-flying activities, Rogers pursued his life-long hobby of buying, restoring and racing vintage and veteran motor cars. He had started at Cranwell with an M-type MG and a chugging Morris Cunard. The latter was 'a deservedly rare model', he remarks. 'You were lucky to get more than 50mph with the hood up.' Among the other cars in his life were (or are) a 1933 Le Mans Aston Martin, a 1930 twin-cam Alfa Romeo ('villainous Italian carburettor, an ignition prone to sudden and unpredictable bouts of condensation, but super roadholding'), a 1904 Darracq and a 1923 Rolls-Royce. But although knowledgeable about motoring history as well as mechanically adept, Rogers is no mere old car buff: he believes that automobiles are meant to be driven. He himself has long held an RAC competitions licence and over the years has participated at club level in most types of motor sport.

In 1988 Rogers took part in the Brighton Run, at the end of which Jeffrey Rose invited him to become Executive Chairman of the RAC Motor Sports Association. Rogers agreed and started in January 1989. Soft-spoken yet hard-headed, he made an immediate impact. He took a grip on safety. The RAC tightened up crowd control and improved its co-ordination of rescue vehicles, including helicopter ambulances. It also drew up a 'comprehensive disaster plan' for Silverstone, which fortunately has never had to be implemented. Rogers put the MSA on a businesslike footing, as well as giving it the direction and leadership that was needed. He separated the government of the sport from its commercial and promotional activities. And at the end of 1989 he recruited John Quenby as his second in command to run everyday operations.

The RAC Motor Sports Association governs the conduct of every sprint, hill-climb, rally and race in the United Kingdom, up to and including the British Grand Prix. It deals with entries, deploys an army of volunteer marshals, administers the rules drawn up by the Motor Sports Council, appoints technical scrutineers, oversees the timekeeping (by means of an electronic beam which measures hundredths of a second) and supervises the judging. Controversy envelops motor racing like spray thrown up by tyres on wet tarmac. So the RAC Stewards are kept busy and it is important that their verdicts are respected. The appointment of such eminent legal figures as Lord Shawcross and, currently, Lord Rawlinson of Ewell to the chairmanship of the appeals tribunal has done much to achieve this end as well as to sustain the RAC's own authority. The Club, to repeat the point, governs motor sport by consent: its only statutory power is to act as the agent of the Department of Transport for the movement of rally vehicles on the public highway. For this reason the RAC needs all the prestige it can muster, especially when issuing permits to its affiliated clubs for some 4,000 competitive events and 350 rallies on public roads annually, as well as 30,000 individual competition licences. Although the licence-holders need the RAC's sanction (not least for insurance purposes), they are not always cheerful givers of the fees which make up nearly half of the Motor Sport Association's £4 million revenue. As Rogers remarks: 'If there's a surly silence you reckon you're doing well. If they gather outside with axes it's – less good.'

Like other activities in which the RAC is involved, motor sport is driven, in more senses than one, by new technology. Sometimes this has been to the detriment of the spectacle, which

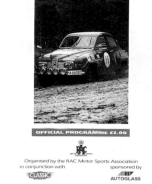

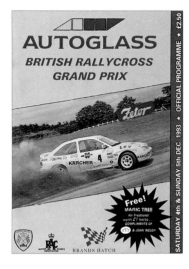

TOP OF THE RANGE

These programme covers illustrate the broad range of work done by the RAC Motor Sports Association. They also show what a colossal task it is for the governing body of British motor sport to keep in touch with the rank and file. Government by consent is a delicate matter, especially when so many enthusiasts, to say nothing of commercial interests, are involved.

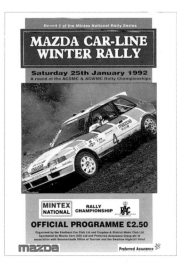

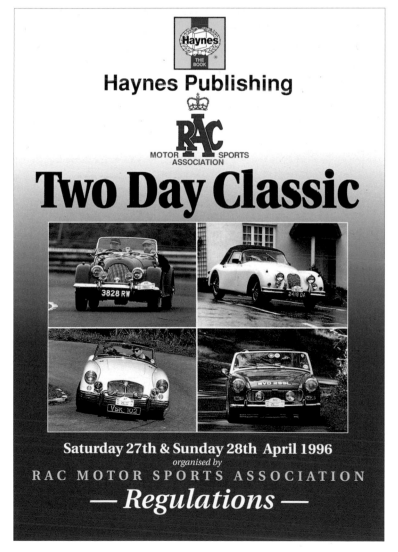

the MSA has at heart. Thus enhanced aerodynamics (now limited) and traction control (now stopped) threatened to change the nature of Formula One races, making overtaking so difficult that competitions were liable to become processions. Similarly rallies are now dominated by a small number of works-supported teams in high-performance cars, while the remaining contestants generally drive lower-powered vehicles which have little or no chance of winning except in their own class. The MSA has recently sponsored a project called 'Racing Ahead' which seeks to provide more races, an improved spectacle and better value for both competitors and onlookers. The Club certainly aims to put on a good show in its own events, such as the RAC Rally, the Classic Car Run and the Veterans' outing from London to Brighton, one hundred years old in 1996. The RAC's virtuosity in mounting such extravaganzas was well displayed when (with French partners) it arranged the Eurotunnel Inaugural Rally in May 1994.

A brilliant cavalcade of vehicles, representing every year of motoring history since 1894, journeyed from Hyde Park to the Champs-Élysées via Le Shuttle. The Chairman himself travelled in the original 1907 Rolls-Royce Silver Ghost, which took the lead. He acted as co-driver to Prince Michael of Kent, who has had a passion for motoring since his childhood – he drove a jeep at the age of seven, had driven over a hundred vehicles by the time he was ten and did much rallying subsequently. It was understandable, therefore, that he should have become President of the RAC when Lord Mountbatten was killed by an IRA bomb in 1979 and that he should have brought such energy and enthusiasm to the task.

As it happened the ground-breaking Eurotunnel odyssey coincided with a challenge to the RAC in the field of motor sport. The AA, which had previously taken no interest in it, now moved into the sponsorship of specific events, plainly recognising this as 'a route to the market'. But the Club's old rival will have to work hard to match the RAC's long-nurtured expertise, which is acknowledged all over the world. On RAC advice during the early 1970s, for example, Japanese motor sport was organised on the British model. More recently the Club's status has been enhanced by the work of Rogers and Quenby, both of whom sit on important committees of the FIA. In 1995, in an endeavour to capitalise on its overseas reputation and on the pre-eminence of the United Kingdom's billion-pound motor sport industry, the MSA set up a unique consultancy. Under the chairmanship of Brian McGivern, RAC International Motor Sports Ltd aims to export 'know-how' about everything from designing circuits to training race officials, from noise control to safety planning. Though they look like mobile billboards, British Formula One cars are in fact safer than ever and progress has been made in matters such as banning obnoxious fuels. Green racing is set to supersede racing green.

In equally good shape are the RAC's clubhouses at Pall Mall and Woodcote Park. The former, as Anthony Sampson said, during the early 1980s resembled the waiting-room at a railway station, while the latter still bore the scars of its long neglect. But between 1980 and 1990, under the direction of Brian McGivern, the perennially youthful Chairman of the clubhouses, £14.2 million was spent on repairs and improvements. About a third of this sum went on Woodcote, which was thoroughly refurbished and equipped with a lavish sports complex, including an indoor swimming pool as well as squash and tennis courts. Not everyone at Woodcote approved of the development, which marginally impinged on the 'Coronation' golf course. Golfers at Woodcote have often tended to regard the place as their club rather than the

MASTERS OF THE ROLLS

*Prince Michael of Kent, President of the RAC, and
Chairman Jeffrey Rose are pictured with the original
Rolls-Royce Silver Ghost, probably the most valuable car
in the world, which they drove from London to Paris on the
Eurotunnel Inaugural Rally in 1994. It illustrated the
RAC's abiding capacity to organise such glamorous events.
But it was, as Rose observed, an automotive pageant the
like of which will seldom if ever be seen again.*

country club of the RAC. In 1987 a number of them, led by Michael Breckon and David Wade (the golf captain), tried to get the planning application rejected. However, the vast majority of members supported Rose, McGivern and the Committee. Breckon and Wade were expelled from the Club and in a subsequent court action the RAC won its case with costs.

At Pall Mall a huge programme of renovation began. It could be carried out with confidence because in 1982 Jeffrey Rose, assisted by Maurice Grainger, the able, abrasive and charismatic Club Surveyor, had brought off an intricate and essential property deal. It involved the construction of new offices within the existing listed front and rear façades of 83/85 Pall Mall (formerly headquarters of the Associate section) next door to the Club. This was done with the co-operation of the Crown Commissioners, who then granted a new lease which the RAC sold to the developers. The Club retained half the basement area, which was converted to become the new Long Bar, buffet and billiards room. Most of the proceeds of the sale were used to buy a new ninety-nine-year lease for the clubhouse itself, giving it security of tenure until 2081 on payment of a peppercorn rent. This turned out to be £1,000 a year and when Rose gently remonstrated, the Crown Commissioners' surveyor replied with a chuckle: 'That is a peppercorn nowadays.'

Much of the renewal at Pall Mall occurred in the bowels of the building. Workmen installed new sewage ejectors and smoke detectors, 240-volt wiring and copper (instead of lead) piping, boilers and central heating. Improvements of this sort continued into the 1990s, with the introduction of up-to-date telephone and computer systems. There was also a carefully phased modernisation of everything from the Turkish bath in the basement to the top-floor bedrooms, most of which were provided with en suite bathrooms. Moreover, all the bedrooms are now available for letting since the last member to reside in the clubhouse died in 1995. He was Allen Brereton, who moved in just after the war, haunted the Club late at night like the Phantom of the Opera, and became still more eccentric in his final years. He lived off tinned goods supplied by Harrod's and heated up in the kettle in his bedroom, supplemented in due course by 'meals on wheels' delivered by the social services. Latterly he ceased to dress and could sometimes be glimpsed flitting along a top corridor wearing only a towel or vest and pants. Recently, too, the office accommodation has been transformed and the main public rooms have been beautifully redecorated. There have been threats from below, in the shape of the Jubilee line, and from above: a hole in the roof cost the RAC £1.25 million. Yet the clubhouse is more palatial than at any time in its history. In terms of service and amenities it resembles a five-star hotel. Moreover, since the handsome profits are ploughed back into the business, the improvements seem set to continue. What was once a disastrous downward spiral has become, thanks largely to McGivern, a triumphant upward spiral.

Particularly distinguished is the Great Gallery restaurant, which provides ample evidence that club catering need not resemble that of Spartan English boarding schools (though it often does). Presided over by the imposing figure of Hans Jahns, and supplied by the talented head chef Philip Corrick and his fifty-strong staff, it might well earn one or even two rosettes in the Michelin Guide, if clubs were included. This all results from teamwork. But Jeffrey Rose, who lists 'dining' as one of his hobbies in *Who's Who*, is at least partly responsible for the excellence of the food. His taste also extends to art. He has encouraged the work of the Paintings

WOODCOTE RISING

From about 1980 Woodcote Park (top) underwent a series of dramatic improvements. The Lounge Bar (centre right) was refurbished several years ago and in 1996 work started on the Cedar Restaurant (centre left). Woodcote is no longer the poor relation of Pall Mall.

KEEPING FIT

For devotees golf is the raison d'être – even the religion – of Woodcote Park. But the elaborate sports complex, with its swimming pool, tennis courts and other amenities, attracts many members, not least because of its unique pair of doubles squash courts.

Committee, consisting of Tim Keown and Ronald Gordon, which has seen to the restoration of nearly all the Club's existing pictures and bought new ones. The Chairman's most notable contribution to the aesthetic side of the clubhouse was the purchase of a painting entitled *La Fête des Paysans* by the nineteenth-century Belgian artist Théodore Gerard in 1994. Rose spotted it at Christie's, correctly estimated that it would fit a blank panel at the eastern end of the Great Gallery and acquired it for £25,000. Admirably lit from the minstrels' gallery, it adds a rich sense of conviviality to the restaurant and is much admired. But at least one member took a dim view of it, complaining that the scene of 'bucolic debauchery ... reflects neither the grandeur of the surroundings nor the sophistication' of the gastronomy. Rose disagrees.

BETTER THAN NEW

At the Pall Mall clubhouse the bad old days of the 1970s are fading into history and members have come to expect the highest standards of elegance, comfort and catering. But as these photographs of the vestibule, the Great Gallery and the swimming pool show, the Club is more palatial now than it was even in Edwardian times.

The tone of the Club has changed since the days of its raffish youth, when members were pleasure-loving patricians, automobile adventurers, novelty-seeking non-conformists, sporting and business pioneers. But something of that atmosphere remains. The clubhouses are alive with activity – squash, snooker, bridge, chess and so on – each supervised by its own subcommittee. Unabashed hedonists still join the Pall Mall Club because of its lavish facilities. Charles Ogden, for example, *Time*'s bureau chief in London, conducted a rigorous investigation of rival establishments. He rejected the Reform because it was 'too gloomy', the Travellers' because it was deserted at midday, the Oxford & Cambridge because it did not provide towels after squash and the Naval & Military because its squash courts were ill-lit – 'I asked for a miner's lamp.' But when he visited the RAC with its 'glorious pool', beside which the other club swimming-baths seemed 'about the size of three bidet bowls', Ogden could only exclaim: 'Eureka!' As in the past, the RAC continues to attract its share of adventurers, ranging from the late Sir Fitzroy Maclean to Colonel John Blashford-Snell. 'Blashers' seems to embody the springtime spirit of the Club, as illustrated in the account of his expedition to Outer Mongolia which he wrote for *Pell-Mell & Woodcote*. When a piston broke in his battered Russian 'Gaz' jeep, he drove across 150 miles of mountainous terrain with 'fumes pouring into the cab and loud back-firings keeping the wolves at bay!... Every few miles we had to burn off the spark plugs on a yak dung fire. Temperatures were freezing and on a diet of boiled mutton, soggy rice and fermented mares' milk, it was no picnic.' Tame though they may be by comparison, the Club's sartorial dissidents also represent a maverick strain. They assert that its fuddy-duddy standards of propriety make the Club 'the laughing-stock of the capital'. Some revolt against the 'tyranny of the tie'. Others insist that taking off their jackets during a heat wave would not lead to 'an orgy in the foyer (though it might liven the place up)'.

In general, though, Brian McGivern, champion of the traditional dress code and guardian of gentlemanly modes of decorum, finds support among the members. They are more respectable – or, at any rate, more orthodox – than the founding fathers of the Club. Typically members today are successful professional men, in their forties, living in London. Many care little about cars; some hardly associate the Club with the motoring organisation; a few belong to the AA. But they have become a more homogeneous body since 1986. Then corporate membership was phased out and the Elections Committee strove harder to realise the ideal,

enunciated by its Chairman, Tim Keown, that members should be 'friends of friends of friends'. According to John Hopkins, for years an editor of *Pell-Mell & Woodcote*, the Club is healthier than it was when boisterous members bombarded each other with bread rolls, but less fun. Others acknowledge that members are now 'a little too serious, too correct, too pompous'.

Yet it is understandable that they should take seemly pride in an institution which has reached such a vigorous maturity. Since the watershed crisis of the late 1970s, indeed, members have been more inclined to cherish its heritage. The psychiatrist Dr Anthony Fry, for example, joined the Club because it offered him 'the style and peace of another age'. The RAC's centenary, toasted with fine wines which the Club began buying for the event as early as 1984, will therefore be a celebration of survival. Many of the overseas automobile clubs founded at about the same time as Frederick Simms and his friends created what became the RAC, have fallen by the wayside and more have lost some of their original functions. Virtually alone, the RAC still carries on the triple role of major national motoring organisation, governing body of motor sport and social club. It is a rich inheritance, which gives the RAC confidence in a future in which the opportunities are expected to match the challenges. So, too, do the extraordinary technological advances of the last few years. They encourage hopes that the centenary will (in the idiom of the managerial minute) 're-inforce RAC group strength' by projecting its 'progressive/modern image'. That image will be most graphically expressed in a panorama of the present depicted on the bare walls of the first-floor rotunda of the Pall Mall clubhouse. The Chinese artist Mao Wen Biao, whose striking mural at the Holland Park Orangery attracted him to Jeffrey Rose's attention, has been commissioned to paint scenes of the RAC's life and work at the time of its hundredth birthday. It is an exciting moment in the Club's history: the end of the motoring century, with its remarkable record of achievement; and the beginning of what promises to be a motoring millennium full of bright prospects for the RAC.

LOOKING FORWARD

*Solidly facing the future, the RAC
remains a monument to the self-confidence
of its founders and to the vitality of the
motoring movement.*

1997 The Centenary

MANUSCRIPT SOURCES

RAC ARCHIVES (RAC)

The essential source for this book is the RAC's own archive, lodged at Pall Mall and Woodcote Park. This consists of an immense collection of documents, holograph letters, business correspondence, personal memoranda, minutes of myriad committees, annual reports, financial accounts, motor racing and rallying records, trial and technical dossiers, press cuttings, scrap books, photograph albums, news letters, pamphlets, exhibition programmes, conference bulletins, route guides, suggestions books, dinner menus, film and slide material, memorabilia and ephemera of all sorts. Particularly valuable for the purposes of this book were the two large files of Frederick Simms's Papers and other documents relating to the founding of the Club, as well as the microfilmed minutes of the RAC Committee over the past hundred years. The Library at Pall Mall also contains a full run of the Club *Journal* plus other annual and occasional RAC publications, as well as a priceless collection of motoring magazines, notably *Autocar* and *Motor*.

OTHER SOURCES

RAC MOTOR SPORTS PAPERS

A vital collection of documents, known as 'the crown jewels', relating to the Club's crisis of the 1970s.

BRITISH LIBRARY

Northcliffe Papers: interesting correspondence on Club and automobile matters with Claude Johnson, Lord Montagu, Arthur Stanley and motoring journalists.

BEAULIEU ARCHIVES

A valuable collection, including Lord Montagu's manuscript diary and the uninhibited correspondence of Montague Grahame-White.

SOUTHAMPTON UNIVERSITY LIBRARY

Several useful files of Lord Mountbatten's Papers relating to his long presidency of the RAC.

VETERAN CAR CLUB OF GREAT BRITAIN ARCHIVE, Ashwell

A miscellaneous collection of the Papers of Frederick Simms.

CHURCHILL ARCHIVES CENTRE, Cambridge

A few letters and documents relating to Winston Churchill, the RAC and automobiles.

LORD ILIFFE PAPERS

Manuscript Memoirs of Edward Mauger, Lord Iliffe of Yattenden.

NOTES

THE TYPESCRIPT of this book contains some 1,750 footnotes. Obviously a volume intended primarily for the general reader should not be burdened by such a weight of reference; so the printed notes have been drastically pruned. In particular, many of the references to internal Club documents and to motoring journals have been omitted. Enough remains to indicate the literature on which the book rests and to suggest lines of further research. Scholars who wish to examine the fully annotated typescript, which is lodged at Pall Mall, should apply to the RAC's Librarian.

The numbers preceding the notes indicate the page number and the line on which the annotated passage begins. The place of publication is London unless otherwise stated.

CHAPTER ONE:

HORSELESS CARRIAGES

13/23   C. Jarrott, *Ten Years of Motoring and Motor Racing* (1956), 1

14/3   C. G. Harper, *The Brighton Road* (1922), 54.

14/4   *P[all] M[all] G[azette]*, 14 Nov. 1896.

14/6   *Automotor [and Horseless Vehicle Journal]* I (17 Nov. 1896), 67.

14/8   *[The] Autocar* I (14 Nov. 1896), 649.

14/42   *Daily Mail*, 16 Nov. 1896.

16/15   *To-Day* (21 Nov. 1897), 82.

18/2   T. Barker, *The Economic and Social Effects of the Spread of Motor Vehicles* (Basingstoke, 1987), 33.

18/11   *Autocar* LXXV (22 Nov. 1935), 990.

18/25   *Times*, 16 Nov. 1896.

18/37   *RAC World*, Dec. 1982.

20/10   St J. C. Nixon, *Romance Amongst Cars* (n.d., 1938), 6 and 12.

20/17   *[Royal Automobile Club] Journal* X (14 Dec. 1905), 606. This journal was first called *Automobile Club Notes & Notices*, then (until the grant of a royal title to the Club in 1907) *Automobile Club Journal*. It will here be abbreviated to *Journal*.

20/18   S. F. Edge, *My Motoring Reminiscences* (1972 edn.), 260.

20/30   V[eteran] C[ar] C[lub of Great Britain Archives, Ashwell], J. T. Norman to Simms, 31 Jan. 1893.

20/33   E. Johnson, *The Dawn of Motoring* (1986), 29.

22/2   *Motor* LXXVII (8 May 1940), 362.

22/4   A. Bird, *The Motor Car 1765-1914* (1960), 65.

22/14   T. R. Nicholson, *The Birth of the British Motor Car 1769-1897* III (1982), 357 and 383.

22/18   *Windsor & Eton Express*, 27 July 1895.

22/35   H. O. Duncan, *The World on Wheels* (Paris, 1926), 682.

22/39   *Journal* XII (30 Aug. 1906), 212.

24/22   *Kent and Sussex Courier*, 4 Oct. 1895.

24/31   *Motor* LXXX (15 Oct. 1941), 190.

24/37   Beaulieu, M. G[rahame]-W[hite] P[apers], E. N. Duffield to M. Grahame White, 26 July 1955.

24/40   [RAC], Simms Papers, 5 Oct. 1895.

26/10   Nicholson, *Motor Car* III, 387.

26/11   H. Barty-King, *The AA: A History of the First 75 Years of the Automobile Association* (Basingstoke, 1980), 24.

26/19   The RAC concluded before publication, on the advice of Captain A. W. Phillips, that Nixon's book 'could not be regarded as a serious and complete history of the Club'. [RAC] Executive Committee Minutes, 16 Feb. 1938.

26/24   E. N. Duffield in G WP, Beaulieu.

26/26   *Daily Graphic*, 5 May 1896. Sir David Salomons kept scrapbooks of such revealing press cuttings, which are still extant at Broomhill.

26/34   *Motor* XLIX (20 Apr. 1926), 536.

26/42   Simms Papers II, 91.

28/15   B[ritish] L[ibrary], Add. MSS 62165B, N[orthcliffe] P[apers], Northcliffe to Montagu, 12 May 1921.

28/18   Harper, *Brighton Road*, 54.

28/24   *Times*, 16 Nov. 1896.

28/30   *Automotor* I, 109.

28/36   Simms Papers II, 91.

30/7   E. T. Hooley, *Hooley's Confessions* (n.d., 1924), 250.

30/13   *Automotor* I (17 Nov. 1896), 43.

30/20   S. C. H. Davis, *Memories of Men & Motor Cars* (1965), 1.

30/42   *Automotor* I (18 Aug. 1897), 472.
32/2   *Journal* XI (22 Feb. 1906), 211. The phrase was Claude Johnson's.
32/2   *Journal* VI (10 Dec. 1903), 589.
32/4   *Autocar* II (31 July 1897), 488.
32/7   Simms Papers.
32/9   Simms Papers, W. Leonard to Simms, 11 Aug. 1897.
32/39   *Autocar* IL (8 Dec. 1922), 1213.
34/9   Simms Papers.
34/25   Simms Papers.
36/5   Duncan, *World*, 657.
36/6   E. Diesel, G. Goldbeck and F. Schildberger, *From Engines to Autos* (Chicago, 1960), 257.
36/10   *Journal* XXVII (27 Mar. 1914), 257.
36/20   F. R. Simms, 'How I Founded the Automobile Club' (1911).
36/25   Simms Papers.
36/33   Simms Papers, draft of letter to *Autocar*, autumn 1897.
38/4   Simms Papers.
38/20   *Automotor* II (15 Dec. 1897), 83.
38/30   *Autocar* IL (8 Dec. 1922), 1207.

CHAPTER TWO:

MOTORING ON THE MAP

39/5   R. Pound, 'High Life before 1914' in J. Canning (ed.), *Living History* (1967), 198. The expression was John Buchan's.
39/9   Private information: Harry Stanley.
39/12   [RAC] Committee Minutes (13 Feb. 1899).
39/19   Beaulieu, G-WP, Duffield to Grahame-White, 26 July 1955.
40/12   Duncan, *Wheels*, 885.
40/28   *The Autobiography of Bertrand Russell 1872-1914* (1967), 26.
40/29   *PMG*, 24 Nov. 1896.
40/39   *Daily Telegraph*, 16 Jan. 1906.
42/2   P. Brendon, *Head of Guinness* (1979), 78.
42/5   'Memoirs of Lord Iliffe of Yattenden', 17. I am grateful to the present Lord Iliffe for allowing me to read and quote from his father's memoir.
42/8   R. Pound and G. Harmsworth, *Northcliffe* (1959), 257.
42/14   BL Add. MSS 62165B, NP, Northcliffe to Montagu, 12 May 1921.
42/23   A. J. M. Gray, 'The Work of the Motor World' in *[The] World's Work* XVI (Nov. 1910), 637.

42/32   M. Pemberton, *The Amateur Motorist* (1907), 203.
44/8   *D[ictionary of] N[ational] B[iography]*.
44/9   *Autocar* XIX (17 Aug. 1907), 489.
44/18   W. Boddy, *The History of Brooklands Motor Course* (1957), 8.
44/37   E. Jepson, *Memories of an Edwardian* (1937), 92.
44/39   F. H. Butler, *Fifty Years of Travel by Land, Water and Air* (1920), 99.
44/42   R. E. Crompton, *Reminiscences* (1928), 195.
46/9   *Autocar* XXXVII (4 Nov. 1916), 475.
46/16   M. Pemberton, *The Life of Sir Henry Royce* (1935), 71.
46/24   *Journal* XXI (23 June 1911), 532.
46/30   W. J. Oldham, *The Hyphen in Rolls-Royce* (1967), xix.
46/41   P. Tritton, *John Montagu of Beaulieu 1866-1929* (1985), 141.
48/5   BL Add. MSS 62279A, NP, Northcliffe to Johnson, 12 Jan. 1912.
48/6   BL Add. MSS 62279A, NP, Johnson to Northcliffe, 7 Jan. 1913.
48/15   E. S. Shrapnell-Smith, 'Five Decades of Commercial Road Transport ...' in *Journal of Institute of Transport* XXII (Feb.-Mar. 1946), 215.
48/41   *Archive[: Bulletin of the RAC Historical Committee]* IV (Winter 1987/88), 4.
50/1   M. Grahame-White, *At the Wheel Ashore and Afloat* (n.d., 1935), 220.
50/4   Nixon, *Romance*, 73.
50/27   *Archive* IV (Winter, 1987/88), 5.
50/29   A. B. Filson Young, *The Complete Motorist* (1904), xxiii.
52/6   R. Kipling, 'Steam Tactics' in *Windsor Magazine* (Dec. 1902), 14.
52/22   *Journal* VI (10 Dec. 1903), 598.
52/26   L. A. Everett, *The Shape of the Motor Car* (1958), 43.
52/39   G. Rose, *A Record of Motor-Racing* (1909), 18.
54/6   T. Hardy, *The Woodlanders* (1964 edn.), 7-8.
54/13   *Journal* IX (23 Feb. 1905), 142.
54/14   A. Griffiths, 'A New Carriage on an Old Road' in *Blackwood's Edinburgh Magazine* CLXVI (Nov. 1899), 658.
54/16   *Journal* VI (10 Dec. 1903), 597.
54/30   Shrapnell-Smith in *Journal of Institute of Transport* (Feb.-Mar. 1946), 217.
54/30   C. Petrie, *Scenes of Edwardian Life* (1965), 91.
54/32   C. W. Morton, *A History of Rolls-Royce Motor Cars I 1903-7* (1964), 80
54/36   *Eastbourne Chronicle*, 19 Nov. 1898.
56/1   Simms Papers II, 69.
56/8   *Autocar* IV (24 June 1899), 542-3.
56/38   J. J. Hissey, *An English Holiday with Car and Camera* (1908), 337.
58/2   Young, *Complete Motorist*, 316-317.

58/11   C. F. Smith, *The History of the Royal Irish Automobile Club 1901-91* (Dublin, 1994), 4.

58/22   *Motor Car Journal* (24 Nov. 1899), 595.

58/26   Edge, *Reminiscences*, 8.

60/13   *Journal*, 22 Nov. 1899.

62/3   Committee Minutes (2 Oct. 1899), 109.

62/12   BL Add. MSS 62165B, NP, Northcliffe to Montagu, 12 May 1921.

62/15   VCC, Johnson to Simms, 11 Oct. 1899.

62/18   *Journal*, 3 Jan. 1900.

62/22   Committee Minutes, 2 Oct. 1899).

62/33   *Journal* XIII (21 Feb. 1907), 178.

62/39   Lord Brabazon of Tara, *The Brabazon Story* (1956), 1.

62/41   'Memoirs of Lord Iliffe', 46.

64/6   *Journal* XIX (5 May 1910), 298.

64/16   *Journal* XIII (21 Feb. 1907), 178.

64/24   *Autocar* CXXXVII (7 Dec. 1972), 20.

64/28   *Automotor* IV (17 May 1900), 416.

64/35   *Journal* XIX (28 Apr. 1910), 286.

66/2   I. Ehrenburg, *The Life of the Automobile* (New York, 1976 edn.), 12.

66/23   F. M. L. Thompson, 'Nineteenth Century Horse Sense' in *Economic History Review* 29 (1976), 62.

68/2   *Journal* VIII (15 Dec. 1904), 463 and 466.

68/5   Churchill [Archives Centre, Cambridge], CHAR 2/18/107-109, Montagu to Churchill, 30 Nov. 1904.

68/11   Grahame White, *At the Wheel*, 227.

68/13   *Automotor* IV (17 May 1900), 408.

68/23   *Autocar* XXXV (13 Nov. 1915), 612.

CHAPTER THREE:

THE PARLIAMENT OF MOTORING

69/5   *Times*, 18 May 1900.

69/13   R. Kipling, *Something of Myself* (1937), 178.

69/17   T. Pinney (ed.), *The Letters of Rudyard Kipling* III (1996), 69 and 60-61.

69/21   Young, *Complete Motorist*, 286.

70/1   *Journal* IX (27 Apr. 1905), 363.

70/5   *Automotor* II (15 Feb. 1898), 195.

70/16   Crompton, *Reminiscences*, 6.

70/25   N. Streatfield (ed.), *The Day Before Yesterday* (1956), 126.

70/26   *Journal* IX (5 Jan. 1905), 3 and II (3 Dec. 1901), 465.

70/28   *Journal* IX (27 Apr. 1905), 363.

70/35   *Daily Graphic*, 5 May 1896.

72/7   F. M. L. Thompson, *Horses in European Economic History* (1983), 101.

72/15   *Journal* II (2 Jan. 1901), 163.

72/17   H. G. Wells, *Anticipations* (1914), 25.

72/23   J. Pettifer and N. Turner, *Automania* (1984), 83.

72/27   Hissey, *English Holiday*, 80

72/40   R. Jefferies, *Hodge and His Masters* (1966 edn.), 6 and 162.

72/41   *Journal* XII (12 July 1906), 26, quoting the *Daily News*.

74/18   *Field*, 29 Dec. 1900.

74/27   D. Cannadine, *Aspects of Aristocracy* (1994), 62.

74/29   J. R. Kellett, *The Impact of Railways on Victorian Cities* (1969), 91.

76/1   *Autocar*, XI (29 Aug. 1903), 264.

76/7   *Fielden's Magazine*, Feb. 1900.

76/15   Young, *Complete Motorist*, 288.

76/16   G. Bourne, *Change in the Village* (1955 edn.), 121.

76/17   *Journal* II (6 June 1901), 340, quoting the AGM of the County Council's Association.

76/20   J. Pannell, 'Motors and Cycles: The Transition Stage' in *Contemporary Review* 81 (Feb., 1902), 185.

76/38   Committee Minutes, 18 June 1902.

78/6   *Journal* II (6 Mar. 1901), 221.

78/8   *Journal* IX (23 Feb. 1905), 148.

78/17   W. J. Crampton, 'An Important Inauguration' (27 Aug. 1902), typescript in the possession of John Crampton who kindly gave me a copy.

78/31   W. J. Bentley, *Motoring Cavalcade* (1953), 35.

78/33   *Journal* IV (25 Sep. 1902), 189, quoting *Weekly Dispatch*.

80/17   Executive Committee Minutes, 19 Mar. 1902.

80/25   *Journal* IV (27 Nov. 1902), 351.

80/30   H. O. Tyman, 'Motoring London' in G. Sims (ed.), *Living London* III (1903), 190.

80/36   *Journal* XV (9 Jan. 1908), 25

82/1   Simms Papers II, 73.

82/17   G. Lowes Dickinson, 'Motoring' in *[The] Independent Review* I (Jan. 1904), 580.

82/23   *Times*, 19 May 1902.

82/37   *Autocar* XV (1 July 1905), 17.

82/41   *Journal* II (2 Jan. 1901), 163.

84/15   *Journal* VI (13 Aug. 1903), 172.

84/16   *Times*, 26 June 1903.

84/27   W. Plowden, *The Motor Car and Politics 1896-1970* (1971), 51.

86/5   *Journal* III (5 June 1902), 229.

86/7   Barty-King, *AA*, 40.

86/12   *Hansard* VIII (1902), 762.

86/15   *The Scotsman*, 30 Apr. 1903. I am grateful to the present Mr Kenneth Balfour for providing this anecdote.

86/19   Executive Committee Minutes, 15 Dec. 1902.

86/32   G. Cornwallis-West, *Edwardian Hey-Days* (1930), 233.

86/36   *Autocar*, XI (29 Aug. 1903), 264.
86/40   *Journal* IX (27 Nov. 1902), 10, quoting M.A.P.
88/11   *Autocar* XII (27 Feb. 1904), 293.
88/27   Publications Committee Minutes, 11 Jan. 1905.
88/36   *Journal* VI (12 Nov. 1902), 492.
88/37   *Motoring Illustrated*, 31 Oct. 1903.
88/40   *Journal* VI (27 Aug. 1903), 251, quoting Motor.
90/6   Smith, *Irish Automobile Club*, 25.
90/20   VCC, Simms to Johnson, 1 Nov. 1901.
90/30   *Journal* IV (27 Nov. 1902), 10.
90/35   *Journal* V (5 Mar. 1903), 228.
92/6   *Journal* IV (7 Aug. 1902), 39.
92/13   P. Brendon, *The Life and Death of the Press Barons* (1982), 34.
92/22   *Journal* V (22 Jan. 1902), 78.
94/17   Committee Minutes, 8 June 1903.
94/27   Edge, *Reminiscences*, 141.
94/32   Committee Minutes, 8 June 1903.
96/8   *Journal* VI (9 July 1903), 35.
96/14   *Journal* VI (9 July 1903), 36.
96/21   B. Lynch, *Green Dust: Ireland's Unique Motor Racing History 1900-1939* (Dublin, 1988), 25.
96/33   *Journal* VI (9 July 1903), 25.
96/36   *Motor Cycling*, 21 May 1902.
96/40   R. Jeffreys, *The King's Highway* (1949), 240.
98/10   *Automotor* VIII (11 July 1903), 716-17.

CHAPTER FOUR:
RAC & AA

99/7   *Journal* VII (28 June 1904), 72.
99/21   Jepson, *Memories*, 91.
100/10 *Journal* XXVII (15 May 1914), 393.
100/15 *Autocar* XXXVII (4 Nov. 1916), 501.
100/22 *The World*, 20 Nov. 1906.
100/26 *Journal* VIII (1 Dec. 1904), 408.
100/37 *Car* VIII (9 Mar. 1904), 70.
100/40 Beaulieu, Montagu's Diary, 4 Nov. 1903.
102/3   Tritton, *Montagu*, 100.
102/30 *Journal* VII (10 Mar 1904), 253.
102/34 *Car* VIII (9 Mar. 1904), 67.
104/1   *Journal* VII (17 Mar. 1904), 310.
104/5   *Journal* VII (5 May 1904), 510.
104/17 *Journal* VIII (18 Aug. 1904), 127.
104/22 *Daily Mail*, 1 Mar. 1905. The Inconsiderate Driving Committee was created some four months before the AA. It was not formed as a response to the AA, as H. Barty-King states (*AA*, 64); rather, the AA was a militant reaction against the moderation of the Automobile Club.
104/26 *Journal* X (10 Aug. 1905), 171.
104/31 *Journal* VII (5 May 1904), 509.
104/32 *Automotor* VIII (24 Oct. 1903), 1140.
106/5   *Journal* VIII (11 Aug. 1904), 115.
106/10 M. Maeterlinck, *The Double Garden* (1904), 140-141.
106/14 C. N. and A. M. Williamson, *The Car of Destiny* (1907), 4.
106/27 *Journal* IX (8 June 1905), 509.
108/10 *Journal* IX (11 May 1905), 392.
108/12 *Star*, 19 Apr. 1905.
108/14 G. Lowes Dickinson, 'The Motor Tyranny' in *Independent Review* XI (Oct. 1906), 15-16.
108/19 C. Emsley, '"Mother, What *Did* Policemen Do When There Weren't Any Motors?" The Law, the Police and the Regulation of Motor Traffic in England, 1900-1939' in *Historical Journal* 36 (1993), 367.
108/38 *Autocar* XV (16 Sep. 1905), 343.
110/14 *Autocar* XV (16 Sep. 1905), 344.
110/22 *Journal* X (8 Mar. 1906), 267.
110/33 Touring Committee Minutes, 29 May 1906.
110/40 *Journal* X (31 Aug. 1905), 245.
112/3   Beaulieu, Montagu's Diary, 15 February 1904.
112/10 Committee Minutes, 27 July 1910.
112/20 *Journal* XII (23 Aug. 1906), 175.
112/32 *Journal* XI (25 Jan. 1906), 72.
114/4   Pemberton, *Amateur Motorist*, 141.
114/11 D. Noble, *The Jubilee Book of the Royal Automobile Club 1897-1947* (1947), 20.
114/19 *Journal* VIII (6 Oct. 1904), 259.
114/30 *Journal* IX (5 Jan. 1905), 2.
114/39 Races Committee Minutes, 12 Oct. 1905.
116/10 *Motor* LXXVII (29 May 1940), 426.
116/12 R. Hough, *Tourist Trophy* (1957), 26.
116/33 Lord Montagu and D. Burgess-Wise, *Daimler Century* (1995), 98.
116/36 C. Wilson and W. Reader, *Men and Machines* (1958), 87.
116/38 Beaulieu, G-WP, Grahame-White to Lawton-Goodman, 1 Dec. 1944.
116/42 A. Bennett, *The Journals*, (Harmondsworth, 1984 edn.), 230.
118/7   L. Edel (ed.), *Henry James Letters* IV (1984), 442-5.
118/10 E. M. Forster, *Howard's End* (Harmondsworth, 1989 edn.), 36.
118/19 *[The] Motorist and Traveller* I (12 Apr. 1905), 395.
118/22 Harmsworth, *Motorists*, 29.
118/23 P. Roberts, *The Motoring Edwardians* (1978), 140.
118/25 *Motorist and Traveller* I (1 Mar. 1905), 158.
118/33 *Journal* X (19 Oct. 1905), 397.
118/41 D. Levitt, *The Woman and the Car* (1970 edn.), 28 and 30.
120/4   D. N. Pigache, *Café Royal Days* (1934), 43.

120/11 RAC, J. S. Critchley Papers, 27 Nov. 1897.

120/21 Noble, *Jubilee Book*, 42.

120/24 P. Magnus, *King Edward the Seventh* (Harmondsworth, 1967 edn.), 519.

120/26 C. W. Stamper, *What I Know* (1913), 65. The memoirs of Edward VII's personal motor engineer were ghost-written by Dornford Yates.

120/34 Beaulieu, Montagu's Diary, 16 July 1904.

122/5 *Journal* XIII (14 Mar. 1907), 291.

122/13 *Journal* XIII (21 Feb. 1907), 182.

122/25 *Westminster Gazette* (11 May 1909), 4.

122/30 *Journal* XVIII (8 July 1909), 18.

122/30 *P[ell] M[ell] & W[oodcote]* (Dec. 1991), 34.

122/40 *Journal* XIV (11 July 1907), 44.

124/1 Davis, *Memories*, 174.

124/13 He was the son of Claude Johnson's erstwhile companion, who was killed during a hill-climb at La Turbie in 1903.

124/25 *Car* XX (20 Feb. 1907), 18.

124/30 *Journal* XIV (21 Nov. 1907), 561.

126/15 [O. J. Llewellyn], *The Autocar-biography of Owen John* (n.d., 1927), 132.

126/18 *PM & W* (Dec. 1985), 32.

126/22 P. Green, *Kenneth Grahame* (1959), 203.

128/7 Relations Committee Minutes, 27 Nov. 1907.

128/11 *Autocar* XX (8 Feb. 1908), 198.

128/27 Earl Russell, *My Life and Adventures* (1923), 295.

128/31 D. Sutherland, *The Yellow Earl* (1965), 4 and 170.

128/31 Beaulieu, G-WP, Lawton-Goodman to Grahame-White, 29 Nov. 1944.

130/11 *Car* XXI (17 July 1907), 440.

130/17 *Motor* XVIII (27 Dec. 1910), 884.

130/21 *Car* XXIX (19 May 1909), 3.

130/24 *Motor* XVIII (27 Dec. 1910), 884.

CHAPTER FIVE:

A PALACE IN PALL MALL

131/13 [Llewellyn], *Autocar-biography*, 122. This protest, published in *Autocar*, may well have been a fraud, written by its mischievous columnist 'Owen John' himself.

131/17 *Journal* XXI (27 Jan. 1911), 66.

131/21 F. R. Cowell, *The Athenaeum: Club and Social Life in London 1824-1974* (1975), 143.

132/13 *Journal* XVI (23 July 1908), 78.

132/20 J. Pope-Hennessy, *Queen Mary* (1959), 105 and 323.

132/28 *Journal* XX (27 Oct. 1910), 265.

132/31 H. Montgomery-Massingberd and D. Watkin, *The London Ritz* (1989 edn.), 27.

132/39 *Journal* XIX (6 Jan. 1910), 5.

134/16 Private information: John Crampton.

134/17 *Journal* XIX (6 Jan. 1910), 6.

136/26 Noble, *Jubilee Book*, 45.

136/12 *Motor* XIX (11 Apr. 1911), 391.

136/18 *Journal* XXI (24 Mar. 1911), 220.

136/26 Private information: Robin Montgomerie-Charrington.

136/27 *Archive* 2 (Sep. 1985), 7.

136/41 P. Fleetwood-Hesketh, 'The Royal Automobile Club' in *Country Life* CL (14 Oct. 1971), 969.

138/17 *Motor* XIX (4 Apr. 1911), 325.

138/20 H. G. Wells, *The Labour Unrest* (1912), 13.

138/22 *Journal* XVI (24 Mar. 1911), 199.

138/23 *Journal* XIX (6 Jan. 1910), 6.

138/25 *Automotor* XII (21 Dec. 1907), 1816.

138/34 J. Halifax, 'The Royal Automobile Club' in *World's Work* XVI (July 1910), 195.

138/37 *Hansard*, 5th series 1933-34, Vol 288, c. 215.

140/4 *Journal* XVII (17 June 1909), 395.

140/11 *Journal* XX (17 Nov. 1910), 337. Cf. D. H. Laurence (ed.), *Bernard Shaw: Collected Letters 1898-1910* II (1972), 935 ff. During the late summer of 1910 Shaw was on a motoring holiday in Ireland, where he found many of the hotels 'revolting' and 'loathsome'. It seems almost certain that the *Journal* was quoting his words.

140/25 E. Wharton, *A Motor-Flight through France* (1908), 32.

140/31 *Journal* XVII (22 Apr. 1909), 255.

140/38 Halifax, *World's Work* XVI, 196.

142/18 *Journal* XVI (26 Nov. 1908), 520.

142/21 *Car* XXIX (19 May 1909), 3.

142/28 *Journal* XVII (6 May 1909), 293.

144/2 *Journal* XVII (27 May 1909), 344.

144/4 M. Thomas, *Out on a Wing* (1964), 236.

144/16 E. F. Carter, *Edwardian Cars* (1955), 87.

144/17 S. B. Saul, 'The Motor Industry in Britain to 1914' in *Business History* V (Dec. 1962), 40.

144/22 Lynch, *Green Dust*, 50.

146/1 D. Thoms and T. Donnelly, *The Motor Car Industry in Coventry since the 1890's* (1985), 63.

146/19 *Westminster Gazette* (20 May 1909), 4.

146/33 Morton, *History of Rolls-Royce*, 223.

146/37 Bird, *Motor Car*, 242.

148/2 *Journal* XXII (13 Oct. 1911), 263.

148/6 Beaulieu, G-WP, Duffield to Grahame-White, 27 Aug. 1955.

148/17 *Journal* XVIII (18 Nov. 1909), 343.

148/28 *Archive* 6 (June 1993), 3.

148/40 Tritton, *Montagu*, 9.

150/16 *Times*, 18 Nov. 1912.

150/24 *Journal* XVIII (23 Dec. 1909), 440.

150/32 *Journal* XVIII (23 Sep. 1909), 211.

152/1 *Motor* XVIII (20 Sep. 1910), 246.

152/2 *Standard*, 1 Apr. 1913.

152/5 Committee Minutes, 15 Jan. 1913.

152/8 Pannell in *Contemporary Review* 81, 192.

152/11 P. Brendon and P. Whitehead, *The Windsors* (1994), 13.

152/31 Committee Minutes, 24 Nov. 1911.

152/39 *Journal* XIX (5 May 1910), 295.

154/5 *Journal* XX (26 Aug. 1910), 70.

154/9 *Journal* XX (8 Dec. 1910), 385.

154/28 *Journal* XXIII (7 June 1912), 584.

154/30 *Motor* XXI (27 Feb. 1912), 158.

154/37 *Autocar* XXVIII (24 Feb. 1912), 403.

156/9 *Journal* XXIV (12 July 1912), 43.

156/14 *Journal* XXIII (15 Mar. 1912), 271.

156/29 *Autocar* XXVIII (23 Mar. 1912), 543.

156/34 *Autocar* XXVIII (9 Mar. 1912), 455.

156/35 Committee Minutes, 15 July 1908.

156/35 Pemberton, *Amateur Motorist*, 308.

156/38 A. Service, *The Architects of London* (1979), 167.

158/11 Viscount Grey of Falloden, *Twenty-Five Years 1892-1916* I (1925), 238.

158/14 D. Gilmour, *Curzon* (1994), 464.

160/4 A. Lejeune, *The Gentlemen's Clubs of London* (1979), 29.

160/26 *Journal* XIX (10 Feb. 1910), 95.

CHAPTER SIX:

PEACE AND WAR

161/17 *Journal* XI (22 Feb. 1906), 207.

161/21 *Journal* XIX (17 Feb. 1910), 112.

162/7 *Morning Post*, 2 Feb. 1912.

162/17 *Journal* XX (15 Dec. 1910), 398.

162/31 *Journal* XXVI (1 Aug. 1913), 83.

162/36 *Journal* XV (28 May 1908), 629.

164/10 Plowden, *Motor Car and Politics*, 96.

164/21 *Journal* XXVI (22 Aug. 1913), 159.

164/32 *Journal* XXII (18 Aug. 1911), 131.

164/35 *Journal* XXVII (30 Jan. 1914), 89.

164/37 *Journal* XXVII (6 Mar. 1914), 190.

164/40 H. Williamson, *Young Phillip Maddison* (1994 edn.), 33.

166/13 *Journal* XX (14 July 1910), 19.

166/14 *Journal* XXiI (14 July 1911), 25.

166/20 *Journal* XXII (21 July 1911), 53.

166/22 *Journal* XXII (28 July 1911), 76.

168/2 Grahame-White, *At the Wheel*, 230.

168/17 J. Rey, *The Whole Art of Dining* (1914), 144.

170/21 *DNB*.

170/31 *Journal* XXIII (26 Apr. 1912), 436.

172/1 BL Add MSS 62279A, NP, Johnson to Lady Northcliffe, 18 Jan. 1910.

172/8 *Journal* XI (26 Apr. 1906), 488.

172/16 C. Ellis, *Military Transport of World War I* (1970), 120.

172/19 D. Noble, *Milestones in a Motoring Life* (1969), 45.

172/22 *Journal* XVI (17 Dec. 1908), 571.

172/35 Noble, *Milestones*, 39.

174/1 Carter, *Edwardian Cars*, 160.

174/13 *Journal* XXVIII (26 June 1914), 545-7.

174/19 S. Van de Casteele-Schweitzer, 'Management and Labour in France 1914-1939' in S. Tolliday and J. Zeitlin (eds.), *The Automobile Industry and its Wonders* (Cambridge, 1987), 58.

174/26 *Journal* XXVIII (11 Sep. 1914), 179.

174/37 *Journal* XXVIII (4 Dec. 1914), 280.

174/39 F. Coleman, *From Mons to Ypres with French* (1916), xvii.

176/10 P. Brendon, *Winston Churchill* (1984), 70.

176/18 *RAC Staff Relief Fund Journal 1915-1919* (n.d.), unpaginated.

176/22 Ibid.

176/25 Montagu and Burgess-Wise, *Daimler*, 159.

176/37 C. Andrew, *Secret Service* (1985), 132.

176/41 A. M. Henniker, *Transportation on the Western Front 1914-1918* (1937), 152.

178/3 D. Winter, *Haig's Command* (1991), 65.

178/5 M. Gilbert, *First World War* (1994), 286.

178/17 *RAC Staff Relief Fund Journal*.

180/5 Ibid.

180/20 Committee Minutes, M[icrofilm Reel] 12-1.

182/2 Committee Minutes, M12-1.

182/8 Private information: C. P. Mason.

182/22 *Car* LII (17 Mar. 1915), 92.

182/28 *Car* LIV (11 Aug. 1915), 3.

182/33 E. S. Turner, *Dear Old Blighty* (1980), 238.

182/37 R. S. Churchill, *Lord Derby* (1959), 260.

182/42 *Autocar* XXXVI (25 Mar. 1916), 404.

184/7 Committee Minutes, M12-1.

184/21 *Journal* XXI (6 Jan. 1911), 2.

184/32 Committee Minutes, M12-1.

184/36 *Autocar* XXXV (6 Nov. 1915), 568.

186/1 *Autocar* XXXV (13 Nov. 1915), 611.

186/14 *Autocar* XXXV (11 Dec. 1915), 731.

186/30 *Autocar* XXXVIII (10 Feb. 1917), 130.

188/8 *Royal Automobile Club: A Record of its Part in War Service* (n.d.), 23.

188/24 Committee Minutes, M12-1.

188/28 Committee Minutes, M17575/4.

190/1 *Autocar* XXXVIII (23 June 1917), 645-6.

190/6 *Autocar* XXV (20 Nov. 1915), 627.

CHAPTER SEVEN:
MOTORING FOR THE MILLION

191/1   L. T. C. Rolt, *Landscape with Machines* (1971), 172.

191/13   *Autocar* XLIX (8 Dec. 1922), 1214.

191/23   J. Stevenson, *British Society 1914-45* (1984), 390.

192/9   R. Church, *Herbert Austin: The British Motor Car Industry to 1941* (1979), 161.

192/11   Z. E. Lambert and R. J. Wyatt, *Lord Austin* (1968), 29.

192/13   Beaulieu, G-WP, Duffield to Grahame-White, 27 Aug. 1955.

192/13   P. Pagnamenta and R. Overy, *All Our Working Lives* (1984), 220.

192/22   T. R. Nicholson, *The Vintage Car 1919-1930* (1966), 268.

192/25   R. J. Wyatt, *The Motor for the Million: The Austin Seven 1922-1939* (Newton Abbot, 1972), 20.

192/31   R. Graves and A. Hodge, *The Long Week-end* (1965 edn.), 178.

192/33   Davis, *Memories*, 101.

194/3   R. Church and M. Miller, 'The Big Three: Competition, Management, and Marketing in the British Motor Industry, 1922-1929' in B. Supple (ed.), *Essays in British Business History* (Oxford, 1977), 163.

194/3   C. F. Caunter, *The History and Development of Light Cars* (1957), 69.

194/9   R. C. Whiting, *The View from Cowley* (Oxford, 1983), 44.

194/12   P. W. S. Andrews and E. Brunner, *The Life of Lord Nuffield* (Oxford, 1955), 112.

194/16   R. J. Overy, *William Morris, Viscount Nuffield* (1976), 68.

194/24   Davis, *Memories*, 114.

194/32   *Motor* LVI (19 Nov. 1929), 867.

194/42   Overy, *Morris*, 104 and 68-9.

196/18   *Motor* XXXV (11 Feb. 1919), 51.

196/26   J. Camplin, *The Rise of the Plutocrats* (1978), 253.

196/29   D. L. Lewis and L. Goldstein (eds.), *The Automobile and American Culture* (Ann Arbor, Mich., 1986 edn.), 129.

196/30   J. Steinbeck, *Cannery Row* (1945), 44.

2196/36   V. Scharff, *Taking the Wheel* (New York, 1991), 138.

196/38   *Car [and Golf]* LXXXI (Dec. 1922), 17.

198/10   Earl of Cottenham, *Motoring To-day and Tomorrow* (1928), 114, 70, 125 and 116.

198/27   P. Brendon, *Eminent Edwardians* (1979), 239-40.

198/29   U. Bloom, *The Log of No Lady* (1940), 18.

198/33   G. Keynes, *The Gates of Memory* (Oxford, 1981), 236.

198/35   V. S. Pritchett, *A Cab at the Door* and *Midnight Oil* (Harmondsworth, 1986), 186.

198/38   V. Brome, *J. B. Priestley* (1988), 148.

200/8   *RAC Staff Relief Fund Journal*.

200/17   Committee Minutes, M12-1.

200/18   S. Cooke, *This Motoring* (1931), 151.

200/34   L. Lee, *Cider with Rosie* (Harmondsworth, 1985 edn.), 190.

200/38   R. Blythe, *Akenfield* (1969), 138.

200/39   J. B. Priestley, *English Journey* (1934), 3.

202/15   *Car* LXXXIII (Sep. 1923), 13.

202/23   Committee Minutes, 2 July 1919.

202/27   *Autocar* LVI (16 Apr. 1926), 664.

202/29   A. F. C. Hillstead, *Those Bentley Days* (1953), 129.

202/34   J-P. Bardou, J-J. Chanaron and J. M. Laux, *The Automobile Revolution* (Chapel Hill, N.C., 1982), xiv.

204/3   BL Add. MSS 62279B, NP, Northcliffe to Johnson, 2 Mar. 1921.

204/11   *Motor* LXXX (17 Sep. 1941), 118.

204/12   *Car* LXXXVII (Oct. 1925), 67.

204/37   *Car* LXXXVII (Nov. 1925), 10.

206/19   Committee Minutes, 7 June 1918.

206/29   *Motor* XXXVI (12 Nov. 1919), 664. Geddes used the phrase and denied that it applied to him.

206/31   Plowden, *Motor Car and Politics*, 126.

208/5   *Motor* XXXVI (20 Aug. 1919), 88.

208/17   *Car* XCII (Dec. 1927), 54.

208/22   The starting wage was £2 a week, and there were various allowances such as a shilling to a Guide who provided his own bicycle.

208/37   Committee Minutes, 3 Apr. 1923.

210/1   Committee Minutes, 5 Mar. 1924.

210/5   *Sunday Times*, 30 July 1939.

210/11   Private information: Harry Stanley.

210/26   *RAC World*, Autumn 1972.

210/28   Russell, *Life and Adventures*, 294.

210/29   Private information: Harry Stanley.

210/30   Private information: Eric Charles.

210/30   Private information: Robin Montgomerie-Charrington.

210/31   Committee Minutes, 16 Sep. 1936.

210/33   Cambridge University Library, Baldwin Papers Vol. 9, 263. Sir William Joynson-Hicks to Baldwin.

210/41   RAC, Commander Armstrong's 'Confidential Report on "THE STRIKE"'.

212/8   Ibid.

212/22   Ibid.

212/25   *Car* LXXXIX (June 1926), 44.

212/28   Committee Minutes, M17575/1, 1932.

212/34   *Autocar* LVI (21 May 1926), 774.

212/36   *Motor* IL (18 May 1926), 692.

214/2   *Autocar* LVI (4 June 1926), 902.

214/8   Churchill, CHAR 1/148/22, Orde to Churchill, 16 Apr. 1921.

214/9   *Motor* XLIX (18 May 1926), 709.

214/24 B. Donoughue and G. W. Jones, *Herbert Morrison* (1973), 139.

214/25 P. S. Bagwell, *The Transport Revolution from 1770* (1974), 263.

214/36 Committee Minutes, M12-2, May 1933.

216/6 Motor LXVII (26. Feb. 1935), 141.

216/10 Committee Minutes, 1 Apr. 1936.

216/25 Grahame-White, *At the Wheel*, 266. Cf. Edward Shanks's attack and Mervyn O'Gorman's defence in, respectively, *Sunday Times*, 2 and 9 July 1939.

218/11 *Motor* LXVII (7 May 1935), 619.

218/13 Committee Minutes, 6 Nov. 1935.

218/21 *Motor* LXXV (7 Feb. 1939), 42.

218/23 Committee Minutes, 1 Nov. 1937.

220/4 Committee Minutes, 2 Dec. 1925.

220/24 *Autocar* LXIII (26 July 1929), 165.

220/32 Committee Minutes, 20 Sep. 1933.

222/13 A. F. C. Hillstead, *Fifty Years with Motor Cars* (1960), 93.

222/19 Hillstead, *Fifty Years*, 174.

224/4 Committee Minutes, 3 June 1925.

224/10 A. Bird and I. Hallows, *The Rolls-Royce Motor Car and the Bentley since 1931* (1984 edn.), 147.

224/15 I. Rendall, *The Chequered Flag* (1993), 102.

224/16 L. J. K. Setright, *With Flying Colours* (1987), 75.

224/26 C. Posthumus, *Sir Henry Segrave* (1961), 167 and 218.

224/30 B. Gunston, *By Jupiter! The Life of Sir Roy Fedden* (1978), 6.

226/4 M. Hamilton, *RAC Rally* (1987), 11.

226/17 P. Drackett, *The Story of the RAC International Rally* (Yeovil, 1980), 32.

226/22 *Autocar* LXXVI (27 Mar. 1936), 542.

226/36 *PM & W* (June 1980), 20.

226/41 *Autocar* LXXVI (29 May 1936), 1016.

228/11 Private information: Robin Montgomerie-Charrington.

228/12 Grahame-White, *At the Wheel*, 234.

228/25 Committee Minutes, M12-2.

CHAPTER EIGHT:

AUSTERITY MOTORING

229/4 T. Harrisson, *Living through the Blitz* (1976), 27.

229/19 *Motor* LXXV (4 Apr. 1939), 335.

229/20 C. Ellis, *Military Transport of World War II* (1971), 9.

229/24 *The Memoirs of Captain Liddell Hart* I (1965), 241.

230/2 Thomas, *Wing*, 212.

230/5 *Observer*, 19 May 1996.

230/12 To quote the title of R. L. Dinardo's book (1991).

230/38 Private information: Lord Abinger.

230/39 Private information: John Crampton.

232/12 Private information: Norman Neale.

232/15 *PM & W* (Sep. 1981), 20.

232/24 Private information: Malcolm Pollock-Hill.

234/32 *Motor* LXXVII (10 Apr. 1940), 264.

236/2 N. Longmate, *How We Lived Then* (1971), 312.

236/12 Committee Minutes, 4 Sep. 1940.

236/24 E. S. Turner, *The Phoney War on the Home Front* (1961), 255.

236/35 Private information: Harry Stanley.

238/2 M. Cocker, *Richard Meinertzhagen* (1989), 207-209.

238/12 Private information: John Crampton.

238/17 M. Gilbert, *Finest Hour* (1983), 843.

238/18 R. Hough, *The Ace of Clubs* (1986), 13.

238/20 Noble, *Jubilee Book*, 143.

238/24 P. Ziegler, *London at War* (1995), 124

238/31 Committee Minutes, 1 Mar. 1944.

238/42 *PM & W* (Spring, 1979), 15.

240/8 Private information: Robin Montgomerie-Charrington.

240/13 *Motor* LXXX (17 Dec. 1941), 360.

240/26 J. Colville, *The Fringes of Power* (1985), 271.

240/28 Churchill, CHAR 20/13, M.201, Churchill to Moore-Brabazon, 19 Oct. 1940.

240/37 *Motor* LXXVII (6 Nov. 1940), 293.

242/3 Committee Minutes, July 1941.

242/11 J. Foreman-Peck, S. Bowden and A. McKinlay, *The British Motor Industry* (Manchester, 1995), 86-7.

242/15 R. M. Ogorkiewicz, *Armoured Forces* (1970 edn.), 161.

242/17 Davis, *Memories*, 205.

242/31 Executive Committee Minutes, May 1942.

244/1 Private information.

244/6 A. Lane, *Austerity Motoring 1939-1950* (1987), 6.

244/21 Committee Minutes, 30 Oct. 1942.

244/25 Executive Committee Minutes, 20 Oct. 1943.

244/34 *Motor* LXXXIII (19 May 1943), 271.

244/38 *Motor* LXXXV (21 June 1944), 377.

244/41 Committee Minutes, 13 Feb. 1942.

246/16 *Autocar* LXXXVI (2 May 1941), 387.

246/18 Committee Minutes, 3 Mar. 1943.

246/32 Private information: J. B. Cowan.

246/34 Private information: John Crampton.

246/37 Private information: Tony Lee.

248/1 Committee Minutes, 5 Nov. 1947.

248/9 Private information: Tony Lee.

248/15 Ibid.

248/16 Beaulieu, G-WP, Andrews to Grahame-White 21 Dec. 1953.
248/18 Private information: John Crampton.
248/28 Committee Minutes, 28 May 1954.
250/5 Lejeune, *Gentlemen's Clubs*, 55.
250/8 Committee Minutes, Aug. 1945.
250/12 Committee Minutes, 29 May 1952.
250/35 *Autocar* XCIV (30 Dec. 1949), 1476.
252/4 M. Sedgwick, *The Motor Car 1946-1956* (1979), 192.
252/11 J. Wood, *Wheels of Misfortune: the Rise and Fall of the British Motor Industry* (1988), 107.
252/14 M. Sedgwick, *Cars of the Thirties and Forties* (1979), 231.
252/35 D. Pryce-Jones, 'Towards the Cocktail Party' in M. Sissons and P. French (eds.), *Age of Austerity* (1963), 213.
252/41 Committee Minutes, 3 Oct. 1945.
254/11 Committee Minutes, 1 Jan. 1947.
254/17 Committee Minutes, 3 Sep. 1947.
254/20 T. E. B. Howarth, *Prospect and Reality: Great Britain 1945-1955* (1985), 70.
254/22 *Autocar* XCII (3 Oct. 1947), 873.
254/27 P. M. Williams, *Hugh Gaitskell* (1979), 152.
254/31 K. O. Morgan, *Labour in Power 1945-1951* (Oxford, 1984), 315-316.
254/38 *Autocar* XCII (19 Dec. 1947), 1135.
254/41 Plowden, *Motor Car and Politics*, 318.
256/16 Private information: Jock Gay.
256/22 Private information: Brian Hall.
256/30 Private information: A. D. Anderton.
256/31 *Autocar* XCII (7 Feb. 1947), 128.
258/6 *Autocar* XCI (27 Nov. 1946), 1037.
258/30 Committee Minutes, 3 Dec. 1947.
258/37 *Autocar* XCII (19 Dec. 1947), 1135.
258/41 L. Stanley, *The Legendary Years* (1944), 83.
260/2 P. Carrick, *Silverstone: The Story of Britain's Fastest Circuit* (1974), 26.
260/30 *Autocar* XCV (19 May 1950), 581.
260/35 Private information: Harry Stanley.

CHAPTER NINE:
BLESSING AND BLIGHT

263/14 R. Barthes, *Mythologies* (1972), 88.
264/2 Bagwell, *Transport Revolution*, 375.
264/3 C.D. Buchanan, *Mixed Blessing* (1958), 89.
264/9 Committee Minutes, 27 Nov. 1945.
264/27 Committee Minutes, 3 Feb. 1954. Cf. *Manchester Guardian* (19 Jan. 1954), which called for a 'New Deal' for roads.
264/35 *Sheffield Telegraph*, 26 July 1966.
264/40 *Autocar* CIV (8 June 1956), 683.
266/2 Committee Minutes, 1 Oct. 1958.
266/17 *RAC World*, July-Aug. 1965.
266/37 Committee Minutes, 2 Nov. 1955
268/6 Committee Minutes, 6 June 1956.
268/10 Private information: Graham Barker.
268/19 Committee Minutes, 6 June 1956.
268/28 Committee Minutes, 5 Apr. 1961.
268/41 Committee Minutes, 4 July 1956.
270/3 [Southampton University, Mountbatten Papers,] MB1/345, Mountbatten to Lt.-Col. B. Ede, 11 July 1960.
272/3 Private information: Harry Stanley.
272/10 MB1/L348, Mountbatten to the Duke of Edinburgh.
272/33 Private information: Harry Stanley.
272/35 Private information: Tony Lee.
272/40 Private information: Michael Limb.
274/5 Committee Minutes, 31 May 1951.
274/10 Private information: Bob Plummer.
274/11 Private information: Jack Hardy.
274/19 Private information: Carl Stewart.
274/19 *Autocar* CVII (20 Dec. 1957), 968.
274/28 J. Morgan (ed.), *The Backbench Diaries of Richard Crossman* (1981), 1019.
276/3 Private information: Edward Wray.
276/12 Private information: Graham Barker.
276/15 Private information: Maureen Preston.
276/27 *Autocar* CX (1 May 1959), 646.
276/28 Private information: Mrs M. A. Worrall.
276/40 Private information: Riley Simister.
276/42 Private information: Barbara Williamson.
278/11 Private information: E. Baker.
278/21 P. Marsh and P. Collett, *Driving Passion: The Psychology of the Car* (1986), 197.
278/22 Private information: Ian Williams.
278/39 Private information: Mark Gatty
280/26 P. Filby, *Amazing Mini* (1981), 23, 10 and 12.
280/34 G. Turner, *The Car Makers* (1963), 181.
282/21 S. Young and N. Hood, *Chrysler UK: A Corporation in Transition* (New York, 1977), 85.
282/39 K. Ross, *Fast Cars, Clean Bodies* (Cambridge, Mass., 1995), 16.
282/39 H. Beynon, *Working for Ford* (1973), 118.
284/35 *Traffic in Towns* (Harmondsworth, 1963), 15. The quotation comes from the preface by Sir Geoffrey Crowther.
286/16 Committee Minutes, 4 Mar. 1964.
286/19 *Daily Telegraph*, 3 Apr. 1977.
286/23 RAC, Andrews File 2, quoted from W. Andrews, 'The Case for Urban Motorways' in Traffic Engineering and Control, May 1961.

286/27 Autocar CXX (13 Mar. 1960), 490.

286/27 Committee Minutes, 4 Jan. 1967.

286/34 RAC, Andrews File 2, 1962.

288/6 B. Castle, *The Castle Diaries 1964-70* (1984), 216.

288/18 J. Jerome, *The Death of the Automobile* (1972), 18.

288/18 Lord Montagu and F. W. McComb, *Behind the Wheel: The Magic and Manners of Early Motoring* (1977), 22.

288/24 R. Nader, *Unsafe at Any Speed* (New York, 1965), 257.

288/28 C. McCarry, *Citizen Nader*, (1972), 68.

288/35 Private information: Jack Williams.

290/4 Committee Minutes, 1 June 1966.

290/28 RAC, Andrews File 1, 22 Feb. 1968.

290/33 For a brief history of the Institute see the final edition of its newsletter, *The Instructor* No. 169, Summer 1992.

292/11 Committee Minutes, 2 July 1969.

292/24 MB1/l346, Andrews to Mountbatten, 8 Apr. 1960.

292/34 Private information: Michael Limb.

292/38 Private information: Dean Delamont.

292/39 Private information: Michael Limb.

292/41 Private information: Norman Austin.

294/8 Private information: Tony Lee.

294/11 MB1/L346, Andrews to Mountbatten, 4 Feb. 1953.

294/13 Private information: Michael Limb.

294/18 Private information: Tony Lee.

294/32 Committee Minutes, 3 May 1967.

294/36 Committee Minutes, 5 July 1968.

296/5 Private information: Eric Charles.

296/7 Private information: John Crampton.

296/11 Private information: John Hogg.

296/12 Private information: Michael Limb.

296/28 Committee Minutes, 4 Dec. 1963.

298/6 C. Lycett Green (ed.), *John Betjeman Letters* II (1995), 492, 315 and 144.

298/11 Committee Minutes, 5 Apr. 1972.

298/25 Committee Minutes, 5 Oct. 1960.

298/34 *RAC World*, 17 May 1965.

298/42 Committee Minutes, 3 Nov. 1965.

300/16 *Autocar* CXXVII (15 Aug. 1967), 51.

300/22 Hamilton, *RAC Rally*, 87.

300/41 Committee Minutes, 2 Apr. 1969.

302/5 Private information: Michael Limb.

302/27 MB1/l346, Andrews to Mountbatten, 4 Jan 1965.

302/30 *PM & W* (Mar. 1990), 36.

302/36 Committee Minutes, 6 Jan. 1971.

304/1 D. Howarth, *The Shetland Bus* (1951), 166.

304/3 Committee Minutes, 5 June 1968.

304/17 Committee Minutes, 3 May 1972.

CHAPTER TEN:

CRISIS IN THE CLUB

305/6 Committee Minutes, 3 May 1972.

305/13 *PM & W* (Mar. 1980), 29.

305/14 Private information: John Crampton.

305/18 Private information: John Hogg.

305/19 Private information: Michael Limb.

306/23 P. Evans, *Where Motor-Car is Master* (1992), 60.

308/14 Castle, *Diaries*, 374-5.

308/24 Private information: Terry Lankshear.

308/31 *Autocar* CXL (17 Aug. 1974), 19.

308/36 P. G. Cooper to A. G. Polson, 29 Aug. 1974. I am grateful to Peter Cooper and Dean Delamont for sending me a copy of this letter.

310/13 Private information: T. H. Lowe.

310/25 Committee Minutes, 8 Sep. 1976.

312/3 *RAC World*, Autumn 1977.

312/17 *Sunday Telegraph*, 3 Apr. 1977.

312/21 Private information: Mrs A. M. Howlett.

312/26 Private information: John Hogg.

314/4 *Times Herald*, 17 Sep. 1976.

314/10 Private information: Neil Eason Gibson.

314/19 Private information: Jack Williams.

314/23 *PM & W* (Mar. 1980), 13.

314/23 Private information: Brian Palmer.

314/24 Private information: John Hogg.

314/38 Committee Minutes, 5 Mar. 1975.

316/4 Private information: Sir Clive Bossom.

316/6 Committee Minutes, 4 June 1975.

316/18 Private information: Michael Limb.

316/29 *Times*, 21 Apr. 1977.

316/37 *Autocar* CXLIV (3 Jan. 1976), 37.

318/5 Committee Minutes, 8 Sep. 1976.

318/13 Private information: Sir Clive Bossom.

318/23 Ibid.

320/1 Committee Minutes, 8 Sep. 1977.

320/14 Committee Minutes, 6 July 1977.

320/18 Ibid.

320/38 Committee Minutes, 7 Sep. 1977.

322/1 *Autocar* CXLVII (3 Sep. 1977), 15.

322/3 *Sunday Times*, 18 Sep. 1977.

322/13 *NYT*, 5 Apr. 1978.

322/15 Private information: Michael Limb.

322/19 Private information: Harry Stanley.

322/25 *Sunday Times*, 28 May 1978.

322/37 RAC Preliminary Report of the ad hoc committee, 24 Oct. 1977.

324/2 *PM & W*, Sep. 1978.

324/18 Private information: Brian McGivern.

324/21 Private information: Sir Clive Bossom.

324/22 Private information: Brian McGivern.

324/40 *PM & W*, Mar. 1978.

324/42 *PM & W* (Dec. 1995), 15.

326/18 Executive Committee Minutes, 3 Oct. 1978.

326/19 *PM & W* (Mar. 1979), 23.

326/34 Executive Committee Minutes (M14-7), Second Report of the ad hoc committee.

328/8 *PM & W*, Sep. 1978.

328/22 *PM & W*, Sep. 1978.

328/34 M[otor] S[port] C[ouncil], Administrative Committee Minutes, 10 Nov. 1977.

330/2 MSC Minutes, 13 June 1978.

330/6 RAC M[otor] S[ports] A[ssociation Archives], n.d.

330/15 RACMSA, Bossom to Motor Sport Council's Specialist Committees, 2 Aug. 1978.

330/25 *Autocar* CIXL (14 Oct. 1978), 19.

330/27 RACMSA, Rose to Bossom, 2 Apr. 1979.

332/22 *PM & W*, (Mar. 1980), 21.

332/39 *PM & W*, 31 May 1978.

334/5 MB1/L351, Lesser to Mountbatten, 7 Aug. 1979.

334/9 MB1/L351, Aarvold to Lesser, 29/30 July 1979.

334/22 Private information: Michael Limb.

334/35 Private information: Alan Levinson.

336/11 *Observer*, 29 June 1980.

336/22 Private information.

336/39 *Times*, 5 July 1980.

336/41 *Daily Telegraph*, 4 July 1980.

338/14 *PM & W* (Sep. 1980), 4.

338/14 *Times*, 25 July 1980.

338/17 Committee Minutes, 25 July 1980.

CHAPTER ELEVEN:

THE TRIUMPH OF TECHNOLOGY

339/3 Evans, *Motor-Car is Master*, 61.

339/9 M. Edwardes, *Back from the Brink* (1983), 227.

339/14 J. Cole, *As It Seemed to Me* (1995), 252.

339/15 M. Thatcher, *The Downing Street Years* (1993), 114.

340/9 Edwardes, *Brink*, 64.

340/10 Pagnamenta and Overy, *Working Lives*, 241.

340/15 T. Garrison, *Mrs Thatcher's Casebook* (1987), 101.

340/16 *Observer*, 25 Oct. 1981.

340/17 M. Adeney, *The Motor Makers* (1988), 292.

340/25 I. Fallon and J. Srodes, *Dream Maker* (New York, 1983), 243.

340/27 *Daily Express*, 9 Oct. 1978.

340/30 Edwardes, *Brink*, 95.

342/9 N. Fowler, *Ministers Decide* (1991), 236.

342/14 N. Georgano (ed.), *Britain's Motor Industry* (1995), 251.

342/22 Lord Young, *The Enterprise Years* (1990), 286.

342/38 R. Morales, *Flexible Production* (Cambridge, 1994), 97.

344/12 *Sunday Times*, 9 Oct. 1983.

344/23 Private information: Mark Gatty.

344/29 Private information: David O'Bee.

344/31 Private information: D. Bland.

344/41 *Road & Car* (Autumn, 1983), 30.

346/2 *Times*, 19 Mar. 1982.

346/7 Private information: P. F. Slade.

346/34 Private information: Charles Lewis.

348/11 Private information: Mervyn Jacobs.

348/15 R. Hallowell, 'The Royal Automobile Club Rescue Services Division: Transformation through Technology' (Harvard Business School Paper, 1991), 3.

348/17 Private information: M. Kirby.

348/19 A. Large, 'Service Excellence through People Empowerment' (1991), 7.

348/39 Private information: Miss O. L. Oram.

350/1 Private information: Jack Williams.

350/5 RACMS Board Paper, 17 Oct. 1985.

350/15 *Which?* (July 1987), 307.

350/19 *Autocar* CLIII (6 Sep. 1980), 16.

350/26 Private information: Jeffrey Rose.

354/30 Private information: Brian McGivern.

354/31 Committee Minutes, 17 Nov. 1983.

354/33 Large, 'Service Excellence', 1.

354/34 Committee Minutes, 17 Nov. 1983.

356/7 Private information: Jeffrey Rose.

356/11 Private information: Norman Austin.

356/39 Private information: Arthur Large.

358/4 Jeffrey Rose's notes of talk with Edwardes, 1984.

358/4 Private information: Graham Barker.

358/18 *Management Week* (May 1991), 88.

358/29 *Newslane* (Apr. 1989), 2.

360/3 Private information: Brian Palmer.

360/5 Private information: Graham Barker.

360/20 Large, 'Service Excellence', 9.

362/4 Private information: Norman Austin.

362/10 Private information: Alec Leggett.

362/30 Maple Report, 1986.

364/20 Committee Minutes, 18 Nov. 1987.

364/23 Committee Minutes, 21 Jan. 1987.

366/3 Private information: Jeffrey Rose.

366/21 *Newslane* (June 1988), 4.

366/25 *Newslane* (June 1988), 2.

366/38 Large, 'Service Excellence', 11 and 3.

366/40 Private information: Arthur Large.

368/1 Private information: Frank Richardson.

368/13 *Newslane* (Jan. 1989), 1.

368/15 Private information: Graham Barker.

368/34 Private information: Martin Connor.

370/2 A. B. Andrews, 'Was it only five years ago...', (*c*. 1990), 12.

370/14 Hallowell, 'Transformation', 10.

372/8 Private information: Jeffrey Rose.

372/14 Andrews, 'Five Years', 13.

374/3 Private information: Frank Richardson.

374/11 *Management Week* (May 1991), 91.

CHAPTER TWELVE:

MOTORING INTO THE FUTURE

375/7 *Autocar* CLXX (31 Dec. 1986), 5.

376/11 Public Policy Committee Minutes, 10 Apr. 1984.

376/36 RAC, Rose to D. D. Barron, 9 Oct. 1990.

378/3 D. Williams *et al*, *Cars and the Environment: A View to the Year 2020* (1992), 3.

378/15 J. J. Flink, *The Automobile Age* (Cambridge, Mass., 1988), 404.

378/23 *Independent on Sunday*, 21 Jan. 1996.

378/31 Williams, *Cars and Environment*, 6.

378/31 *Evening Standard*, 24 June 1994.

378/39 'North York Moors National Park: Impact of Car Usage Study 1994/5', 1 and 38.

380/5 'Paying for Roads: A Radical Review' (May, 1993),

380/9 'Paying for Motorways: RAC Response to Government Green Paper' (Aug. 1993), 6.

380/26 Private information: Emma Rothschild.

382/7 *Independent on Sunday*, 15 Sep. 1994.

382/8 *Evening Standard*, 15 May 1996.

382/15 *Guardian*, 22 July 1995.

382/38 *Car Dependence* (1995), 13 and 109..

382/40 G. P. Maxton and J. Wormald, *Driving Over a Cliff?* (Wokingham, 1994), 50.

384/3 *Car Dependence*, 126.

384/14 *Observer*, 18 June 1995.

384/18 *Guardian*, 26 Apr. 1996.

384/18 *Economist* (22 June 1996), 19.

384/23 J. Rose, 'Whatever the policy, cars are here to stay' in *The House Magazine* (22 July 1995), 19.

386/15 *Newslane* (June 1991), 3.

386/36 Private information: Elizabeth Robson.

386/36 Private information: Stewart Pinney.

386/39 Private information: G. Hopper.

386/42 Private information: Martin Connor.

388/1 Private information: John Greaves.

388/5 Private information: A. B. Andrews.

388/12 *Marketing* (23 May 1996), 10.

388/38 Private information: John Bidgood.

390/4 *Newslane* (Mar. 1994), 1.

392/4 Committee Minutes, 22 June 1994.

392/23 Private information: David Livermore.

392/30 Committee Minutes, 11 Oct. 1995.

392/35 Private information: Neil Johnson.

392/36 Committee Minutes, 21 July 1993.

394/1 Private information: Neil Johnson.

394/22 Ibid.

396/6 Committee Minutes, 11 Oct. 1995.

396/13 Private information: Neil Johnson.

396/19 Private information: Brian Palmer.

396/26 *Sunday Telegraph*, 3 Apr. 1977.

396/27 *Management Week* (June 1991), 23.

396/39 *Newslane* (Aug. 1991), 3. Women are also safer because they drive less than men.

398/2 *PM & W* (Mar. 1984), 47.

398/6 *PM & W* (June 1993), 28.

398/16 'Roads to the Future', (video, 1996).

398/22 N. Johnson, 'Keynote Speech', (Feb. 1996).

398/28 *Financial Times*, 5 Feb. 1996.

398/34 *Daily Express*, 3 Feb. 1996.

400/21 *Financial Times*, 1 May 1996.

402/8 *Archive* 12 (Mar. 1996), 3-4.

402/18 *PM & W* (June 1992), 24.

404/22 Committee Minutes, 19 July 1995.

408/11 *PM & W* (Dec. 1994), 39.

408/22 *PM & W* (Dec. 1990), 33.

408/34 *PM & W* (Sep. 1983), 35.

408/35 *PM & W* (Mar. 1990), 42.

410/17 Committee Minutes, 11 Oct. 1995.

BIBLIOGRAPHY

A FULL BIBLIOGRAPHY would merely duplicate the notes, so what follows is a short list of the most important and useful books relating to the RAC and the history of motoring over the past century. These works were published in London unless otherwise stated.

Adeney, M., *The Motor Makers* (1988)

Bagwell, P. S., *The Transport Revolution from 1770* (1974)

Barker, T., *The Economic and Social Effects of the Spread of Motor Vehicles* (Basingstoke, 1987)

Barty-King, H., *The AA: A History of the First 75 Years of the Automobile Association* (Basingstoke, 1980)

Bird, A., *The Motor Car 1765–1914* (1960)

Boddy, W., *The History of Brooklands Motor Course* (1957)

Buchanan, C. D., *Mixed Blessing* (1958)

Caunter, C. F., *The History and Development of Light Cars* (1957)

Church, R., *Herbert Austin: The British Motor Car Industry to 1941* (1979)

Cottenham, Earl of, *Motoring To-day and Tomorrow* (1928)

Davis, S. C. H., *Memories of Men & Motor Cars* (1965)

Drackett, P., *The Story of the RAC International Rally* (Yeovil, 1980)

Duncan, H. O., *The World on Wheels* (Paris, 1926)

Dunnett, P. J. S., *The Decline of the British Motor Industry* (1980)

Edge, S. F., *My Motoring Reminiscences* (1972 edn.)

Edwardes, M., *Back from the Brink* (1983)

Evans, P., *Where Motor-Car is Master* (1992)

Flink, J. J., *The Automobile Age* (Cambridge, Mass., 1988)

Flower, R. and Wynn Jones, M., *One Hundred Years of Motoring* (1981)

Foreman-Peck, J., Bowden S. and McKinlay, A., *The British Motor Industry* (Manchester, 1995)

Georgano, N. (ed.), *Britain's Motor Industry* (1995)

Grahame-White, M., *At the Wheel Ashore and Afloat* (n.d., 1935)

Harmsworth, A. (ed.), *Motorists and Motor-Driving* (1902)

Hough, R., *Tourist Trophy* (1957)

Jarrott, C., *Ten Years of Motoring and Motor Racing* (1956)

Jeffreys, R., *The King's Highway* (1949)

Levitt, D., *The Woman and the Car* (1970 edn.)

Lynch, B., *Green Dust: Ireland's Unique Motor Racing History 1900–1939* (Dublin, 1988)

Marsh, P. and Collett, P., *Driving Passion: The Psychology of the Car* (1986)

Maxton, G. P. and Wormald, J., *Driving Over a Cliff?* (Wokingham, 1994)

Montagu, Lord and Burgess-Wise, D., *Daimler Century* (1995)

Nicholson, T. R., *The Birth of the British Motor Car 1769–1897* III (1982)

Nixon, St J. C., *Romance Amongst Cars* (n.d., 1938)

Nixon, St J. C., *The Simms Story* (n.d., 1955?)

Noble, D., *The Jubilee Book of the Royal Automobile Club 1897–1947* (1947)

Oldham, W. J., *The Hyphen in Rolls-Royce* (1967)

Overy, R. J., *William Morris, Viscount Nuffield* (1976)

Pettifer, J. and Turner, N., *Automania* (1984)

Plowden, W., *The Motor Car and Politics 1896–1970* (1971)

Richardson, K., *The British Motor Industry 1896–1939* (1977)

Rose, G., *A Record of Motor-Racing* (1909)

Smith, C. F., *The History of the Royal Irish Automobile Club 1901–91* (Dublin, 1994)

Tritton, P., *John Montagu of Beaulieu 1866–1929* (1985)

Turner, G., *The Leyland Papers* (1971)

Williams, D. *et al.*, *Cars and the Environment: A View to the Year 2020* (1992)

INDEX

Page numbers in *italic* refer to picture captions